World Heritage   *Archaeological Sites and Urban Centres*

A joint co-publication by

The United Nations Educational, Scientific and
Cultural Organization (UNESCO),
7, Place De Fontenoy, 75007 Paris, France
and
Skira Editore spa, Palazzo Casati Stampa,
via Torino 61, 20123 Milan, Italy

World Heritage

Archaeological Sites and Urban Centres

Skira

pages II and III
Angkor, Cambodia

page VII
The Sistine Chapel, Vatican City

pages X and XI
San'a, Yemen

page XII
Persepolis, Iran

Design
Marcello Francone

Editing
Marco Abate

Layout
Serena Parini

Translations
Antony Shugaar

Iconographical Research
Massimo Zanella

First published in Italy in 2002 by
Skira Editore S.p.A.
Palazzo Casati Stampa
via Torino 61
20123 Milano
Italy

Printed and bound in Italy. First edition
Skira ISBN 88-8491-393-4
UNESCO ISBN 92-3-103869-9

Distributed in North America and Latin America
by Rizzoli International Publications, Inc. through
St. Martin's Press, 175 Fifth Avenue, New York,
NY 10010.
Distributed elsewhere in the world by Thames and
Hudson Ltd., 181a High Holborn, London WC1V
7QX, United Kingdom.

This book was first published
exclusively for IntesaBci

The year 2002, which the General Assembly of the United Nations has officially declared the 'International Year of World Heritage', also marks the thirtieth anniversary of the World Heritage Convention. These official events confer a special significance on the commitment that IntesaBci has made by sponsoring, in conjunction with Skira, the publication of this 'catalogue raisonné' of the Cultural and Natural World Heritage Sites inscribed on UNESCO's World Heritage List.

Over the past thirty years, the World Heritage Convention has achieved considerable success on the international stage. Today the states that belong to this important international juridical instrument for the protection of the world heritage are 174 in number: we are not far short of the total number of states on the planet.

This means that all of the societies on earth, in their complex historical and cultural diversity, have recognized and defined in juridical terms the importance of the protection of the world's cultural and natural heritage and have chosen to share the universal principles expressed by the World Heritage Convention. In short, they have chosen to share in the re-

sponsibility of safeguarding on a global scale the sites protected by the Convention.

In a world that continues to be riven by ethnic and ideological conflicts, closely linked to cultural traditions and questions of identity, this is an achievement not to be taken lightly.

In the past thirty years, 730 cultural and natural sites have been inscribed on the World Heritage List. Of these, 544 are cultural, 130 are natural, and 44 are mixed. Another 1,300 sites have been inscribed by their respective nations in the 'indicative lists'. This is a substantial number of properties, though so much remains to be done, especially for the protection of properties or sites that do not exactly fit the definition of 'cultural heritage' as it has been formulated in the European and Western context, and for which a great deal of work remains undone.

The existing World Heritage List, all the same, clearly betrays a problem of 'equilibrium' among the various regions and the various categories of properties and sites. The fact that roughly half the properties and sites classified are in Europe is certainly an indicator of that continent's cultural wealth, but it also undermines the 'world' relevance of the list, its intercultural nature, and its utility for the defence of cultural and natural heritages in regions of the world that enjoy more limited technical and economic resources to be invested in the effort to preserve them.

Moreover, a number of other imbalances can easily be noted if we examine the categories inscribed on the list. While some categories, such as classical archaeology or Baroque architecture for example, are well represented, others, of no lesser importance, are almost or entirely absent, as is shown by the extremely small number of sites related to prehistoric archaeology or sites dating from the nineteenth and twentieth centuries.

But these problems can also be solved, given time. The work that the UNESCO World Heritage Centre is carrying out, under the supervision and encouragement of the International World Heritage Committee, is proceeding in this direction. Certainly, the action that UNESCO can perform has its limits, particularly clearly delineated in the 'zero-growth' funding that the various states are appropriating for the organization. That is why, in the course of its most recent assembly, in June of 2002, the World Heritage Committee approved a proposal for the creation of a 'Programme of Partnership', addressed to organizations and the private sector, for the reinforcement of the action of protection and conservation of the world cultural and natural heritage. This programme concerns the array of organizations and agencies that are directed, by institutional statute or programmatic choice, to encourage conservation: local agencies, research and educational institutions, non-governmental organizations, foundations, banks, and corporations. Over the course of the coming years, the World Heritage Centre will attempt to reinforce the existing network of entities that identify with the mission that the World Heritage Committee and Convention have entrusted to us. It is a partnership to which IntesaBci has already given an initial contribution, reinforcing our activity of protecting the World Heritage Sites.

Francesco Bandarin
Director
UNESCO World Heritage Centre

The foundation in 1972 of the World Heritage Committee sanctioned the creation of an international and non-partisan organization and instrument, explicitly dedicated to the identification, documentation, and safeguarding of the cultural, artistic, and environmental heritage of humanity. The work of the past thirty years has expanded the 'catalogue' of sites to more than seven hundred, featuring an array of monumental complexes, archaeological areas, environments altered by human intervention, large and small urban settlements, temple sites, individual artistic monuments, and untouched natural areas, which — in their entirety — constitute an ideal tour of the history, cultures, and manifold creative expressions of humanity and the world environment.

The project that the publishing house of Skira, in conjunction with the general headquarters of UNESCO and IntesaBci, has undertaken calls for the creation of a rich and detailed analytical fund of information and images regarding an emblematic selection of the more than seven hundred sites identified by the international organization. In order to justify better and present the selected sites, they have been classified, not by nation or by time period, but rather by category: the first volume features archaeological areas, including places of worship, urban settlements, historic and architectural complexes, and will be followed by two other volumes, one dedicated to individual monumental complexes, of varying scale, and another devoted to environmental areas altered by the hand of man, in which the human intervention is intimately linked to the state of nature, and untouched natural areas.

The classification of the themes calls for in-depth explicatory files, in which the history, the monumental stratifications and the emblematic structures of the individual site being treated are all taken into consideration, in many cases further documented by detailed boxes concerning historical figures, critical problems, and individual monuments. The richness and the variety of the illustrations offer a possible independent visual approach to the volume and to the sites, with the assistance of specific captions, while the appendix offers a list of the sites identified by UNESCO, with the specific motivations and characteristics, in the context of the thematic categories indicated above. The sites described in the volume are not included in this list.

The identification and selection of sites from an enormous and extremely diversified heritage, dating far back in time and scattered across the globe, inevitably required drastic decisions, since each potential site had fundamental reasons for being considered unique and important, worthy of examination, description, and documentation; the choices were difficult and made reluctantly, and even so required painful exclusions. All the same, the reasons for the selection of the core group of forty-six sites described and illustrated in this first volume find a logical justification in the goal of documenting the development and the various operative modes that human cultures have amassed over time concerning the problem of how to organize built space, both for sacred use and as inhabitations and urban centres, as well as with respect to the natural environment: in other words, how the *forma urbis* — in a broader sense as the form of the city but also as the form of place, built and/or transformed by man — has engaged humanity, both in a theoretical and ideal sense and as a practical application in the adaptation and radical transformation of the natural landscape.

The interventions can in reality be modifications within the context of a natural site, which still maintains the prevalent role, as in the case of the fascinating and mysterious petroglyphs in the desert of Nazca in Peru: carvings and paths marked in the rocky expanse to plot out a sort of rationalization of astral space and the cycle of the seasons. A similar logical underpinning can be found in the monolithic structure of Stonehenge in Great Britain, or else, as is the case with the Caves of Ajanta in India, the natural site is substantially preserved as it originally was, while still intervening with decorative modifications, such as wall paintings, sculptures, and carvings that transform it into a sacred place, where religious faith, collective memory, and natural grandeur find an absolute unity, as was true for the monumental Buddhas of Bamyan in Afghanistan, and as is still true in the extraordinary site of Petra in Jordan, where the red rocks of the desert gorges provide a metaphysical value to the temple and funereal architecture of the civilization of the Nabataeans. Sometimes human constructions can be camouflaged by a natural appearance, as happened with the emblematic case of the burial mounds of Asian cultures, documented here by the burial site of the first Chinese emperor in Xi'an, arranged as a city, enlivened by thousands of terracotta soldiers and then covered by a man-made hill.

Certainly, areas of worship, cities of the gods, often combined with the sites of economic and political power, have marked the development of human civilizations as they organized and consolidated into states, which necessarily display a rational and emblematic organization, the physical projection of a cosmic order. In this sense it is possible to understand the complex organization of the temple areas on the opposite bank of the Nile from the city of Thebes: the buildings of Luxor and Karnak, on the one hand, and the necropolises of the kings and the queens, on the other, but also the linear distribution of the pyramids in the religious settlement of Teotihuacán in Mexico and the sacred areas of the Maya cities of Copán and Chichén Itzá, also in Mexico. The vertical element of the pyramid or the step structure, a genuine staircase communicating with heaven, looms over the remarkable structure of the sacred city of Angkor, immersed in the rainforests of Cambodia, much as the raised platforms, adorned with ramps and forests of decorated columns, marked the site of Persepoli in Iran, the ancient centre of Persian political power. On the other hand, the sacred area of Paestum, the Acropolis in Athens, and the Imperial Forums in Rome all reveal an organization of space, built in close connection with the urban area proper, in which the equilibrium among the architectural structures and the open spaces follows proportional and idealized logic that, centuries afterwards, could be found in the Campo dei Miracoli of Pisa, a genuine sacred citadel, alongside the urban spaces; quite different as a solution when compared with the space recognizable in Ravenna, an ancient late-imperial city, in which the sacred areas were incorporated in the connective tissue of the city itself. A special adaptation of the temple area in the modern age can be glimpsed in the Museumsinsel (Island of Museums) in Berlin: a full-fledged acropolis of the North, a 'sacred' citadel of museums and culture, which borrows its form and architectural distribution from ancient typologies.

And it is precisely in the Mediterranean area, from Europe and Northern Africa all the way to Asia Minor, that the *forma urbis*, in its Western version, finds concrete form in an orthogonal layout that, even in its diverse variants, has been handed down over the centuries: from Pompeii to Leptis Magna in Lybia, from Hierapolis in Turkey to Palmyra in Syria and to Baalbek in Lebanon, providing clear evidence of the common culture, first Hellenistic and later Roman. As a counterpoint to the Mediterranean urbanistic concept, aside from the previously mentioned sacred cities of Angkor, Teotihuacán, Copán, and Chichén Itzá, the decision was made to emphasize the diverse characteristics of such complex urban settlements as Cuzco, a capital of the Inca civilization that was totally transformed by the superimposition of Western construction systems, or the better preserved Machu Picchu, perched high on the slopes of the Andes, or else the city of Kandy in Sri Lanka, organized around its pagoda with the holy relic of the Buddha's tooth, or to an even greater degree in the alternation of gardens and pavilions of the imperial capital of Kyoto in Japan, in the stratification of the capital of Yemen, San'a, or in the complex network of lanes, houses, shops, and balconies of the Casbah of Algiers.

Historical and religious transformations, changes in economic conditions, technical and structural inventions, have all served to modify the ancient conditions of the *forma urbis,* with the consequential transformation into fortified citadels such as Russian kremlins and, especially, in the walled monasteries of Novgorod, the city of Alexander Nevsky, Suzdal and Vladimir, or as in areas quite distant from each other, in the cities of Salamanca and Cordoba, in Spain, centres of study and learning, or in the more distant Damascus in Syria, Cairo in Egypt, Marrakesh in Morocco, and Bukhara in Uzbekistan, versions each original and exceptional in the variety of solutions adopted of the *forma urbis* in the various acceptations of Islamic culture.

Missing from the narrow array of sites selected are such noteworthy examples as the Forbidden City of Beijing or the Kremlin in Moscow, since they can be considered, however large and complex they may be, unified monumental areas more than urban centres; all the same the Vatican City represents once and for all that peculiar condition of the aggregation of buildings into the form of a city. Even such remarkable structures as Avignon, Bruges, Istanbul, Strasbourg, and Venice were rejected in favour of unified urban centres that may well be less well known, as is the case with the Renaissance jewels of Pienza or Ferrara, capital of the Este duchy, or the Vicenza of the Renaissance and the Venetian district of Palladian villas, as well as the fortified city of Ragusa, now Dubrovnik in Croatia, a genuine Venetian enclave in the Balkans, or the historic centres of cities in Mitteleuropa such as Prague, Bamberg, and Cracow, where the medieval personalities fade, without interruption, into the great period of European Baroque. To conclude this ideal tour of the meaning and form of the cities, we selected the unique cases of the Cuban capital, Havana, where the Spanish colonial culture is amalgamated with the modernity deriving from European and American culture, with astounding instances of eclectic, modernist, and Art Deco architecture,

and Brasilia, a capital that was designed and built from scratch, in which architectural functions and forms, decorative choices and urban spaces represent emblematically the transposition into reality of the ideal concepts of the future city.

The volume concludes with a list of the archaeological sites and urban areas protected by UNESCO's World Heritage Convention, to provide documentation of the richness and importance of cultural diversity, which should be studied, understood, and safeguarded as an irreplaceable treasure of all humanity.

The Publisher

Contents

ICELAND

NORWAY

SWEDEN

FINLAND

Novgorod

RUSSIA

Suzdal and Vladimir

Northern Ireland

IRELAND

DENMARK

ESTONIA

LATVIA

LITHUANIA

UNITED KINGDOM

NETHERLANDS

BIELORUSSIA

Stonehenge

BELGIUM

Berlin

GERMANY

CZECH REP.

POLAND

Cracow

UKRAINE

Bamberg

Prague

SLOVAKIA

FRANCE

SWITZERLAND

AUSTRIA

HUNGARY

MOLDOVA

Salamanca

PORTUGAL

Vicenza

SLOVENIA

ROMANIA

Ferrara

CROATIA

Pisa

Ravenna

BOSNIA

YUGOSLAVIA

SPAIN

Pienza

ITALY

HERZEGOVINA

Cordoba

Rome

Dubrovnik

BULGARIA

VATICAN CITY

MACEDONIA

ALBANIA

Pompeii

Paestum

GREECE

TURKEY

Athens

EUROPE Europe

Apostolic Palaces, Vatican Museums, Saint Peter's Square and Basilica

The Vatican City extends along the right bank of the Tiber, between the furthest slopes of Monte Mario to the north and the Gianicolo to the south, on the area of the ancient '*ager Vaticanus*'. With a surface area of just 0.44 square kilometres (about one-sixth of a square mile), it is the smallest state on earth, but as it is the seat of the head of the Catholic Church and because it houses the most important church in the Christian world, it has for centuries been a destination for pilgrims. Moreover, its concentration of masterpieces of art and antiquities makes it one of the greatest artistic and cultural attractions in Rome and Italy. UNESCO has declared the entire Vatican territory a World Heritage Site.

The expression 'Vatican' is commonly used to indicate both the 'Holy See' and the territorial entity that lies in the heart of Rome. The document that lies at the origin of the creation of this tiny state, the Lateran Treaty, was signed between the Holy See and Italy on 11 February 1929 and took effect on 7 June of the same year. Along with the Treaty, the Concordat was also stipulated, in order to regulate relations between the Holy See and the Italian Government. These two diplomatic instruments have taken the name of 'Patti Lateranensi', or 'Lateran Pacts', because they were signed in the Lateran Palace by the Prime Minister of Italy, Benito Mussolini, and by the Vatican Secretary of State, Pietro Cardinal Gasparri.

And although the Lateran Treaty is a unique and historically important document which put an end to the 'Roman Question', created by the occupation of Rome by Italian troops in 1870, the Concordat is an agreement that the Holy See has established not only with Italy but at numerous other times with various countries around the world.

It is not only the treasures housed here that make the Vatican the most sensational compendium of all that the arts have produced on Italian soil from the Etruscan era to the present day. Even the containers of those collections, the product of the uninterrupted sequence of building projects beginning from the imperial period, recapitulate the architectural conceptions of the last five centuries, with memorable models created by artists such as Bramante, Raphael, Michelangelo, and Gian Lorenzo Bernini. The ideological motivations that, together with their functional counterparts, underlie the history of the construction of this complex, from the gardens — metaphors for paradise — to the enclosure walls that protect the complex, are all evidence of the determination to create the residence of the vicar of Christ as a citadel of faith, wisdom, and beauty, and as a projection of the 'celestial city'.

The Basilica of Saint Peter's, with the adjoining apostolic palaces and other smaller buildings, covers roughly one-third of the total area of the Vatican City, but by the terms of the Lateran Pacts it also includes numerous areas and edifices located in Italian territory: the three Basilicas of Santa Maria Maggiore, Saint John Lateran, and Saint Paul outside the Walls, with their adjoining buildings, a number of *palazzi* in Rome that contain various papal offices — chancellery, datary, etc. — and the villa and the Palazzo of Castel Gandolfo, on Lake Albano, which is the site of one of the oldest astronomical observatories in Europe (the Specola Vaticana) and the summer residence of the Pope.

Even if we ignore these peculiar territorial characteristics, the State of the Vatican City presents a number of distinctive features that cause it to differ from any other state, particularly as a result of its intrinsic connection with the Holy See, whose independence it is entrusted to preserve. It therefore acts always and exclusively through the offices of the latter, which is not considered a territorial entity and exercises its sovereignty over the State itself, which therefore has a derived juridical stand-

Aerial view of the Vatican City.

Opposite page
The dome of the Basilica of Saint Peter's; it was designed by Michelangelo Buonarroti (from 1546 on).

The Torre di San Giovanni (Tower of Saint John) and the Mura Vaticane (Vatican Walls) built during the papacy of Nicholas V.

Panoramic view of the Palazzi Apostolici from the dome by Michelangelo; it is possible to recognize the Sistine Chapel (bottom right), the Cortile del Belvedere, designed by Donato Bramante for Julius II Della Rovere (top right), the Pinacoteca Vaticana (Vatican Picture Gallery) by Luca Beltrami (top left), while at the bottom is the Casino of Pius IV.

ing, not an original one. And unlike all other states, whose constituent features are their territory, population, and sovereignty, the State of the Vatican City lacks the last of the three as it is under the authority of the Holy See.

Like the Catholic Church, it is governed by canon law; its supreme body is the head of the Church, the Pope; its institutional goals are not, as they are in all other states, the regulation of the collective life of its citizens, but rather the assurance of independence of the Holy See from all external interference. Despite all this, the Vatican State presents itself to the outside world like any other state in the form of an elective monarchy, whose leader — the Pope — has full executive, legislative, and judiciary powers.

The generic term Musei Vaticani, or Vatican Museums, refers to a complex of institutes located in part in the Vatican and in part in the Lateran (the latter museums are also called the Musei del Laterano, or Lateran Museums). Among the most important institutions are the Museo Pio-Clementino (the Museum of Pius and Clement), the Museo Chiaramonti (the Chiaramonti Museum), the Museo Gregoriano Egizio (the Gregorian Egyptian Museum), the Museo Gregoriano Etrusco (the Gregorian Etruscan Museum), the Museo Cristiano (the Christian Museum), the Museo Profano (the Profane Museum), and the Pinacoteca (Picture Gallery).

Although, in their present-day form, these institutions were organized between the eighteenth and the twentieth centuries, their origins date back to the Humanistic period.

In 1471 Sixtus IV offered to the Roman people the oldest collection of art still in existence: the Museo Capitolino (the Capitoline Museum).

After becoming Pope, Julius II Della Rovere (1503-13) transferred the renowned statue of *Apollo* from his own see as cardinal of San Pietro in Vincoli to the Vatican; because of the courtyard in which it was placed, it became known as the *Belvedere Apollo*. Soon, that first work of art was joined by other numerous and extraordinary items, to the point that the courtyard in which the works were assembled was renamed the 'Cortile Antiquario delle Statue', or 'Antiquarian Courtyard of Statues', and the popes were soon obliged to organize new exhibition spaces.

A halt in the creation of the museums came with the reign of Pius V (1566-72), a stern standard-bearer of the spirit of the Counter Reformation, who not only closed the Antiquarium, but abolished from the Vatican a great portion of the collections, donating statues to the Museo Capitolino and even to private individuals like Maximilian II and Francesco de' Medici.

However, the impulse towards collecting was unstoppable, in part because of the new archaeological finds that were continually being dug up in Rome in the dominions of the Church that were too important for the Popes to ignore. The Biblioteca Vaticana (Vatican Library), too, as accompaniment and commentary upon its main works, had accumulated over the course of the centuries a rich and important collection of smaller items (coins, vases, inscriptions, ivories, bronzes, etc.) which required cataloguing and ordering. Thus, in 1756 under Pope Benedict XIV (1740-58), the first nucleus of the Musei Vaticani, the Museo di Antichità Cristiana (Museum of Christian Antiquities), came into being, along with — at the behest of the same Pope — the Galleria Lapidaria.

Ten years later, in 1767, Clement XIII (1758-69), with the assistance of the Cardinal Albani, founded the Museo Profano, a collection of coins and medallions of great interest.

The intensification of research and archaeological digs brought to the Vatican a great number of artworks — Egyptian, Greek, Etruscan, and Roman — so that Clement XIV

The Casino of Pius IV was commissioned by Paul IV Carafa from Pirro Ligorio between 1558 and 1561; next to it, Pius XI ordered the construction of the present-day headquarters of the Pontificia Accademia delle Scienze (Papal Academy of Science).

The Pinacoteca Vaticana, designed by Luca Beltrami, was built in 1932 for Pius XI Ratti.

Aerial view of the Giardini Vaticani (Vatican Gardens) and the Palazzo del Governatorato, built for Pope Pius XI Ratti in 1931.

(1769-74), in 1771, and his successor, Pius VI (1775-99), were able to found an exceptional sculpture museum named after the two Popes, the Museo Pio-Clementino. It was largely housed in specially constructed buildings.

After Napoleonic troops confiscated many works of art during France's imperial expansion, and their subsequent, though partial, restitution, Pope Pius VII (1800-23) succeeded in founding a new museum that took his surname, Chiaramonti. Along with the Museo Pio-Clementino, it constitutes the most magnificent and fundamental complex of sculptures that exists on earth. Pius VII was also responsible for the creation of the Pinacoteca (Picture Gallery) and the Medagliere Vaticano (collection of coins and medallions).

The current level of splendour of the Vatican Museums was attained under Pope Gregory XVI (1831-46): in 1836 he established the Galleria degli Arazzi (Gallery of Tapestries), which was added to the Galleria dei Candelabri; in 1837 he opened the Museo Etrusco (Etruscan Museum), in 1839 the Museo Egizio (Egyptian Museum), and in 1844 the Museo Profano Lateranense (literally, the Lateran Profane Museum), dedicated to early Christian art. Finally, Pope Pius XI (1922-39), aside from his considerable contributions to the Museo Etrusco and the Museo Egizio, inaugurated the Museo Missionario (Missionary Museum).

The original core of the Biblioteca Apostolica Vaticana (Vatican Apostolic Library) consists of the codices of Greek and Latin texts assembled by Pope Nicholas V, who installed the library on the ground floor of his own building in the Vatican, with an entrance from the Cortile del Pappagallo and a view overlooking the Cortile del Belvedere. Soon the number of codices grew to well over 2,000, and Sixtus IV had a new library prepared, decorated with frescoes by Melozzo da Forlì, Antoniazzo Romano, and Domenico and Davide Ghirlandaio.

The progressive and incessant increase in the number of codices over the course of the sixteenth century led Sixtus V to commission Domenico Fontana, in the years 1587-89, to erect the building that still houses the institution, and which, constructed in the place of the partitioning staircases in the Courtyard of the Belvedere as it was designed by Bramante, cuts straight across that courtyard. The Biblioteca Apostolica is rightly considered the most important library on earth in terms of the value of its collections, which over time have seen a steady increase in their patrimony, not only through purchases and similar acquisitions, but also through donations from the libraries of aristocratic Roman families, princes, and prelates.

Among the manuscripts (over 60,000), there are fragments of the codices of Virgil's work from the third and fourth centuries, the autograph copy of Petrarch's *Canzoniere*, illuminated codices by the most illustrious miniaturists of the Renaissance, and Bible codices from the fourth and fifth centuries. The documentary section proper of the collections was separated during the papacy of Pope Paul V, thus leading to the creation of the Archivio Segreto Vaticano.

Inside the Vatican City, aside from the buildings and the museums or religious institutions usually included in the course of a tour, there are others of equal importance but, since they are difficult to gain access to, are less well known. Among them are the Collegio and the Camposanto Teutonico to the west of Saint Peter's, two institutions founded in A.D. 799; the first of the two is the headquarters of the Istituto di Studi Archeologico-Storici (Institute of Archaeological and Historical Studies) and includes a small museum and a library of archaeology and ecclesiastical history with some 45,000 volumes.

Overlooking the apse of the Basilica Vaticana is the little Church of Santo Stefano degli Abissini (Saint Stephen of the Abyssinians),

The Cappella di San Pietro or Confessione di San Pietro (Saint Peter's Chapel or Saint Peter's Confessional) in the Vatican Grottoes built for Pope Paul V Borghese. It was richly adorned in polychrome marble during the reign of Clement VIII between 1592 and 1605; the eighteenth-century stuccoes are by Giovanbattista Maini; the altar holds the relics of the Saint and Apostle.

THE SISTINE CHAPEL

Begun by Giovanni de' Dolci in 1477, the chapel was supposed to be finished by the end of the summer of 1481, when work began on the decoration of the walls. It was used for the first time on 9 August 1493 on the anniversary of the election of Sixtus IV.

The room, which measures more than 40 metres in length, and roughly 14 metres in width is covered by a depressed barrel vault, joined to the perimeter walls with webs and pendentives, and illuminated by large windows, six of which line each of the long walls. Two other windows in the far wall were filled in during the time when Michelangelo was preparing to paint the *Last Judgement*.

The chapel was built to house the most important functions of the liturgical calendar of the papal court, which required a setting capable of expressing the *majestas papalis* (papal majesty) to the eyes of the select guests. Among them would be the college of the cardinals, the generals of the various monastic orders, but also foreign diplomats serving in Rome, the officials of the papal bureaucracy, the senators and conservators of the city of Rome, and then all the patriarchs, princes, and other eminent personalities visiting at the time.

A transenna, or openwork screen, which still divides the room into two parts, separated these guests to the 'papal chapel' proper from the crowds admitted to the functions.

Work continued well past the spring of 1482, at least on the Cosmatesque mosaic floor and the reliefs on the railing which, it should be noted, was moved back to a location closer to the entrance, possibly in the late 1550s. The mural decorations, inspired by medieval examples, delimit and punctuate the processional path from the entrance as far as the railing, beyond which the space is sacred. The design of the flooring also reproduces in this sector the formal scheme established by the choreography of the ceremonies: it indicates the positions of the throne, and the ceremonial chairs of the cardinals, and even the location and movements of the celebrants.

The painted decoration began with the altar wall, following a working plan that was then extended to the other walls. The decoration of this first sector was undertaken by Perugino and his workshop: the plan called for, in the upper section, portraits of the *First Four Popes*, at the centre, the *Nativity* and the *Discovery of Moses*, and then at the lower level, two trompe-l'oeil painted tapestries framing the altarpiece, and a fresco depicting the *Assumption of the Virgin Mary*, to whom the chapel is dedicated. These frescoes were completed by the end of the autumn of 1481. The ceiling was then decorated with a star-spangled sky, similar to that of the Chapel of the Scrovegni in Padua.

The first four scenes of the *Life of Christ*, which was portrayed entirely on the northern wall, were already finished in January 1482 when their decorative scheme was extended to the rest of the chapel. Each section called for portraits of two Popes at the summit, a narrative scene in the middle, and a painted tapestry in the lower section.

The contract for the other scenes from the *Life of Christ* and the seven other scenes from the *Life of Moses*, which correspond to the first ones on the southern wall, was signed in October of 1481 by Cosimo Rosselli, Sandro Botticelli, Domenico Ghirlandaio, and Perugino, who undertook to complete the work by no later than March 1482.

In May 1504 a serious diagonal fracture compromised the ceiling of the chapel, which became unusable for several months, leading Julius II to decide in 1506 to assign Michelangelo to a new campaign of decoration, though work did not begin prior to 1508.

At the centre of the ceiling are nine *Stories from Genesis*, five of which, beginning from the altar, are dedicated to the *Creation*. In the pendentives are painted, in the place of the *Apostles* that were originally called for, seven *Prophets* and five *Sibyls*, while in the lunettes and webs are depictions of the *Ancestors of Christ*. In the corner pendentives are portrayed four miraculous events in favour of the chosen people. Work was completed in 1512.

The *Last Judgement*, the design of which had been discussed by Michelangelo and Clement VII in September 1533, but which had not been approved until April 1535 under Paul III, was worked on from spring 1536 and unveiled in 1541.

Opposite page
The Sala Regia, which was commissioned, along with the Cappella Paolina (Pauline Chapel), by Pope Paul III Farnese from Antonio da San Gallo the Younger in the second half of the sixteenth century.

The Biblioteca Apostolica Vaticana (Vatican Apostolic Library), one of the world's most important libraries, was built and installed during the papacy of Sixtus V, between 1587 and 1589 by Domenico Fontana.

Commissioned by Pope Julius II Della Rovere, Michelangelo Buonarroti frescoed the vault of the Sistine Chapel between 1508 and 1512 with the Stories of the Genesis, and with alternating figures of Prophets and Sybils in the spandrels. This is the imposing figure of Zachariah.

Details of the elegant Casino of Pius IV de' Medici, Pirro Ligorio's masterpiece, formed by two buildings with an enclosed elliptical courtyard in the centre; the fronts of the entrances are adorned with bas-reliefs in stucco in imitation of ancient ones, while on the interior are preserved frescoes by Federico Barocci, Santi di Tito, and Federico Zuccari.

built by Leo III with the title of Santo Stefano Maggiore and then conceded in 1479 by Pope Sixtus IV to Coptic monks, and almost entirely rebuilt in the eighteenth century by Pope Clement XI. To the right of the church a vast staircase leads to the Palazzo del Governatorato (1931), where various civil service offices are located; in the area to the left is the Studio del Mosaico (Mosaic Studio), founded to execute the mosaic decoration of Saint Peter's, and a small railroad station, linked by a short spur to the Rome-Viterbo railway line.

Behind the Palazzo del Governatorato there extends over the slopes of the Monte Vaticano a broad green area, characterized, like other Italian gardens of the sixteenth century, by an alternation of meadows and groves, artificial grottoes and fountains.

In the depression to the north-east, the outlines of which are marked by the building of the Pinacoteca Vaticana (Vatican Picture Gallery) and by the brickwork wall of the Courtyard of the Belvedere, stands the mansion built by Pius XI to house the Pontifica Accademia delle Scienze (Papal Academy of Science), set adjacent to the so-called Casina di Pio IV, unquestionably the most attractive architectural complex in the gardens. The building was actually begun by Pope Paul IV, who entrusted its construction (1558) to Pirro Ligorio, who completed the project, with assistants, in 1561. It comprises two distinct buildings and two side pavilions. The smaller building, surrounded by a fountain, has a base adorned with mosaics and opens above into a Doric loggia; the larger building, on the other hand, has a front decorated with ornamental and figured stuccoes, and frescoes by Federico Barocci, Santi di Tito, and Federico Zuccari inside.

Lastly, there is the Church of Sant'Anna dei Palafrenieri, the parish Church of the Vatican City which was begun in 1572 by Vignola for the Confraternita dei Palafrenieri della Corte Papale (Confraternity of the Grooms of the Papal Court) and was completed after the architect's death by his son Giacinto Barozzi. It was later given a Baroque façade, and it owes its importance to the fact that its interior is one of the first in Rome to have had an elliptical plan.

Hemicycle of Saint Peter's Square built by Gian Lorenzo Bernini between 1656 and 1657; the two arms comprise 284 columns and 88 pillars which support a trabeation crowned by 140 statues of saints and the heraldic crests of Alexander VII Chigi, who commissioned the work.

The large façade was built by Carlo Maderno between 1607 and 1614 for Paul V Farnese.

Saint Peter's Basilica

Saint Peter's was founded in the early Christian era as a longitudinal basilica with five aisles, with a transept, apse, and large atrium with quadriporticus. The edifice, built at the behest of Constantine, was begun in A.D. 315 over the tomb of Saint Peter, which was incorporated into the apse area of the building. The apse area, after about 1,000 years, was subjected to a lengthy renovation which, entrusted by Pope Nicholas V in 1452 to Bernardo Rossellino, over the course of the following two centuries led to a total revamping of the basilica's structure and appearance. Within the context of the sixteenth-century cultural project of a *renovatio imperi*, designed to emphasize the magnificence of ancient Rome, Pope Julius II, the previous Cardinal of Saint Peter who was elected to the papal throne in 1503, inaugurated a massive artistic project that called for the refoundation of the entire basilica, along with the decoration of the Stanze Vaticane and the Sistine Chapel and the construction, entrusted to Michelangelo, of Pope Julius's own tomb. The project was commissioned from Bramante who, beginning from the area of the dome and maintaining the massive walls built here by Rossellino fifty years

before, proceeded in 1506 to demolish a great deal of the building to the north. The planimetric typology, of clear Eastern and Byzantine influence, designed by Bramante for Saint Peter's proved optimal from a functional and static point of view, inasmuch as it made it possible to construct a colossal structure that was at the same time light.

In 1515 supervision of the work passed, during the papacy of Leo X, to Raphael, with the assistance of Fra Giocondo and Giuliano da Sangallo, though they were soon replaced by Antonio da Sangallo the Younger. Raphael developed a majestic design based on a Latin-cross plan, which was also carried forward by his successor. Subsequently, Michelangelo, commissioned by Pope Paul III, returned to the Greek-cross plan that Bramante had designed, and explored new solutions for the dome whose symbolic value, covering as it did the tomb of Saint Peter, already seemed fundamental in the first fifteenth-century designs for the renovation of the basilica. Michelangelo built only the tambour whose high horizontal fascia, punctuated by the twinned columns and the windows with pediments that are alternatively curved and rectilinear, serves as a transition between the huge mass of the basilica and the dome, which was finally built, along with the lantern, by Giacomo della Porta.

Carlo Maderno, in 1606, after winning the competition ordered by Pope Paul V, finally returned to the Latin cross and, in 1614, built the monumental façade. The church was consecrated in 1626, and in 1656 Pope Alexander VII took up the problem of renovating the area in front of the basilica. Lorenzo Bernini, who was entrusted with this difficult task, resolved the problem by building two enormous hemicycles with Doric porticoes linked to the church through a trapezoidal plaza that frames the façade between two inclined perspectival backdrops. This was a theatrical masterpiece

on Bernini's part; moreover the colonnade of Saint Peter's is pervaded by a powerful symbolic significance: it represents the Church's embrace of all Christianity.

The Vatican Palaces

The first settlements here are documented in the fifth century A.D., while digs have yielded fragments dating back to the papacies of Leo III and Gregory IV (first half of the ninth century A.D.). It is believed that the earliest origin of the present *palazzo* was the Palatium novum built by Eugene III (1145-53) and then rebuilt by his successor Innocent III, who established the first Palatine Chapel.

With Nicholas III Orsini, the *palazzo* was enlarged to the north on the hill; the north-eastern wing was added, with monumental loggias open to the exterior.

After the return of Gregory XI from the captivity in Avignon (1309-77), the papal headquarters were permanently located in the Vatican, but it was only under Nicholas V (1447-55) that the complex took on its current, magnificent layout. During his reign a new residence, with a square plan and a courtyard, was designed (the Vatican Palace), with the Courtyard of the Parrot (Cortile del Pappagallo) at its centre; before his death, however, only the three-storey northern wing of the complex was built, with several reception rooms. The chapel, which is called the Cappella Niccolina and dedicated to Saint Lawrence and Saint Stephen, was frescoed by Fra Angelico.

Sixtus IV (1471-84) established the Public Library (Biblioteca Pubblica) and ordered the reconstruction of the chapel that still bears his name (Sistine Chapel), while Innocent VIII (1484-92) ordered for himself the Villa del Belvedere, which was completed in 1487 by Giacomo da Pietrasanta on top of the Belvedere Hill. It was decorated by such renowned masters as Mantegna and later in-

Opposite page
Detail of the top of the hemicycle built by Bernini with statues of saints, apostles, and pontiffs; in the background, behind Maderno's façade, rises the dome designed by Michelangelo.

Above the Confessione di San Pietro (Saint Peter's Confessional) and beneath the dome, stands the great bronze baldachin built at the behest of Pope Urban VIII Barberini and designed and constructed by Bernini between 1624 and 1633; in the foreground is the bronze statue of Saint Peter attributed to Arnolfo di Cambio.

Detail of the tambour of the dome with the giant twin columns, built by Michelangelo between 1546 and 1564.

corporated into the constructions by Bramante and those later erected by Pius VI for the Museo Pio-Clementino.

Alexander VI (1492-1503) returned the papal residence to the Palace of Nicholas V, which had been enlarged and reinforced by the construction of the Borgia Tower (Torre Borgia), and frescoed by Pinturicchio.

The fundamental turning point in the architecture of the Vatican came with Julius II Della Rovere. The Papal State took on at that time the status of a European power, and artworks were also expected to manifest this new and exceedingly ambitious conception of the successor to Saint Peter: examples of this can be found in such major works as the decoration of the ceiling of the Sistine Chapel by Michelangelo (1508-12), the new Saint Peter's, work on the Vatican Palaces, and the tomb of Julius II himself.

The first project of the pontiff was the Belvedere Courtyard, built by Bramante starting in 1505 and intended to link the Belvedere Palazzetto, erected by Innocent VIII between 1485 and 1487 on the north slope of the Vatican Hill, with the old papal palace.

The projects of Bramante corresponded to the idea that the papal residence of the Vatican could rival the imperial palaces on the Roman hills, inspired by the descriptions of Tacitus and Suetonius of the Domus Aurea of Nero, the ruins of the Temple of Fortune in Palestrina, and Hadrian's Villa in Tivoli. This project was pursued for about 50 years, until the reign of Sixtus V.

Behind the great niche of the Belvedere, and placed off the axis with respect to the north side of the Courtyard of the Pine Cone, is the Octagonal Courtyard (Cortile Ottagono), the site of the collection of antiquities of Julius II, linked to the Palace of the Belvedere, which can also be reached by the remarkable spiral staircase built by Bramante in 1510.

Also part of the expansive project of Julius II for the Vatican was the construction of a four-storey façade, in place of the medieval façade, on the front facing east (that is, towards the city) of the old papal palace, which was also begun by Bramante. Although it still exists, it has lost its original functions as a façade — the first façade treated with loggias in the Renaissance — and constitutes the west wing of the courtyard of San Damaso. The celebrated decoration of the interior of the loggias, in stucco and fresco, done by Raphael (who also contributed in part to the architectural completion of the loggias) and his pupils, was not completed until the reign of Julius II's successor, in accordance with the original intentions of the pontiff, and depicting *Scenes from the Old and New Testaments*. Following the period of stagnation marked by the papacy of Clement VII, ravaged by the Sack of Rome in 1527, came a new period of enlargement of the palace on the part of Paul III (1534-50): Baldassarre Peruzzi and Antonio da Sangallo completed, though without respecting Bramante's compositional plans, the eastern corridor undertaken under Julius II but never completed. The large exedra of the Courtyard of the Pine Cone was raised with a fourth floor during the reign of Julius III by Girolamo da Carpi, while Michelangelo replaced Bramante's circular staircases inside the exedra with a double flight of stairs.

In 1560 Pirro Ligorio began work, in accordance with the plans of Bramante, on the three-storey corridor on the western side of the Courtyard of the Belvedere (Cortile del Belvedere) — completed in the upper section, that of the Gallery of Maps (Galleria delle Carte Geografiche), in 1578 by Ottaviano Mascherino for Gregory XIII — and applied a semi-circular canopy over the exedra of the Courtyard of the Pine Cone (1562).

Ottaviano Mascherino was also responsible for the design of the large two-storey exedra, which is still called the Belvedere, and the con-

In the foreground is the monumental fountain built in 1613 by Carlo Maderno for Paul V Borghese; in the background is the massive structure of the dome.

The statue of a bishop-saint on the balustrade of Gian Lorenzo Bernini's colonnade, which rings Saint Peter's Square.

struction of the so-called Tower of Winds (Torre dei Venti, 1576-79).

In 1589 Domenico Fontana built a new palace for Sixtus V, destined to contain the papal apartments and the offices of the Secretary of State; it was later completed by Taddeo Landini in 1595. By this point, completely departing from the design of Bramante, he also built the new wing of the Library, which was completed in 1588.

In subsequent papacies there were few and fairly insubstantial modifications, with the exception of the restructuring of the Royal Staircase (Scala Regia), entrusted by Alexander VII to Gian Lorenzo Bernini (1663-66), and the important and largely late eighteenth-century additions, done by Michelangelo Simonetti and the Camporeses; Raffaele Stern was responsible for the design and construction of the Neo-classical building known as the New Wing, or Braccio Nuovo (1817-22), which was destined to hold the Museo Chiaramonti.

Dubrovnik

Dubrovnik, situated upon a rocky spur of the Dalmatian coast, is washed by the Adriatic Sea on three sides. Surrounded by powerful walls, it has been a prosperous trading port since the thirteenth century as well as an important maritime power that, in its control of the sea routes of the Mediterranean, came second only to Venice. Despite the fact that it was badly damaged in 1667 by an earthquake, and more recently by the conflict between Serbs and Croats, the city has managed to preserve intact its ancient urban fabric which earned it the appellation of 'Slavic Athens'.

Its origins date back to the first half of the seventh century, when the inhabitants of the Graeco-Roman colony of Epidaurus (the present-day Cavtat), invaded by Slavs and Avars and destroyed by an earthquake, selected this little island separated from the coast by a small body of water, and founded there a settlement that they called Laus, from the Latin term 'lausa', or rock, hence the name Ragusa, as Dubrovnik was called until the fifteenth century. On the nearby mainland, at the foot of the mountains, shortly thereafter the Slavs founded Dubrava (which in Slavic means an area abounding in oak trees). The two settlements established increasingly close ties, and in the twelfth century they were joined physically as well, with the filling in of the channel that once separated them; the body of water was transformed into the present-day Stradun, the broad and elegant main thoroughfare of the city.

As early as the thirteenth century, Ragusa was a major trading town, thanks to the port situated at the eastern extremity of the peninsula, around which stood the cathedral and the administrative centre of the city. After falling under the dominion of the Byzantine empire and the Republic of Venice, the city had become part of the Croato-Hungarian Kingdom in 1358, but it had preserved completely autonomous rule, with the sole obligation of paying a tribute to the king and backing him with the city's fleet.

Rebuilt and reinforced repeatedly between the eighth and the seventeenth centuries, the enclosure walls defended the liberty of the Republic of Dubrovnik for centuries, becoming over time its principal symbol. These walls are an imposing complex some two kilometres in length surrounding the entire old city, formed by an outer ring and an inner ring of solid stone walls, and by a series of towers, bastions, and auxiliary fortifications: to the north, the fortress of the Minčeta, with its enormous and magnificent tower; to the south, the Bokar, which protected the Pile Gate and the City Bridge; to the east, the tower of Saint John, built between 1346 and 1557 to protect the port, which was closed at night-time by chains. Outside the external ring of walls, built by the Tuscan architect Michelozzo, and composed of lower walls with ten semi-circular bastions, stood two separate fortresses, Fort Revellino, built in the sixteenth century in the eastern zone, and Fort Lovrijenac, looming atop a cliff, 46 metres (about 150 feet) above sea-level. Four gates linked the city to the exterior: two led to the port while the two Pile and Ploce gates, opening respectively to the west and the east and both overlooked by the statue of Saint Blaise, patron saint of the city, offered access to the *terra firma* across one stone bridge and one wooden bridge, which was raised every night.

The Republic governed a very limited territory: including the city, a narrow strip of coast (which during the city's greatest period of prosperity and power extended for some 120 kilometres, or about 75 miles), and a few islands to the south; all the same, its mercantile fleet put it in a position of great importance in the political context of the Mediterranean in the Middle Ages. The city's commercial routes brought it considerable wealth, which resulted in the con-

View of the historic centre of Dubrovnik.

Opposite page
The view of the Old City from the sea shows the enclosure walls still intact. They were built from the eighth century and renovated on several occasions up to the seventeenth century.

The old port basin was defended by the Fortress-Gate of Saint John, built between 1346 and 1557, and currently the site of the Maritime Museum and the City Aquarium.

View of the port, still bounded by the sixteenth-century Venetian towers and city walls; the monumental Cathedral stands in the centre.

THE GOVERNMENT OF THE ANCIENT REPUBLIC OF DUBROVNIK

The Republic of Dubrovnik had a rigidly oligarchic nature, which offered only aristocrats the right to become members of the Grand Council, the supreme governing body, the Lesser Council, which exercised executive power from 1238 on, or the Senate, or to attain the elective office of Duke or Rector, who remained in office for only one month (with the exception of the years of Venetian rule, the Rector was always a Ragusan). In fact, the Government of the Republic was quite enlightened and willing to take decisions in favour of progress and social justice: in 1317, the first pharmacy, still in operation, was opened in the city; in 1347 a hospice was opened, followed, in 1377, by a quarantine colony, and in 1432 an orphanage; in 1418 the slave trade was abolished. In 1436 Dubrovnik was equipped with a 20-kilometre aqueduct, which allowed the construction of two splendid Renaissance fountains: the Great Fountain, built by Onofrio della Cava between 1438 and 1444, and the Little Fountain, built in 1441 by Petar Martinov, an octagonal basin with sculpted panels from which a column rises.

The Fortress of the Minčeta is located so as to defend the city on the northern side that faces the mountain.

The Fortress called Bokar protected, in the city's complex defensive system, the Pile Gate and the access bridge leading to the city centre.

The distribution of the buildings inside the Old City is based on a grid of perpendicular streets, in keeping with the ancient model.

In 1420 ancient Ragusa, then under the control of the Republic of Venice, was equipped with important public buildings, including the Civic Tower.

struction of prestigious civil and religious buildings. Among those buildings was the monastery of the Franciscans, which was begun in 1317 in a transitional style between Romanesque and Gothic, and of whose original structure, destroyed in the earthquake of 1667, there now remains only the splendid cloister with capitals decorated with zoomorphic motifs. In the interior is one of the oldest pharmacies in Europe, and a museum that contains its inventories, recipes, laboratory instruments, and old books, along with other valuable liturgical objects, paintings, and illuminated codices.

When, in 1420, Dalmatia became part of the Republic of Venice, only Ragusa, thanks to its defensive walls and negotiating skills, managed to preserve its status as an independent city. Italian art was in any case well accepted in the Dalmatian city and left a clear mark on the new palace of the Rectors, built in the Gothic style that flourished between 1435 and 1441 to a design by Onofrio della Cava. In it, visitors can admire a number of masterpieces, such

as the two capitals by Onofrio, one of them depicting Justice and the other the Rector of the Republic who administers that justice, the loggia with its Gothic vaults with ribbing, and the bust of the merchant Miho Pracat (1638), the only monument that the strict Republic permitted to be erected to an ordinary citizen.

With the passage of time, local artists replaced Italian artists, even though Renaissance art itself, at the time the cutting edge throughout Europe, continued to be imported from the opposite shore of the Adriatic Sea. This allowed the creation of a magnificent piece of architecture in the Sponza Palace, built in the sixteenth century and used for centuries as a customs building, mint, and city trading house, a fine example of a harmonious hybrid of Gothic architecture and Renaissance architecture.

The flourishing existence of the 'Slavic Athens' suffered a cruel blow in 1667, when an earthquake destroyed most of the city centre and decimated the population.

Between 1435 and 1441 Onofrio Della Cava built in Flamboyant Gothic style the new Palace of the Rector (on the right) from which rises the Civic Tower, while on the northern side rises the Customs Building in Venetian Flamboyant Gothic.

Between 1671 and 1713, the cathedral took on Baroque forms and its well-endowed Treasury, which consisted of 138 reliquaries, was accommodated in the magnificent chapel designed by Marino Gropelli and painted by Mattei Matejevic. Between 1705 and 1717 Gropelli also rebuilt the Church of Saint Blaise, which features on its main altar the sixteenth-century gilt statue of the patron saint of Dubrovnik holding a small model of the city in his hand. After the earthquake, the fourteenth-century Dominican church was also rebuilt.

The museum contains splendid liturgical objects and paintings, and the exceedingly well-stocked library was founded in the thirteenth century and was one of the largest and finest in Europe.

After the earthquake came the last large-scale development plan completed within the walls of Ragusa, which definitively lost its status as an independent republic in 1808 when it was conquered by Napoleon, a status that it had fiercely preserved and defended for centuries.

Detail of the interior courtyard of the Palace of the Rector, by Onofrio Della Cava, in which Gothic capitals support Renaissance arches.

Facing the Church of San Salvatore which the Neapolitan architect Onofrio Della Cava built in the first half of the fifteenth century, there is a monumental public fountain known as the Great Fountain of Onofrio.

Opposite page
Aerial view of the grid of roofs in the old city, from which there emerges the Baroque building of the cathedral, erected between 1671 and 1713 after the terrible earthquake of 1667.

Bamberg

Bamberg, a city in Upper Franconia (Germany), has been featured in the World Heritage List of UNESCO since 1993 for its important architectural and artistic monuments, which make this German city a singular urban and cultural crossroads.

The historical events of Bamberg date back to the early Middle Ages: it was founded as a settlement of the Slavs, an Indo-European people from Eastern Europe that began migrating westward from the fifth century; it came under Frankish rule, and subsequently passed to the counts of Babenberg, who gave it its name. It was not until the wedding of the Holy Roman Emperor Henry II to Cunegund of Luxembourg in 997 that the city attained any renown. The Saxon emperor received the Bavarian city as a wedding gift and decided to transform it into a new holy city because, like Rome, Bamberg stood on seven hills and had a river running through it. The emperor's idea was to build a powerful Christian bulwark to defend Germany from the pagan peoples that lived in the territories to the east. In order to set this project in motion, he decided to build a cathedral; around 1003-04 the cornerstone was laid for the construction of the *Dom*, whose present-day appearance, however, was the result of a Gothic reconstruction, following the disastrous fire that destroyed it in 1185. Beginning in 1215 construction resumed on the cathedral, and by the second half of the thirteenth century, work could be said to have been finished. The unmistakable shape of the four-towered *Dom* is the symbol of the city and one of the finest examples of German Gothic architecture, which reached its culmination in the decoration of the portals at the base of the towers, dating back to 1235, where one may admire statues of the *Virgin Mary Adored by Saints George and Peter* and of *Henry II* and *Cunegund*. The interior still clearly contains the remains of the Romanesque edifice, clearly visible in the eastern choir, while the new Gothic architecture clearly shaped the western choir, called the *Peterschor*. The new choir has at its centre the tomb of Pope Clement II, Bishop of Bamberg from 1040 to 1047 and the only Pope buried north of the Alps. The cathedral also features the renowned *Statue of the Horseman*, a masterpiece by an unknown master of the thirteenth century, which has risen to become a symbol of the world of medieval chivalry.

In contrast with the upper city, at the foot of the hill the city of the merchants and bourgeoisie developed over the centuries to become a rival and antagonist to the stronghold of religious power. The separation and the profound conflicts of interest that separated the upper city, the base of episcopal power, from the lower city also led to terrible consequences, such as witch hunts and persecution of heretics which, at the turn of the seventeenth century, brought an immense fortune into the coffers of the Bishop Johann Georg Fuchs von Dornehaim, the result of confiscations from the victims of the Ecclesiastical Tribunal.

The Altes Rathaus was built on an islet in the middle of the river Regnitz at the end of the fourteenth century. Its location on the water was selected as a neutral zone in which the representatives of the two opposing factions would meet to discuss and resolve the problems of the city. From this islet it is possible to admire the remarkable zone of Bamberg called Klein Venedig (Little Venice), an old fishing quarter characterized by tall houses with curving-pitch roofs.

With the rise to power of the bishop-princes of Schönborn in the seventeenth and eighteenth centuries, a remarkable building fever took hold in Bamberg that shaped the city in the new Baroque style; the bishops

Aerial view of Bamberg.

Opposite page
The city, founded on the banks of the river Regnitz, has maintained its historic centre practically intact; in the foreground is the roof of the Baroque structure of the Altes Rathaus, the old City Hall.

Portal with telamons, reclining figures of the rivers, and the princely heraldic crest.

At the centre of the river Regnitz, on an islet that linked the episcopal city with the mercantile city, the Altes Rathaus was built in the fourteenth century, and between 1744 and 1756 a larger building was added to it.

went so far as to offer tax breaks to private citizens who renovated their homes in the Baroque style. This renewed interest for architecture on the part of the Schönborns contrasted with the absolute prohibition to '…build new castles or repair, with spending of money, of old castles…'. This prohibition was violated with various subterfuges by Bishop Lothar Franz, who in 1693 decided to transform his own residence into a setting worthy of his rank, in the wake of the construction that was going on in Würzburg under the supervision of the architect Johann Leonhard Dientzenhofer, who was transforming the town into a Baroque capital. The Neue Residenz, built between 1695 and 1704 with austere and classical façades, clearly betrayed the determination of the bishop-prince to create interiors decorated in the new style that was sweeping through the courts of Europe.

As a result of the fiscal encouragement offered by the bishop, numerous Baroque private homes were built, principally around the Judenstrasse and the Concordiastrasse, zones inhabited by the well-to-do bourgeoisie who, in response to the Baroque luxury flaunted by the Schönborns in the upper city, were willing to rebuild their homes. The principal characteristic of the buildings on the Judenstrasse is the elegance and homogeneity of the façades built from the early years of the eighteenth century. The fulcrum of the upper city is the Domplatz, overlooked by the chief buildings that characterized and which are still the pride and joy of the city of Bamberg: the Neue Residenz, the Alte Hofhaltung, and the magnificent cathedral.

On the hill to the north of the cathedral, stands the complex Benedictine Abbey of Michaelsberg, founded by the Holy Roman Emperor Henry II the Holy (at the turn of the twelfth century); despite the Baroque renovations of the interior, it has preserved its exterior Romanesque-Gothic appearance.

The Archiepiscopal Residence called the Neue Hofaltung — Neue Residenz — was begun in 1608 and completed in 1704; in the Kaisersaal are conserved ten splendid view paintings by Bernardo Bellotto.

HENRY II THE GOOD

Henry, the son of Duke Henry of Bavaria and Giselle of Burgundy, was born in Bavaria in 973. The future Holy Roman Emperor was given a fervid religious life by Saint Wolfgang, the bishop of Ratisbon. In 997 he married Cunegund of Luxembourg and, to commemorate their wedding, the Duke of Bavaria gave him the city of Bamberg. Following the theories that he had learned at the school of Saint Wolfgang, Henry decided to establish the city as a new bulwark to protect the Faith against the paganism that was still quite widespread to the east of Germany, by establishing an ecclesiastic principality to govern the city.

In 1002 he became the King of Germany, and two years later he also received the crown of Italy, thereby extending his dominion over the Italian peninsula; in 1013 he fought and defeated Ardouin of Ivrea, winning for himself the imperial crown. He was solemnly crowned Emperor of the Holy Roman Empire in 1014. His entire life was devoted to the protection of the Church and the well-being of religion; he devoted great energy to the spread of the Benedictine Rule, co-operating with the principal centres of the reformation of the time — Cluny, Montecassino, Camaldoli, Einsiedeln, and Verdun — for a return to ecclesiastical and social discipline. During the last years of his life, the emperor expressed the wish to enter the Benedictine order; for his devotion to the order of Saint Benedict, Pope Pius declared Henry II the patron of the Benedictine Oblates at the end of the nineteenth century. He died in 1024 and was buried, along with his wife Cunegund, in Bamberg cathedral; thanks to the imperial couple's exemplary life together, they were both beatified in 1146.

Opposite page
View of the apse of the cathedral founded by the Holy Roman Emperor Henry II in 1003, rebuilt after the fire of 1185 by a master of the Upper Rhine region in Gothic style (1215-25).

The Virgin Mary, part of the statuary group depicting the Visitation *placed in the choir of the cathedral: this is a major work from the thirteenth century based on the similar group conserved in the Cathedral of Reims.*

View of the right portal of the cathedral, the Marienpforte, in Romanesque style (c. 1235) in the lunette of which is depicted the Virgin Mary with Christ Child, and the Imperial Couple of the Founders Henry II and Cunegund.

Berlin, Die Museumsinsel (The Island of Museums)

With the inauguration on 3 August 1830 of the Königliches Museum (Royal Museum, later renamed the Altes Museum), built by Karl Friedrich Schinkel in Berlin on the island in the River Spree from 1824, the first public museum complex in Germany was created. The Altes Museum was one of the first buildings in Europe built expressly as the site of a museum, and was ordered by King Frederick William III to display publicly the crown art collections.

The area selected by the architect, in the Lustgarten, for the construction of the building made use of an undeveloped plot of land facing the City Hall and thus closed off the square formed by the buildings of the Castle, the Arsenal, the Cathedral, and the Museum.

The façade derived from the front of Greek temples is set on a high socle, access to which is provided by a broad staircase lined by sculptures. Along the façade run eighteen sandstone, Ionic columns in a giant order, supporting the attic along which extends the inscription: *FRIDERICUS GUILELMUS III STUDIO ANTIQUITATIS OMNIGENIÆ ET ARTIUM LIBERALIUM MUSEUM CONSTITUIT MDCCCXXVIII* (Frederick William III dedicates this museum to the study of antiquity and the liberal arts 1828).

The Museum of the Lustgarten, as soon as it was completed, proved to be too small, and in fact it was decided to start construction of another building in the area adjoining to the north; for this purpose the Crown purchased the land adjacent to the Museum, so as to have space for new buildings. In 1841, the year following the coronation of the new sovereign Frederick William IV, it was ordered, by Royal Decree, that the entire island of the Spree should be transformed into a 'haven for art and science'. This established the programmatic concept that informed and would guide the construction of the so-called Island of Museums.

The first step towards the creation of the museum-island was the construction of the Neues Museum, which stood behind the building erected by Schinkel. The design of the project was entrusted to the architect Stüler, a pupil of Schinkel's; work on the new building extended for many years because of the clayey soil which created considerable static problems, as had already been the case with Schinkel's structure. The ceremony of the laying of the cornerstone took place in 1841 and the project was not finished until 1859. In this new building, the collections of the Egyptian art treasures and the Ethnographic Cabinet were installed. The ground floor was used for the exhibition of sculpture, while the upper galleries housed the collection of miniatures, drawings, and prints (Kupferstichkabinett, now at the Kulturforum), as well as a collection of models reproducing renowned pieces of medieval architecture.

Seriously damaged during the Second World War, the Neues Museum will be reopened in 2006 with the integration of the works from the Egyptian collection, currently exhibited in the castle of Charlottenburg in the former Western Zone.

The year 1861 marked the entry into the collections of the Prussian state of the Wagener collection of contemporary German art. Such a bequest entailed a new museum, the Nationalgalerie, built between 1866 and 1876 to plans by Stüler, with construction by Johann Heinrich Strack,

Aerial view of the Museumsinsel of Berlin.

Andokides, Attic Amphora with Scenes of Battle, a splendid example of Greek ceramic production with red figures on a black background (fifth century B.C.), conserved in the Altes Museum.

Opposite page
The Berlin architect Karl Friederick Schinkel, built, at the behest of Frederick William III, the Rotunda of the Altes Museum: a Neo-classical version of the Pantheon of Rome (beginning in 1824).

Opposite page
Along the Kupfergraben stand, in the foreground, the side of the Bodemuseum, designed by Ernst Eberhard von Ihne between 1897 and 1904, and in the middle distance the propylaea of the Pergamonmuseum, built between 1907 and 1930.

Dominating the eastern side of the Island of Museums, the Nationalgalerie was designed by Stüler, and built between 1866 and 1876, in forms reminiscent of the Parthenon in Athens in order to house collections of German art of the modern era.

Considered one of the masterpieces of Karl Friederich Schinkel, the Altes Museum with its monumental Ionic façade dominates the ample space of the Lustgarten and closes off to the south the Island of Museums.

Hedwing Schulz-Völker, the main staircase of the Neues Museum: this watercolour depicts the installation and decoration of the museum (destroyed by bombing during the Second World War), executed by Stüler between 1841 and 1859.

in a site to the east of the Neues Museum. In this way, for the first time contemporary paintings entered the museums of Berlin, long excluded from the context of the royal collections.

With the advent on the throne of Kaiser Wilhelm II, the new project for the construction of the Museum of the Renaissance found financing. The building, set at the tip of the Island of Museums, was constructed to plans by the architect Ernst Eberhard von Ihne, Court Counsellor for Construction; work began in 1897 and the building was solemnly inaugurated in 1904 with the name of Kaiser Friedrich Museum, in honour of the first 'protector' of the Museums of Berlin. The decoration of the façades, which overlooked the Kupfergraben, is openly Neo-Baroque. The two-storey building is punctuated, on its façade, by Corinthian giant-order sandstone semi-columns, between which are giant windows, with continuous arched lintels on the ground floor, and architraves on the second floor. The building is dominated by the looming mass of the dome, set atop a tambour with an elliptical plan, divided by pilasters between which are set oval oculi. The Bodemuseum is currently closed for restoration, and is expected to reopen in late 2005; it will then house the collections that belonged to the Prussian Medal Collection, the Numismatic Cabinet, the Museum for Byzantine Art, and the Sculpture Collection.

The discovery of the magnificent Altar of Zeus near the hill of Pergamum, in Asia Minor, between 1878 and 1886, and its successive transportation to Berlin, created the need to build a structure in which to display one of the greatest examples of Greek architecture and sculpture. The project was assigned to the architect Fritz Wolff, who built the first nucleus of the museum between 1899 and 1901, at the same time as the construction of the Kaiser Friedrich Museum.

Work on the Pergamonmuseum was begun by the architect Alfred Messel in 1907, on the west side of the island, amidst enormous financial constraints and delays caused by the outbreak of the First World War. It was not until 1930 that the building could be considered finished, thanks to the immense devotion of Ludwig Hoffmann, following the death of Messel in 1909; the construction of this museum concluded the architectural process that unfolded on the Museum Island over the course of a century. Badly damaged by Allied bombing raids during the Second World War, the Pergamonmuseum was reopened in 1954. The restoration of the entire complex will be finished in 2010.

Panoramic view of the reconstruction of the Altar of Zeus Sother and Athena Nikephoros, from Pergamum in Asia Minor, a masterpiece of Hellenistic art. The Pergamonmuseum was built between 1907 and 1930 to accommodate it.

The dominant theme of the magnificent altar of Pergamum, built at the behest of Eumenes II to commemorate his own dynasty, is the frieze depicting the Titanomachia: the cosmic struggle between the Titans and the gods of Olympus, is a recurring allegory for the battle between reason and irrationality, between order and chaos.

Stonehenge

The imposing monument of Stonehenge stands in an area noted for it megalithic relics, to the north of Salisbury in the country of Wiltshire. Due to its complexity, its impressive remains and the fantasies that it has inspired over the centuries, it represents the point of departure for Britain's national heritage. This English complex, which has prompted a vast bibliography (often fantastic or at least fanciful) and which has been studied by numerous researchers and scholars, still constitutes one of the most enigmatic of mysteries whose interpretation poses considerable problems. Different explanations are offered even for the meaning of the word *Stonehenge*: if there are no doubts about the first part, *stone* (meaning 'stone', or 'rock'), matters stand differently for the second part, *henge* (from the Anglo-Saxon term *hon*, from which comes *hang*, 'hang', or 'suspend'). Stonehenge would thus mean 'hanging stones', alluding to a system of architraves, or 'suspended stones'. Even though the megalithic construction may appear to be imposing to our modern eyes, we should keep in mind that of the original complex there remains on the site no more than a portion, consisting of a giant *cromlech* (literally, 'curved stone') and other monoliths dating back to various phases. The most recent and thorough archaeological investigations have allowed reconstruction of the later events on the site which belong fairly clearly to three main phases of construction. In the most ancient phase, which dates to just before 2000 B.C., the zone had no megaliths, but was occupied by a circle of small wells carved into the earth, surrounded by a concentric ditch and a large berm, with a diameter of roughly 90 metres (295 feet). Inside some of these wells remains have been found that have led archaeologists to suppose that they were cremation tombs. The second phase, which dates

from the turn of the millennium, coincides with a megalithic stage in the full sense of the word; on the interior of the circle of wells stood two *cromlechs*, or concentric circles of stones. These were made up of unhewn monoliths of various heights and a particular type of stone called Bluestones (these were eruptive rocks, dolerites and rhyolites) that came from the Prescelly Mountains in the region of Pembrokeshire, some 300 kilometres (about 200 miles) from Stonehenge. Today there remains only a small portion of the double circle of stones, even though certain excavation finds have cast doubt on the certainty that the circles were ever completed. During the third and final phase, which dates from the first centuries of the second millennium B.C., the erection of the structure that is still considered the most important occurred: the so-called 'sarsen circle', or 'outer circle'. This consisted of thirty sarsen monoliths (blocks of sandstone which came from an area to the north of Wiltshire, in the Marlborough Downs), which stood 4 metres (13 feet) fixed vertically in the ground and linked by stone architraves. On the interior of the circle, arranged so as to form a horseshoe, stand five triliths, also made of sarsen, formed of two vertical support stones rising some 7 metres (23 feet) and a horizontal architrave that lay snug atop the two monoliths thanks to a very precise tenon-and-mortise system. In the area between the outer circle of monoliths and the triliths and the inner horseshoe formed by the latter, the Bluestones of the double *cromlechs* of the preceding phase were moved and relocated, leaving only the housing of the original positions. At the centre of the system, at the focal point of the horseshoe, there lies a flat and elongated stone, 5 metres (about 16 feet) in length, called the 'altar stone'. To the east there is an access road at the centre of which looms the so-called 'Heel Stone', which

Panoramic view of the site of Stonehenge.

Opposite page
Detail of one of the five trilithic elements in the inner circle.

Detail of the monoliths.

Aerial view of the sacred complex made with a series of cromlechs *(curved stones), probably on the site of an ancient necropolis.*

has given rise over the centuries to heated discussions; it stand 5 metres (about 16 feet) above ground level, and it leans slightly towards the monument. Between this block and the outer circle is the 'Slaughter Stone'. Despite the fact that numerous studies have focused on the Stonehenge complex, it continues to pose numerous problems. First and foremost, the question of the transportation and erection of the stone blocks of enormous size and weight by a prehistoric society that was certainly not technologically advanced. In the second place, debates still rage over the function that the site was meant to serve. On the one hand its placement in an area with numerous barrow tombs suggests that it was a holy place, but on the other, recent studies on the orientation of the entire monument have led to the hypothesis that it was a sort of astronomical observatory for the study of lunar phases and eclipses. While there is no question that on the summer solstice the sun rises exactly over the summit of the Heel Stone and that other major stones in the complex have locations with equally precise orientations, it should not be excluded that this had to do with sun worship. According to some scholars, moreover, considering the movement of the sun for each year, in the same period and the same place, the sun rises slightly to the right; when the Heel Stone was positioned it cannot have marked the rising of the sun at the summer solstice with its summit, since it does today, thousands of years later.

THE LEGENDS OF STONEHENGE:
THE 'DANCE OF THE GIANTS'.

In his *Historia Regum Britanniae*, Geoffrey of Monmouth (1100-54) tells of an episode that he dates to the year 475. He linked this episode to the origin and the history of the monument of Stonehenge, which had been handed down in this form for centuries. The story tells of the conflict between the kingdom of the Breton Vortigern, elected King of England, and the Saxons and their King Hengist. Since the two parties had agreed to make peace, they agreed to meet, unarmed, near the site of Stonehenge; here, treacherously, the Saxons drew their daggers and assassinated King Vortigern and hundreds of noble Bretons. Aurelius Ambrosius, successor to Vortigern, decided to erect a monument to commemorate the massacre, a monument that Geoffrey of Monmouth identifies as the complex of Stonehenge. A decisive role was played by the wizard Merlin, a figure who would in this case link the fame of the monument to the cycle of King Arthur and the Round Table; Merlin suggested to the king that he utilize for the construction of the monument a number of large stones, known as the 'Dance of the Giants', which were found on Mount Killarus in Ireland. These stones, which the 'Giants' had brought over from Africa, were said to have marvellous properties and to cure all ills. The Bretons therefore took ship and sailed towards the mountain in question, and were obliged to fight the Irish people in order to seize the Dance of the Giants, which were then repositioned according to their original layout on Salisbury Plain.

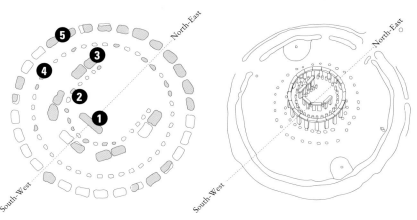

Picture of Stonehenge between 2100 and 1100 B.C.:

1 Altar stone
2 Blue horseshoe stones
3 Five horseshoe triliths
4 Inner circle
5 Outer circle

Trilith elements of the outer circle.

Athens, Acropolis

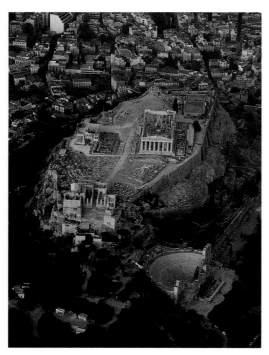

Aerial view of the Acropolis.

Opposite page
Detail of the south-eastern corner of the temple dedicated to Athena Parthenos, known as the Parthenon, and designed by Ictinus and Callicrates between 447 and 432 B.C.

'And it is but meet that the city, when once she is sufficiently equipped with all that is necessary for prosecuting the war, should apply her abundance to such works as, by their completion, will bring her everlasting glory. ... So then the works arose, no less towering in their grandeur than inimitable in the grace of their outlines, since the workmen eagerly strove to surpass themselves in the beauty of their handicraft. And yet the most wonderful thing about them was the speed with which they rose'. Thus Plutarch (first to second centuries A.D.) in his *Life of Pericles* (12, 4-13, 1 *passim*) describes how the Athenian statesman conceived and laid the groundwork for his great creation, around the middle of the fifth century B.C.: he decided to reconstruct, even bigger and more beautiful than before, the sacred buildings of the Acropolis, which had been sacked and burned by the Persian King Xerxes in 480 B.C., before being defeated by Themistocles in the great naval battle of Salamis. In fact, the hill that was one day to house the Parthenon, once the site of the royal palace in Mycenaean times, had become a sacred site dedicated to Athena, the goddess after whom the city had been named, and to other cults, such as those of Erechtheus and Poseidon, at the time of the birth of the Athenian *polis*, an event that is lost in the mists of the so-called Hellenic Dark Ages. Here, in 1886 and 1887, a number of sculptures of great quality were discovered, in part now in the Museum of the Acropolis (among other items, the *Blond Ephebus* and the enigmatic *Rampin Horseman*). The first building to which the Athenians turned in the larger project of reconstruction was the Temple of Athena (448-432 B.C.), the Parthenon, which we find described for the first time with this name in an oration by Demosthenes in 355 B.C. The name was probably given to the temple because it featured in its cella a statue of ivory and gold of Athena *Parthenos* (or virgin), which stood 12 metres tall. This artwork, now lost, was by Phidias; other scholars have suggested however that the temple took its name from a room placed behind the cella which housed during the Panathenean Games the virgin maidens (*parthénoi*) entrusted with serving the goddess. The architect was Ictinus, assisted by Callicrates, but it would seem that Phidias also made considerable contributions to the design; Phidias was the artistic adviser and personal friend of Pericles, and had been appointed by him the superintendent of all the works on the Acropolis. The temple, built entirely of Pentelikon marble and originally painted in encaustic in shades of red, light blue, and gold (like all the other monuments of the Acropolis), is surrounded by columns, eight on each of the fronts and seventeen on each of the long sides. The selection of a layout whereby the columns on the long sides were twice as many plus one as the columns on the short sides already constituted per se a major innovation with respect to the more elongated plans of earlier archaic constructions. The great mastery with which the project was designed is clearly documented by the refined optical corrections meant to obtain an effect of lightness: the horizontal lines (stylobates, pediments, and the cornices of the long sides) are slightly convex because of a very minor curvature; the columns are not vertical, but imperceptibly inclined towards the interior of the structure: the corner columns are slightly stouter than the others, and the intercolumnars of the corners are slightly narrower in order to attenuate the angular contrast. The cella (*naos*) *in antis*, which is to say, preceded and followed by a colonnade, occupies a considerable portion of the stylobate: on the interior it is split up into two parts, one of which is larger, split into three aisles by double rows of

Doric columns, and contains the statue of the goddess, while the other is smaller, and contained the great peplus embroidered with mythical scenes, readied after months of work by the *Ergastines*, aristocratic maidens selected to perform this honourable task, and offered to Athena during the Panathenean Games. The columns of the peristyle were in the Doric order, as were the triglyphs and the metopes of the external frieze. The latter, totaling ninety-two in number, are now largely in the British Museum of London, and depict the war between the Athenians and the Amazons (*Amazonomachia*) on the western side; the sack of Troy (*Ilioupérsis*) on the northern side; the revolt of the Gigantes against the Gods of Olympus (*Gigantomachia*) on the eastern side; and the battle between Centaurs and Lapites (*Centauromachia*) on the southern side. Moreover, with an original blend of Doric and Ionic elements, the Parthenon featured another frieze, which ran unbroken along the external walls of the cella and depicted the great procession in which the entire city, on the occasion of the Panathenean Games, brought the goddess Athena the peplus woven by the *Ergastines*: a long line of horsemen, men, women, maidens, old men, and priests walks towards deities enthroned high above the entrance to the cella. The deities are depicted on a larger scale than the humans, but their very human gestures and poses and their seated position undercuts that difference. The pediments too featured a refined scuptural decoration, the component parts of which are now scattered around the world: on the eastern pediment (the main one) was depicted the birth of Athena, while on the opposite pediment was depicted the struggle between Athena and Poseidon for dominance over Attica. What we can admire today is the result of a long history of destruction and plunder: with the advent of Christianity the temple was

1. Parthenon (Temple of Athena Parthenos)
2. Temple of Athena Nike
3. Propylaea
4. Pinacotheca
5. Temple of Erechtheum
6. Statue of Athena Promachos

PHIDIAS AND THE INVENTION OF THE 'CLASSICAL' STYLE

Phidias (*c.* 490-*c.* 430 B.C.) was not satisfied with directing work on the Acropolis, nor did he execute only the gold and ivory statue of Athena for the cella of the Parthenon; it is quite likely that he conceived the subjects for the entire decoration of the temple, as well as executing the models, which were then translated into marble by his assistants. All the same, a careful analysis of the nineteen surviving metopes, all depicting scenes from the *Centauromachia* (or battle of the centaurs), the panels of the frieze, and the statues of the pediment, clearly reveals the fundamental aspects and the strong sense of the new that permeated the style of Phidias, which marked the definitive obsolescence of the rigid and archaic figurative language. The sculptures and the reliefs appear to be dominated by a powerful psychological tension, but the movements depicted preserve a controlled and harmonious cadence; the lines are softer than in earlier sculpture and the shaping of the nudes takes on a more plastic modulation dominated by a lively sense of the flesh; the female figures are enveloped in mantles and peploses with a flowing drapery, executed with detailed folds that in some cases adhere to the body 'beneath', revealing a painstaking attention to anatomical detail and the movement of the body thereby displaying an emotional involvement in the action. But Phidias was also a brilliant innovator in terms of compositional layout and organization, as is shown by the way in which he resolves the problem of the decoration of the pediment, whose triangular shape creates a number of problems: at the centre, where the image of a deity traditionally stood out, the sculptor placed a number of figures instead, which with their movements determined the rhythm of the sculptures in the lateral segments. He left a profound mark on the figurative culture of his time with the birth of a Phidian mannerism, one of the greatest representatives of which was Callimachus, who sculpted the balustrade around the little temple of Athena Nike; all the same, Athens, as was so often the case in its 1,000-year history, was not a grateful mother to this genius son of hers. The target of resentment and envy because of his friendship with Pericles, he was first accused of embezzling some of the gold and ivory entrusted to him for the great statue of Athena Parthenos and, subsequently, of impiety. He was imprisoned, and is said to have died in prison (though, according to a second version, he fled to Elis).

Phidias and his workshop produced the entire plastic decoration of the Parthenon for Pericles; in particular, the eastern pediment with the birth of Athena, and the western pediment, with the battle between Athena and Poseidon, from which come the two statues of the Attic rivers, Cephisus and Ilissus, now in the Museum of the Acropolis.

Opposite page
To Callicrates alone is attributed the design of the Temple of the Erechtheum, dedicated to Athena Polias and built between 421 and 405 B.C.; on the southern side is a loggia supported by six female figures called Caryatids.

View of the Acropolis from the level of Athens: high up looms the bulk of the Parthenon, on the left of the complex of the Propylaea and the Temple of Athena Nike, and down below are the structures of the Theatre of Dionysus.

Western front of the Parthenon, a monumental example of the Doric style created by Ictinus and Callicrates.

Internal view of the Propylaea: spectacular entrance to the plateau of the Acropolis, built by Mnesicles beginning in 437 B.C.

Opposite page
The little Ionic temple with a double front dedicated to Nike Athena was built to overlook the western slope of the cliff of the Acropolis between 427 and 425 B.C. by Callicrates.

Before the devastation wrought by the Persians, the Acropolis of Athens was already decorated by temples and sculptures, fragmentary evidence of which still survive, such as this fragment of the pediment frieze with a sea monster with three bodies, made of painted limestone (560-550 B.C.), now conserved in the Museum of the Acropolis.

Detail of the west pediment of the Parthenon on which the sequence of methopes and triglyphs on the frieze is clearly visible.

transformed into a church and many of the metopes were chiselled away; then, under Turkish dominion, it was transformed into a gunpowder magazine and was shelled in 1687 by the Venetian fleet; finally, in 1801 Lord Elgin purchased and carted off to London a considerable portion of the sculptural decoration, with the intention of saving it from certain destruction. Once the architectural section of the Parthenon was complete, work continued on the construction of a new monumental entrance to the Acropolis, the Propylaea (437-433 B.C.), the creation of the architect Mnesicles, who skilfully managed to blend Doric and Ionic elements in it. Set at the westernmost extremity of the plateau, they are composed of a central body reached via a magnificent staircase, a double-façade vestibule divided into aisles by two rows of three Ionic columns each, and two lateral wings, one of which (the northern wing) contains the picture gallery which

once housed famous paintings. To the right of the Propylaea, on a south-western bastion of the hill, was erected — between 424 and 420 B.C. — in all likelihood to plans by Callicrates, the little Temple of Athena Nike. The building, exceedingly graceful with its four elegant Ionic columns on both fronts, was adorned above the architrave by a continual frieze depicting the battle between Greeks, Persians, and Amazons, in the presence of the gods; the pediments may have depicted an *Amazonomachia* and a *Gigantomachia*. Around it was built a marble balustrade, several panels of which are now housed in the Museum of the Acropolis: the decoration in relief portrays Athena Nike and a group of Nikai who, as a symbolic token of victory, raise terrestrial and naval trophies and lead bulls to the sacrifice. The last great temple built on the Acropolis in the fifth century was the Erechtheum, probably designed, also along Ionic lines, by Philo-

cles. It was set to the north of the Parthenon, where it was thought the tomb of the mythical founder of Athens, King Cecrops, was located, on the site where the ancients believed that the struggle between Athena and Poseidon had taken place: even in classical times, the olive tree was still pointed out that had supposedly been caused to sprout by the goddess, along with the mark of the trident, struck against the ground by the god to cause a salt-water spring to bubble up. The temple thus housed in a single building a number of different cults, a factor that affected its structure, giving it an irregular plan. The Erechtheus presented a central structure with a hexastyle portico on the eastern front and four columns set against the wall on the western front. The eastern zone of the central structure contained the

wooden simulacrum of Athena Polias, which was thought to have fallen from the sky; the western section, split up into a number of rooms, was dedicated to the cult of Erechtheus, a mythical king and religious reformer who was identified with Poseidon, the hero Butes, and the god Haephestus. Many other monuments and artworks by famous artists were present on the Acropolis, some added after the fifth century, and among them also the great bronze statue, now lost, of the *Athena Promachos* (protectress), 7 metres tall, and set before the Propylaea in an almost central position. The monumental entrance to the esplanade of the Acropolis was provided with an entrance that imitated a temple façade, and was set next to the Pinacotheca, the first public museum in history.

Opposite page
Detail of the trabeation and of the supporting elements (fluted shaft, capital, and abacus) of the Parthenon, built in the Doric style by Ictinus and Callicrates.

The Temple of the Erechtheum, designed in the Ionic style by Callicrates, was connected to a sanctuary in which was conserved the olive tree sacred to Athena.

Detail of one of the female figures supporting the trabeation of the loggia of the Erechtheum, known as Caryatids because the women of Caryae were considered the most beautiful in the Greek world.

Ferrara

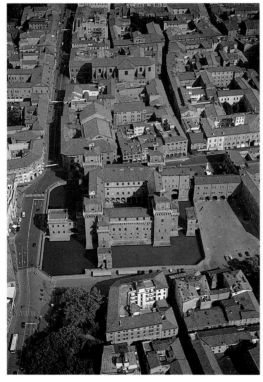

Aerial view of the Este Castle and the historic centre.

Opposite page
Maestro Niccolò and his assistants were responsible for conceiving and decorating with sculpture the Cathedral of Ferrara between 1120 and 1150; in particular, the lunette of the portal with Saint George and the Dragon. *In the Gothic loggia, the* Virgin Mary and Child *was done by Cristoforo da Firenze (1427).*

Ferrara, along with the enclosure walls that surround the city for 9 kilometres (5 and one-half miles), still possesses, virtually unaltered, the main urbanistic features and the buildings that connote both the medieval period and the Renaissance period, during which, respectively, the city established itself and experienced the height of its glory. The church of San Giorgio, whose present-day appearance was established during the Renaissance with the crucial contribution of the architect Biagio Rossetti (1446-1516), was, from the seventh century onward, the cathedral of Ferrara and the centre of the first inhabited nucleus of the city, which was built at the branching of the River Po into its two emissaries, the Volano and Primaro. Stripped of its original role in 1135, following the construction of the new cathedral, in 1417 it became the headquarters of the Order of the Olivetans and an important centre for the production of illuminated codices. The campanile by Rossetti here has an eminently urbanistic function, because it is the first architectural feature that can be seen from the plain by those who approach the city from the south-east.

An important relic, practically unaltered, is the layout of the fortified *castrum* (roughly seventh century) in the area around the Via San Pietro, with a series of narrow parallel streets, characterized by a horseshoe shape, with the base along the Via Ripagrande. From the *castrum* another fortified system ran, which can also be easily identified from the grid of the streets which, with the interruption of the areas of the Duomo and the Castello Estense, runs all the way to the zone of the Via Garibaldi.

The artery that presently corresponds to the Via Carlo Mayr-Via Ripagrande documents the old course of the River Po, which was then filled in, on the left bank of which ran the Via Grande, mirrored in the river, with its storehouses, trading emporiums, port facili-

ties and shops. Even today the Via delle Volte remains unaltered, running parallel to the last-mentioned road, served as a service road for the riverfront buildings along the Via Grande: it is characterized by a series of round arches and pointed arches, which date back to the thirteenth and fourteenth centuries, and in some cases by holm-oak beams, which supported the passageway, raised about the narrow and tight street level, between the buildings facing the river and private residences.

Among the various monumental complexes, certainly the oldest is the cathedral, built at the beginning of the twelfth century, when the need was felt to move the cathedral from the church of San Giorgio towards the centre of town which was by this point developing in that direction. In 1135 it was consecrated and dedicated to San Giorgio, or Saint George, the patron saint of Ferrara. The successive integrations and modifications that were made in the thirteenth and fourteenth centuries created the harmonious synthesis of Romanesque and Gothic that marks the exterior of the building and gives the façade its structure with three cusps of equal height, which has been interpreted as a symbolic reference to the Holy Trinity.

A great deal of the sculptural decoration is certainly the work of Nicholaus or Niccolò, a master who was active in northern Italy from 1120 to 1150, whose name appears carved in the lunette of the portal with *Saint George on Horseback, Depicted As He Spears the Dragon.* In the middle of the tripartite little loggia of the vestibule is placed a *Virgin Mary with Christ Child* executed by Cristoforo da Firenze in 1427. In the tympanum and the underlying fascia is a depiction of the *Last Judgement.* Alongside the two lateral doors are depictions of the Marquess Alberto d'Este, portrayed in pilgrim's garb, returning from Rome where he obtained from Pope Boniface IX formal recognition of the establishment of the Uni-

Detail of the complex structure of Este Castle, still surrounded by the defensive moat.

The Marquess Nicholas II d'Este commissioned Bartolino Ploti da Novara to build the princely residence, begun in 1385.

*Opposite page
Biagio Rossetti was responsible for the conception in the late fifteenth century of the Palazzo dei Diamanti, built on the main intersection of the so-called Addizione Erculea, with its two fronts sheathed in rough-hewn faceted ashlars.*

versity of Ferrara in 1391; on the left is a bust of Clement VIII, under whose papacy Ferrara came under the direct government of the Church in 1598. The southern flank, now covered with the plaster of shops, bears an important statutory decree carved into marble slabs, ordered by the Council of Wise Men of the city in 1173. Midway along the wall was set the Door of the Months, closed in 1717; the handsome panels with depictions of the months of the year are now conserved in the nearby Museo del Duomo (Museum of the Cathedral). The semi-circular apse dating from 1498 was the work of Biagio Rossetti, while the shape and design of the campanile, begun in 1412 and left unfinished, is traditionally attributed to at least a contribution from, among others, Leon Battista Alberti. The interior was renovated by Francesco Mazzarelli (between 1710 and 1712). In the bowl-vault of the apse is the fresco of the *Last Judgement,* a work by Sebastiano Filippi, known as Bastianino (1577-80), strongly influenced by Michelangelo's *Last*

Judgement in the Sistine Chapel. But there can be no question that the emblem of the city *par excellence* is the Castello Estense, begun in 1385 at the behest of the Marquess Nicolò II to plans by Bartolino Ploti da Novara, architect, among other things, of the castles of Pavia and Mantua.

It is connected with the old residence of the marquess, across from the cathedral, with a walkway, the 'Via Coperta', transformed at the behest of Duke Alfonso I into the so-called 'Camerini di Alabastro', or 'Alabaster Dressing Rooms', and then adorned with paintings by Giovanni Bellini, Titian, and Dosso Dossi.

In order to 'schivar la noia' — literally, drive away boredom — the Marquess Alberto V d'Este ordered the construction in 1385 of Palazzo Schifanoia, a 'delizia', or peaceful refuge from daily worries. The palace is the sole survivor of the numerous d'Este 'delizie' built within the walls.

Borso was the chief admirer of the *palazzo*.

THE FERRARESE SCHOOL
During the reign of Leonello d'Este, between 1441 and 1450, the court of Ferrara, one of the most vibrant and prosperous in all of northern Italy, enjoyed an especially fertile atmosphere, characterized by a remarkable open-mindedness. Among those who had significant influence on the local artistic culture, we should mention the relationships and encounters with personalities such as Pisanello, Leon Battista Alberti, Jacopo Bellini, Piero della Francesca, and the young Mantegna; also extremely stimulating were the strong ties to Flanders whereby Ferrara was able to offer hospitality to such artists as Rogier van der Weyden, whose dramatic focus on the emotional life of his characters left a profound mark on the artistic research being carried on at the d'Este court. These are all elements that helped to contribute to the formation of a genuine Ferrarese visual language, which established its independence a few years later under the rule of Borso (1450-71): the exasperated and incisive line that was typical of the court was accentuated and emphasized still further, resulting in an extreme emotional tension, and in an illusory realism that even came to pervade fantastic subjects. The three great masters of the 'officina ferrarese', or 'Ferrarese Workshop', who took on a stylistic quest based on common characteristics, although with autonomous artistic processing that did not necessarily come to the same conclusions, were Cosmè Tura (*c.* 1430-95) and the young Francesco del Cossa (*c.* 1436-78) and Ercole de' Roberti (*c.* 1450-96).

The beloved residence of the Duke Borso d'Este, the Palazzo of Schifanoia was adorned, beginning in 1471, with a cycle of paintings of the months; here in particular is the month of April, painted by Francesco del Cossa, subdivided into the deities that protected each month (Venus), the three signs of the Zodiac (Taurus), and scenes of courtly life.

To it the marquess, beginning in 1471, newly elevated to the title of duke, consecrated the most solemn celebration of his lordly reign: the cycle of frescoes of the Salone di Mesi (Hall of the Months). Despite centuries of neglect (in the eighteenth century the building even housed the Manifattura Tabacchi, where tobacco was processed) that buried the memory of this masterpiece in oblivion, only to return around the middle of the nineteenth century and effectively damage part of the frescoes, the sequence of images has preserved intact its remarkable evocative power. The frescoes on the walls of the Salone, which measures 25 by 11 metres (82 by 36 feet), are divided into twelve vertical panels, one for each month of the year, and three horizontal zones: the higher part is dedicated to the pagan gods, depicted on triumphal chariots; the central part is dedicated to the signs of the Zodiac, with symbolic figures in keeping with the astrological ideas of the time; the lower part celebrates the saga of Borso d'Este and praises his achievements and deeds in every period of the year. The cycle is considered to be a full-fledged visual epic poem

on the magnificence of Borso d'Este, inspired by the learned and refined supervision of the renowned court Humanist, Pellegrino Prisciani, who was capable of producing the best from the members of the painterly Ferrarese 'officina', or workshop, Francesco del Cossa (1435-78) and Ercole de' Roberti (1450-96).

The most important historical and urbanistic feature is the Renaissance section of the city, to the north of the thoroughfare of Corso Giovecca-Viale Cavour, corresponding to the so-called Addizione Erculea (literally, Ercole's Addition). This zone of expansion of the city to the north, strongly encouraged by Duke Ercole I d'Este and commissioned from Biagio Rossetti, intended to double the urban area, enclosing within new walls the development of the urban structure in accordance with modern and rational rules. The new grid of broad straight arteries, perpendicular to each other, was meant to splice into the various roadways of the medieval part of the city with the goal of surrounding the d'Este Castle (Castello Estense), hitherto at the northernmost edge of the city, and placing it in the new centre, as the

Panoramic view of the cathedral consecrated to Saint George (San Giorgio) in 1135, in which the Romanesque structures blend harmoniously with the additions from the Gothic era and the Renaissance.

Maestro Nicolò and assistants, lion with the head of a calf between its paws and on its back a telamon supporting the porch of the cathedral (first half of the twelfth century).

The elegant Renaissance façade of the Church of San Francesco was the work of the architect Biagio Rossetti, inspired by the design by Leon Battista Alberti for the façade of the Church of Santa Maria Novella in Florence.

The complex of the Charter House in Ferrara, left unfinished, to which a Baroque portal was added.

Opposite page
View of the Piazza del Municipio (town square); in the foreground note the pillar-bearing lion of the portal of the cathedral.

fulcrum of the modernized plan of the city. Work continued on the massive project for just under a decade from 1490. In order to anchor the Addizione Erculea some twenty aristocratic *palazzi* were built in those years, along with twelve churches, and many of those buildings still stand. At the intersection produced by the two main arteries, Via Ercole d'Este and the Corso di Porta Po and the Corso di Porta Mare, stand, facing each other, the two most important monumental civic edifices of the Addizione Erculea: the Palazzo dei Diamanti and the Palazzo Prosperi Sacrati, both by Rossetti. The symmetry of the two buildings, accentuated by the presence of a corner balcony on each, pointing towards the intersection, underscores and emphasizes the most evocative intersection in the entire Ferrarese city layout. The Palazzo dei Diamanti, the construction of which Rossetti oversaw beginning in 1493, was commissioned by Prince Sigismondo d'Este, the brother of Ercole I, in order to add luster to the new zone, and it was completed in 1567 at the behest of Luigi Cardinal d'Este. The façade is sheathed in over ten thousand ashlars made of white stone, rough-hewn into diamond shapes; the effect of intense lu-

minosity of the surface is obtained through the various structure of the orders of the 'diamonds': in the lower rows, closest to the street surface, the peak of the pyramids is slightly turned downward; in the middle rows, the peak of the pyramids is perfectly centred; in the upper rows, it is raised slightly upward.

In the planning of the Addizione Erculea a specific role was accorded to the Piazza Ariostea, at the time, the Piazza Nuova, specially built as a ring of greenbelt, tree-lined and grassy back then, just as it is today, as well as the skilful inclusion of the existing d'Este residence of Belfiore, later destroyed, of which only a few traces survive; it housed the splendid and renowned *studiolo* of the Marquess Leonello d'Este (1441-50), with the celebrated pictorial cycle of the *Muses*, inspired by the Humanist Guarino da Verona, now largely housed in the Picture Gallery, or Pinacoteca Nazionale Ferrarese. Across from it stands the Certosa (Charter House), an imposing monastic complex founded by Borso d'Este in 1452. Within it stands, its silhouette gloriously intact, the church of San Cristoforo, begun in 1498, a sort of great architectural sculpture by Rossetti.

Paestum

It was the Greek colonists of Sybaris, originally from Peloponnesian Achaea, who founded Poseidonia at the beginning of the seventh century B.C. as a trading base in the Tyrrhenian Sea, accessible overland from the mother colony on the Ionian Sea, without having to circumnavigate Calabria; it was built not far from the Silaris, or Sele, a river that was then navigable, in the midst of a rich but marshy plain, similar to that of the mother city.

The area of the city, still undergoing excavation, occupies two limestone plateaus overlooking the sea, which once lay closer in, surrounded by a single solid enclosure wall, almost 5 kilometres (3 miles) long, built by the Greeks and later restored under Italic and Roman rule. In the four principal directions — towards the sea, to the north towards the extraurban sanctuary of Argive Hera, to the east, and to the south, towards the *kora* — the four main entrance gates open out. The city's structure is based on the typical scheme of orthogonal blocks whose main axis is the Via Sacra which, beginning from the southernmost gate, the Porta della Giustizia, connects the two temple areas dedicated to Hera and Athena. Nowadays, unfortunately, the path is crossed by the state road, Statale 18, opened in 1829.

Documentation of the flourishing period in which it was a trading emporium, which lasted until the end of the fifth century B.C., is provided by three monumental temples. In the first half of the sixth century B.C., the building known as the Basilica was erected; it is more commonly known as the Temple of Hera, who was the patron goddess of the Achaeans since the Trojan War. The renovation undertaken around 540-530 B.C. produced the Doric forms, the nine columns on the front with the typical swollen shape of this style, and an unusual division of the cella into two aisles: preceded by a vestibule to which an *adyton* corresponded on the opposite side, it features two niches in the far wall, which have led scholars to hypothesize that the temple was also consecrated to Zeus. Dating from the following century is the nearby Temple of Neptune, 460 B.C., which was actually also consecrated to Hera, a masterpiece of the classical age and in the Doric style which, according to archaeologists, was a reference to the Temple of Zeus at Olympia. Rising from the base are the six columns of the façade and the fourteen columns of the long sides, which support a massive architrave with decoration consisting of metopes and triglyphs; the interior space is articulated from a pronaos offering access to the cella, divided into three aisles by a double order of Doric columns, and from an *opistodomos*, which also features two columns *in antis*. In front of the principal façade of both temples stand the altars for the cults. The last area of worship inside the city was given monumental forms as early as the sixth century B.C.; at the end of that century the Temple of Ceres was erected, though it was actually consecrated to Athena. It too is Doric and has six columns in its façade, and is likewise articulated into a pronaos opened by columns in the Ionic style, which precedes the cella; typical of the Doric style is the architrave with metopes and triglyphs, while one characteristic feature of the temple is the jutting cornice decorated by a coffer motif. Also referring back to the Greek phase of the settlement is the underground sacellum, surrounded by a rectangular enclosure (third century B.C.) and covered with a double-pitch roof. According to the bronze and ceramic vases uncovered on the interior, it dates from the end of the sixth century B.C.; less certain is the interpretation of this environment: some think it is a place for the worship of the nymphs, others believe it to be a *heroon*, a monument dedicated to the founder of the homeland of Poseidonia, Sybaris, after

Archaeological view of the sacred area of Paestum.

Opposite page
Interior of the so-called Temple of Neptune, actually dedicated to the goddess Hera, characterized by a double Doric colonnade (460 B.C.).

THE HERAION AT THE MOUTH OF THE SELE

The Sele is one of the most important rivers on the Tyrrhenian coast, both in terms of the expanse of its watershed and in terms of the number of emissaries; it presently feeds the main aqueduct providing the water supply of Apulia. In antiquity it was even more important, as it marked the boundary between the *kora* of Poseidonia and the district of Salerno subject to the Etruscans. The construction of the temple served the function both of marking the ownership of the territory, but also establishing contact with the natives for purposes of trading.

The sacred precinct was created with the foundation of the colony in the form of an open-air ash altar upon which sacrifices were performed. Quite early in the course of the first half of the sixth century B.C., construction began on a *hekatompedon*, a temple that extended 100 feet in length, the ruins of which have been found beneath the foundations of the new and monumental peripteral temple dating from the end of the sixth century B.C., with eight columns on the front, a cella with a single aisle with an entry portico and an *adyton*, a room opening behind the statue of the deity, arranged in the centre of the hall, for use by the priests. On the exterior two monumental altars and a *thesauros* were created, the latter being a building in which to preserve the votive offerings, upon which it was erroneously believed that the thirty-six slabs of architectural ornament were placed, the metopes, depicting scenes from the Greek myths, such as the Twelve Labours of Hercules, episodes from the Trojan War, and the Voyage of Jason and the Argonauts, who were thought to have been the founders of the sacred precinct.

The façade of the so-called basilica, a monumental temple dedicated to the goddess Hera, in the colonnade of which it is easy to see the entasis, or the characteristic swelling of the archaic wooden columns.

Opposite page
Eastern front of the so-called Temple of Ceres, actually dedicated to Athena, in the classical Doric style.

Detail of the double order of Doric columns that divided the naos of the Temple of Neptune into three aisles.

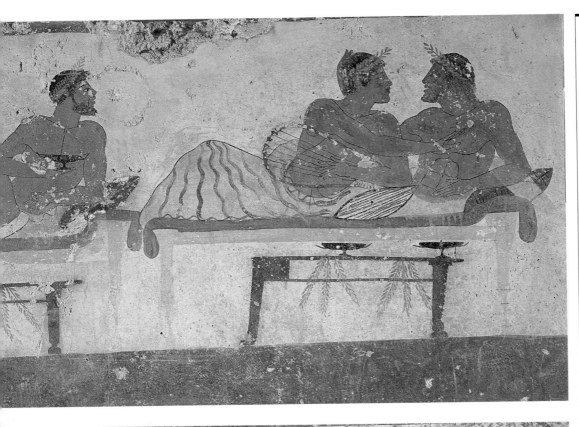

THE TOMB OF THE DIVER

Of particular value are paintings of the tomb known as the 'Tomba del Tuffatore', literally, 'Tomb of the diver,' discovered in 1969 in a casket tomb, dating back to 480-470 B.C. To the present day it remains the only fresco from classical times originating from a Greek city. Along the sides are depicted male characters lying on beds, before whom there are *kylikes* set on low tables; on the short sides is painted, on one side, a large garlanded *krater* set on a table from which a youth is walking away with an *oenochoe*, the vase that is used to pour into the goblets the wine drawn from the *krater*, and, on the other, a procession composed of a naked young man with a light-blue mantle over his shoulders who walks, preceded by a flute player, and followed by a bearded pedagogue leaning upon a cane. The banquet scene is completed by the painting that occupies the entire interior façade of the ceiling slab, which gives the tomb itself its name: a young diver is plummeting through the air towards a body of water. The structure not entirely unlike a diving board from which the diver is leaping may well represent the columns placed by Hercules at the edge of the inhabited world to mark the limits of what humans can know. The image, therefore, is a remarkable metaphor for death. The depiction and the composition of the figures, especially those of the members of the symposium stretched out on their *klinai*, are organic to Greek culture, as is shown by the scenes scattered on the figured ceramic of the same period, but the custom of decorating with wall paintings the interior of the tomb is clearly Etruscan-Italic; suffice it to consider the tombs of the seventh and sixth centuries uncovered in Capua and especially in Etruria proper, in Tarquinia, Cerveteri, Veio, and Chiusi. This document shows the complex social structure of Poseidonia around the fifth century, the centre from which a new form of politics and new culture was spreading to the surrounding indigenous communities and at the same time a city in a close and osmotic relationship to the Etruscan and Campanian centres to the north of the river Sele.

Among the tombs unearthed at Paestum, the best known is the 'Tomb of the Diver' (480-470 B.C.), in which a funeral banquet is depicted, along with a splendid image of the soul of the deceased diving into the sea of oblivion.

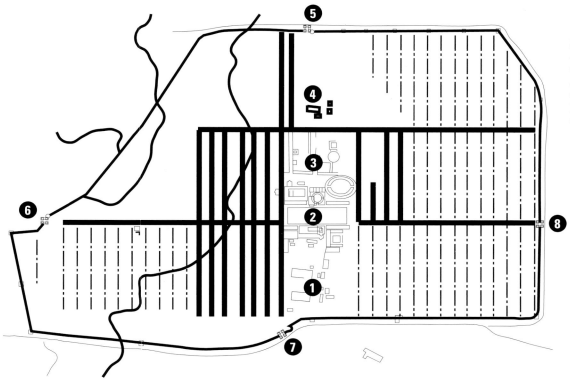

1. Temple of Hera
2. Forum
3. Agora
4. Temple of Athena
5. Golden gate
6. Sea gate
7. Justice gate
8. Mermaid gate

Panoramic view of the so-called basilica, which has for the most part preserved its architectural structures.

its destruction (510 B.C.). Around 400 B.C. the city fell into the hands of the Lucanians. In 273 B.C. Rome founded the Latin colony of Paestum, from *Paiston,* the Lucanian name for the city. Dating back to this period is the arrangement of the area between the two sacred areas on a line with the road that linked the Sea Gate, or Porta Marina with the Mermaid Gate, or Porta della Sirena into the form of a Roman Forum: a rectangular plaza bounded by a Doric portico. It was lined by shops, but also by the *Macellum,* or slaughterhouse, to the south, beneath which have been uncovered the foundation of an archaic Greek temple; the Curia, the building in which the Senate met, recognizable also from the semi-circular exedra; to the north the *Capitolium,* the most important temple of the Latin colony, set atop a high podium that supported the cella, surrounded by columns only on three sides, and adorned high up by triglyphs and metopes, upon which are carved scenes

of combat and running Maenads; to its right is the *Comitium*, the place for assemblies of the citizenry, with a circular plan enclosed in a rectangular perimeter. Behind the forum it is possible to make out the western curve of the amphitheatre. It was built between the first century B.C. and the first century A.D. in an area that was already built up with leisure-related buildings, such as the gymnasium, and in which recent excavations seem to have uncovered the site of the Greek agora. This hypothesis would seem to be confirmed by the discovery of a meeting place that was in operation from the end of the fifth century to 273 B.C., when it was buried after the foundation of the Latin colony.

Excavations were carried out intermittently under the Bourbon kings, but it was not until the years between 1907 and 1914, and again after 1928, that excavations were undertaken systematically. In 1998 UNESCO named the archaeological zone as a World Heritage Site.

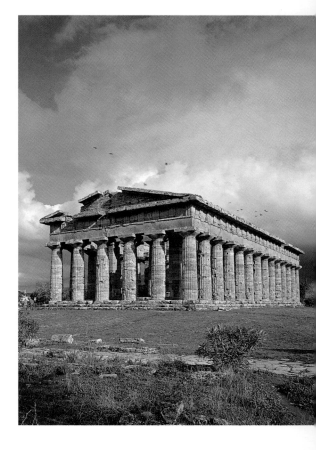

Pienza

The history of the little Tuscan town of Pienza, near Siena, is closely tied to the figure of Pope Pius II: in 1459, the Pope ordered construction of a huge project for the renovation and beautification of his home town, Corsignano, and from that time forth the town took, in his honour, the name of Pienza. In 1462 the complex project could be said to be finished, to the point that Pius II decided to commemorate the event by appointing the small town to the prestigious status of episcopal see. Currently the little town, which preserves its original appearance virtually intact, constitutes one of the most noteworthy and charming documents of the urbanistic ideals and the architectural style of the Italian Renaissance.

The documents show that the Pope commissioned the Florentine architect and sculptor Bernardo Rossellino (1409-64) to work on Pienza: Rossellino, formerly the palace engineer of Pope Nicholas V in Rome, was an admired and close colleague of Leon Battista Alberti, for whom he supervised the construction of Palazzo Rucellai in Florence. It would appear from the terse account given by the Pope himself that Pius II had originally asked Rossellino simply to design a church and a *palazzo*, or mansion, which was going to be the site of his summer residence. The architect's proposal, which met with the full support of the client, instead went well beyond his initial task: in fact, he presented the Pope with a wide-ranging plan that covered the entire urbanistic plan of the city and its individual monumental structures. In fact, his design called first of all for an intervention affecting the basic layout of Corsignano, involving the creation of a new *piazza* that would become the focal point of the town, and that would host its most important buildings, including the Duomo, or cathedral, and the papal palace. At the same time, Corsignano would be equipped with new public buildings, such as an inn, a hospital, and a series of twelve houses for the people. Along the main road would be built the mansions of the prelates of the papal court, who arranged at their own expense to rebuild existing buildings or to construct new ones.

Rossellino's plan fitted in harmoniously on the medieval grid of the little town, which stood surrounded by defensive walls on a hilltop: its simple road structure was in fact maintained virtually intact, consisting in a main thoroughfare that connected the two main gates, and from which a dense network of secondary roads branched out. The new town square was set tangential to the main thoroughfare at the point where it curved slightly, extending towards the Valley of the River Orcia: the main square's trapezoidal form and the asymmetrical arrangement of the buildings allowed the architect to create a fluid connection with the old town, or *borgo vecchio*, upon which the square opened out without any apparent interruption. On the space thus identified stand the Duomo, or cathedral; Palazzo Piccolomini, the Pope's mansion; the Palazzo Vescovile or episcopal residence; and the Palazzo Pretorio, or civic building: the square thus contains all of the most important buildings in the city's life. These buildings, all dating from the time of Rossellino, are each characterized by a special architectural idiom that clearly distinguishes their different functions: they have in common a basic stylistic unity, based on an adherence to the vocabulary of the Florentine Renaissance and a uniform decorative style, both sober and delicate, that enlivens the façades.

The cathedral stands at the far end of the square and constitutes a clear variation on the model of the Tempio Malatestiano designed by Leon Battista Alberti in Rimini: the façade is tripartite and distributed over two orders linked by sharply jutting pilaster strips. On

Aerial view of the town, or borgo, *of Corsignano, later Pienza.*

Opposite page
One of the sides of the main square lined by the magnificent Renaissance façade of the cathedral, designed by Bernardo Rossellino from 1460.

The Gothic apse of the cathedral stands on the steep hillside, flanked on the left by the elegant Renaissance loggia of the Palazzo Piccolomini.

View of the Italian-style gardens overlooking the loggia of the Palazzo Piccolomini.

Pope Pius II Piccolomini was responsible for the idea of reconstructing his birthplace, the town of Corsignano in thorough-going Renaissance style: the project was entrusted in 1460 to Bernardo Rossellino.

The skyline of Pienza seen from the surrounding countryside.

the pediment, of clearly classical inspiration, that serves as a crown there is a tondo with the heraldic crest of the Piccolomini family. The interior, divided into three aisles, instead stands out considerably for its variation from Renaissance forms, presenting a cross vault set on tall clustered pillars: the fact that the three aisles are all the same height has suggested a contamination with models from the German area (*hallenkirche*), probably familiar to Pius II from his stay in Austria as apostolic legate. The solemnity of this luminous space is increased by the sobriety of the decoration, bounded by a wooden choir and with five altarpieces, similar in shape and size, painted by the most important Sienese artists of the period, including Vecchietta and Matteo di Giovanni.

Palazzo Piccolomini too shows the clear influence of Leon Battista Alberti, borrowing — with significant modifications in the layout — the stately model of the Palazzo Rucellai in Florence: in Rossellino's building there is an

internal courtyard and a three-order loggia that opens out over a hanging garden and the surrounding panorama, particularly beloved to Pius II.

The harmonious overall effect of the piazza is enhanced by a few ingenious devices. The terracotta paving is modulated by a grill of travertine inserts which mirror the perspectival scheme of the painterly constructions by Piero della Francesca, establishing the geometric space of the square. The trapezoidal layout gives the cathedral, set at the peak of the visual pyramid, a certain monumental grandeur, standing out from the isolation created by the insertion of the two roads that open out towards the panorama behind.

The importance of Pienza in art history can be fully understood only if we consider it in the light of the refined Humanistic culture of its commissioner and its creator, both profoundly immersed in the milieu of Neoplatonism and closely tied to the leading intellec-

Closing the square before the Duomo, or cathedral, is the Palazzo del Pretorio dominated by the Torre Civica, or Civic Tower.

From the porticoes of the Palazzo Comunale it is possible to glimpse the façade of the Palazzo Piccolomini, inspired by Leon Battista Alberti's design for Palazzo Rucellai in Florence.

*Opposite page
Bernardo Rossellino designed for the inner courtyard of the Palazzo Piccolomini a fully Renaissance structure.*

tual personalities of their time. Beginning from this presupposition, it has been possible to hypothesize that the architectural structure of the city of Pius II harks back to mathematical and philosophical modules and to cosmological and astronomical references that are difficult to grasp, thought easily accessible to those who were endowed with sufficient culture. In the wake of such conjectures and in the light of the evident complexity of the architectural and urbanistic project, a number of scholars have gone so far as to suggest that Leon Battista Alberti himself took an active role in the conception and design of the town: while on the one hand there is no doubt that on other occasions he made use of Rossellino as a trusted implementer of his work, we cannot rule out that he knew personally and spent time with Pius II, who clearly expressed his own admiration for the architect.

Pisa, Campo dei Miracoli (The Field of Miracles)

Pisa's Piazza del Duomo, or Cathedral Square, commonly known as Campo dei Miracoli (literally, Field of Miracles), is the site of one of the most important monumental complexes built in medieval Italy: the unusual nature of its exquisite individual buildings and the harmonious space in which they are set as a group have contributed to their great renown over the centuries.

The current appearance of the square began to take shape between the eleventh and thirteenth centuries, over a span of time marked by the flowering of the powerful maritime Republic, which was engaged in highly profitable trade throughout the Mediterranean and involved in the struggle against the Saracens. The economic and cultural vitality of the city, which was in constant contact with various civilizations, is reflected in the architecture of the Campo dei Miracoli, in which elements of varied provenance are merged into a complex and original visual language.

The foundations of the monumental plaza were laid to commemorate the victorious expedition of 1063 to Palermo against the Muslim forces there, culminating in the sacking of the city by Pisan troops. For the construction of the new cathedral, dedicated to the Virgin Mary in thanksgiving for Her protection, an area was selected adjoining the city walls and set on the northern edge of the city grid. This area was free of existing buildings and large enough to allow the construction, over time, of an architectural complex on a grand scale consisting of the city's basilica, a baptistry, a monumental campanile, and a burial ground.

The construction of the Duomo, or cathedral, was begun in 1064, and required three phases of construction. The first, the work of the architect Buscheto, involved the general definition of the layout, and ended in 1118 with the consecration of the building by Pope Gelasius II. Successively, Rainaldo made a

major modification to the original plan, extending the body of the church by adding the first three bays that now exist and the first order on the face. The façade was completed around the middle of the twelfth century with the addition of the remaining floors. The interior is divided into five aisles arranged on a Latin-cross plan and an elliptical dome sits over the transept. The space thus defined is reminiscent in its grandeur and the distribution of the rooms of the model of the Roman early Christian basilica, but renewed with the introduction of several elements of striking modernity: the use of exceedingly tapered columns made of polished marble, monumental pointed-arch arcades and the insertion of the *gynaecum matroneum*, or women's gallery, over the nave gave the Duomo an unprecedented grandeur. The church contains a number of artworks, including the famous pulpit by Giovanni Pisano; the apse has frescoes attributed to Ghirlandaio and, in the vault of the apse, there is a magnificent mosaic of *Saint John* by the Florentine Cimabue dating from 1301.

The elegant and renowned elevation of the Duomo features a lower order of small blind arches adorned with elegant geometric decorations in marble and mosaic; above it rise four orders of loggias that can be entered, crowned by a coping with statues. The façade is characterized by an extraordinary sensibility for chromatic and luministic values: the wall covering is modulated by a delicate decoration in horizontal bands of white and black marble, while the motif of the galleries, of Lombard derivation, is here interpreted in a powerfully plastic context, creating a lively interplay of light and shadow. The dome with its extrados, which adheres to the same ornamental vocabulary, harks back to Islamic models.

The distinctive architectural and decorative themes set forth in the Duomo became a fun-

Aerial view of the Campo dei Miracoli in Pisa.

Opposite page
The 'Leaning Tower' of Pisa, in reality the campanile of the cathedral, was built beginning in 1173 by Bonanno Pisano, who also executed the bronze doors of the church, but it was not completed until well into the fourteenth century because of the problems of sinking ground that had already emerged during construction.

Opposite page
Following the victories of the Pisans in Africa in 1088, the treasure of the cathedral had expanded considerably, and in 1104 the architect Busketus or Busketos was compared to the legendary Daedalus in the epigraph dedicating the façade, built in fact in the early years of the twelfth century.

Around 1153 Deotisalvi began to build the baptistry across from the cathedral; the building was completed in the fourteenth century and was decorated with Gothic spires and pinnacles.

The Cathedral of Pisa was begun in 1064, financed by the immense plunder seized with victories in maritime wars, and was consecrated in 1118.

THE PULPITS BY NICOLA AND GIOVANNI PISANO

The buildings in the Campo dei Miracoli contain two major works of sculpture that attest to the early role that Pisan art played in the nascent Gothic civilization. The two pulpits by Nicola and Giovanni Pisano, carved fifty years apart, are both evidently based on classical models: in both, the orchestration of the compositions in the relief panels and the plasticity of the figures attests to a profound knowledge of Roman funerary art, known from the Roman sarcophagi at the time displayed in the cathedral and later transferred to the Camposanto, or graveyard. In the older of the two works (1260), by Giovanni Pisano and placed in the baptistry, the solemn figures are carved in broad planes and evoke, among other things, in the stately cadence of the drapery and the vigour of the treatment, a possible adoption of models of sculpture from the court of the Holy Roman Emperor Frederick. The pulpit executed at the turn of the fourteenth century by Giovanni's son and pupil, Nicola, is characterized, instead, by the exuberance of the sculptural forms, which practically form the architectural structure, and by a lively and almost confused treatment of the planes, enlivened by effects of the light. The full-relief and extremely stylized figures accentuate the expressivity of the whole.

Opposite page
The cathedral building is characterized by five aisles and a tripartite transept; the interior spaces are separated by granite columns in similar forms but different sizes, and adorned with capitals in a composite style.

Giovanni Pisano, pulpit of the cathedral, 1301-1310.

You enter the Campo dei Miracoli through the Gate of Santa Maria from where you glimpse the bell tower behind the transept of the cathedral.

The distribution of the buildings in the Campo dei Miracoli follows the arrangement of the stars in the constellation of Aries.

Sculptural group from the eighteenth century with little cupids bearing the heraldic crest of the Administration of the Cathedral, or Opera del Duomo.

damental point of reference for the development of the successive Tuscan Romanesque and they set the pattern for all the other constructions built on the site in the years that followed. In 1152 the architect Diotisalvi began work on the baptistry, which was not finished until the end of the fourteenth century with the completion of the last decorative work. The traditional circular plan features in the elevation a double order of galleries surmounted by a curious conical dome covered on the exterior by a hemispheric dome cap. In this evocative atmosphere, Byzantine and classical influences are mingled, as seen in the rich decoration of the main portal. On the exterior, the decorative elements are the same as on the Duomo: the blind arches and the loggia are accompanied here by cusps and aedicules, finely worked with reliefs and fret-

work in the Gothic style. The charming internal hall features an exquisite pulpit by Nicola Pisano and a thirteenth-century basin for full-immersion baptism; the altar features decorations in coloured marble in an eclectic style, mingling motifs of Cosmatesque derivation with others of Arab-style imprint.

Isolated behind the Duomo stands the renowned bell tower with its circular plan, begun in 1173 by Bonanno Pisano: here too an order of small blind arches serves as the base for a loggia. The notoriety of this construction is due, even more than to its historical and artistic value, to its peculiar inclination. Recently efforts have been made to halt the sinking of the earth by consolidating the foundations, which already manifested itself during the construction of the tower and which has become worse over the centuries.

Deotisalvi and Nicola
Pisano, internal space of
the dome of the baptistry,
c. 1153.

THE FRESCOES IN THE CAMPOSANTO

At the end of the thirteenth century work began in the Campo dei Miracoli on the last structure of this exceptional complex: Giovanni di Simone began work in 1278 on the construction of the Camposanto, which is designed as a long marble enclosure punctuated by the traditional motif of the little blind arches. A broad quadriporticus opens on to the ancient cemetery, which, in accordance with tradition, had been filled with earth brought back from the Holy Places in Jerusalem. The Camposanto, which possesses a significant collection of ancient sarcophagi, Greek and Etruscan vases and fragments of architectural decorations from the Romanesque and Gothic periods, was the subject of an impressive campaign of painting that lasted for more than two centuries. A great number of highly renowned artists were summoned to take part in the remarkable enterprise, among them only a single Pisan, Francesco Traini. The preference of the city commissioners for painters from elsewhere, for the most part Tuscans, attests both to the refined taste of the Pisan milieu and, above all, the great financial commitment to the construction and completion of the Campo dei Miracoli.

On the walls of the Camposanto were frescoed a number of important cycles of sacred subjects, dedicated to *Stories from the Old Testament* and to episodes from the *Life of Christ* and the *Lives of the Saints*. Among the most renowned fourteenth-century masters involved in the project were Taddeo Gaddi, Spinello Aretino, and Antonio Veneziano. In the fifteenth century came Benozzo Gozzoli, who was assigned the frescoes that had previously been offered to Mantegna and for which Botticelli and Vincenzo Foppa had also been considered as candidates. The most evocative painting of this extraordinary collection is the fourteenth-century *Triumph of Death*.

Buonamico Buffalmacco,
Ten Young People in the
Orchard, *detail of the*
Triumph of Death, *c.
1336, in the monumental
Camposanto, or
graveyard.*

*Giovanni di Simone
designed the
monumental
Camposanto, or
graveyard of Pisa,
adorned with important
cycles of frescoes
(beginning 1278).*

Pompeii

The city of Pompeii, situated to the north of the mouth of the river Sarno (Sarnus, in ancient times), on one of the spurs of the southern slope of Mount Vesuvius, in the province of Naples, dates its foundation to the sixth century B.C. The Greek influence that was unquestionably strong in the little town forms part of a much broader pattern of cultural contributions from certain Greeks who settled, first on Ischia, and then on the acropolis of Cumae and on the hills of Pozzuoli and Naples. Following periods of alternating fortune, the city became a Roman colony in 80 B.C., taking on the official name of *Cornelia Veneria Pompeianorum*. The ruins of the city, which became a World Heritage Site in 1997, constitute a priceless and unique piece of documentation for the reconstruction not only of architectural and urbanistic aspects of the site, but of society and everyday life in a specific moment of Roman antiquity. In A.D. 62 a violent earthquake seriously damaged Pompeii and other cities in Campania; it had not yet been completely rebuilt when, in August of A.D. 79, the terrible eruption of Mount Vesuvius entirely buried the city in a thick blanket of ash and fragments of volcanic debris, suffocating its flourishing life. The earliest reports of the existence of Pompeii, which had been forgotten throughout the Middle Ages and confused with Stabiae in the Humanistic tradition, are documented in the sixteenth century, when the architect Domenico Fontana, during work for the reclamation of the Sarno valley, happened upon a number of painted walls and fragments of inscriptions. Excavation work, however, only began in 1748 under King Charles of Bourbon, increasing in scope and pace in the first half of the nineteenth century. In the 1860s, the archaeologist Giuseppe Fiorelli divided the city, in accordance with a convention dictated by convenience of topo-graphic indication, into nine 'regions', numbering the *insulae* (or blocks, constituted by a number of buildings surrounded by streets that followed an orthogonal layout) as well as the houses, and adopting a nomenclature that is still used today. To date, the excavations have unearthed some two-thirds of the urban area, equal to 44 hectares (about 110 acres), and sectors of the *suburba*, or outlying areas. The south-western part of the city with the zone of the forum constitutes the most ancient nucleus, where the earliest traces of life date back to the sixth century B.C. In the fifth century B.C. the city experienced a further expansion based on a clear Hippodamean layout, constituted by two main thoroughfares known as *cardines* (Via di Stabia and Via di Nocera) intersected by two *decumani* (Via di Nola and Via dell'Abbondanza). The urban layout created in this way a succession of isolated blocks with an elongated shape and an orthogonal plan; it is interesting to note that in the eastern part of the city some of these blocks were not occupied by buildings, thus revealing a regulatory plan that would establish in advance the successive development of the settlement. It is important to keep in mind that Pompeii was a prosperous trading centre that was becoming progressively wealthier, which would necessarily entail a steady territorial expansion, thanks to its strategic position. It stood in fact at the centre of a network of roads that linked the settlements of the Salerno district and the Sorrento peninsula, making it a strategic intersection for the land and sea traffic between southern Campania, Etruria, and Magna Graecia. Also dating back to the fifth century B.C. is the earliest phase of construction of the city walls, while the three successive construction phases take us up to the Samnite period. The gates of the ancient settlement, dating back to the Samnite and Roman era, have interior courtyards

View of the area of the Forum of Pompeii.

Opposite page
One of the principal thoroughfares of the ancient city was the Via dell'Abbondanza, shown here at the intersection with the Via Stabiana.

In the southern part of the city, close to the city walls, are the structures of the amphitheatre and the odeon, shown here from high atop the bleachers.

The rich archaeological documentation of the site of Pompeii reveals the numerous variants of the typologies of Roman homes; here we see the marble inserts of the floor of the triclinium in the House of the Faun.

and lateral bastions were built to reinforce them. Also in the Samnite period, the forum was built, with porticoes and imposing buildings, some of them dedicated to worship, others public in nature, such as the immense three-aisle Basilica, the podium of the Temple of Jove, the Temple of Apollo with its quadriporticus, and the older Macellum, or large provision market; from the same period comes the layout of the complex of the so-called Triangular Forum with a quadriporticus and with the open-air theatre which clearly takes its inspiration from the architectural stage design of the great Hellenistic cities. In the urbanistic context of the time we also find the first layout of the Stabian Baths. After its inclusion within the boundaries of the empire, Pompeii, now officially a colony, continued to expand its collection of public buildings: the façade of the Capitolium, the Temple of Venus Pompeiana, the Odeon and the amphitheatre, the Stabian Baths, the Forum Baths, and the Baths of the House of Lime. At the end of the first century B.C. the aqueduct was built with the

'castellum aquae' to supply water from the River Sarnus (now Sarno) to the baths, private homes, and public fountains. A number of buildings, such as the Temple of Vespasian, part of the portico of the forum, and the Central Baths, date from after the earthquake, as do various elements of reconstruction, left however incomplete when, in A.D. 79, the volcanic cone of Mount Vesuvius exploded, interrupting all activities in the ancient settlement. Aside from the considerable interest of the urbanistic development of the city, Pompeii should also be recognized as by far the richest source of documentation of wall painting from the second century B.C. until the eruption of Mount Vesuvius in A.D. 79. The use of painting in Pompeii, even though it was a provincial town, was not limited to monumental buildings, but was found as well in the houses of every class of society, workshops, and stores. The monumentality of the architectural structures and the richness of the decorations of the houses, at times to the point of ostentatious luxury, allows us to form an idea

The load-bearing structures of the Arch of Tiberius mark the entrance to the paved Via di Mercurio; Mount Vesuvius looms in the background.

Detail of the civil and sacred buildings that adorned the side of the area of the forum.

*House of the Vettii,
detail of the fresco with
Cupid on a Chariot
Drawn by Dolphins.*

*Villa of the Mysteries,
detail of the frieze
frescoed with scenes of
the rites of the Eleusinian
mysteries.*

THE PAINTED DECORATION

The exceedingly rich pictorial archive of Pompeii in Roman times has long constituted the only surviving documentation of the entire painterly experience of the ancient world. This led, in a clear tendency towards Romano-centrism, to an excessive appreciation of the Pompeiian style of painting, which was later debunked through the study and understanding of Hellenistic painting, of which the Roman painting is only a sort of revision. That said, we do not wish to understate the remarkable beauty of the frescoes, some of which are remarkably well preserved, that decorate the mansions, houses, and shops of the city of Pompeii. Surely inspired by Hellenistic models, the Roman wall paintings are conventionally divided into four 'styles', or, to be more accurate, decorative schemes. The first style (from *c.* 200 to 90/80 B.C.) is called the 'marble encrustation' style inasmuch as it aims to recreate with stuccoes and paint the chromatic effects typical of marble facing, as we find in the 'House of the Faun'. The second style, which established itself in the Age of Augustus, is called the 'architectural framing' style: the walls are divided by painted architectural elements, between which we find painted scenes. This is the case with the 'Villa of the Mysteries', on the walls of which is developed a pictorial cycle that represents the initiation of brides into Dionysian rites. The third style (from the end of the first century B.C. to about the middle of the first century A.D.), known as the 'royal wall' style, is distinguished by the subdivision of the wall into coloured zones in which slender and fantastic architectural elements are distributed. Within the panels that are punctuated by these there are isolated figures or false paintings that reproduce famous compositions of a mythological or epic character; illustrious examples of this style include the 'House of Marcus Lucretius Fronto' and the 'House of Lucius Caecilius Jucundus'. The fourth and last style, which spread in the Julian-Claudian age, developed the illusionistic and perspectival view of painted architecture, making it the protagonist of decoration, as we see in the frescoes on the walls of the 'House of the Vettii'.

Opposite page
House of the 'Golden Bracelet', detail of the fresco with nightingale and rose-bush.

The fundamental element of the Roman domus was the presence of the peristyle: a garden/courtyard that provided light to the interior rooms; this is the peristyle of the House of the Gilded Cupids.

The House of Loreius Tiburtinus was embellished with a viridarium (garden/fruit orchard) equipped with an irrigation system.

of what the residential quarters of Rome, the capital, must have been like; unquestionably the models of life but also the various customs must have been copied from the metropolis. In order to trace the development of this pictorial decoration, suffice it to consider the construction history and the various artistic schools that over time have accompanied that history. The house, the essential module of a larger settlement, has been preserved in all its various forms, and in Pompeii, better than elsewhere, its process of development has been manifest. The first type, the more fundamental and ancient sort of house, is well represented by the 'House of the Surgeon' and the 'House of Sallust'. These houses were constituted by a door and an access corridor (*ostium* and *fauces*) and developed around a central courtyard, called the *atrium*, from which the bedrooms (*cubicula*) radiated like spokes. At the far end of the atrium, hard by the entrance, was the *tablinum* which opened with a large window

on to the *viridarium*, the most intimate and sacred room in the house, where the family members generally gathered. At either end of the atrium opened out two other rooms, rather elongated in shape, known as *alae* (wings). Finally, in a setback position, was the *hortus* (garden), reached via one or two lateral corridors. The Italic house of this first period, entirely surrounded by high walls with high loopholes, seems to resemble a full-fledged fortress. Certainly less austere is the mansion-house of the second century B.C., which was developed in keeping with the Hellenistic style. Representative of this second typology were the 'House of the Faun', the 'House of the Labyrinth', the 'House of Pansa', and the 'House of Marcus Epidius Rufus', this last house featuring a podium before the entrance and a Corinthian atrium. Among the outlying villas, the ones of greatest interest, the 'Villa of Diomedes' and the 'Villa of the Mysteries', date back to the Samnite Era.

Ravenna, the Early Christian Buildings

The first centuries of the Christian era were for the Emilian city of Ravenna a time of exceptional political and cultural growth, and likewise a time of extraordinary architectural and artistic development. Ravenna was the capital of the Western empire in the fifth century, the capital of the Kingdom of Italy under Theodoric, and it was also very important in the Byzantine era, as the capital of the exarchate and a port of primary relevance. From the monumental appearance of the city at the time, significant relics survive, major documents scattered throughout the urban fabric and in the area immediately surrounding Ravenna. This splendid series of buildings provides a mute testimonial of the development of an original visual language in the sacred architecture and the figurative art of a crucial historical period. Between the fifth and the seventh centuries there developed in the field of art a transition from the tradition in late antiquity, derived from a classical matrix to a new idiom, created in the wake of the new views introduced by the Christian religion. On the path towards the definition of new architectural typologies and effective iconographic and stylistic solutions in the field of figurative art, the art of Ravenna placed itself on a plane of absolute importance, merging in a stately and original visual language concepts taken from antiquity with an understanding of the nascent Christian and, especially, Byzantine art.

The sacred buildings of Ravenna document a thorough reflection on the two fundamental themes of early Christian architecture, the basilica plan of the earliest Roman churches and the central plan exemplified by classical models, conventionally utilized in baptisteries and mausoleums and, more rarely, for churches. These buildings with brick exteriors present elevations of extraordinary solemnity, in which the clear structure of the volumes is accompanied by a delicate treatment of the surfaces, subtly modulated by tenuous processions of fine blind arches and by simple ornamental motifs. On their interior, these buildings contain extraordinary treasures: renowned wall mosaics which, with their refined figural scenes and their profusion of ornamental inserts, testify to the imperial richness of the art of Ravenna.

In 402 Honorius, threatened by the advance of Alaric, designated Ravenna as the capital of the Western Roman Empire, a title that had previously accrued to Milan. Dating back to the early imperial era is the foundation of the Basilica Ursiana, founded on the site of the present-day Duomo, or cathedral, and demolished in the eighteenth century to make room for the new building. Few traces remain of its ancient splendour, among them the original columns made of pink granite and an ambo from the sixth century. What has been preserved intact, however, is the building known as the Mausoleum of Galla Placidia (425-430): the little edifice once stood close to the Palatine Church of Santa Croce, which no longer exists. The Latin-cross plan is covered by a central dome which is joined by the four barrel vaults that cover the four arms of the structure. The interior presents a rich mosaic decoration across the entire surface of the ceilings: the mosaic complex, inspired by the theme of redemption, develops in various figured panels, which alternate with fields crowded with refined geometric and plant-themed motifs. In the dome, a sky spangled with golden stars welcomes the apparition of the Cross, while in the corbels are the symbols of the Four Evangelists. In the lunettes instead are arranged the figures of the *Apostles*, a *Saint Lawrence* and a splendid panel with the *Good Shepherd*: here the naturalistic style and the plasticity of form reveal a profound classical influence. In one of the side arms there is a lunette decorated with *Two Stags Drinking*: the scene, with its subtle symbolic meaning, is

Aerial view of the complex of San Vitale and Galla Placidia.

Opposite page
The interior of the so-called mausoleum of Galla Placidia is one of the masterpieces of the art of Ravenna for its splendid mosaics executed around A.D. 450 depicting Christian allegories.

The brickwork Church of San Francesco, heavily renovated between the eighth and tenth centuries, contains several Christian sarcophagi from the fifth century.

GALLA PLACIDIA

Galla Placidia was the daughter of the Emperor Theodosius and the sister of Honorius; she was an ambitious and clever woman, and she played an active role in the political events of her time. She was taken prisoner in 410 by the Visigoth Alaric, and she was wedded to his brother-in-law Ataulfus, a future king; she was sent back to Rome after the death of her husband, where General Constantius asked for her hand in marriage, later to become emperor alongside Honorius in 421. Galla Placidia, who had always exerted a powerful ascendancy over her weak-charactered brother, probably tried to impose her own will on the question of the succession, and came to disagreements with him that brought brother and sister to breaking point. She therefore took refuge in Constantinople with her daughter Honoria and her son Valentinian, who was acclaimed emperor at the age of five (423). His mother ruled in his place as regent. According to tradition, Galla Placidia had a mausoleum built in Ravenna as a resting place for herself and for her children; it is likely, however, that she is buried in Rome, where she died in 450.

Detail of the eagle, symbol of Saint John the Evangelist, set in the dome of the mausoleum of Galla Placidia.

Detail of the star-spangled vault in the atrium of the mausoleum of Galla Placidia.

Exterior of the so-called mausoleum of Galla Placidia. The simplicity of its form contrasts with the exceedingly lavish decorative array of the interior.

Exterior view of the Imperial Basilica of San Vitale consecrated in 547 by the Bishop Maximian; the hexagonal plan and the structural models are distinctly Byzantine.

Opposite page
Detail of the presbytery and the mosaics in the apse, with the Emperor Justinian and the Bishop Maximian Presenting Offerings, c. 556.

framed by a precious arabesqued background with gilded vine clusters.

Also dating back to the fifth century is the Baptistry of the Orthodox, in ancient times joined to the Basilica Ursiana: this building with an octagonal plan is covered by a dome built with a technique dating from ancient Rome. The walls are entirely covered with mosaics and stuccoes of classical inspiration, which create an optical illusion of a gallery with triple arches. At the centre of the dome is the scene of the *Baptism of Christ*, which features the personification of the River Jordan, copied from ancient models: all around are arranged, in the eight sections of the ribbed vault, the figures of the Twelve Apostles.

With the fall of the Western Empire in A.D. 476, Ravenna was for a brief period the capital of the kingdom of Odoacer, but he was later replaced by Theodoric, who in 493 established his residence in the city. The Ostrogoth king, who had been educated in the imperial court of Constantinople, where he had been held as a hostage in his youth, kept the spirit of the late Roman tradition alive in the city.

Dating from the first few years of the reign of Theodoric is the Baptistry of the Aryans, built along with a new cathedral, since lost, to satisfy the religious needs of the royal court, whose official religion was, in fact, Aryanism. The building closely copies the model of the Baptistry of the Orthodox, which it echoes down to the selection of subjects for the mosaic decoration. An important new feature is seen, however, in the cycle of the baptistry of Theodoric: the light-blue and green backgrounds of the imperial mosaics, which by referring in abstract terms to the colours of meadows and the sky maintained a residual realism, are here replaced by a uniform gilded surface. Thus begins the process of formal abstraction that was to characterize the successive development of the mosaic art of Raven-

THE MAUSOLEUM OF THEODORIC

At the edge of the ancient city stood the mausoleum of Theodoric, an extraordinary example of a monumental sepulchre built for a barbarian king. The massive building is made out of large hewn stones in Pietra d'Istria, and it presents on the exterior a twelve-sided plan on two orders, punctuated in the lower section by deep arches. The interior is distributed over two storeys, the lower on a cross-shaped plan, the upper on a circular plan; the evocative hall is covered by a massive stone dome made from a single monolith. In the mausoleum are merged in an original manner motifs deriving from imperial Roman architecture with original elements of barbarian derivation, such as for instance the unusual roof and the frieze with its scissor formation used in the cornice.

Theodoric's mausoleum was built in A.D. 520 with the use of Pietra d'Istria, or Istrian stone. The model of imperial Roman tombs was overlapped with elements of the barbarian tradition: for example, the monolith that serves as a roof for the construction.

Sant'Apollinare in Classe was built near the imperial military port of Classe, long since silted up. The church, built at the behest of the Bishop Ursicinus, was consecrated in A.D. 549 by Bishop Maximian.

The brickwork front, dating from the seventh or eighth century, and adorned with marble columns, is known as the Palazzo di Teodorico (Palace of Theodoric). It is in fact the atrium of the Church of San Salvatore a Calchi, no longer in existence.

na, which will attain in its later results compositions of transcendent evocative power.

In the Archiepiscopal Chapel (Cappella Arcivescovile), a small oratory adjacent to the bishop's palace, a partially preserved mosaic complex confirms the popularity of this style: in the vault of the main hall the symbols of the Apostles and the Four Angels that support a tondo with the monogram of Christ stand out against a precious golden background. In the undersides of the arches are set, like so many gems, medallions with *Busts of Saints*, depicted frontally against delicate light-blue backgrounds. The splendid vestibule of the chapel presents a barrel vault decorated with splendid and refined motifs of white lilies intertwined with birds.

Also reserved to the Aryan cult was the Basilica of Sant'Apollinare Nuovo, built in accordance with the model of Roman basilicas with three aisles. The majestic interior, punctuated by twenty-four columns in Greek marble with acanthus-leaf capitals, is characterized by the extraordinary height of the nave, now

covered by seventeenth-century coffers. The building, which underwent considerable renovation in the Renaissance, still conserves a number of major mosaics that date from its foundation. On the walls of the nave are arranged three successive decorative strips, in which the gold of the backgrounds is animated by vivid and brilliant fields of light blue and green. In the upper strip are arranged numerous scenes from the *Life of Christ*, while the intermediate zone features figures of *Saints* and *Prophets*. The third order of mosaics was partially destroyed on the occasion of the passage of the church to the Catholic liturgy following the defeat of the Ostrogoths: new scenes were installed replacing the ones that had been cancelled, although a few significant fragments do survive. In particular two splendid sections were preserved with a view of the city of Classe, the old port of Ravenna, and with the elevation of the Palace of Theodoric: the royal residence, of which not a trace survives, is presented here as a magnificent building in the

The Neonian Baptistry or Baptistry of the Ortodos, was adorned with mosaics around 450 at the behest of the Bishop Neon.

The interior of the Church of Sant'Apollinare in Classe is subdivided by two lines of twelve columns in Greek marble adorned with Byzantine capitals and concluded by a mosaic apse, depicting in its centre a gem-studded cross, an allegory of Christ, and, below, Saint Apollinaris Praying Surrounded by Twelve Sheep, *an allegory of the Apostles.*

Opposite page
Detail of the mosaic depicting Civitas Classis (the old port of Classe) in the Church of Sant'Apollinare Nuovo. The mosaic decoration of the church was mostly executed during the rule of Theodoric.

Pages 100-101
Detail of the Baptistry of the Aryans built during the reign of Theodoric (493-526), depicting the Baptism of Christ with the Personification of the River Jordan.

Angle view of the apse area of Sant'Apollinare in Classe.

classical style, adorned with precious drapery embroidered in gold. It is possible that the original composition depicted two processions of Ostrogoth dignitaries moving from the city towards the *Virgin Mary Enthroned* and the *Saviour*, still preserved on the far ends of the walls. In the second half of the sixth century, at the behest of the Bishop Agnellus, in place of the original mosaics executed under Theodoric, the two renowned strips were executed depicting the *Procession of Martyrs* and the *Procession of Virgins*. The long processions are formed by figures all arranged on the same plane, in a flat paratactic progress: the attitudes and the costumes are repeated identically throughout, creating an original effect of redundancy and magnificence and, at the same time, abstraction. All realism in the background is lost; all descriptive connotations are lost; these mosaics find their essence in the purity of the chromatic and linear values and in the harmonious rhythm of the composition: this is the typical style of Byzantine art, which found a fertile ground for development in sixth-century Ravenna.

In A.D. 540 the Ostrogoth King Vitiges lost his dominion over the city and was driven out by the victorious troops of Belisarius, emissary of the Empire of Byzantium. The city then became the capital of the Byzantine Government in Italy; Ravenna was the seat from the end of the sixth century of the residence of the exarch. The exceptional church of San Vitale is the largest of the Byzantine monuments in the city and fully documents the splendour of the renewed imperial grandeur. The octagonal layout of the building is enlivened on the exterior by the presence of a polygonal apse, flanked by two side elements. In an asymmetrical position with respect to the axis identified by the zone of the presbytery or sanctuary there are two entrances, in ancient times preceded by a portico. On the interior eight large corner piers accommodate double-order exedrae stacked with arches, while above them rises a broad hemispherical dome. The church, founded in 526 and consecrated more than twenty years later (548), clearly shows strong Byzantine influence in its later phases of construction and decoration. The interior space has no unequivocal axial direction, and is con-

tinually multiplied by the interplay of solids and voids and by the luminous effects created in the lateral exedrae: this distinctive quality has led some scholars to compare the church of Ravenna with that of Saint Sofia in Constantinople. Clearly Byzantine in style is the splendid decorative apparatus, consisting of wall coverings in precious marble and exceedingly elegant fretwork capitals; covering the walls is an extraordinary cycle of mosaics, which culminates in the two renowned panels with Justinian and Theodora. In the vault of the apse, the Christ *Pantocrator*, depicted as a beardless variant, is represented between two angels in the act of extending a crown to Saint Vitalis while on his left, the Bishop Ecclesius, founder of the church, offers him a gift of a little model of the building. In the cross vault, adorned with festoons of fruit and flowers, four angels support the Mystical Lamb, standing out against an exceedingly rich decoration of volutes of acanthus over the hues of blue and green.

In 549 the Church of Sant'Apollinare in Classe was consecrated, a huge building with a basilica plan, erected in the small town that housed the military port of Ravenna. Preceded by a portico and equipped with an elegant cylindrical campanile dating from the ninth century, the church is subdivided into three aisles punctuated by a precious marble colonnade, while the apse presents a significant expanse of the ancient mosaic decoration. Here a composition of an evidently symbolic nature depicts the *Transfiguration of Christ*: the image of the Saviour is replaced by a resplendent cross, typical of the tradition of Ravenna, while the three Apostles witnessing the miraculous scene are symbolized by three young sheep. In the lower part, the protobishop Apollinaris is surrounded by twelve sheep, a clear reference to the number of Apostles.

Rome, the Imperial Forums

According to a tradition handed down by Latin historians, the foundation of Rome was the work of Romulus, and it took place in 753 B.C., a date that is now considered reliable. The first nucleus of the city developed on the Palatine, one of the seven hills of classical Rome. The marshy area that extended from the Palatine to the Capitoline was reclaimed, and here the Roman Forum was built, initially the site of commercial activity, and later the nerve centre of city life. As early as the Republican era, Rome — *caput mundi* — had acquired such great importance that the ancient main square, the Roman Forum, was no longer large enough to meet the demands of the intense public life that went on there. From then on, from the age of Julius Caesar until the age of Trajan, over a period of about 150 years, the executive centre of the Roman state experienced numerous and progressive urbanistic interventions that expanded its boundaries, until it finally covered an area of some 90,000 square metres (968,400 square feet). The forums were where the city's life was centred; in addition to judicial and financial functions, commercial activities were pursued there, at least the more prestigious ones. In order to give the forum a less cluttered feeling, Julius Caesar decided to move away the humbler commercial activities, which is to say, those that involved foodstuffs, while allowing the more important transactions to continue to be conducted there (for instance; not that it was a custom among senators to keep their private strongboxes here). In the interior of the forums there also stood the principal temples of the city, endowing the place with a powerful religious significance. This area of the city was also the site of honorary functions, if we consider the abundant number of statues and inscriptions intended to do honour to the figures who represented the state. The Imperial Forums sometimes served as the setting for recreational and cultural activities, such as spectacles and games, or educational pursuits, as is shown by the presence of schools, museums, and libraries. The chief function was in any case to transmit to citizens and subjects, on the occasion of official events, a clear political message: the manifestation of the grandeur and majesty of the Roman state.

Caesar's Forum

The political importance of an urbanistic intervention intended to make available greater space for a capital city like Rome had been clear for some time, and in 54 B.C. Caesar ordered that work got under way. The lands surrounding the previous forum were almost entirely occupied by public buildings and private homes; as a result, a series of demolitions became necessary in order to open up a broad new space; this operation added greatly to the project's overall costs. After Caesar's assassination by a group of conspirators in 44 B.C., work was continued by Octavian. The open plaza had a fairly elongated rectangular shape (160 by 75 metres, 525 by 46 feet) and was bounded on three sides by a double portico of columns. The eastern side was lined with taverns while the western side was occupied by the temple dedicated to Venus Genitrix, already inaugurated in 46 B.C., in compliance with a vow taken by Caesar prior to the battle of Pharsalus against Pompey (48 B.C.). Today we can admire roughly a third of the surface area of the Caesar's Forum. The temple of Venus presented eight columns on the front and nine on the sides, while the far wall was blank. The statue of Venus, which stood prominently in the apse, was by Arcesilaus, a famous sculptor desired by the dictator himself. The connection between the Julian Forum and the Republican square was constituted by the Curia which was moved from its original loca-

Aerial view of the Imperial Forums with the Colosseum in the background.

Opposite page
The Church of San Lorenzo in Miranda makes use of part of the original walls and stands on the site of the Temple of Antoninus and Faustina Deified, the hexastyle Corinthian front of which remains.

The Arch of Titus with its simple forms stands before the massive bulk of the Colosseum.

View of the hemicycle of Trajan's Market inside Trajan's Forum, built around the beginning of the second century A.D.

tion and placed against the plaza's south-west portico. The architectural project encouraged by Caesar had the connotations of a dynastic sanctuary that developed the propagandistic theme of the Gens Julia, in accordance with a monarchic tendency that was taking root on the example of Hellenistic kingdoms. Already from the dedication of the temple to Venus, there is a clear reference to the dictator's family which, according to tradition, descended from the goddess and progenitrix. Moreover, at the centre of the square an equestrian statue was erected, probably, as one source tells us, depicting Alexander the Great, though his head was replaced by a bust of Caesar.

Augustus's Forum

On 1 August 2 B.C., the new forum was inaugurated by Augustus, opening out on the north-eastern side of the Julian Forum. Once

again, the project was conceived as the fulfilment of a vow, made by Augustus during the battle of Philippi against the assassins of Caesar (42 B.C.). Atop a high podium in the Italic style, along the north-eastern side of the square, rectangular in shape (125 by 18 metres) and bounded by porticos matching the scheme inaugurated by Caesar, there rose the imposing temple dedicated to Mars Ultore, or Avenger. The walls of the cella were punctuated by pillars preceded by columns and terminating in a raised apse, on the interior of which were set the statues of the cult: Mars, Venus, and Julius. Mars and Venus also appeared on the pediment of the temple where the personifications of Rome and Romulus, the mythical founder of the Eternal City, or Urbs, were also depicted. The forum had a strong military imprint and at the centre of it stood the chariot drawn by four horses driven by Augustus *princeps*, at the base of which the Senate had ordered the placement of an inscription that bore the title of Father of the Fatherland (*pater patriae*). In the niches of the porticoes were placed statues of the *summi viri*, or those men who with their deeds had made the republic great. Here, in the Temple of Mars Ultor, the Senate assembled for important decisions that involved declarations of war or peace treaties. The plaza covered an immense area (roughly a hectare, or two-and-a-half acres) and the excavations done in the 1920s unearthed only the eastern part. Almost all of the buildings that overlooked the square were made of white marble from Luni (Carrara), the use of which became common from the time of Caesar, and even more so with Augustus, who boasted that he had found a city made of brick and left a city made of marble. The monumentalization of the new forum adhered to a number of very specific directives, as was typical of Augustus's political programme. The new emperor wanted, on the one hand, to present himself as a direct descendant of the dictator-monarch, and hence the inclusion of the statue of Caesar amongst the greats of Roman history, and on the other hand as a continuer of the ancient tradition, hence the reference to Romulus.

Vespasian's Forum

Between A.D. 71 and 75, Vespasian, with the revenues from the submission of Judea, ordered the construction — to the south of the Forum of Augustus, in the area of the *macellum*, the ancient marketplace — of a third plaza. This plaza, with a square plan and extending in width some 160 metres (525 feet), was porticoed on four sides, and was not a full-fledged forum, since it is not evident that it was ever used to perform administrative, judicial or commercial activities. The monument built by Vespasian, one of the loveliest in Rome

1. Temple of Divine Trajan
2. Trajan's Column
3. Trajan's Forum
4. Trajan's Market
5. Temple of Venus Genitrix
6. Caesar's Forum
7. Augustus's Forum
8. Temple of Mars Ultore
9. Nerva's Forum or Forum Transitorium
10. Temple of the Peace
11. Temple of Septimius Severus
12. House of the Vestals
13. Temple of Antoninus and Faustina
14. Basilica of Maxentius
15. Arch of Titus

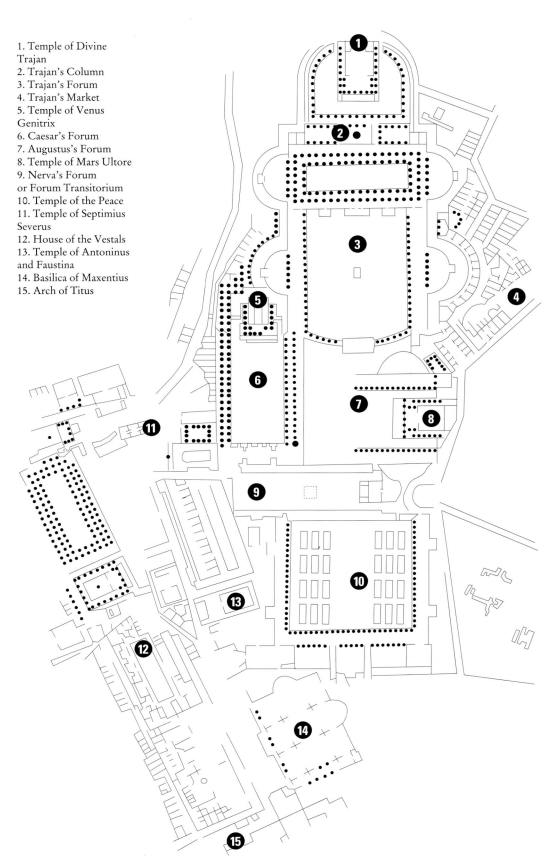

*The Arch of Septimius
Severus, built in A.D.
203, dominates the
northern portion of the
Imperial Forums; in the
background on the left
you can see the
Tabularium of the
Capitolium
(Campidoglio).*

TRAJAN'S COLUMN: A NEW VISUAL LANGUAGE OF PROPAGANDA AND CELEBRATION

Ever since the Hellenistic era, columns had been used as supports for commemorative statues but, whereas, on the one hand, the column built by Trajan tends to continue a tradition (at the summit in fact is a statue of the emperor), on the other hand, it is strongly innovative. Never before had a continuous decorative band been created that covered the entire surface of the column along a spiral path (the adjective refers specifically to the spiral or snail-shell shape). Through a door in the base, access can be obtained to a room where at first the ashes of the emperor and his consort were placed. Above this base, the column proper rises, consisting of nineteen cylindrical blocks of white marble, reaching an overall height of 29.78 metres (about 98 feet), corresponding to 100 Roman feet. The continuous figured depiction on the column illustrates the two wars waged and won by Trajan against the Dacians, one in A.D. 101-102 and the other in A.D. 105-106. The narration of the two military campaigns is interrupted by the allegory of *Victory,* depicted in the act of writing the history. All of the episodes must have been clearly identifiable to the Roman people, and indeed we might speak of a figured exemplification of a report on a war. In the scenes in relief, although quite low but so well modelled by the artist that it confers an extraordinary depth of perspective, we can clearly detect a powerful educational intent. First of all we note the determination to produce propaganda and to celebrate the *res gestae* of Trajan, while no less evident is the wish to transmit the ethical and political values upon which the empire was based in this period.

Trajan's Forum closes the eastern side of the area of the Imperial Forums: here in particular are ruins of the Basilica Ulpia, and in the background the column-sepulchre, built in A.D. 113 and adorned with a frieze depicting the Dacian Wars; on the right, the Church of Santa Maria in Loreto.

*Detail of the trabeation of
the temple built in
Nerva's Forum and
completed in A.D. 98.*

*Detail of the monumental
coffered vaults of the
basilica of Maxentius built
at the beginning of the
fourth century A.D.*

in the first century A.D., as Pliny the Elder informs us, was almost entirely swallowed up by the modern city, and few traces survive. All the same it is possible to reconstruct its plan through the invaluable documentation of the *Forma Urbis*, a monumental plan of ancient Rome engraved on marble slabs in the second century A.D., under the rule of Septimius Severus. The open space of the huge square must in all likelihood have been organized as a garden and it was possible to admire within its precinct magnificent works by the most famous Greek sculptors of the classical era, such as Polycletus and Myron. Moreover, Vespasian enriched his monument with outstanding works of Hellenistic art (such as the Galatians of Pergamum) which he had plundered during his conquest of Greece and Asia Minor, creating a sort of museus *ante litteram*. Adjoining the square, he had ordered the construction of a temple dedicated to peace to commemorate his victory over the Jews; in it he had placed the booty that he had brought back from Jerusalem. Also evident in this case is a powerful determination to glorify the new Flavian dynasty which had not only defeated the external enemies of

Rome, but, with the end of the Civil Wars, had also restored stability to the interior of the Empire.

Nerva's Forum or Forum Transitorium

In A.D. 84, Domitian, the last of the Flavians, decided to monumentalize the narrow strip of land that separated the Forum of Augustus from the Forum of Vespasian. Hence the name of Forum Transitorium by which it is commonly known, since it occupied a stretch of the Argiletum that was a through path, or transitory way. At the extremity of the forum, on the short side to the north-west, Domitian had built a temple dedicated to Minerva, his favourite goddess. Restricted by the narrow space available, the architects were obliged to develop a false colonnade solution for the square, a solution that was quite successful. The death of the emperor interrupted the work which was continued by the el-

Detail of the remains of the trabeation and columns of the Temple of Castor and Pollux.

derly Nerva who, in A.D. 97, inaugurated the forum, dedicating it to himself.

Trajan's Forum

With the construction of the Forum Transitorium, all of the area between the Roman Forum and the hills that rose behind it was now fully occupied. Thus, when Trajan decided to build a new forum of his own, he had to come up with a daring solution that entailed the excavation of a hillside saddle that connected the Capitoline to the Quirinal. In this way he obtained a vast area whose monumentalization constituted a strong link between the two most intensely representative urban nuclei: the Forum and the Campus Martius. Trajan, for his monumental project, disposed of enormous financial resources that he had procured during his recent conquest of Dacia and so he decided to entrust the project, on which work began in A.D. 107 and ended in 113, to the most famous architect of the time, Apollodorus of Damascus. Trajan's project revealed, right from its area plans, original characteristics that differentiated it from the projects of his predecessors, who had all built forums in which there was a strong integration between plaza and temple. Trajan, a soldier-emperor, had in fact transferred into his architectural conception the principles of his politics, and decided to create a plaza that resembled the general quarters of a legionary camp. The forum is immense (roughly 85 by 300 metres, or 280 by 984 feet), clearly making it the largest of the imperial plazas. The basilica closed off the side opposite the entrance while libraries were placed where the archives were located in military camps. One reached the plaza from the southern side through a triumphal arch whose rich sculptural decoration referred back to the emperor's military ideology; it depicted statues of the defeated Dacians, and in counterpoint, portraits of Tra-

Detail of the low relief on Titus's Arch depicting the Entry of the imperial court into Rome through the Porta Triumphalis. *The arch was raised to commemorate Titus's victory during the military campaign in Judea in A.D. 70. The aménora stolen from the Temple in Jerusalem is clearly visible.*

Opposite page
Detail of the plinth and burial chamber in the Trajan Column in which the ashes of the emperor and his consort were placed.

View of the Lacus Curtius on the Via Sacra.

jan's generals, while on the summit of the arch was set the emperor's chariot, flanked by trophies. At the centre of the plaza, the emperor had an equestrian statue erected with his own portrait on it, in a clear imitation of the model of Caesar. Even now only certain portions of the area have been unearthed, during the demolitions of the 1930s, and most of the entire complex remains buried beneath the modern city. More visible, on the northern side, is the powerful five-aisle basilica which could be entered through three entrances. Behind the basilica were the libraries, two symmetrical buildings in which texts in Latin and Greek were conserved. In the niches, still visible in the walls of the buildings, were inserted wooden cabinets where important volumes were kept. The two libraries flanked the marble column that had been conceived as a sepulchre for the emperor and his wife Plotina. From the courtyard one reached the porticoed area where Hadrian built a temple in memory of Trajan (who died in A.D. 117), a perspective backdrop to the entire complex, probably already planned in Apollodorus's original design. Trajan's Forum, one of the most important centres of the city's public life, is the last of the great Imperial Forums that left a clear monumental imprint on the urbanistic layout of ancient Rome.

Vicenza and the Palladian Villas

The bulk of the Palladian basilica with its nave like an inverted ship's hull characterizes the city's skyline.

Opposite page
Aerial view of the historic centre.

The earliest documentation preserved of the city of Vicenza, even though it boasts an exceedingly ancient foundation on the part of the Euganeans between the eleventh and the seventh centuries B.C., refers to much later eras and is linked to the presence of the Veneti people, who later joined forces with the Romans and built in the city, which had become a Roman *municipium* under the name of *Vicetia*, both temples and civil buildings, a large theatre and an aqueduct; even now it is possible to detect in the urban fabric the distinctive grid of the Roman *castrum* arranged around the *cardo* and *decumanus*, identifiable with the present-day Contrada Porti, Contrada del Monte, and Corso Palladio. It is safe to assume that where Piazza Erbe and Piazza Biade now stand, the city's forum must have been located. During the Middle Ages the city was devastated by barbarian invasions, later becoming the seat of a Longobard Duchy and finally part of the Carolingian Empire. At the end of the long struggle between the Guelphs and the Ghibellines, the city won independence with the status of a commune, a status that it enjoyed until it was annexed to the Serenissima, or Republic of Saint Mark, as Venice was known, at the beginning of the fifteenth century, marking on the one hand the advent of a period of peace and prosperity, and on the other a general alienation of the city's aristocracy on the part of Venetian families. The latter, cunning entrepreneurs that they were, after confiscating most of the farmland in the surrounding countryside, began intense agricultural cultivation, testing out new knowledge in the field of drainage and irrigation and investing extensively in a sector that had been generally overlooked until then. The decision made by the Venetians to diversify their economy by increasing the wealth of the hinterland proved to be farsighted and astute in the light of the situation that developed nearly a century later. With the menacing expansion of the Ottoman Empire, the waters of the Mediterranean became increasingly dangerous for Venice, hindering trade with the East considerably; following the discovery of America, the bulk of maritime trade shifted towards the Atlantic Ocean. The true and sole source of wealth for Venice, as an alternative resource to maritime trade, thus became the extensive agricultural lands of the hinterlands, to which it turned greater and greater attention. The Venetian mercantile aristocracy converted itself into a landed aristocracy, without ever forgetting the elegance and refinement that had accompanied its most prosperous periods in the Lagoon City. The great architect for the requirements of this new clientele, and the creator of an innovative architectural language capable of conjugating practical necessities with an exceedingly refined aesthetic taste was Andrea di Pietro della Gondola, known as Palladio (1508-80), who was responsible, among his other great achievements, for renewing the monumental appearance of the city of Vicenza. After making numerous trips to Rome in the company of the Humanist Gian Giorgio Trissino and enriching his own cultural knowledge with a direct study of Renaissance and ancient architecture, Palladio returned to Vicenza where he received his first important commission. In 1546 the plans that he had submitted for the renovation of the basilica were selected during the course of a competition which received submissions from such renowned architects as Sanmicheli, Sansovino, Serlio, Giulio Romano, and others. The basilica, a Gothic building constructed by Domenico da Venezia beginning in 1449, was the seat of the city council, the tribunal, and the administrative offices. Between 1481 and 1494, Tommaso Formenton surrounded the building with loggias that soon showed

Andrea Palladio built the Loggia del Capitaniato in Piazza dei Signori around 1570. It includes clear references to the classical world with which Palladio was deeply cognizant.

Flight of columns in the Palladian basilica following Palladio's modifications in 1549. The building was originally a civil building known as the Palazzo della Ragione.

Opposite page
Andrea Palladio's masterpiece, Palazzo Chiericati, was built beginning in 1550. The tripartite front and the rich sculptural crown presuppose the broad space before it that accentuates the theatrical effect of the whole, which is now the Civic Museum.

Vicenza and the Palladian Villas

signs of structural collapse. Palladio suggested, with an innovative solution, that the existing structure could be incorporated into a new loggia structure with two orders of Serlian windows culminating in a balustrade. Even though this was an extraordinary public work, as was the Loggia del Capitano, built in 1571 to commemorate the victory at Lepanto, Palladian Vicenza boasted above all a great many palazzi, or private mansions, some of them only begun, but all the product of the cultural ambitions and renewed pride of the aristocracy of Vicenza. Some of them featured loggias and giant-order porticoes with strong chiaroscuro contrasts, such as Palazzo Chiericati and Palazzo Porto Breganze al Castello, while others were modelled with less pronounced projections, as was the case with Palazzo Valmarana al Pozzo Rosso and Palazzo Thiene. Aside from a few projects that he undertook for Venice, all of Palladio's activity took place in Vicenza, where it culminated with the design of the new city theatre, which the architect presented to the members of the Accademia Olimpica in 1580 just before his death; the theatre was actually built by his pupil Vincenzo Scamozzi. Palladio founded a new architectural typology for theatres, although he did incorporate significant references to the Vitruvian model of the ancient theatre. The Teatro Olimpico comprises an elliptical *cavea* surmounted by a Corinthian colonnade to accommodate the audience, and a *proscaenium* equipped with a fixed *scaena* that was meant to represent a view of Vicenza in either modern or classical form. In contrast with ancient open-air theatres, Palladio designed a roof to cover the entire structure; Scamozzi, who took over the supervision of the project after Palladio's death, did not embrace the original plan entirely, allowing himself a few variants.

Opposite page
View of the fixed scaenã *and* cavea *in the Teatro Olimpico commissioned from Andrea Palladio by the Accademia Olimpica; it was only inaugurated in 1585.*

Vicenza is also rich in fine examples of Gothic architecture, among which we should mention the church of San Lorenzo, and the Palazzo da Schio, characterized by elegant balconies and three-lobed multi-light windows.

View of Piazza delle Erbe.

In 1549 Andrea Palladio began work on the renovation of the Palazzo della Ragione, known as the basilica, in which the architect applied Serlian windows.

View of the entrance hall and Loggia d'Ercole in Palazzo Leone Montanari, built for Bernardino Montanari in the mid-seventeenth century.

The Room of the Four Continents in Palazzo Leone Montanari is the setting for a series of paintings by the Venetian Pietro Longhi.

THE TYPOLOGY OF THE VILLA

With the decline of trade on the Mediterranean Sea and the consequential increase in investments in the agrarian economy of Venice's hinterland, the Venetian aristocracy also began to commission Palladio to design and build villas in the countryside. These villas were more than just *loci amoeni*, pleasant places in which to pursue leisure activities and mental concentration; they were full-fledged executive offices for great farming estates. And so the architect had to take into account in the initial design stage the final use of the building, the requirements of the clients, to whom he had become a trusted professional, and the morphological characteristics of the place where he was going to build. The result that Palladio achieved was to constitute an absolute novelty in the wider genre of villas; throughout the fifteenth century and up to about 1540, the villa had been a set of distinct and separate structures, but now it attained a unitary combination of sections directed towards the harmonious operation of the agrarian corporation. At the centre was the owner's private residence, characterized by a temple-façade with pronaos surmounted by a pediment; on either side of the central structure extended the porticoed wings, which were called *barchesse*, which could accommodate agricultural equipment and products. These *barchesse* could extend to a considerable degree, as in Villa Emo at Fanzolo and Villa Barbaro at Maser, or else they could have a more compact structure as in Villa Pisani at Montagnana, or even be configured as quarter circles, as in Villa Badoer at Fratta Polesine. Palladio adopted a different solution for Villa Capra, known as La Rotonda, atop a hill not far from Vicenza. This particular site, which the architect himself called *belvedere*, imposed the design of a Greek-cross central plan, characterized by four short wings extending outward, emphasized by raised hexastyle pronaoi.

Andrea Palladio was responsible for the redevelopment of the typology of the villa: one of the best known of his villas is Villa Foscari at Mira known as La Malcontenta, whose Ionic façade overlooking the canal was built before 1560.

The return to Roman typologies and a new spatial relationship can be seen fully developed in the Loggetta Valmarana, designed by Palladio as the front of a Tuscan order temple, overlooking a canal.

Palladio's unquestioned masterpiece is Villa Capra known as La Rotonda: built between 1550 and 1551, it combines a central plan with the theatrical exaltation of the four façades with Ionic pediments.

Cracow

The valiant Prince Krak, who supposedly challenged and beat the dragon that lived in a cave at the foot of the Wawel hill, is the legendary founder of the city which spreads along the banks of the Vistula, and was the capital of Poland from the eleventh century to the sixteenth century. From a fortified village located at the crossroads of the ancient amber route towards the Baltic Sea and the road that led from Kiev to Prague, Cracow grew into a splendid and refined European capital, enjoying its greatest period of splendour and prosperity under the Jagiellon dynasty (1386-1572). Its renown and prestige, nonetheless, began to spread under Casimir the Great (1333-70), the founder of a university that soon became one of the most important centres of culture in central Europe, accepting students and scholars, including Filippo Buonaccorsi, who introduced Humanism here. Relations with Italy, for that matter, had always been and always were lively and rich in cultural cross-pollination, from as early as the late Italian Renaissance, as is documented by the activity of the Venetian painter Tommaso Dolabella (1598-1650) all the way up to the commission to design and build the imperial palace entrusted to two Italian architects, Bartolomeo Berrecci and Francesco the Florentine, by Sigismund I the Elder, who married none other than the Princess of Bari, Bona Sforza. Interaction with Italy continued with the renovation between 1682 and 1684 of the Palazzo San Cristoforo, the present-day site of the Historic Museum of Cracow, upon which the decorator and architect Baldassarre Fontana (1658-1729) worked, supervising the creation of the stuccoes (garlands and scenes from antiquity). No less fertile were artistic relations with Germany, which brought to the Polish capital Veit Stoss, the great sculptor of Nuremberg. The city's decline began with the transfer of the capital to Warsaw at the end of the sixteenth century, and lasted until 1815, when the city, following the Congress of Vienna, was made an independent republic. Beginning in 1846, under Austrian rule, Cracow returned to its status as the leading cultural and artistic centre of Central Europe, establishing itself as the third most important city in the Austro-Hungarian Empire after Vienna and Budapest. Following the Nazi occupation, which resulted in the death of 15,000 Poles, the city was conquered by the Soviet Marshal Konev in January 1945. A few kilometres from Cracow, Auschwitz constitutes another site of the memory of humanity, a testimonial to a tragic and painful recent past that, only with the election to the papal throne of Karol Wojtyla in 1978, found a moment of serene national redemption.

Cracow established its urbanistic layout on four core areas: the medieval centre, which developed around the market square; the Wawel, the hill that has been inhabited since the Palaeolithic and the site of the imperial palace, the urban district of Kazimierz, a quarter built at the behest of Casimir the Great, and the quarter of Stradom.

Stare Miasto is the old city, characterized by the rigid grid of perfectly orthogonal streets, the result of the layout ordered by Boleslaw the Chaste in 1257 when he decided to unify the various peoples scattered around the hill of the Wawel. All that remains now of the medieval enclosure walls is the Gate and the little wall that was built in 1499 near the main city gate. The heart of ancient Cracow is the Market Square, one of the largest medieval squares in all of Europe, lined with elegant buildings, whose internal core is constituted by a Gothic agglomeration of buildings built at the end of the fourteenth century, and later renovated with Renaissance façades. The Gothic Tower from 1383 remains the only

Aerial view of the city.

Opposite page
The appearance of the historic centre of Cracow has maintained the eighteenth-century transformations so clearly linked to the culture of Central Europe.

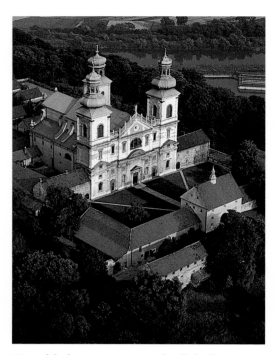

View of the baroque church of the so-called 'Monastery of the hill'.

A fortified village defending the Vistula River, founded by Casimir and transformed at the end of the sixteenth century by Italian artists.

THE WAWEL

The limestone hill that looms over Cracow is the Wawel, one of the most important sites in all Poland, for its historical and political significance as well as for its artistic value. The complex is characterized fundamentally by two buildings, the castle and the cathedral. Traces of fortifications are documented as far back as the ninth century, even though the construction of a complex with its own identity, later destroyed by fire in 1499, only dates from the reign of Casimir III the Great. It was Sigismund I who undertook its reconstruction beginning in 1502. The masterpiece of the Italian architects who worked on the project was the airy and elegant Renaissance courtyard. The building contains some of the most important art treasures of Poland, such as the collection of tapestries created by Flemish master weavers in the mid-sixteenth century, the collection of Oriental art, and the royal treasury with the Crown Jewels. The other structure that characterizes the complex is the Cathedral of Saint Wenceslaus. Built in the Gothic style between 1320 and 1346, it contains the splendid tombs of the Polish kings and, in the sacristy, the treasure consisting of precious reliquaries, manuscripts, and royal insignia.

Entrance of the cathedral in which elements of the Gothic tradition merge with Renaissance models of Italian origin, dominating Wawel hill.

Courtyard of the imperial residence designed and built by Bartolomeo Berrecci and Francesco il Fiorentino, upon commission from Sigismund I the Elder and his wife Bona Sforza.

Main hall of the Collegium Maius, the original nucleus of the ancient university of Cracow, founded by Casimir the Great.

THE LADY WITH THE ERMINE

The collection of the Czartoryski Museum was the product of the refined sensibility and the stubborn determination of the Princess Czartoryska, a member of one of the oldest and most enlightened aristocratic families of the land. The painting by Leonardo da Vinci, at first known as the *Belle Ferronière*, was purchased in Italy by her son Adam Jerzy, around 1800. The panel depicts Cecilia Gallerani, a favourite of Lodovico the Moor, and was executed by Leonardo between 1489 and 1490. This is one of the artist's best known works, a clear indication of Leonardo's genius and a fundamental point of transition in pictorial portraiture. There is of course no shortage of female portraits in European painting in the second half of the fifteenth century, but there had never been such a perfect synthesis between the requirements of traditional iconography of the individual viewed in silhouette and the indications of internal motion, of a state of mind that constituted, in Leonardo's work, an unrelenting quest, both in theoretical and practical terms, with a pictorial execution that is imperceptibly perfect, and here raised to the level of a masterpiece. The elegance of the turning body is a harmonious dialogue of equilibriums rendered still more absolute and elegant by the black background. Here painterly technique lacerates all and any determinism, becoming the instrument of expression of an indefinable sentiment.

The painting by Leonardo (1485-90) known as The Lady with the Ermine, *a portrait of Cecilia Gallerani, lover of the Duke of Milan Lodovico the Moor, is the masterpiece of the Czartoryski Museum.*

View of the fortified citadel from the large square laid out in the nineteenth century.

The richly decorated Baroque balustrade and door of the Church of the Apostles seen from the doors of the ancient Church of Sant'Andrea.

relic of the City Hall, which was demolished in 1820. Among the neighboubouring buildings, it is worth mentioning the so-called Gray House, the oldest building in the city, which was built between the thirteenth and fourteenth centuries, with internal Renaissance variants, and which hosted in 1574 the naming of the first elected king in Poland.

On the same square stand the two towers of the Parish Church of Our Lady of the Assumption, founded by the Bishop of Cracow in 1222, destroyed by the Mongols in 1241, and rebuilt in the Gothic style beginning in 1355. Certainly one of the most interesting buildings, with a plan featuring a nave and

two side aisles, it features elements of great artistic value, such as the vaults over the nave, frescoed by Stanislaw Wyspianski and Józef Mehoffer (1889-92), the marvellous stained-glass windows of 1370, the Marian altar frontal by Veit Stoss, possibly his greatest masterpiece, and one of the greatest polyptychs in Europe, carved out of limewood between 1477 and 1489. Other art treasures in the Czartoryski Museum include collections of historic and archaeological documents, arms and armour, but the museum owes its fame in particular to its collection of paintings, the most important in Poland, which boasts works by Cranach the Elder, Lorenzo Monaco, Lorenzo Lotto, Mattia Preti, Strozzi, and Rembrandt, thus spanning art history from the fourteenth to the eighteenth centuries, including all of the fundamental variants of the European schools, and especially the jewel to which it largely owes its fame: the renowned work by Leonardo da Vinci, *The Lady with the Ermine*.

A cultural tradition that can still be measured in the halls of the Jagiellonian University, and in its oldest nucleus, the *Collegium Maius,* a building made of stone and terracotta with a handsome courtyard lined with Gothic arches that features a priceless *mappamondo* dating from 1510, bearing the earliest indication of the American continent. A cultural tradition that finds a modern-day incarnation in the artistic career of Tadeusz Kantor, a stage director and theorist of Polish theatre, painter and set designer, who died in 1990, and the founder of the theatrical troupe Cricot 2, which since 1980 has been based in this Polish city. Kantor was an intellectual who focused on the creation of avant-garde theatre and art, reflecting the obscenities of war in a comic drama devastated by nihilism, vividly echoing a venerable Polish culture that Cracow still recounts in its streets.

A Catholic city and a city of avant-garde culture, popular traditions and historical and artistic traditions, both architectural and natural dramatic settings, Cracow today finds itself facing the historical and political challenge posed by the fall of the Berlin Wall for all of Eastern Europe.

The market square, one of the largest in Europe, is dominated by the façade of the Church of Our Lady of the Assumption, with its twin towers.

Prague

The historic centre of Prague, which was named part of the World Heritage of Humanity in 1992, represents in an exemplary manner that cultural stratigraphy that has made the city an elegant and refined equilibrium of architectural and natural charms, both historic and literary.

It has a lively natural morphology, which takes the form of slopes and bodies of water that animate a human landscape that is rarely invasive, and spans the centuries in various architectural styles, but always in harmony with the natural lay of the land; its recent and remote history — lively, tragic and painful — has been devoted to the quest for a national identity; its cultural vitality is recounted in literary (Kafka, Hašek, Hrabal) and musical (Smetana, Dvořák) harmonies in which formalism, stylistic research, and folk culture interact with an almost embarrassing nonchalance, and capture the Western soul with all the echoes of a deep-rooted Jewish culture; all of these are factors that make Prague an indispensable chapter of European history.

The earliest known settlements date back to the upper Palaeolithic, even though a true urban centre did not take form until the tenth century. An early documentation can be found in the chronicle of a journey made by the merchant Ibrahim Ibn Ya 'qub, a Jewish councillor to the Caliph of Cordoba, dated 965. A crossroads for trade between the Russians and Slavs, Turks, Muslims, and Jews, Prague still strikes the visitor as a city of 'stone and whitewash'. Sixteenth-century sources attest to the presence of Jews as early as the end of the tenth century and the present-day Jewish Quarter (Židovské Mešto) constitutes a fascinating voyage through the history of this people and its Yiddish traditions. The *Staronova´ synago´ga* is the oldest building in the quarter (Josevof). Built between 1270 and 1275 in a transitional style between Romanesque and Gothic, it represents one of the most interesting and oldest examples of Jewish architecture in all Europe.

Also in the Jewish quarter is the old cemetery, which in a charming and evocative atmosphere gathers some 11,000 graves which, for lack of space, were stacked as many as twelve tombs high. Used as far back as 1439, it features the headstones of such important individuals as Rabbi Jehuda ben Bezalel, known as Rabbi Loew, who died in 1609 and whose name is linked to the fantastic figure of the Golem, the creature made of mud and animated by the rabbi's cabalistic wisdom.

Židovské Mešto is one of the four citadels that form Prague along with the Old City (Staré Mešto) on the curve of the River Moldau, the Malá Strana (literally, 'small part') on the left bank of the river, and the Hradcany, the castle sector.

With the rise to power of Charles IV, a lover of art and a man of culture, Prague became the capital of the Holy Roman Empire and was soon surrounded by an architectural and cultural ferment to which the university — founded in 1348 — offers clear testimony. This golden period, however, was followed by a darker period, in the wake of the monarch's death, which coincided with the explosion of the Hussite revolution, that was the result of the proud preaching of Jan Huss, who established a new national creed that made Prague the centre of the first Protestant Church in Europe. A cultural revival was led by the remarkable personality of Rudolf II (1576-1612), who, in tones and with tastes that differed sharply from his predecessor's, attracted to his court astronomers such as Tycho Brahe and Johannes Kepler, artists like Giuseppe Arcimboldo and philosophers of the calibre of Giordano Bruno. The history of Prague followed its path towards the conflict with Austria that was to subject it to the

Aerial view of the historic centre.

Opposite page
View of the city from the hill of Malá Strana; the double towers of the Cathedral of Tyn rise above the town in the centre.

domination of Vienna until 1918, with the notorious 'defenestration of Prague' as perhaps the best-known episode. Recent history teems with events that hold places in the most vivid memories of Europe: the Second World War, the Nazi Occupation, Communism and the 'Prague Spring', all these are only steps along the troubled historical path that led to the birth of a new and autonomous state, the Czech Republic, events that explain very well some of the shifts in stylistic direction in its architecture and cultural movements that affected it. These moments in history can be deciphered in the urbanistic layout and the architectural, as well as literary, style.

Perhaps the finest documentation of Prague in the Middle Ages, both in civic and artistic terms in the old centre is the City Hall. Founded in 1388, it owes its renown to the astronomical clock set on its tower, a true prodigy of medieval mechanics, capable of attracting the attention of travellers as early as 1410. On the same square stand the two towers of the Church of Tyn, one of the most significant Gothic buildings in Prague. Built from 1365 on, it houses the remains of the astronomer Tycho Brahe.

The Gunpowder Tower, the Jewish Ghetto, the Royal Castle, and the Charles Bridge are only a few of the attractions of this 'ancient chapter' in the Bohemian capital.

A learned and refined city, Prague accepted a Baroque that redesigned the outlines of plazas, exquisite façades, and roads, constructing a stage setting that adhered to the natural 'theatricality' of the territory, so rich in modulations, grafting delicately on to the medieval fabric of the city, especially the old city. A symbol of renewed imperial power, Baroque conferred upon the city a distinctive appearance which finds in the façade of the Church of Saint Nicholas one of its most elevated expressions, as in the decorative element,

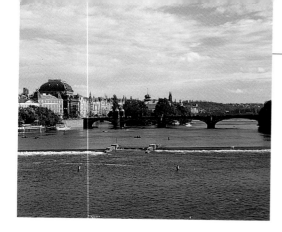

The course of the Moldau, dominated by the bulk of the Národní divadlo (National Theatre), built between 1868 and 1881 to the Neo-Renaissance model of the Staatoper of Vienna.

The agglomeration of buildings beneath the castle, with the Moldau in the background and the New Bridge.

Opposite page
The Church of Sv. Mikuláš (Saint Nicholas), a masterpiece of Prague Baroque, was built by the Jesuits to plans by Christoph Dientzenhofer between 1703 and 1713, while the dome was the work of his son Killian Ignatz, 1737-52.

View of the Karlóv Most (Charles Bridge), which was designed and built by Peter Parler, on a commission from the Emperor Charles IV in 1357 as the centrepiece of the royal road over the Moldau. Its Gothic structure is supported by sixteen pylons and is adorned by thirty-one statues erected between 1706 and 1714.

THE BRIDGES OF PRAGUE

Beginning in the twelfth century, Prague could already boast a number of exemplary works of civil engineering. The millers banded together and widened the bed of the Moldau, adding locks to make its flow more powerful, so that it rivalled the largest rivers in Europe in appearance. The two banks were linked, after the Judith Bridge (1158-72), collapsed in 1342, by the renowned Charles Bridge (1357-83), a true masterpiece of medieval engineering, executed, on a royal commission, by the Swabian architect Peter Parler. The bridge, over 500 metres (about 1,640 feet) in length, terminates at either end with two towers, two on the castle side, the smaller of which dates back to the previous bridge; during the seventeenth century, it was embellished with a series of statues that, long blackened by time, help to construct the atmosphere and appeal that we think typical of Prague. Craftsmen's booths and street artists enliven the stroll, making this one of the most attractive and charming tourist attractions in the city. Two hanging bridges, no longer in existence, were built during the reign of Francis I. The Legions Bridge, made of granite, replaced one of the two bridges at the end of the century.

In 1846 the first viaduct was built for the railroad line. The construction materials became iron, cement, and later, reinforced concrete. The Nusle Bridge represents one of the most interesting architectural creations in Prague. Built as a result of the thriving commercial activity of the Vltavin city, today these bridges contribute to the attraction of the city.

Opposite page
The fairy-tale spires of the Týnský chràm (Cathedral of Tyn) built beginning in 1365, dominate the great square of the Staré Mĕsto (Old City).

a possibility of urban furnishing, still alive in the façades of the buildings that surround the City Hall Square.

And once again its political events are reflected in its artistic history.

Austrian domination naturally imposed certain stylistic preferences. Vienna was close at hand, as was the Viennese school of Otto Wagner, frequented by many Bohemian students, including Jan Koteřa, professor at the Prague Institute of Art and the founder of the Prague Art Nouveau style, a style that in its early results made heavy use of the floral motifs of decoration, of coloured glass, ceramics, and decorative plasters, and later moved towards considerations of functionality and logical construction of buildings. Art Nouveau is also represented starting with the Paterka House (1899) by Koteřa, and culminating in a modernist creation by the same architect in the Urbánek House (1911). The avant-garde impulses of movements such as Expressionism, Fauvism, and Cubism did not

fail to leave their mark on the architecture of buildings of the early twentieth century. The Cubist school of expression formulated into façades structured with broken surfaces, subdivided into diagonals that accentuated luministic effects (the Rašín Riverside Houses of the architect Josef Chochol, 1911-13).

One of the most important architectural characterizations, precisely because it was a reflection of independence-oriented impulses towards a quest for a national identity, was Rondocubism, which replaced corners, spires, and the colour grey, considered so many symbols of Germanism, with a 'rotundity' and a softer modulation of spaces, and especially the use of colour, considered to be a distinctive feature of Slavism.

Through the experience of Constructivism and Functionalism, and the work of another great Czech architect, Jože Plečnik, Prague moved towards the Soviet Occupation of which Saint Wenceslaus Square remains a moral and architectural memory.

The City Hall of the Old City is known especially for the astronomical clock built in 1410 and modified over time, equipped with a mechanism with self-moving figures that emerge from two small side windows.

Detail of the façade of the Obecnì dóm (House of the People), the most prestigious building of the early twentieth century in Prague, built between 1903 and 1911, with decorative motifs inspired by the Viennese Secession.

Novgorod

Novgorod, which stands on the banks of the River Volkhov in the prosperous region known as the Golden Ring is one of the oldest cities in Russia. From the Middle Ages to the nineteenth century, it was a much-respected trading, political, and religious centre, as is evident from its buildings, harmoniously located one next to the other.

Situated along the ancient trading route that linked Central Asia with the Baltic and Scandinavian countries, as early as the ninth century the city was already the centre of a vast region that included a great deal of northern Russia and the Siberian lands. It was then that a group of adventurers came to Novgorod from Scandinavia, settling there and, with the consent of the inhabitants, taking over the city's government. They were commanded by Rurik, the leader of the Variags (as the Russians called the Scandinavians who came to their lands), the founder of a dynasty of dukes, grand dukes, and czars that was to play a leading role in Russian history until the sixteenth century. Following his death, the city was incorporated into the new state founded by Duke Oleg, who established his capital in Kiev and founded a realm that was destined to enjoy great prosperity thanks to its control of trade between the Baltic and the Black Sea. The foundation of this region's wealth was the export of the valued pelts of mink, Arctic fox, and squirrel, animals that abounded in this northern land, as well as wax and linen, the cultivation of which was particularly well suited to the local climate. In the sixteenth century, the Como-born aristocrat Paolo Giovio visited Novgorod, and was impressed by the beauty and richness of its land, which not only produced grains, but also 'excellent linen and hemp for cables, as well as great quantities of cowhide and huge masses of wax'.

The city's prestige won official recognition in the eleventh century, when it was decided that the first-born son of the Duke of Kiev should live there in order to govern, the highest authority of a state that, because of the power attributed to the popular assembly (the *veche*), was configured not as a realm but as a republic. Following the glorious victories over the Swedish invaders won in 1147 by Alexander Nevsky, Prince of Novgorod, and over the Tatars of the Golden Horde at the turn of the thirteenth century, the city was conquered by the Duke of Moscow in 1471. A series of harsh ordeals began then for the ancient republic: part of its population, suspected of harbouring seditious intentions, was deported and replaced with Muscovites, and a century later, Novgorod was almost completely destroyed by Ivan IV the Terrible, who massacred its 60,000 inhabitants.

And yet even now the city preserves the splendid evidence of its artistic and cultural development, the result of the fertile exchanges with other lands, its central territorial location, and its singular combination of social structure that combined princely and democratic traditions. For these reasons, we find coexisting in the churches, in the monuments, and in the icons of what was one of the oldest and most important Orthodox religious centres, the Byzantine-influenced style of Kiev, European Romanesque and Gothic art, and the most original and authentic 'Russian spirit'.

Novgorod is divided into two parts by the River Volkhov: the settlement on the eastern, or right bank, the ancient Torgovaya Storona, is dominated by the Market and the Royal Palace, while the settlement on the western, or left bank, the ancient Sofiyskaya Storona, surrounds the vital heart of the city, the Kremlin; these follow the rolling curves of the hill that overlooks the river. In the buildings that compose it, all the significant events of the city's

Aerial view of the Kremlin of Novgorod.

Opposite page
Apse of the Church of the Trinity in the Monastery of the Holy Ghost. Built in exposed brick in the second half of the sixteenth century.

Opposite page
*The market square, one
of the largest in Europe, is
dominated by the façade
of the Church of Our
Lady of the Assumption,
with its twin towers.*

THE FRESCOES OF THEOPHANES THE GREEK IN THE CHURCH OF THE TRANSFIGURATION

The most important series of frescoes in Novgorod is unquestionably the one that the Byzantine master Theophanes the Greek executed before 1378 in the Church of the Transfiguration, the temple that housed the most precious relic in the city, that is, the icon of the *Virgin of the Sign* who, according to legend, saved the city in 1169 from the army of Suzdal. The surviving fragments of these frescoes, especially the one in the dome with the colossal image of the Almighty enthroned and surrounded by angels, represent the intense use of colour and monumental style, charged with expression and '*terribilità*', that gave rise to the rebirth of Russian painting.

Abel *and* Enoch, *details
from the pictorial cycle
painted by Theophanes
the Greek in 1378 in the
Church of the
Transfiguration.*

Church of Saint Blaise (Vlasij), dating from the beginning of the fifteenth century.

Church of Saints Peter and Paul, whose construction dates back to the first decade of the fifteenth century, built on the left bank of the River Volkhov.

Cathedral of Saint George (Yuriev), built before 1195.

Cathedral of Saint Sophia, dating back to the middle of the eleventh century.

public life took place, from the assemblies of the *veche* to the election of the princes, as well as all administrative, social, and religious activities. The solid ring of city walls, interrupted by the porticoed gallery of white stone from which rises the gleaming bell tower, protected the residence of the Archbishop and especially the cathedral, dedicated to Saint Sophia and built by Prince Vladimir between 1045 and 1050. Inside it took place the great receptions for foreign ambassadors and the princes of Muscovy, bishops were named, the city chronicles were compiled, and the medieval treasuries were housed. Also built in white stone and crowned with delicate Byzan-

tine domes, it conserves an icon stall, built in 1528 that illustrates scenes of the *Last Judgement* and the principal Orthodox holidays.

On the other side of the waters of Lake Miachen formed by a bend in the river, stand the small Church of the Annunciation, built in 1179 in the vicinity of the quarter of Arkhazi, and the Church of Saint George, built in 1119. Forming part of the monastery complex of Yuriev, founded in 1030 by Prince Yaroslav the Wise, the Church of Saint George is most striking for the magnificence and splendour of the frescoes that line its interior, which are products of its status as the long-term burial site of the princes of Novgorod.

Suzdal and Vladimir

To the east of Moscow, between the rivers Moskva and Volga, there stretches a region that for its age-old wealth is known as the Golden Ring. This is where Vladimir and Suzdal are located, two cities that conserve relics of an era in which they guided Russian history and elevated Russian art to greatness.

Suzdal

Suzdal was the place in which for seven centuries masterpieces were accumulated and treasured, to the point that it was fair to call it a full-fledged 'museum- city', formerly the direct property of the Soviet Government, which prohibited the construction of new buildings that might alter the pristine nature of its exquisite urban fabric, dominated by onion domes, studded with daring arches decorated with stacked orders (*kokosniki*), over which loomed the pyramidal spires that crowned the bell towers like so many tents of the nomads of days gone by. Founded in 1024 among the rolling hills through which wound the meandering course of the river Kamenka, the city was chosen by the powerful Prince of Kiev, Vladimir Monomakh, as his residence. In the twelfth century the Fortress of the Kremlin was built there, on the interior of whose walls stood, safe and well defended, the Cathedral of the Nativity of the Virgin Mary on the site of the Cathedral of Our Lady of the Assumption, which collapsed but which had originally been built at the behest of Prince Vladimir, and, in the centuries that followed, the cusped bell tower and the Episcopal Palace. The church, built between 1222 and 1225, is an exquisite example of the white stone architecture that made Vladimir and Suzdal so splendid in the twelfth and thirteenth centuries. The building preserves its original layout, the rich reliefs on the exterior and, above all, the splendid Golden Doors, whose leaves are sheathed in heat-gilded sheets of copper, and feature, in the rectangular panels, exquisite illustrations of scenes from the Old Testament.

The artistic flowering of north-eastern Russia was brusquely interrupted at the beginning of the thirteenth century by the invasion of the Tatars. In 1238, Suzdal was conquered and put to the torch, but it soon recovered. It was then that the city enriched itself with magnificent buildings, foremost among them the great monasteries that controlled vast tracts of land and inestimable wealth, standing alongside the others around the Kremlin: among those constructed were the Monastery of the Intercession (1364), the Monastery of the Enlightened Jevfimi, or Saint Euphemius (1350), which contains various churches built between the fifteenth and seventeenth centuries, and the religious complex dedicated to the Saviour and to Saint Eutimius, the monk from Suzdal who founded it to the north of the city. This latter religious complex was built in the fourteenth century in the general manner and function of a fortress, and in the sixteenth and seventeenth centuries the primitive wooden buildings of which it was composed were gradually substituted by stone structures. The imposing enclosure wall, more than one and one-half kilometres (one and one-quartes miles) in length, thus appeared, punctuated by twelve monumental access towers; the principal tower, 22 metres (72 feet) tall and crowned by a dome, is polygonal in shape and embellished with an elaborate decoration. Then the main church of the complex was built, named for the Transfiguration, an austere and monumental building in the tradition of the churches of Suzdal in white stone, decorated with cycles of sixteenth- and seventeenth-century frescoes. Finally, at the beginning of the sixteenth century, the church dedicated to the Nativity of Saint John the Baptist was built, with its pe-

Aerial view of the Cathedral of the Assumption of Vladimir along the course of the River Klyazmia.

Opposite page
Detail of the tip of the wooden Church of the Transfiguration.

The Cathedral of Saint Dmitry in Vladimir was built on land given to the Church by Prince Vsevolad at the end of the twelfth century, and was renovated several times.

View of one of the more than thirty monastic complexes in the area of Vladimir and Suzdal.

View of the three apses of the Church of the Deposition.

The Monastery of Spaso Yevfmiyev (Saint Euphemius) in Suzdal, with the Cathedral of the Transfiguration and the bell tower built in the fifteenth century.

culiar polygonal campanile surmounted by an elegant dome made of silver-plated boards of poplar wood, further embellished in the seventeenth century with niches, blind arches, and semi-columns; it was here that Prince Vasily III and his wife Solomonia came to pray during their visits to Suzdal.

Although it fell victim, first to Polish occupation (1608), and later to Tatar occupation (1644), as well as to an outbreak of the plague (1654), Suzdal continued to enrich itself with splendid churches, like the Church of Saint Nicholas (1770), in which the traditional motifs of wooden buildings and the local decorative elements are blended; or the Church of the Emperor Constantine (1707), its façade entirely decorated with bas-reliefs, flanked by the smaller winter church dedicated to Our Lady of Sufferers; or the Church of the Resurrection (1720), flanked by the 'warm c hurch' of the Virgin of Kazan (1739) and by the splendid bell tower decorated with niches and majolicas.

Vladimir

The neighbouring city of Vladimir, the official capital of Russia and seat of the Great Prince of Kiev from 1157 to 1238, was even more powerful than Suzdal. It boasts some of the oldest works of art in the country. In fact both the city's defensive walls and the imposing central tower, built in white stone in 1158-64 at the behest of Prince Andrei Bogolyubsky, and featuring the splendid Golden Gate, date back to the twelfth century.

It was once again Andrei Bogolyubsky who ordered the construction, as the main church of the principality of Vladimir and Suzdal, of the Cathedral of Our Lady of the Assumption (or Our Lady of the Dormition). The prince had it built in noble form on the high hill that overlooks the river Klyazma, near his own palace and the palace of the bishop, with the intention of conferring upon the city the elevated status of capital and upon himself political supremacy. The church, co-

147

Panoramic view of the bell tower of the church of the Alexandrovsky Monastery in Suzdal, built in the seventeenth and eighteenth centuries.

Façade and bell tower campanile of the Church of Divine Love (Bogolyubovo) from the early seventeenth century.

vered on the exterior by reliefs carved into the white stone, gilded friezes, and colourful paintings, was built between 1158 and 1160 and was originally surmounted by a huge golden onion dome, to which four more were later added. This church, which long housed the famous and venerated icon of the Madonna of Vladimir (now in the Tret'yakov Gallery in Moscow), possesses noteworthy artistic treasures, such as the giant gilded iconostasis offered at the end of the eighteenth century by the Tsarina Catherine II it stands a full 25 metres (82 feet) tall and especially the fresco of the Last Judgement painted in 1408 by Andrei Rublëv.

Another jewel of the medieval art of Vladimir is the Church of the Intercession on the River Nerl, built in harmonious form, in 1165, by Prince Andrei, who was in quest of spiritual comfort from his grief over the death of his young son in battle. We certainly cannot forget the small building surmounted by a

dome of the Cathedral of Saint Dmitry, which encloses in its interior splendid frescoes from the twelfth century and features on its exterior one of the most eloquent documents of Russian sculpture from the Middle Ages. The entire upper order, in fact, is decorated with more than one thousand cut stones that teem with characters whose symbolic meanings have been established only in part: the Biblical figure of King David is present on all three elevations, while Alexander the Great and Samson appear, respectively, on the southern and western elevations; on the northern façade, seated on a throne, is a depiction of Vsevolod, the Prince of Vladimir who around 1190 had the cathedral built as his palatine church. The churches of the city also commemorate other members of Vsevolod's family: his wife, Maria Svarnov, buried along with other noblewomen in the monastery of the princesses that she founded, and his son, the great warrior Alexander Nevsky.

Details of the frescoes with scenes from the Last Judgement painted in 1409 by Andrei Rublëv in the Cathedral of the Assumption (or Cathedral of the Dormition) of Vladimir.

Cordoba

There is a popular tradition according to which the name of this city, built at a ford across the Guadalquivir River in the region of Andalusia, is linked to 'el Cortheb', a Punic term that indicated a leather press. However questionable that may be, historians agree that the town actually was founded by Phoenicians as a small commercial trading post. In the second century B.C. it became a Roman colony after its conquest in 152 B.C. by the Roman consul Claudius Marcellus. With the establishment of the *Pax Augustea*, which spanned the latter part of the first century B.C. to the first century A.D., the city, by this point having been subjected to complete Latinization, became the capital of Hispania Ulterior. In A.D. 711, after having suffered invasions by Vandals and Goths, it was conquered by the Arabs, and in 756 it became the capital of an emirate under Abd al-Rahman I and in turn a caliphate in 929 with his indirect successor Abd al-Rahman III. Thanks to the work of the particularly active and enlightened dynasty of the Omayyads, Cordoba enjoyed its most flourishing period between the ninth and tenth centuries, attaining an almost fairy-tale splendour. Towards the second half of the tenth century, the city must have boasted a population of roughly half a million people, and among the polyglot and especially turbulent populace, there was a class of numerous aristocrats who loved and patronized the arts and literature. These culture-loving nobles, with the benevolent protection of the caliph as well, summoned to Cordoba a vast group of physicists, philosophers, historians, mathematicians, geographers, astronomers, and so on. The city also enjoyed flourishing industries (for trade with India, three official languages were spoken) which are commemorated even today with the names of certain quarters, such as the *Pergamineros* (parchment makers), *Perfumistas* (perfume

makers), *Zapateros* (cobblers), *Silleros* (seal makers), and so forth. Drawing a parallel with Byzantium, Cordoba occupied an intermediate position between the East and West and, in a period that was certainly anything but luminous for Europe, the city on the River Guadalquivir kept alive a corner of civilization with its rich flowering of culture. Historians disagree concerning the actual statistics of the size of Cordoba during the caliphate, but a few numbers provide some sense of the expanse and magnificence of its territory: 22,000 houses, 600 mosques, 900 public baths, and 100 schools. The city was divided into roughly twenty-one districts with lovely, evocative names: *Jardín de las Maravillas* (garden of wonders), *Tiendas de los Vendedores de Albahaca Dulce* (shops of the vendors of sweet basil), *Mesquita del Regocyo* (mosque of joy), etc. The Alcazaba, a fortress with turreted walls, was located in the heart of the city. Aside from the royal palace, which was embellished and adorned, furnished with gardens and rendered lovely by dancing jets of water, the caliphs also built numerous houses and gardens, both within and without the city walls. With Abd al-Rahman I, driven by an extraordinary passion for flowers and plants, the gardens of Cordoba and of all the realm were enriched with various species of seeds from Syria and other distant lands. With the crisis and fall of the caliphate of Abd al-Rahman and the invasion in 1031 by the Almoravids and the Almohads, Cordoba experienced a gradual but inexorable decline that culminated in its destruction in 1236 when it was conquered by Christians. The city, a product of successive stratifications, has essentially preserved its Moorish layout in the welter of chaotic alleys and lanes and the small white houses that overlook them. Particularly interesting is the *Judería*, the old Jewish ghetto, one of the most ancient and picturesque

Aerial view of the city.

Opposite page
View of the gardens in the interior of the complex of the Alcazar.

View of the side of the cathedral from the Guadalquivir River.

The Juderìa, *the ancient Jewish ghetto, one of the oldest sections of the city, has preserved its medieval layout, in which the houses are arranged around patios.*

Opposite page
The Mosque of Cordoba was completed by Abd al-Rahman on the site of the Visigoth Church of Saint Vincent around A.D. 800 and was transformed into a Christian church after the Reconquista: this is the so-called Gate of San Miguel.

quarters in the city, which has maintained its distinctive medieval plan. Here we find a succession of little streets lined with white houses that are bursting with an explosion of colourful flowers that enclose the lovely *patios*. The Jewish quarter features one of the most celebrated monuments of Cordoba, the great cathedral-mosque completed by Abd al-Rahman III, and begun by his ancestors. On the site where the imposing structure was erected, as early as A.D. 748 stood the Visigoth Church of Saint Vincent, a place of worship for both Muslims and Mozarabic Christians. In 785 Abd al-Rahman confiscated the property of the Mozarabic Christians and built a new and majestic mosque, which was inaugurated the following year. The speed with which work was completed can be explained in part by the fact that a number of existing structures in the old basilica were incorporated in the new building, such as the north-west corner of the prayer hall. The plan of the entire building was also to some extent conditioned by the layout of the old basilica: instead of the large courtyards with narrow porticoes, typical of the traditional plans of eastern mosques, here the proportions were inverted, and we find a fairly small courtyard surrounded by porticoes of considerable breadth, wider even than in the Omayyad mosques of Syria. In the new mosque, not only was the layout of the Church of Saint Vincent incorporated, but a number of Visigothic elements can be noted as well. Another feature that violates the norm, as it were, is the *mihrab*, a sort of Islamic main altar oriented towards Mecca, here unusually elongated and facing south. The mosque built at the emir's behest consisted of a large hypostyle hall divided into eleven aisles, covered by double-pitch roofs, with ten rows of columns running north-south, and a courtyard, the *sahn*. The mosque underwent extensive renovation and enlargement over the years that followed.

Particularly significant was the work undertaken at the behest of Abd al-Rahman II, which called for the extension southward of the aisles, which in turn required that the *mihrab* be moved to the end of the new wall, with two doors and three domes across from it. The façade on the north side, with pillars and horseshoe arches, instead, dates back to the last caliph of the Omayyad dynasty. The largest expansions undertaken on the mosque occurred during the reign of al-Hakim II. At the time, the capital of the caliphate had reached its apex of development, and every Friday a vast number of the faithful were summoned to prayer, by this point so numerous that they could no longer be contained inside the mosque. Once again, therefore, it became necessary to enlarge it; for the second time the southern wall was demolished and the eleven aisles were extended still further in that direction. Under the Minister al-Mansur, it was necessary to expand in a new direction, because by this point the building was almost abutting the banks of the River Guadalquivir: eight columns were added to the east and the courtyard was enlarged, reaching its present-day size. The problem, once the mosque attained such vast dimensions, consisted in the fact that a system with simple arches would have created a building that would be too low and therefore unstable. The solution adopted, probably borrowed from the ancient Roman aqueducts, called for a building with double rows of stacked arches, thus creating an evocative forest of 850 columns topped by capitals in a wide variety of styles (some Roman columns, some Gothic columns, and the rest Arab). Until the reign of al-Hakim II the decorations had been relatively sober and restrained, but from that point on they began to become notably showy. Under the dome of the central aisle lobate arches were introduced, typi-

View of one of the sides of the mosque, with the Gate of San Esteban in the foreground.

This column topped by an angel stands at the entrance to the city.

Opposite page
Interior of the mosque-cathedral, in which the two-toned horseshoe arches of the Arab culture coexist with the Altar of the Crucifix.

cal of the Abbasid Empire, which with a network of ribbing formed geometric figures. From Constantinople expert mosaicists were summoned whose work can still be admired in the *mihrab*, in the dome, and in some portions of the walls. In the wooden ceilings, on the other hand, Mesopotamian influences can be detected. At the time of the General al-Mansur, towards the second half of the tenth century, the mosque of Cordoba was the largest and most majestic mosque in all the Islamic world. It had external walls with buttresses and merlons and various access doors. The main entrance was through the Puerta del Perdón (Gate of Forgiveness), which was flanked by a turreted wall and by handsome porticoes, which led in turn to the Patio de los Naranjos (the *sahn*), which had been embellished with luxuriant orange trees, palm trees, and burbling fountains. From the courtyard one entered the Puerta de las Palmas (Gate of Palm Trees), known also as the Puerta de las Bendiciones (Gate of Blessings), and one reached the interior of the mosque, looking out over the eleven original aisles. After the Christian reconquest, in 1236, the mosque was transformed into a church dedicated to Our Lady of the Assumption. In the sixteenth century, to plans by Hernán Ruiz, the ecclesiastical authorities decided to build the Chapel of the Canons amidst the Muslim columns.

ABD AL-RAHMAN AND THE CALIPHATE OF CORDOBA

During the ninth and tenth centuries, with the occupation of Muslim Spain by Abd al-Rahman I (756-788), a member of the surviving branch of the Omayyad dynasty, the Emirate of Cordoba represented the most important political and social structure. Thanks to a sober and intelligent administration, the city attained its greatest splendour, though there were numerous contradictory elements. First of all, although various religions and races were tolerated, policies in general were quite violent and cruel; moreover, despite the flourishing and prosperous economy, there were profound tensions between elements of Hispanic and Eastern culture. With Abd al-Rahman III (912-961), who declared himself Caliph in 929, thus establishing his independence from Baghdad, the Omayyad Caliphate in Spain reached its high point. With the powerful Commander al-Mansur the territory of the Caliphate extended to the north, reaching Santiago de Compostela. Despite a succession of victorious military campaigns which accompanied the steadily growing splendour of the caliphate, under Abd al-Rahman III unity was precarious and largely spurious. The hybrid population, composed of Arabs, Berbers, Christians, Jews, and Muslims, must have been exceedingly difficult to govern, and indeed with the death of al-Mansur in 1002 came a rapid crisis.

Opposite page
Interior of the dome of the mihrab *of the mosque.*

In the interior of the ancient mosque is the Arch of Maksourah.

Salamanca

Celtic origins confirm the antiquity of the city known in Roman times by the name of Helmatica. The invasion of the barbarians, the Vandals and Visigoths, marked a dark interlude that only returned to documented history from the twelfth century on. Moorish rhythms and versions of the more commonly experimented themes of Western architecure, from Romanesque to Gothic, from Renaissance to Baroque, endow Salamanca with the charm of a cultural city and the solidity of deep-rooted cultural traditions, worthy of preservation, that led to its inclusion on the World Heritage List in 1988.

An interesting document of its Roman history remains in the Roman bridge, built between the first and second centuries A.D. Among the Romanesque structures are the Church of San Cristobal (1145), the Church of San Giulian, the Church of San Martin, and the Catedral Vieja (Old Cathedral, begun in 1152), which, along with the Catedral Nueva (New Cathedral) constitutes the magnificent complex of the Catedral. A brief reference to the finest features of the oldest part of the monument must include the octagonal lantern of the Byzantine-influenced apse, the thirteenth-century frescoes by Sánchez de Segovia (1262), the thirteenth-century Madonna in Limoges enamel, and a polyptych by Nicolò di Fiorentino (1445). The Cat-

edral Nueva, begun in 1513, which combines Renaissance and Baroque elements on a Gothic plan, stands out for its massive tower (rising 110 metres, or about 360 feet), which joins a structure that is developed externally in compact lines, enriched by the dialogue of spires and balustrades, by the side portals and the terminal elevations of the transept and adorned with reliefs, statues, and Flamboyant Gothic decorations. We should also mention the choir designed by the Churriguera brothers, the Capilla Mayor (the main chapel), the Capilla Dorada (literally, the Golden Chapel), and the Capilla del Sudario (the Chapel of the Shroud).

The heart of the city remains the Plaza Mayor, or main square, a genuine jewel of Spanish Baroque and one of the most elegant plazas in all of Spain. Designed by the Churriguera brothers on a trapezoidal plan, it establishes an elegant elevation that develops a uniform structure of buildings over three storeys, punctuated by arches adorned with medallions that depict the sovereigns of Spain and figures from Spanish history, such as Cervantes, Columbus, and Cortes. The renowned university founded in the twelfth century remains a living monument to its cultural heritage. This school was a filter for the spread of the far more advanced (at the time) Arab culture, and it presents a sumptuous façade that faces on to the patio. The venerable study halls with their refined ceilings,

View of the cathedral from the Rio Tormes.

Detail of the Baroque sculptural decoration which adorns the Plaza Major, designed by the Churriguera brothers, adorned with the portraits of the monarchs of Spain.

Opposite page
View of the Roman bridge over the Rio Tormes and the historic nucleus of the city, dominated by the cathedral, begun in 1152.

Monumental entrance to the university, founded in the twelfth century.

Side of the cathedral, in which it is possible to see the load-bearing structure of the Gothic architecture with flying buttresses and spires.

Opposite page
View of the campanile of the cathedral.

160

the lecture room of canonical law with a portrait of Charles IV by Francisco Goya, the library, richly decorated by Alberto de Churriguera, are just a few of the treasures that can be found in this splendid building. Lastly, mention should be made of San Esteban, the monastery where Christopher Columbus stayed and which possesses a *retablo* considered to be one of the greatest masterpieces of Jose Benito de Churriguera.

Details of the external structure of the cathedral in which buttresses and Gothic windows coexist with the Romanesque apse.

Opposite page
The ribbed interior of the dome of the lantern on the Torre del Gallo in the cathedral.

Detail of the portal named 'de Ramos', with the Crucifixion of Saints Peter and Paul *in the so-called 'plateresco' style.*

THE CHURRIGUERA FAMILY

The term *churriguerismo* was developed to indicate the late and most flamboyant forms of Spanish Baroque, nourished by the wooden sculpture of Catalonia and the forms of expression of Italian Baroque, conceived and interpreted by the Churriguera family, which worked both in Madrid and Salamanca. As architects and sculptors, they created the most spectacular and expressive school of the early Spanish seventeenth century, beginning with the head of the family José Simón, and his five sons José Benito, Joaquín, Alberto, Manuel, and Miguel. The best known was unquestionably José Benito, who began to work in Salamanca after the notoriety that he had won in Madrid. In Salamanca he executed the *retablo* (large altarpiece, with monumental dimensions) for the Church of San Esteban from 1693 to 1696. He was considered the 'Spanish Michelangelo', perhaps for the versatility of his genius and for the power of his architectural and wooden stage settings. The constructors of complex altar machinery, extremely lively in the splendour of the decoration, making extensive use of the dynamic properties of the spiral column derived from Bernini and the vine cluster technique that enlivened its sculptural and chromatic effects, the Churrigueras made a deep mark on the history of Spanish art under the patronage of Philip V.

ASIA Asia

Angkor

At the end of the ninth century, Yaso-varman I (889-900) was the first to build his capital on the present-day site of Angkor, a variant form of the Sanskrit term *Nagara*, which means 'royal city, capital', inaugurating a tradition that was to last for the next five centuries. Many of his descendants imitated him so that there sprang up many different Angkors, arranged one alongside the other, until a monumental centre had been created extending over roughly two hundred square kilometres. For centuries, the kings worked to build temples in which they themselves were venerated and which even now perpetuate their memory, to perfect great irrigation works and construct dams (true masterpieces of hydraulic technology which are no longer visible), as well as concentrating on general political and cultural expansion: in the twelfth century the Khmer civilization spread throughout all of South-East Asia, reaching from the coast of Vietnam to central Burma (Myanmar), and from Laos to the Malay Peninsula. The reign of Jayavarman VII between 1181 and 1219 represented the high point of the empire, but also the beginning of its long and slow decline: the progressive shrinkage of the Cambodian empire to its homelands under the incessant advance of neighbouring populations, the suspension of work on water control, the crisis of a society divided by caste, exhausted by warfare and by the lavish fury for construction of the sovereign, and the massive conversion to ascetic Buddhism of the population, undermined the power that for centuries had made a show of its Hinduism. In 1431 the ancient capital of Angkor was abandoned because it could no longer be defended; the kings moved further south to present-day Phnom Penh and the temples were swallowed up by tropical vegetation, only to be freed from it again in the twentieth century by a French archaeological

mission (1933-72). Since 1992 Angkor has been a World Heritage Site.

In the monumental complex of Angkor the same urban layout returns, with few variants, in the various 'capitals': at the heart of each 'royal city', protected on four sides by an enclosure wall, stands the main temple; to the north of it, the royal palace, then the residential quarter; last, but not least, the *barays*, whose geometric shape had a magical significance, enormous artificial basins created through imposing hydraulic works which made it possible to irrigate the rice paddies in the six months of the dry season. The urban structure reflected the cosmology of the Khmer universe, which had its roots in Indian culture: the enclosure walls and moats corresponded to the mountain range and the ocean that bounded the world, at the centre the pyramidal temple enclosed the idol, the *linga*, the ideal centre of the world, the eternal emblem of the earthly king who is the direct emanation of the deity; the bridges that cross the moats, lastly, bring the two worlds — the divine world and the human world — into communication. All the Khmer buildings that have survived to the present day are religious buildings. In contrast with the urbanistic layout, the great temples differ from one another in their decoration, plan, and setting: they contain the greatest artworks of the Khmer empire, which experienced its period of greatest splendour between the second half of the ninth century and the beginning of the twelfth century. King Indravarman I (877-889), who completed the process of unification begun by Jayavarman II (802-850), ordered the construction in the Angkor region of the first great stone monuments. The first temple of classical Khmer architecture is the Prah Ko, which stood on the Mount Mahendrapura to house, as tradition would have it, the souls of the ancestors of the sovereign; dedicated to the god Shiva, the building was made of brick, with

View of the Bayon Temple.

Opposite page
Ruins of a colossal gopura. A gopura is a monumental portal-tower of a temple.

View of Angkor Wat with, in the foreground, one of the pools that surround the early twelfth-century monastic complex.

Detail of a gopura on the eastern façade of Temple IV East, dating from the end of the twelfth century.

Bottom, section of the Bayon Temple.

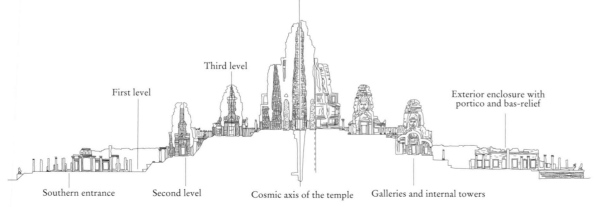

First level

Third level

Exterior enclosure with portico and bas-relief

Southern entrance

Second level

Cosmic axis of the temple

Galleries and internal towers

Detail of a high relief from the central tower of Pré Rup, depicting an apsàra, *a celestial dancer, from the end of the tenth century.*

ANGKOR-MANIA

Abandoned in 1431, Angkor was 'discovered' in 1863 by Europeans through the posthumous publication of the notebooks and drawings of the French naturalist Henri Mouhot, who in 1858 happened upon the ruins of the ancient Khmer capital. When some of the finds of sculpture and architecture were brought from Angkor to Paris by Delaporte a few years later, casts and statues depicting a five-headed giant with ten arms, a many-headed dragon, a lion tensed and ready to leap, wound up at the Universal Exposition of 1878 surrounded by charts and drawings; in conseguence, France was swept by Angkor-mania, with collectors, architects, sculptors and writers all fascinated by Khmer art. Although French colonial policy in the East had not found the wealth that had been hoped for in Cambodia, as the exquisite pieces, the casts, and souvenirs from Angkor began to make their way into Gallic museums and collections, France was increasingly conquered by the magic of Khmer art. And so, in time, Angkor began to be not only the destination for increasingly frequent archaeological expeditions, but also a full-fledged river of tourists. In the autumn of 1907 more than two hundred European tourists reached Angkor, for the most part colonials from Phnom Penh or Saigon, while beginning in 1912 'all-inclusive' voyages were organized, but only lasting two days: it was possible to stay in stilt huts but it was necessary to bring one's own linen, provisions, and cooking utensils. In the 1920s, travel agencies made it possible to visit the city in any season, and the fad for cruises made its way even to Angkor, which also became a destination for important artists, such as the author Pierre Loti, who after his short stay in 1901 was to write *Un pèlerin d'Angkor*, and the actors Charlie Chaplin and Paulette Goddard (1936). The seduction exerted by Angkor awakened interest for Cambodian civilization as a whole: when in 1924 King Sisovath came to France bringing with him the Royal Dance Troupe, Rodin dedicated an entire series of drawings to the girls, and in order to finish it, he followed them as far as Marseilles. But it was on the occasion of the Colonial Exposition of Paris in 1931 that the iconography of Angkor finally entered fully into the collective imagination: a monumental reconstruction of Angkor Wat was presented and the advertising industry seized on it.

Detail of the western entrance of Angkor Wat, dating back to the first half of the twelfth century.

The two-storey pavilion of Preah Khan, a Buddhist monastic complex built during the reign of Jayavarman VII at the end of the twelfth century.

Opposite page
View of the ruins in the central section of Angkor Wat. The pavilions that form the sacred complex are still visible.

frames and casements in laterite, a stone with a warm brick-red colour, which characterized the oldest Khmer architecture. In the structure, from exterior to interior, there was a succession involving a large square enclosure with turrets, a second enclosure that rose to a higher level, and finally a rectangular platform equipped with six tall square towers, arranged in two rows: the first row of three towers was consecrated to the male ancestors, while the second row was consecrated to the female ancestors, since in the Khmer culture women and men had the same rights; on each tower we find a figure in bas-relief, a 'guardian' that oversees the repose of the ancient ancestors. In A.D. 881 Indravarman I ordered the construction of a second temple, more imposing and articulated, the Bakong: it too was dedicated to Shiva, whose representative on earth was in fact none other than the sovereign, and once again it stood on a mountain and was surrounded, besides the enclosure wall, by a large artificial lake. Access was possible thanks

to two raised entrances that crossed the basin of water: the balustrades of the two suspended walkways were shaped like serpents. The Bakong is the first large stone monument which combines the step pyramid and the tower sanctuary: of the five storeys of the complex, constituted by as many concentric terraces, the first three are decorated at the top with stone elephants, the fourth is decorated by twelve turrets, while on the top storey is the principal sanctuary surmounted by five roofs crowned by a lotus flower. At the base of the entire edifice are located eight turreted sanctuaries and as many crouching lions guarding the entrance stairs. Suryavarman II (1113-50, the 'Protector of Victory') succeeded in building in thirty years Angkor Wat (1122-50), that is, the 'sanctuary city', the largest architectural creation in all of Asia and highest expression of Khmer art, to the point that it is known as the 'Cambodian Parthenon'. Dedicated to Vishnu, the temple constitutes in all likelihood the sovereign's mausoleum: this hypothesis is

Central group on the north side in Preah Khan, end of the twelfth century.

View of the western enclosure wall of the complex of Angkor Wat, dating from the first half of the twelfth century.

proven by the entrance oriented to the east and the countless bas-reliefs that read from left to right, just as in Hindu funerary ritual. Set on a pyramidal base with a square plan, surrounded by three concentric series of galleries, punctuated by columns and set at an increasingly elevated level, there are five enormous towers, more than two hundred metres tall, in the shape of lotus blossoms, with the centre tower slightly taller than the other four: they evoke the silhouette of Mount Meru, 'the mythical golden mountain' of Hinduism, the heart of the universe and the site of the deity. On the interior, the visitor's eyes are greeted by the sight of miles and miles of decorations, sculpted mouldings and bas-reliefs that cover the entire interior wall of the second-storey gallery. There are visual descriptions of ancient Indian poems, episodes of court life and scenes of battle. But the masterpiece is the depiction of the Indian creation myth of the 'churning of the ocean of milk', which occupies a wall roughly a hundred metres long. In

order to obtain the drink of immortality, the *amrita* or ambrosia, gods and demons agree to a truce and together thrash the waves of the ocean of milk, making use of the serpent Vasuki, which is rolled up like a rope around a mountain: at one end and at the other end of the giant cobra, ninety-two demons and eighty-eight gods pull in alternation, in order to obtain a rotating movement. The referee of the dispute is Vishnu, depicted both with human features and in one of his incarnations, the turtle. Hundreds of female figures with calm and smiling faces and a hieratic expression, adorned with exquisite jewellery, appear on the pillars, on the architraves of the doors, on the exterior walls and the interior walls of the galleries: these are the *apsàras*, celestial dancers, and the *dévatas*, female deities who dispense the joys of paradise.

Following the death of Suryavarman II in 1150 there was a period of 30 years of political instability but the future Jayavarman VII (1181-1219) led the recovery of the Khmer

people, who once again gained independence. At the end of the twelfth century, this ruler, known as the 'builder king', built his own capital, the giant Angkor Thom, 'Angkor the Great', the 'Great City', and Khmer art regained its ancient splendour. In its ten-mile enclosure wall there are five monumental gates, each of which is served by a bridge lined with fifty-four colossal statues: on the left, with a serene expression, are the gods; on the right are the demons, their faces twisted in grimaces, and — oddly enough — Western eyes; they all embrace the body of the mythical serpent Naga, recognizable by its seven heads, progenitor of the Khmer and spirit of the waters. At the centre stands the Bayon temple, a pyramidal building over which loom fifty-four towers, upon each of which is carved four Cyclopean faces of the god-king. The wall of the gallery of the external portico is decorated with bas-reliefs that depicts battle scenes, but especially scenes of everyday life of the populace of the time, described in a spontaneous and realistic visual language: with this king, who converted to Buddhism, Khmer art abandoned mythology and became profane. Among the numerous Buddhist religious buildings built at the behest of the newly converted King Jayavarman VII, special note should be paid of the immense Monastery of Ta Prom, dedicated by the king to his own mother: this is the most charming and evocative place in the ancient city, intentionally left by the archaeologists in the same condition in which it was discovered in the second half of the nineteenth century.

Detail of the exterior wall of the complex of Angkor Wat; the covered walkways are quite visible.

Detail of a bas-relief with scenes of everyday life, from the outer portico of the Bayon Temple built at the behest of Jayavarman VII at the end of the twelfth century.

Xi'an

Imagine the amazement of an unwitting farmer in a Chinese commune in Xi'an (pronounced 'ssi-an') in March 1974, when, as he was prodding the ground to dig a well, he unearthed fragments of clay statues. Fortunately, the impromptu archaeologist had the sense to alert the local superintendency straightaway.

This was the beginning of the excavation of one of the largest archeological complexes so far discovered in China: the mausoleum that Qin Shi Huangdi began to prepare for himself around 220 B.C. Qin was a ruthless sovereign and military genius who had the merit of reunifying China after centuries of political fragmentation.

The ancient Chinese used to believe that the soul was composed of two parts: the *bo*, which died with the body of the deceased, and the *hun*, which was destined to continue on a journey to the Afterworld.

It was the practice of the nobility to have themselves buried with a retinue of servants and favourite horses and objects. In order to obviate the costs involved, aristocratic families soon began to have clay surrogates made of the objects the deceased wished to have buried with them on their final journey. These funerary figurines, known as *mingqi*, are responsible for a very large proportion of our knowledge of Chinese statuary. In most cases, they are no more than twenty centimetres (eight inches) tall. However, one of the exceptional aspects of the find in Xi'an is the greater than life size of the statues, some of which stand 190 centimetres (6 feet 2 inches) high.

Xi'an ('City of Peace in the West') is the ancient Chang'an ('Long-lasting Peace'), which was the capital of the Chinese empire for several centuries and dynasties, long before Beijing replaced it. This is why hundreds of trenches have been found less than one kilometre from the city walls and just a few hundred metres from the tomb of the emperor, which contained the collections of objects buried with Qin. The terracotta army, drawn up in ranks to protect him on his final journey, filled the four main trenches.

Trench no. 1 covers 14,260 square metres (3.6 acres) and is 5 metres (16 feet) deep. Although it was the first to be investigated, the excavation is far from complete: only one-third has so far been explored. To judge by the concentration of soldiers found to date, it should hold around 6,000 overall with a great many bronze weapons. So far an entire battalion has been unearthed, consisting of three rows of sixty-eight soldiers that form the vanguard. The 'corps' is formed by thirty-eight rows of chariots which alternate with members of the infantry; then comes the rearguard of three rows of foot-soldiers. The entire battalion is surrounded by a ring of foot-soldiers facing outwards to defend the formation.

On 23 April 1976, two years after the discovery was made, archaeologists found Trench no. 2 at a distance of 20 metres (65 feet) to the north-east of Trench no. 1. The second trench was in the form of a square covering 6,000 square metres (1.5 acres), and measuring 124 metres (134 yards) along the east-west axis, and 98 metres (106 yards) north-south, but of the same depth. This trench, however, contained a much richer collection of troops, including kneeling and standing archers, horses and eighty chariots. This trench is still being excavated.

But the discoveries were not yet over. On 11 May 1976, Trench no. 3 was found 25 metres (27 yards) north-east of Trench no. 1, but this was slightly smaller. It measures 29 metres (31 yards) east-west, 25 metres (27 yards) north-south and covers a total of 529 square metres (621 square yards). It contains the strategic heart of the army and has been excavated completely: it contained the High Command chariot, i.e. the mobile headquarters, which was escorted by sixty-four foot-soldiers armed with ritual weapons.

Top view of a battalion of foot-soldiers.

Opposite page
The face of a soldier.

So far over 2,000 soldiers and 40,000 bronze weapons have been brought to light. Surprisingly, no one soldier resembles another. The sculptors took the enormous trouble of infusing each figure with a unique identity.

Production

Each statue is composed of a combination of dye-stamped and hand-modelled parts, i.e. they are 'personalized'. The clay used is composed of local loess, which was washed and cleaned of impurities, before being mixed with quartz sand.

The craftsmen produced the various parts of the horses separately, joined the parts together and then covered them with a layer of clay. When fired at a temperature of between 950-1050°C, the hole in the stomach of each figure served as an air-hole. This made the material in the statues extremely hard and, even today, if they are struck, a strong, rounded note is produced.

Next the figures were coloured, first with a neutral tint. Today they have lost almost all their original polychromy but, at the time, the artists had an enviable palette of colours at their disposal: red, pink, dark green, rosy green, rosy violet, light blue, black, two hues of white and even rosy brown.

The terracotta army is a highly faithful reproduction of military science at the end of the third century B.C. For example, the presence of foot-soldiers in Xi'an has already been discussed on several occasions but the existence of independent infantry in China was the result of a huge leap in strategy in the fourth century B.C. Originally, foot-soldiers were only mobilized to aid the movements of the war chariots, with approximately ten being assigned to each chariot. The arrangement of the foot-soldiers in the terracotta army demonstrates, however, that the foot-soldiers were still used for this purpose but that they were completely independent. The nimble fingers of the sculptors succeeded in differentiating the soldiers by ethnic group, military rank and age; the faces of the younger soldiers are softer, less hollow and with eyes still capable of smiling, whereas the foreheads of the older soldiers are wrinkled to indicate weariness and steadfastness.

The generals wear a double tunic that reaches down to their feet and is covered by a coloured piece of armour made from elements like fish scales; they also have a head-dress in the form of a cock's comb and some hold a sword, resting the handle against their stomach. The officers wear lighter armour that protects only the trunk of the body, or longer armour made from wide links. The lower-ranking officers were fitted with lighter equipment as the vanguard had to be fast-moving: their deployment could decide the outcome of a battle. They did not wear armour, only a cloak, and carried two weapons: a sword in one hand and a halberd in the other. Their hair was either tied up in a bun, held down in six plaits or hidden beneath the *jiezi* (conical cap).

The identity of the artists

The names of the artists were hidden in unseen corners of the statues, and so far eighty-seven have been identified. It is probable that each had his own apprentices and assistants to form a workshop of a dozen or so people, and this suggests that hundreds of artists were required to produce the terracotta army. The names so far identified refer to craftsmen who worked in the kilns in the capital and in local ceramics workshops whose output was less uniform.

An arsenal of parade weapons

The trenches form an arsenal of different dress weapons: long, short, for throwing, *ge* (hatchets), *ji* (halberds), *mao* (pikes), crossbows and a multitude of bronze arrow tips. Archaeologists have found two superb items: gold hooks, rather like small sickles, that measure 65 centimetres (23 inches) long and 3.5 centimetres (1.5 inches) wide, which were invented by the Wu people around the end of the fourth century B.C. There were also sixteen different types of *bo*, which are a sort of long-handled pike measuring 38 centimetres (14 inches); they were cited in historical sources but their appearance, until these were found, remained a mystery.

All the weapons were made from bronze, are still sharp and little oxidized. Once they were dug up and cleaned, they shone as though they had only recently been buried. Close examination revealed that they had been given a layer of chrome as an antiseptic and to prevent oxidation. The parallel marks left by the sharpening process suggests that a machine with a sort of rudimentary grindstone was used. Motifs similar to flames were stamped on the *bo*, which imply that vulcanization was used.

The mausoleum of the emperor

The mausoleum of Qin Shi Huangdi is a terraced, pyramidal mound, originally 115 metres (374 feet) high and large enough to cover 2,000 square metres (half an acre), however, the passage of time has eroded it to only 76 metres (247 feet) and 1290 square metres (one-third of an acre). It was built on the same model as the bastions of the capital, with three enclosure walls and a gateway and guard tower on each side. The mound contains some 200 trenches as follows: 100 or so are variously sized stalls to accommodate 500 horses; these, however, were real and were buried alive for sacrificial reasons. One trench holds the remains of rare animals which probably lived in the emperor's private park of zoological wonders. And in November 1980, two half-size chariots were dug up composed of 3,000 pieces and made from bronze with inlays of gold and silver. They weigh approximately one ton.

The sculptors took the enormous trouble of infusing each figure with a unique identity.

Opposite page
Picture of the trenches during the excavation.

Kyoto

Kyoto, capital of Japan for over 1,000 years, still preserves its ancient urban fabric, despite the fact that fire destroyed most of the wooden monuments that made it famous for centuries. Fortunately, its architectural, artistic, and spiritual tradition is documented by numerous civic and religious buildings and by the splendid parks and gardens that have survived to the present day.

Located in a favourable geographic position at the centre of the country but in communication via the Kamo River with the coast and the great port city of Osaka, Kyoto was founded by the Emperor Kammu, who moved there in A.D. 794; he named it Heian-Kyo, 'city of peace', and thus began the first Heian period, that is, 'time of no wars', which lasted until 1185. Renamed Kyoto, which means 'capital', it was the seat of political power until the turn of the seventeenth century, and of the imperial court until 1868. The urbanistic model that shaped the design of the city was that of the capitals of ancient China, adapted to the configuration of the territory and the Japanese national culture. Kyoto had a centre enclosed by a defensive wall with a double moat, criss-crossed by broad perpendicular streets, on the interior of which were built palaces, temples, and private homes to original designs: wooden and terracotta roof tiles were accompanied by traditional covering in tree bark; the masonry elements of stone and clay were abandoned in favour of wood; pillars became the main load-bearing structures and the walls were mere curtains, used to articulate the interior spaces; lastly gardens were created that, in combination with miniaturizing criteria for vegetal elements, rocks, little rocks and tiny streams, harmonized the architecture with the landscape.

Dating from the first Heian period is the great Buddhist temple of Daigo-ji, which contains various pagodas and monasteries and over 100 rooms. Samboin, the principal monastery, with its five-storey pagoda, its rooms adorned with wall paintings and decorated sliding walls, even today is the site of evocative ceremonies, such as that in which the participants, dressed in sixteenth-century costumes, sit under the blossoming cherry trees to re-enact the encounters between the military chief Toyotomi Hideyoshi and his lovers.

Linked to the esoteric Buddhism of Tendai and Shingon, which cultivated ideals of hermitage and transcendence, was the construction of the monastery of Enryaku-ji, with its three thousand buildings harmoniously set in the remote forest of Mount Hiei, only a very few of which still stand. For centuries, beginning with its foundation in 788, it was one of the largest temple complexes on earth, and many founders of Buddhist sects were educated here.

A bloody civil war marked the conclusion, in 1185, of the Heian period and the beginning of the Kamakura period, which ended in 1333. The transfer of power from the court to the military, a consequence of the creation of the shogunate, provoked a radical transformation of Japanese society, and thus of culture and art. There was

View of the Kiyomizu-dera, early Heian period, ninth century.

Sculpture depicting Siddhartha in meditation, from the Sukacutel period, early seventh century.

Opposite page
Detail of the mouth of a fountain in the form of a dragon.

View of one of the pavilions of the Kiyomizu-dera, early Heian period, ninth century.

Golden Pavilion, (Kinkaku), Muromachi period, late fourteenth century.

a general sobriety in the structures and the decorations of the new residences which, in line with the 'warrior style', were girded with moats and palisades, and gardens were replaced by training grounds. The best example of this architectural typology is represented by the Kozan-ji which, erected in the twelfth century on Mount Toganoh, features the oldest Japanese tea garden: according to tradition, its founder, the priest Myoe, planted here the seeds of a plant brought from China by a Zen master. The tea ceremony (*cha-no-yu*), which is also of Zen origin, contributed to the modification of the residences: the unadorned simplicity and the modest dimensions of the tea room and the tea pavilion led to the construction of intimate, small buildings, with light beams and pillars, and surfaces that opened to the exterior by means of sliding structures (*shoin*).

During the Muromachi period (1392-1573), the spectacular and decorative style of

the Yüan and Ming dynasties was imported from China. This can be seen in the splendid temples of the Ginkaku-ji or Silver Pavilion, built in the first half of the fifteenth century for a sophisticated little group of artists and monks, and the Rokuon-ji (Kinkaku-ji), on the hills of Kitayama. Here, at the edge of a large pond, stands the Golden Pavilion, a three-storey reliquary building, with broad surrounding verandas (a faithful copy of the original, which was burned down in 1950), in which lacquered decorations and gold-leaf contrast with the willowy simplicity of the structures and austere bark roof coverings. Alongside the temples are the Zen gardens, first and foremost the gardens of Ryoan-ji and Saiho-ji; the latter is known as the Temple of Moss because it is covered by a thick carpet of 120 varieties of moss.

The Kyo-o-gokuku-ji (To-ji) Temple, the oldest temple in the city, was built in A.D. 796, at the same time as the foundation of the

THE TEMPLE OF BYODO-IN

At a distance of 15 kilometres (about 10 miles) from Kyoto, on the western bank of the Uji River, stands one of the most elegant and refined buildings in all Eastern architecture. This is the Temple of Byodo-in, originally the country home of the noble Minamoto-no-Toru. The *Amidado* (Temple of the Amida Buddha), which is reflected in the waters of the magnificent pond of the monastery, features interior rooms that are richly decorated with polychrome lacquer, encrustations of mother-of-pearl, appliquées of gilt copper, and painted chests of drawers. Here is the Pavilion of the Phoenix, formed from a series of structures that overlook at different levels the lakeshore, famous for the two phoenixes that spread their wings over the roof and the large statue of the Buddha, attributed to the sculptor Jocho. It stands three metres (ten feet) tall, and is surrounded by fifty-two wooden images of *Bodhisattvas*, that is, those who, although they are capable of attaining enlightenment, tarry on the threshold of *nirvana* to aid other men to find the path to perfection.

Detail of strips of paper with votive values, left by the faithful near the temples.

Rear view of a pavilion in the Hoodo enclosure, late Heian period, end of the eleventh century.

THE ZEN GARDEN OF RYOAN-JI

Kyoto still houses many gardens, introduced in the Muromachi period by the masters of the Zen Buddhist sect, in which the classical elements of the Japanese garden, such as islands, little bridges, and lakes, were not only distributed in such a way as to be visible from various points of observation but took on specific symbolism. Thus, by replacing water with sand or gravel and laying out stone slabs or rocks over it to symbolize fords, islands, and other salient features, the dry garden was created. The most celebrated is certainly the garden of Ryoan-ji, dating from the second half of the fifteenth century, which presents — in a rectangular space surrounded on three sides by earth walls and on the fourth side by the corridor of the Hojo building — fifteen rocks of various shape, arranged on the white sand in five groups, each of which is composed of, respectively, five, two, three, two, and three rocks. According to the most common interpretation, they represent a tiger with her cubs, swimming across the sand river towards a terrible dragon.

Zen gardens in Ryoan-ji Monastery, first half of the sixteenth century.

Pagoda of the Kiyomizu-dera, early Heian period, ninth century.

Golden Hall of the Kiyomizu-dera, early Heian period, ninth century.

ancient capital Heian-kyo to protect the entire nation from evil spirits. For that reason it was built in the eastern zone, near the four gates that marked the principal access routes. Even today, these gates constitute exceedingly prestigious elements of the complex, along with the *kondo*, or great hall, the *kodo*, the reading room that contains the earliest Japanese statues from the school of esoteric Buddhism, the *jikido*, or refectory, the *daishido*, or residence of the founder of the Shingon Temple, and the *gojunoto*, the five-storey pagoda that stands 57 metres (187 feet) tall, the tallest pagoda in Japan.

Another of Kyoto's architectural treasures is Kiyomizu-dera Temple on the top of Higashiyama hill. Although it has been destroyed several times, it has been rebuilt on nine occasions. The current building is seventeenth-century and considered one of the boldest wooden constructions in the world: the main room exploits the slope of the hill and the wooden terrace — supported by 130 pillars, each 15 metres tall — projects over a gorge, giving a suberb view of all Kyoto. Both followers of Buddhism and Shintoism honour this place, and drink the water that gushes from the mouth of the metal dragon over the entrance.

Petra

The ancient city, as the name itself suggests, stands in a natural amphitheatre formed by high cliffs, a place made even more secure by the narrow gorges of pink sandstone that surround it and by the one, enchanting means of access, the narrow fissure of the Siq, almost 2 kilometres (one and one-quarter miles) long, but at certain points only 2 or 3 metres (6 to 10 feet) wide, and bounded by sheer walls rising nearly 100 metres (330 feet) straight up. Legend has it that this was the 'sesame' that Ali Baba had the power to open. In a naturally fortified position (the first defensive walls were not built until the first century B.C.), rich in water even though it is surrounded by desert, Petra was for centuries the meeting point of the most important routes used by the camel caravans that transported precious cargoes of spices between the Mediterranean and the Near East, Africa, India, and possibly even China. The city was founded by the Nabataeans, a Semitic population originally from northern Arabia that settled in the region in the eighth century B.C.: serving as commercial middlemen, they changed from a semi-nomadic people to a sedentary community, and they founded their capital and their kingdom which, after their victory in 312 B.C. over the Diadochi Antigonus Monophthalmus and Demetrius Poliorcetes, was consolidated and enlarged, prospering greatly until the second century A.D. Despite the fragmentary reports from ancient sources, such as Diodorus Siculus and Strabo, and the numerous inscriptions, for the most part carved in rock, we do not know that much about the lifestyle, social organization, and commercial activity of the Nabataeans, while we have much more detailed information about their deities, their form of worship, and their religious life. As far as we can reconstruct, their society had a relatively simple organization: the state was run by a hereditary monarch, and the king could have more than one wife; the queen played a sufficiently important role that she was sometimes depicted on coins, alongside the sovereign. It is well known that the population was organized by tribes; in the epigraphic documentation, mention is made of priests and soothsayers and often, as a demonstration of their importance on the social scale, builders or carvers of monuments. The Nabataeans, who had remained independent over the centuries, though linked to the political fortunes of the Ptolemies and the Seleucids, were unable to withstand the imperialist policies of the Romans. In A.D. 106 Trajan annexed the Nabataean Kingdom, which thus came to form part of the new province of Arabia: the designation of the city of Bostra as the capital and the establishment of safer caravan routes, controlled by Palmyra, along with the numerous earthquakes that hit the zone triggered a period of slow decline for the city, which was not halted either by its designation as an Archiepiscopal See, nor as capital of the province of Palaestina Tertia under Diocletian, nor with the Arab conquest in 636, because Petra remained in any case distant from the pilgrim road to Mecca. It was not until the time of the Crusades that its strategic position for the defence of Jerusalem and the construction of an important Crusader fortress returned it in part to its ancient splendour: Li Vaux Moise, or the Valley of Moses, is what the Crusaders called it; while the Bedouin called it Wadi Musa, or Torrent of Moses, in the centuries of oblivion.

The magic begins as one walks through the Siq, the gorge formed by the torrent, the Musa, which the Nabataeans blocked with a dam and channelled: as we move forward in space we are moving backward in time to another dimension and another space, where the numerous monumental documents tell us about different periods in the city's history.

View of the rock-cut tombs of Petra.

Opposite page
View of the gorge of Petra, with, in the foreground, the façade of the Khazneh el Foroun (Treasury of the Pharaoh), from the Hellenistic period.

View of the theatre built in Roman times by carving out the mountainside.

One of the numerous rock-cut tombs that characterize the canyons of Petra.

Stele with anthropomorphic stylized frieze adorned by geometric cornices in Nabataean style and inscriptions.

Along the rock walls of the Siq we see a succession of inscriptions, niches, and small votive altars, but we also see, badly damaged by atmospheric erosion, the reliefs and sculptures that depict a caravan of men and camels: these are Nabataeans (for that matter, almost devoid of a figurative culture). As we emerge from the canyon the dramatic effect is powerful: the first building that we encounter, the best-known building in Petra, is the Khazneh el-Faroun, or the 'Treasury of the Pharaoh', an imposing façade standing nearly 40 metres (about 130 feet) tall, cut directly from the rock of the mountainside. In a good state of preservation, it presents an elaborate architectural form: on the lower floor is a portico with six columns, crowned by floral capitals and surmounted by a fronton, as if to form a pronaos; the third floor is divided into three parts at the centre is a tholos with the conical roof, surmounted by an urn, and on either side, two half-frontons, supported by columns. An architectural and sculptural decoration of the highest qualitative level adorns the architectural elements and the front of the building. Among the friezes, largely decorated with plant motifs (flowers, vine clusters, and garlands of berries and leaves), it is possible to make out the sculptures in more-than-life size of the standing Dioscuri, near a horse and in heroic nudity (aside from the chlamys draped over their bodies). Nine other large relief figures decorate the upper order: the most important effigy is the draped female deity, carved at the centre of the tholos who, by the attributes she holds in her hands, a cornucopia in her left hand and a *patera*, or shallow dish, in her right hand, can be identified as the Egyptian Isis or Greek Tyche, but she is also identifiable as al-'Uzza, the supreme female deity of the Nabataean pantheon; the other figures in the niches of the upper order are Winged Victories, or Nikai and Amazons, dressed in short tunics and distinguished by axes, the usual attribute of their iconography. The Khazneh is the only rock-cut building in

The Via Sacra, *bounded by the remains of the colonnade from Roman times; in the background, the Palace Tomb and the Corinthian Tomb.*

Sequence of tombs carved out of the red rocks of Petra with typically Nabataean decorative details.

THE 'DISCOVERER' OF PETRA

'So you will never know what Petra is like, unless you come out here. … Only be assured that till you have seen it you have not the glimmering of an idea how beautiful a place can be'. These words were written to a friend by Thomas Edward Lawrence, the legendary Lawrence of Arabia, who launched the revolt in the desert that, between 1917 and 1918, contributed to the defeat of the Ottoman Empire. For that matter, many of the scenes in the movie made by David Lean about the life of this English adventurer were shot in Petra. But the rediscovery of the city by the Western world had been accomplished a century before, in 1812, by Johann Ludwig Burckhardt. The young Swiss explorer, an expert on Arab culture, had already visited Baalbek, Palmyra, and Damascus, and had heard people speak of a 'lost city' hidden among the mountains of the Wadi Musa; in order to overcome the mistrust of the Bedouin and find this lost city, he converted to Islam with the name of Sheik Ibrahim and pretended that he wanted to sacrifice a goat on the tomb of Aaron, the brother of Moses, which he knew was in the area surrounding the mysterious city. But his Bedouin guides still did not trust him; they feared that the white 'wizard' wanted to lay his hands on the precious treasures hidden in Petra, and so perhaps they toyed with him, answering his insistent questions at random, attributing every monument to an imaginary Pharaoh, a trick that left many traces in the place-names of Petra.

Petra that presents absolutely no Nabataean element and which, in terms of its general design, its decoration, and the carved reliefs attests to links exclusively with the Alexandrian world and the Hellenistic artistic tradition of the second half of the first century B.C. The programme of figuration, entirely linked to Hellenistic and Roman funerary symbolism, and the plan and the organization of the interior space suggest an intended use as a sepulchre, possibly for Aretas III, the ruler who was responsible for the process of Hellenization of his people (in fact, he used Philhellene as an attribute). Just before we enter the urban structure, we might notice the monumental façades of other rock-cut tombs, such as the Corinthian Tomb, in which the stylistic elements of the lower order, more typically Nabataean, contrast with the Hellenistic elements of the upper order, which borrow motifs from the Khazneh, or the magnificent and solemn Palace Tomb, or else the simpler Silk Tomb, named for the extraordinary chromatic effect of the veins in the rock from which it was carved. This latter belongs to the type that is most common in Petra, tombs shaped like towers, with the front decorated with a stepped frieze (depicting two small opposed stairways) or merlons arranged in one or more rows, elements clearly of Eastern derivation, either Assyrian or Persian; the architectural spaces, instead, are marked by semi-columns or pilasters surmounted by characteristic Nabataean horned capitals. The two types of rock-cut façades, the more complex type and the simpler type, are from the same period: the thirty-four fronton or temple tombs should be attributed to the royal house and the court, which took inspiration from Western, Hellenistic or Alexandrian and Roman models, which were widespread in the first century B.C. throughout the Hellenized Near East; instead the more than 600 tombs of the more sober variety can be attributed to the middle classes which were more conservative in their tastes and therefore preferred Eastern shapes and styles. Whereas the cliff-side funerary architecture, with tombs with richly plastered or painted façades, represents the most distinctive expression of the Nabataean civilization, recent archaeological excavations have also unearthed entire quarters of homes, both built and cut into the rock, but which presented no architectural decoration in their façades. There are also noteworthy relics from Roman times: at the southern edge of the valley stands the first-century A.D. theatre, carved almost entirely into the rock, which could hold more than 8,000 spectators, while at the end of the Siq open out the ruins of the colonnaded way, a road lined with high columns on both sides, which was reached via an arch. Set on a promontory that overlooks the Valley of Petra to the west, accessible via a sort of sacred stepped way cut into the rock, is another

building with an imposing façade carved out of the rock: this is ad-Dayr. The architectural scheme mirrors that of the Khazneh, but in a less articulated and elaborate manner, just as the decorative ornaments, horned capitals and continuous Doric frieze, in which the metopes have been replaced by disks, are typically Nabataean: the austerity and simplicity of the complex join to demonstrate the original local version of elements of the Hellenistic tradition. Because of the characteristics of the architectural structure, the building has been compared to the Library of Celsus in Ephesus, dating from the reign of Hadrian (A.D. 117-138). The structure of the interior is devoid of any funereal installation whatsoever, but it does present a platform set in an open niche in the far wall, bound by pillars and a stucco arch with cornice; moreover, along the side walls the remains of two benches have been uncovered, comparable to cult-related *triclinia*.

The rock-cut tomb of Ed-Deir offers ornamental solutions inspired by late Hellenistic architecture.

Opposite page
The large building known as the Tomb of the Urn, or Doric Tomb, is part of the complex of monumental tombs that lie on the western slope of the el-Khubtha massif.

The funerary triclinium and Tomb of the Garden. The triclinium stands in front of the porticoed building seen in the photograph, which, at one time, would have been covered by a vault.

The Caves of Ajanta

In India's western state of Maharashtra, whose capital is Bombay, or Mumbai, stands the extraordinary sacred complex of Ajanta: in a rocky river valley, the semi-circular flank of a hill is dotted with some thirty caves, dug out of the cliff face and arranged on several levels. The dating of this important Buddhist settlement is difficult to determine, since the religious centre itself was active from the first century B.C. to the seventh century A.D., and over the course of those centuries continual extensions and embellishments were undertaken. During that period, various reigning dynasties succeeded one another in the Deccan region, the most important of which was the Vakataka dynasty, closely linked to the great Kingdom of the Gupta. After a long period of neglect, the Ajanta Caves, by this point heavily covered by dense vegetation, were rediscovered by chance in 1817 by an English soldier involved in military manoeuvres. The caves, architecturally structured, contain a significant complex of sculptures, statues, and reliefs and, most important, an exceptional collection of fresco-type paintings. The paintings of Ajanta constitute one of the highest examples of Indian painting, of which only very rare specimens survive. The chief value of this site consists precisely in the fact that it contains similar works of exceptional artistic quality and historic importance.

The rooms of the caves, a typical expression of the rock architecture of the Deccan, correspond to two specific traditional typologies of the sacred sites of Buddhism: five of them are in fact *caityas* (sanctuaries) while the rest are *viharas* (monasteries). The temples feature an elongated rectangular plan with apses, and in the terminal niche generally feature a *stupa*, a reliquary in the form of a mound. Inside, punctuated by decorated pillars, the walls are covered with small sculptures rich in naturalistic motifs. The portals of the *caityas* are monumental sculptural and architectural structures, enlivened by columns and countless statues of the Buddha. In Cave 19 a large arched window, which illuminates the interior vault, surmounts a finely worked jutting aedicule. The *viharas* were places reserved for teaching and meditation and contained the lodgings of the monks: the cells were arranged around a central cloister, which could be reached from richly decorated façades. On the interiors, which in some cases were incomplete, a splendid array of sculptures and paintings were illustrated with an extraordinary profusion of themes and motifs and sacred subjects proper to the Buddhist tradition. Here the images of the Buddha and the illustrations of the principal episodes of his life alternate with numerous figures of the *Bodhisattvas*, compassionate humans who had reached an exceedingly high level of wisdom and were ready to assist the other creatures of the world when needed. The sacred paintings alternate with symbolic, animal, and vegetal motifs.

These paintings were probably done in the *fresco secco* technique, on dry plaster, spreading the paints on a multi-layer preparation that made it possible to smooth the rocky wall and fix the mineral pigments. The style of the paintings at Ajanta, which underwent considerable development over the centuries, stands out for the extraordinary elegance of the finely stylized figures and for the narrative vitality of the scenes, described with an acute spirit of observation. In the older paintings, the narrative compositions develop longitudinally in separate panels, in a pattern that vanished after the fifth century, when the episodes began to be arranged without interruption across the entire wall in evocative overall views. The great artistic maturity expressed in these pictorial cycles appears evident in the softness of the chiaroscuro contrasts and in the refined use of colour.

Panoramic view of the Caves of Ajanta.

Opposite page
Fresco on the far wall of Cave 17, depicting a palace scene with the king and queen in a loving embrace, surrounded by two cupholders, from the Vakataka dynasty, fifth to sixth centuries.

EPISODES FROM THE LIFE OF THE BUDDHA IN THE PAINTINGS AT AJANTA

In the paintings that adorn the caves are narrated countless episodes linked to the hagiography of the Buddha: many of them refer to the collection of stories known as *Jatakas*, in which, according to tradition, the Buddha himself narrated stories of his previous incarnations. In one of these stories, the Buddha was an elephant that died, offering his tusks to an evil hunter. Numerous paintings were also devoted to the life of Siddhartha, beginning with the fantastic episode of the *Dream of Maya*: to the future mother of the Buddha there appeared in a dream a white elephant, a symbol of purity and gentleness, which she welcomed into her womb. The dream was interpreted as a premonition of the birth of a king who would abandon glory in order to become a monk and save all the creatures of the earth.

Detail of the frieze in Cave 17, with eight Buddhas (upper strip) and pairs of dampati *(lovers) in the lower strip; Vakataka dynasty, fifth to sixth centuries.*

Detail of the frescoes with 'Buddha strip' decorations.

Detail of the figure of the Sikyamuni Buddha depicted in the mudra *(symbolic gesture) of preaching.*

Opposite page
Portico of one of the caves, carved under the Vakataka dynasty, fifth to sixth centuries.

Persepolis

On the slopes of Mount Zagros, now called the Kuh-e-Rahmat (Mount of Mercy), in the Fars region of Iran, once stood the monumental city Persepolis. The Greek name, meaning 'City of the Persians', indicates its origin but also commemorates its importance; it was in fact one of the capitals of the far-flung Persian Empire, along with Susa, the winter capital, and Hagmatan, the summer capital. It was the seat of the government for most of the year, and it was a sacred place where magnificent ceremonies were performed in honour of the sovereigns. The inscription uncovered in the foundations of the southern wall, dating from 518 B.C., tells that the city was built at the command of Darius I the Great, at the behest of 'Ahura Mazda, along with all the other gods'. Work went on for another 100 years, so that all the successors of Darius, Xerxes I, Artaxerxes I, and Artaxerxes II, took part in the city's foundation. In another inscription found on the foundations of the citadel, the decision of Xerxes I, made under the grace of the gods, to complete the project begun by his father is commemorated.

The city stood on a natural plateau that had been enlarged by building a terrace enclosed by retaining walls that contained the entire structure, while the elevation was covered by a double staircase with two flights of stairs. The *propylaeum*, built during the reign of Xerxes I and called the 'Gate of All Peoples', consisted of a hall extending 25 metres (82 feet) on each side, whose wooden roof was supported by four colossal columns each 20 metres (66 feet) tall. Their base features a phytomorphic, or plant-like,

decoration, while the corolla capital supports a double-scroll element adorned by monstrous animals. Two giant human-headed winged bulls still protect the surviving uprights on the western side. The part of the platform that was accessible to the people, and which was therefore official in nature and function, ends in two enormous halls: the *Apadana* and the Hall of the Throne, also called the 'Hall of the Hundred Columns'. The Apadana, the audience hall, is a structure typical of Persian royal palaces; the same structure is found in Susa and in the ancient capital of Cyrus II the Great, Pasargadae. Built at the behest of Darius and completed during the reign of Xerxes I, it could be reached via two staircases, one to the north and the other to the east, whose parapets still feature reliefs depicting the Medean and Persian soldiers and 'honour guard'; the procession continues along the base, which rises 2.6 metres (eight and one-half feet) high, with a parade of offerings including subjects, court dignitaries, and representatives of the twenty-three nations under Achaemenid rule. Thirteen of the seventy-two columns that supported the roof still stand. Porticoes surrounded the great hall on three sides, and adjoining it were various storehouses. Slightly to the east is the second great building on the terrace, the Hall of the Throne. Planned by Xerxes I, it was completed under his son Artaxerxes I at the end of the fifth century B.C. The square building possessed eight entrance doors. On the northern and the southern sides, the stone pillars are still decorated by high reliefs that depict the sovereigns on their thrones in the presence of their subjects, while on the western and eastern entrances are carved scenes of battle against

General view of the palace area of Persepolis.

Detail of a zoomorphic capital of the columns of the Apadana (sixth to fifth centuries B.C.).

Opposite page
View of the great hypostyle hall of the Apadana (audience hall); in the foreground is one of the monumental bulls set to guard the northern entrance to the throne room.

One of the two access ramps to the Apadana with a frieze depicting soldiers, warriors, and foreign emissaries.

'Gate of All Peoples', seen from the propylaea of Xerxes I, flanked by two winged and human-headed bulls.

ANCIENT PERSIA

Modern Iran corresponds almost completely to the Persian realm at its origin during the middle of the sixth century B.C., when Cyrus II became king, a descendant of the royal house of the people of the Medes, the first Indo-European ethnic group to settle in the plains of the 'Fertile Crescent'. The conquests that led to the surrender of the Medes, of Asia Minor, and of Mesopotamia, with the Babylonian Empire (539 B.C.) and Syria with its Phoenician cities, won the appellation of 'Great' to the forefather of the dynasty of the Achaemenids. Upon his death, the empire passed into the hands of Chambyses II (529-521 B.C.). To restore order in the land, Chambyses's successor, Darius I the Great (521-485 B.C.), divided his territory into twenty satrapies, administrative and military circumscriptions ruled by a satrap who was sworn to obey the Great King. He then devoted himself to the further expansion of the empire by conquering southern Russia and subjecting the Scythians. He extended his power over the Greek cities on the Anatolian coast, requiring them to pay him tribute. The revolt of these latter peoples triggered the Persian Wars. The first Persian War, fought in 490 B.C., resulted in the victory of the Athenians at Marathon. The successive Persian Wars, waged and lost between 480 and 478 B.C., were undertaken by his son Xerxes (485-465 B.C.). With the last of the Achaemenids, Artaxerxes I (465-424 B.C.), Darius II (424-404 B.C.), Artaxerxes II (404-358 B.C.), and Artaxerxes III (358-338 B.C.), the Persian Empire slowly declined until the definitive defeat of Darius III by Alexander the Great in 331 B.C. Upon the death of the Macedonian sovereign, the empire was divided among his generals, and the territory of ancient Persia passed under the power of Seleucus. During the reign of Antioch II the Seleucid (261-246 B.C.) the Iranic plateau achieved independence, creating the Kingdom of the Parthians commanded by Arsaces, the founding father of the dynasty of the Arsacids, and, from A.D. 226, by the Sassanids. The Roman emperors fought against these sovereigns repeatedly but without ever winning. The Battle of Yarmuk, in 636, opened the Iranic territory to the rule of the Muslim Arabs.

Details of one of the columns with double-scroll capitals from the propylaea of Xerxes I (485-465 B.C.).

Plan.
1. Xerxes' gate
2. Apadana
3. Hall of the Throne
4. Darius's Palace
5. Hall of the Council
6. Xerxes' Palace
7. Treasure
8. Xerxes' Harem

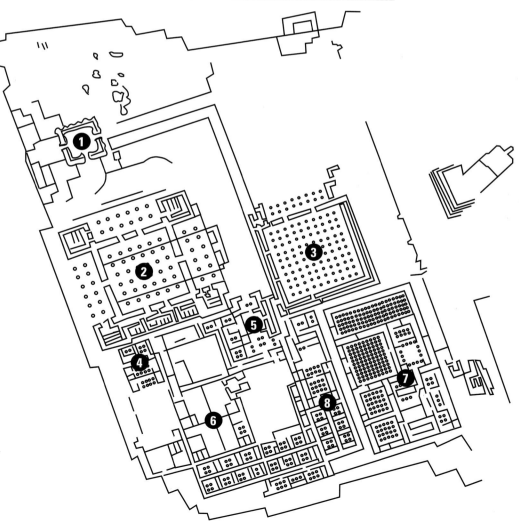

Details of several inscriptions in cuneiform characters on the palaces of Persepolis.

CUNEIFORM TABLETS

Under the ruins of the palace, described as the Treasury, hundreds of clay tablets were discovered, marked with inscriptions in cuneiform characters. The wedge-shaped impressions in the fresh clay (*cuneus*, Latin for wedge, hence the name) could be arranged in various combinations to form syllables and then words; after the tablets were sun-baked, they were stored in the royal archive, where they survived to the present day thanks to the fire that destroyed the city. They were mostly written in ancient Persian, a language that derives from the family of Indo-European languages, and in a few cases in the Elamite and Babylonian languages. They are of great importance because their translation has enabled the reconstruction of everyday life in the imperial city and therefore, the culture, the society, and the economy of the Persian people. From them we learn that Persepolis was inhabited by people from every corner of the empire, sculptors from Egypt, goldsmiths from Caria, and decorators from Susa. Some mention the month and year in the reign of Darius or Xerxes in which a certain structure was built, the number of workers, and their pay. We have records of the tributes paid, their quantity and their nature, by every satrap of the Great King, and the correspondence from governors to the king concerning political and administrative problems. Other tablets contain instructions for performing certain rites or ceremonies in honour of the gods or the kings.

Opposite page
High relief of the Tripylon (Palace of the Council) depicting Xerxes walking, accompanied by his fan-bearer and his parasol-bearer.

monsters. The northern portico, the main one, is flanked by two enormous bulls. Inside there remain the bases of the immense columns that supported its roof, while in the past it must have housed some of the precious gifts and treasures given to the sovereign by his subject peoples. The magnificence of the empire is expressed by the endless processions of mythical characters and scenes carved on to the parapets, the basements, and the door jambs and uprights of the buildings. Each personage is characterized in the clothing, hair style, and type of tribute that he brings to the king: gold and silver vases, weapons, jewels, and animals depending on provenance, but always in the same repetitive attitude that gives the scene a sense of solemnity and a grandiose impression.

The monumental complex continues with the royal apartments, built as needed and as ordered by the sovereigns, without following any preset plan. Thus, the Palace of Darius, *Tokara*, is followed by the Palace of Xerxes, *Hadis*, twice its size, and flanked by the Palace of the Council, called the *Tripylon*, since it has three entrances, and by the Harem of Xerxes, linked to his palace and the site of the apartments of the queen. Shifted to the east was the Treasury, the archive of the realm.

The splendour of the city literally went up in smoke with all its wooden structures during the great fire that Alexander the Great ordered in 330 B.C. after he conquered the Persian Empire, thereby extending his territories all the way to the Indus.

The ruins that can still be toured today were unearthed between 1931 and 1939 by an expedition financed by the Oriental Institute of the University of Chicago. Their immense importance has led to their being included on the World Heritage List since 1979, the second year of UNESCO's activity.

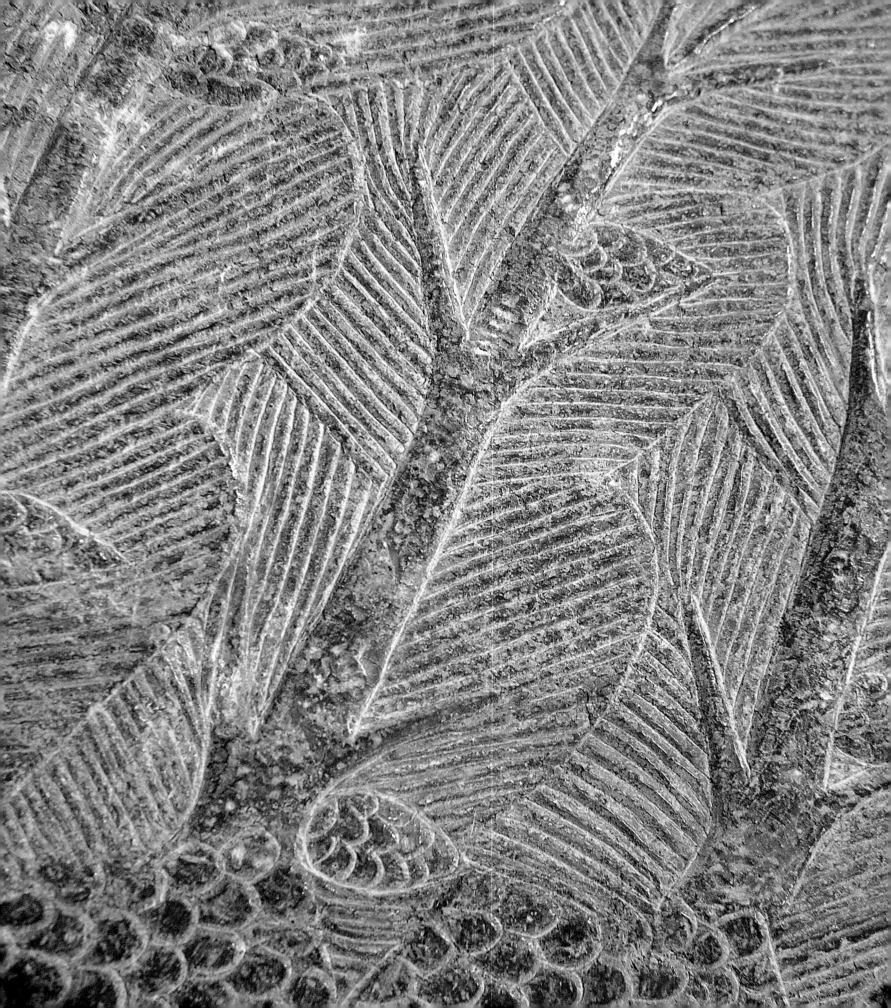

Detail with an Assyrian soldier bringing prisoners of war who are in turn proffering gifts; frieze of the access ramps of the Apadana.

Detail with camel driver; frieze of the access ramps of the Apadana.

Large bas-relief with a lion attacking a bull on the entrance front of the Apadana.

Opposite page
Detail of a tree top engraved on the access ramps of the Apadana.

ROYAL TOMBS

About five kilometres (three miles) to the north-west of Persepolis lies Naqs-i-Rustam in the Valley of Husain Kuh. Here, carved in the high rock wall, are the tombs of the Persian kings. The first king to select this valley as his final resting place was Darius I. The façade of his tomb carved in the rock presents an enormous cross at the centre of which stood a false colonnade with animal-shaped capitals. Between the two central columns is the access door to the funerary chamber carved deep into the rock. In the central panel over the entrance is a relief depicting the king standing on a three-step pedestal before an altar. The king's hand hints at a gesture of adoration towards the sun disk which looms over him, a symbol of the god Ahura Mazda. He is surrounded by twenty-three figures representing the nations subject to Darius. In the side panels appear soldiers and the Persian imperial guard. The façade is further decorated with a trilingual dedication in cuneiform characters, enumerating the nations that belong to the realm and glorifying the role of the sovereign. Traces of pigment on the background and on the reliefs show that all of the façade or a part of it was painted. His successors, Xerxes, Artaxerxes I, and Darius II imitated the choice of the Great King not only in the place but also in the decoration of the entrance. Therefore the rocky ridge presents a series of cruciform façades quite similar to one another. Artaxerxes II, instead, preferred to build himself a monumental tomb on the slopes of the mountain facing the terrace where Persepolis stood.

201

Baalbek

Baalbek stands in the highest part of the fertile Békaa valley (*al Biqa'*), an agricultural region irrigated by the waters of the Litani river that divides the highlands of the Lebanon and the Anti-Lebanon, midway between the Nile and the Euphrates, along one of the chief trading and caravan routes between Mesopotamia and Egypt, and Palmyra and Jerusalem. Founded by the Phoenicians, Baalbek never rivalled Byblos, Tyre, or Sidon in terms of trade, but it was always a sacred city: brought into the Hellenic world by Alexander the Great and the Seleucids (323-64 B.C.), it took the name of Heliopolis, 'city of the Sun', and reached its greatest degree of splendour in the centuries of Roman domination (64 B.C.-A.D. 312), when it was known by the name of 'Colonia Julia Augusta Felix Heliopolitana', which Augustus had given it in A.D. 15. Here we find temples that are some of the greatest constructions of Roman architecture to have survived to the present day. Under Constantine the sites of pagan worship were abandoned and closed, and Theodosius (A.D. 379-385) ordered the construction of a great Christian basilica, adapting for this project the ancient material that was found on the site, as was a long-standing practice; in the seventh century, with the advent of Islam, the Roman monumental area was transformed into an Arabic fortress that took the name of Qalaa. From the sixteenth century, the Ottoman conquest brought about a progressive abandonment, which was hastened by numerous earthquakes, such as the one in 1759. After its rediscovery by the Western world in the nineteenth century, the first restoration campaign began in 1898, at the behest of Wilhelm II, the Emperor of Germany and King of Prussia (1888-1918), who had chanced to visit the site while he was travelling to Jerusalem.

Over the course of roughly 200 years, the Romans made the sanctuary of Baalbek so magnificent that even today the Lebanese insist that even in Rome, with the exception of the Colosseum, there is nothing comparable: one need only wander among the temples, discover that one is only as tall as the plinths of their columns and consider the size of the staircases that lead to the places of worship in order to gain a full sense of its grandeur. In all likelihood the complex was planned as a whole around the time of Octavian Augustus; it was during his rule that the Temple of Heliopolitan Jove was begun. It stood on the highest point of the hill upon which the city lay, and it covered an area much larger than what had been occupied by the altar of Baal; inside the cella was a great statue of Jove and all around extended a monumental portico with fifty-four columns, each of them 20 metres tall, and with a diameter of over 2 metres, rivalling the columns of Selinunte. All that remains of the Temple of Heliopolitan Jove, the largest temple in the Corinthian style in antiquity, as immense as the Baths of Diocletian in Rome, are six columns: eight may have been taken by Justinian for the basilica, now the Mosque, of Saint Sophia in Istanbul; the others were destroyed or were stolen. The sanctuary was especially important to the emperor Trajan (A.D. 98-117), who built the great court in front of the Temple of Jove, an enormous square surrounded by twelve exedrae, eight rectangular and four semi-circular: the idea of the small courtyard standing before the main courtyard of a temple was a Semitic idea, but it was borrowed by the Romans, who transformed it into a sort of Pantheon, where each exedra was dedicated to the worship of a deity of Olympus. Facing the exedrae stood a portico with columns made in pink granite from Aswan in order to protect the faithful who took part in the religious ceremonies and sacred meals. The strong feelings

Aerial view of the archaeological area of Baalbek.

Opposite page
Detail of the Corinthian half-columns and architrave in the Temple of Bacchus and Mercury.

*Ruins of the great
courtyard, built for
Trajan, A.D. 98-117,
before the Temple of
Heliopolitan Jove.*

The temple built by the Emperor Antoninus Pius, A.D. 138-161, was dedicated to Bacchus and Mercury.

View of the cella of the Temple of Bacchus and Mercury, adorned by Corinthian semi-columns.

that Trajan had for this place are documented, not only by the works that he ordered, but by the accounts of his devotion: it is said that before he left to wage war against the Parthians in the east, the emperor consulted the oracle of Baalbek concerning his destiny, and that in response the oracle presented him with a vine shoot that had been torn to bits. Trajan died in Cilicia on his way back from the war, and only his remains arrived in Rome. Another emperor from the western provinces like Trajan, Antoninus Pius (138-161), ordered the construction of a temple that, because of its decorations depicting Dionysian scenes, grape vines, garlands, and pomegranates, is generally considered to be a Temple of Bacchus; all the same, the presence, on the ceiling, of a sculpted eagle clutching two serpents in his talons, a symbol of Mercury, led many scholars in the past to attribute this temple to the messenger of the gods, the third member of the triad venerated in Baalbek. Standing in a less elevated position and in smaller dimensions than the Temple of Jove, this is the best preserved building, the greatest example in Baalbek of the skill and decorative richness of an art that, alongside the Western forms of the splendid Corinthian columns, the cornices, and the friezes, presents characteristics of the local tradition, especially in the depiction of the deities: in the ceiling of the peristyle, Mars, Victory, Diana, and Tyche are still recognizable from their attributes, although the faces have been cancelled by the iconoclastic furore of the Muslims. Only partially conserved is the Temple of Venus, which was built at some

Detail of the enclosure walls of the large square in front of the Temple of Jove.

In the foreground, sacred enclosure from the time of Trajan, and in the background, the six magnificent columns in the Corinthian style of the Temple of Heliopolitan Jove built during the reign of Augustus, first century A.D.

Detail of a mosaic floor with a female head, from the imperial era.

distance from the other two at the turn of the third century A.D. under Septimius Severus (A.D. 193-211). It stands out for its original round plan, unusual in Roman architecture with the exception of the Pantheon (rebuilt by Hadrian, A.D. 115-127 over a previous building ordered by Agrippa in 27 B.C.): beyond the rectilinear front with its portico with four columns, the concave surfaces that shape the podium and the cornice, linked to it by columns, harmonized with the convex surface of the central structure of the cella. Even when construction of the temples was complete, the Roman emperors continued to take an interest in Baalbek: Caracalla (A.D. 211-217), the last of the Severi, adorned it with a monumental entrance, a staircase that leads to the propylaea, a portico with twelve columns, at the centre of which stood a tympanum, while two towers flanked it at either extremity; indeed Philip the Arab (A.D. 244-249) connected this solemn entrance with the large courtyard through a hexagonal courtyard, a singular space created, once again, with exedrae and columns.

WHERE THE GODS MEET AND MINGLE: RELIGIOUS SYNCRETISM AT BAALBEK

Baalbek means 'Lord of the Bekaa' and derives from Baal, deity of the Canaanites and the Phoenicians, whose cult had spread among various other peoples, taking on various forms and being assimilated into existing cults. As Baal-Hadad, he was the god of atmospheric phenomena and fertility, and was assimilated into the annual cycle of the seasons: venerated as Adon, 'the lord', at the end of the summer he was destined to vanish into the afterlife or world beyond, whence he would re-emerge at the beginning of spring. This ancient agricultural myth of Eastern cultures would pass into Greek culture and give rise to a similar myth, the legend of Adonis, fought over and shared between Aphrodite, goddess of love, and Persephone, queen of the underworld. In the meantime, the figure of Baal underwent a further evolution and became the principal deity of the Phoenician Olympus, replacing his father El as the god of the sky, just as Zeus had taken the place of Chronos. Baal was venerated in Baalbek, in fact, as the 'lord of the sky', along with his wife Astarte, goddess of fertility, whose cult included sacred prostitution, and a son, possibly Aliyan, guardian of the spring and subterranean waters. In Hellenistic times, Baal was assimilated to Helios, the sun god, whence the city took its name of Heliopolis. With the establishment of the *pax romana*, the sanctuary became one of the most important in the empire: the Romans continued the practice of religious syncretism and identified the Phoenician triad with Jove, Venus, and Mercury, dedicating solemn and magnificent temples to them.

Sarcophagus whose cover consists of a sleeping lion, while on the sides, framed by an architectural cornice, are depicted scenes of sacrifice, from the third-fourth centuries A.D.

View of a hypostyle room with large cross vaults in the monumental complex of Baalbek.

Damascus

amascus, in Syria, is a priceless city, like its exquisite and renowned fabrics, and a city with thousands of years of history, yet still keenly alive, one of the most ancient of the sites still inhabited in the Near East (it is mentioned in Egyptian and Mesopotamian sources dating back to the turn of the second millennium B.C. and in the Bible story of Adam): the old city has been a World Heritage Site since 1979. Dominated to the west by Mount Qasiyun and bounded to the east by the desert, Damascus was founded, with the name of Palmyra, in an oasis, exceedingly fertile thanks to the presence of the River Barada, a meeting place for cultures and caravans. It was the capital between the eleventh and seventh centuries B.C. of an Aramaic kingdom that was often at war with the kings of Israel; the city was temporarily conquered by King David; later, defeated twice by the Assyrians, it was definitively conquered by Nebuchadnezzar in 600 B.C. It fell into Persian hands in 530 B.C.; in 333 B.C. it was annexed to the empire of Alexander the Great by his lieutenant Parmenion, establishing a link to the Western world for the next ten centuries: dating back to this period is the second urban nucleus, regular and Hellenistic in its layout, which lay just to the east of the Aramaic centre; the two adjoining areas were unified by the Romans, who enclosed the city in a single ring of enclosure walls when they took control of it (64 B.C). Damascus therefore shared the fate of Byzantium until, after the brief interval of rule by the Sassanid Parthians (614-635), in 636 it sealed its fate permanently as part of the Arab world, becoming the prestigious and monumental capital of the Omayyad caliphs. From that point on the city's fortunes varied: in 750 the Abbasids shifted their capital to Baghdad, and between the tenth and eleventh centuries Damascus found itself in the sphere of influence of the Fatimids of Egypt, until Salah ad-Din, the famous Sultan Saladin (1138-93), champion of Islam and skilful politician in the events of the Third Crusade (1189-92), restored it to its role as the capital of Syria and Egypt by founding the Ayyubid dynasty (1174-1260). The city then began to expand outside the enclosure walls and enjoyed a period of particular economic prosperity, which continued despite its loss of capital status under the Mameluke dynasty (from the second half of the thirteenth century until 1516), and despite the devastation wrought during the Mongol incursions (1260 and 1401): the skilful Damascene artisans specialized in the production of luxury goods, objects made of metal as well as cloth, which, much sought after by the markets of the West, crowded the warehouses of the ports of southern France, Genoa, Pisa, and Venice. Under Ottoman rule, which snatched Syria and Egypt away from the Mamelukes, Damascus experienced a gradual decline, as it lost out to other, more strategically important sites, in economic and military terms, in the immense Turkish Empire. After the First World War and the dissolution of the Ottoman Empire, the League of Nations gave France a mandate over Syria: Damascus rebelled against the occupying French army in vain and, in 1926, it was even bombarded. The French began work on an ambitious project to modernize the city's layout, under the supervision of Michel Ecochard, who did his best to salvage and restore as many monuments as possible and establish a close link between the historic nucleus and the modern city. Since 1946 Damascus has been the capital of an independent Syria.

The old city

Damascus preserves a few traces of its long history prior to the Arabic conquest, and by and large these traces date back to the reigns of

Aerial view of the old city.

Opposite page
Façade of the great Omayyad Mosque, dating from 706.

View of the internal courtyard of the great Omayyad Mosque from the eastern side, dating from the eighth century.

Northern portico and minaret of the great Omayyad Mosque, dating from the eighth century.

THE MOSAICS OF THE GREAT MOSQUE

Originally, the courtyard of the building was decorated with a high marble socle above which the walls were covered to the ceiling by a vitreous mosaic that was clearly of Hellenistic inspiration (it originally covered more than 4,000 square metres, or about one acre, the largest mosaic decoration ever made). Even now the side of the western portico that overlooks the courtyard preserves a certain expanse of the original mosaic decoration, a panel more than 30 metres (90 feet) long and over 7 metres (21 feet) tall, with depictions of clusters of houses, palaces, and pavilions set in a luxuriant vegetation and here and there overlooking a stream. There is absolutely no depiction of human beings, evidence that the Byzantine mosaicists summoned to decorate the building may have used classical images from the late Hellenistic and Roman traditions, but they were guided by specific instructions bound up with the new Muslim faith. The progressive accentuation of the adversion to images that developed in the Muslim world later led to the entire mosaic decoration being hidden under a layer of plaster, and it was not uncovered again until 1928. Other mosaic fragments with identical inspiration have been uncovered in the Bab al-Barid, or western door.

Internal view of the haram *(hall of prayer) in the Great Mosque.*

Detail of one of the corners of the haram *in the Great Mosque.*

Septimius Severus and his son Caracalla (A.D. 197-217). Under the Romans, who unified the Aramaic and Hellenistic nuclei, the city was first of all provided with enclosure walls, a circuit running about 6 kilometres (almost 4 miles) that can still be identified, despite the presence of a few later buildings, which bounds the old city; in the square enclosure walls there were seven gates (the southern gate and the eastern gate, the oldest one, now called Bab Sharqi — in Arabic 'bab' means gate — still survive), while the north-western side was reinforced by a *castrum*, a fortification that was modified and reutilized as a military structure by the Ayyubids (the citadel). From east to west the Roman city was crossed by the decuman, the so-called *via recta*, mentioned in the *Acts of the Apostles* and coinciding with the present-day route of the road called Shari Madhat Pasha, a road that was originally lined with columns, and which still preserves one of the three monumental arches. Completing the Roman ruins are the remains of the Temple of Damascene Jove, which stood on the area of the Aramaic sanctuary dedicated to the god Haddad, a temple of which the propylaea and the so-called 'triumphal arch' survive, and to conclude, the aqueduct, still in operation. At the end of the fourth century, during the reign of the Emperor Theodosius, on the area of the ancient Temple of Jove there stood a Byzantine church dedicated to John the Baptist and, since A.D. 706, the Great Mosque, or the Mosque of the Omayyads, built at the behest of al-Walid, the sixth Omayyad caliph. With a vast square extending before it, the building represents a fundamental model for successive Islamic architecture: the complex presents an external courtyard, bounded by a massive wall and flanked by three minarets in different styles from which the *muezzin* would summon the faithful to prayer. The inner courtyard has three sides with a covered

Opposite page
Detail of one of the walls with mosaic decoration in the Omayyad Mosque.

Typical courtyard of a madrasa *(Muslim theological school) made from large basalt blocks.*

The Mosque of Sinān Pasha was built during the Ottoman period.

double portico and the centre of it is covered by a dome of ablution for the rituals that precede the prayer, while adjoining the porticoed side is the Bayt al-Mal or the Dome of Treasure, a small octagonal pavilion covered with refined mosaics (mostly the product of restoration), surmounted by a dome that stands on eight Corinthian columns: this structure was meant to contain the goods of the community. On the fourth side of the internal courtyard stands the mosque proper, subdivided by arches into three parallel aisles, cut on a perpendicular line by a transect, the central part of which was covered by a wooden dome that was destroyed in 1401. The arrangement of its component elements is reminiscent of the Christian churches of Syria and Armenia and represents a significant example of Omayyad art that continues, through the master craftsmen employed, the tradition of Byzantine art. The urban fabric underwent important transformations with the rise to power of the Abbasids: the urban centre ceased to be a unified organism, and was divided up into autonomous quarters, each equipped with its own institutions, mosques, public baths, markets, police corps; in this way, the rectangular blocks from the Hellenistic grid were transformed into the characteristic Islamic urban fabric with its typical progressive branchings ending in blind alleys, in accordance with an organization of space that mirrored the separation of society into ethnic groups or crafts guilds. The chief concern of Saladin (1138-93) and his successors, the Ayyubids, was to return Islam to a strict orthodoxy: from this goal derived the establishment of many theological schools, in Arabic, *madrasas*, sober structures made of basalt and limestone, like the Madrasa al-Aziziya, near the Great Mosque, which houses the mausoleum of the great Saladin. In the twelfth century, while in the old city the subdivision tended to be into quarters protected by separate walls and gates, the new reorganization took place according to religious confession — Christians and Jews in the eastern zone, Muslims in the western zone — and expansion be-

gan to push outside of the ancient layout of walls that in the centuries that followed, with the Mamelukes and the Ottomans, was to lead to the creation of new suburbs. This meant the progressive abandonment of the historical centre, in which there were no more significant construction projects: the sole exception, perhaps, came in the eighteenth century, when the governors of the Azem family, who were responsible for a lively cultural and economic revival, ordered the construction of two magnificent caravanserais to the south of the Great Mosque, Khan Sulayman Pasha and Khan Asad Pasha, and in the immediately surrounding area, their own private palace, the Azem Palace. Of the two caravanserais, originally structures with a central courtyard with stables and storehouses on the ground floor and lodgings for travelling merchants on the upper storeys, Khan Asad Pasha still survives, and is used as a market (*suq*); it was once covered by a dome that has since vanished. Azem Palace, built around 1750 and restored in the 1970s, is a lovely example of a Syrian house of the time, divided into a public part, the *salamlik*, and a private part, the *haramlik*, inaccessible to guests, against whom no fewer than three doors protect it. The structure of the *haramlik* has been preserved: it is articulated around a large paved courtyard, adorned with porticoes and fountains; the interior halls feature stupendous ceilings made of inlaid wood and furnishings from the eighteenth and nineteenth centuries, and an interesting example of a bathing area divided into many small spaces with different temperatures, documentation of a tradition that is thousands of years old.

The minaret of the Omayyad Mosque dominates the old city of Damascus.

General view of the Tomb of Yahai, from late Roman times, conserved in the National Museum of Damascus.

Palmyra

'Palmyra is a city famous for its situation, for the richness of its soil and for its agreeable springs; its fields are surrounded on every side by a vast circuit of sand, and it is as it were isolated by Nature from the world, having a destiny of its own between the two mighty empires of Rome and Parthia, and at the first moment of a quarrel between them always attracting the attention of both sides'. Thus Pliny the Elder (first century A.D.) describes in his *Naturalis historia* (Book V, xx, 88; translation by H. Rackham, Loeb Edition) the rich and prosperous caravan city that the Romans called *Palmyra* (or 'city of palm trees'), but whose ancient name, attested in the tablets found at Mari (eighteenth century B.C.), and still used in Arabic, was Tadmor, 'city of date trees' (according to some, however, the name comes from *damar*, 'destruction', while others derive it from *tatmor*, which means to bury or cover up). Set in the middle of a vast oasis in the Syrian desert in the midst of a ring of gently rolling hills and lying on the trade route that linked Syria with the port cities of the Mediterranean on one side and with Mesopotamia on the other, the city owed its prosperity and importance to the exploitation of the rich caravan trade: probably it was already flourishing in the Hellenistic era, but it reached its apex between the first and the third centuries A.D. In particular, Palmyra established itself as the most important market for Eastern products and the leading caravan city of the empire, falling heir to a role that had previously been performed by Petra, beginning when the emperor Trajan in A.D. 105-106 incorporated it into the new province of Arabia, resulting from the annexation of Nabataea, a client state that controlled much of the trade with the East. Over the course of the third century A.D., with the advent of the Sassanid dynasty on the Parthian throne (A.D. 226), and the re-

sulting resumption of hostilities against the Romans, Palmyra also took on an important strategic and military role: taking advantage of this new situation the Palmyrene noble Septimius Odaenathus (Udhainat) succeeded in dominating the four tribes that controlled the city and seizing power, obtaining support and recognition from Rome, as an ally in the struggle against the Sassanids. When the Emperor Valerian was defeated and captured by the King of the Parthians, Shapur I in A.D. 260, Odaenathus took a stand in defence of the empire and Valerian's son, Gallienus (260-268), winning a series of military victories that warranted him the titles of *Dux Romanorum*, 'commander of the Romans', and *Corrector totius Orientis*, 'special commissioner for all the East'. This nomenclature indicated a generic supervisory role over the East, but not actual rule, which was the province of Roman governors, thus creating conflicts in jurisdiction and personal animosity, which only became worse when, with successive campaigns waged between 262 and 267, Odaenathus managed to conquer the area bounded by the Taurus Mountains on one side and the Arabian Gulf on the other, creating a practically autonomous state on the eastern borders of the empire. The political adventures of Odaenathus came to a sudden end in A.D. 267, when he was killed along with his son from his first marriage, Herod, in a palace conspiracy conducted by a few relatives and a Roman governor. He was succeeded on the throne by his younger son from his second marriage, Vaballathus (Wahballath), under the regency of his mother Zenobia. A resolute woman of great ambition, a lover of luxury but energetic in her conduct of military affairs, she carried on her late husband's policy of expansion: thanks to the advice of the Neoplatonic philosopher and rhetor Cassius Longinus, whom she invited to her court as her son's

View of the archaeologycal site.

Opposite page
View of the so-called Tetrapile, twinned pairs of Corinthian columns on bases, late second and early third centuries.

Great Colonnade on the caravan road.

The theatre still has only the first floor of the fixed scaena *and shows many similarities with the theaters of Sabratha and Leptis Magna.*

Opposite page
Closure plaque on a tomb ornamented with a relief of a banquet scene. The limestone low relief was found in the necropolis in Palmyra and is now kept in the local museum.

praeceptor, and thanks to the good offices of the General Septimius Zabdas, she conquered all of Syria and extended her dominion as far as Egypt and Anatolia, taking advantage of the difficulties that were plaguing Rome and the unrest that was spreading through the East. When the queen took the title of Augusta and affirmed her independence from Rome, the Emperor Aurelian (270-275), who had up to this point countenanced all of her undertakings, reacted promptly: he defeated the Palmyrene army repeatedly, first in Antioch and later in Emesa (Homs); he then laid siege to the city and then took it. Zenobia was captured and taken to Rome (autumn of 272), where she was paraded 'decked with jewels and in golden chains, the weight of which was borne by others' (Scriptores Historiae Augustae, *Life of the Deified Aurelian*, Chapter 34) in the triumph that was held in A.D. 274. Palmyra, which was spared at first, made an attempt at rebellion and was quickly sacked and plundered, and the city walls were destroyed. It was the beginning of the city's decline: the great trade routes shifted further north and the city was reduced to nothing more than a military garrison controlling the desert, to the point that the Emperor Diocletian had a huge encampment built for the Roman soldiers in the garrison (the so-called Diocletian's Camp). This remained the function to which Palmyra was relegated when it passed, in 634, under Arab dominion, as is documented by the construction of a castle atop a hill in the seventeenth century at the behest of the Emir Fakhr ad-Din.

Although they were of Arabic descent, the Palmyrenes developed a civilization of Aramaic language and culture, with strong Hellenistic and Parthian influences: for that matter, the city's basic nature as a great emporium of goods of all sorts and a major crossroads for people from all over, made it a place of cultural syncretism, blending and mixing East with West, as is documented as well by fascinating archaeological finds, all of which date back to the city's period of greatest splendour (first to third centuries A.D.). For example, where-

Ruins of the sacred enclosure built in the late first and early second centuries in the heart of the city.

as the architecture, painting, and mosaics seem more closely tied to Western culture, the sculpture, represented essentially by votive, ritual, and funerary reliefs, shows evident traces of Eastern influence: the taste for the exaggerated bas-relief is neither Greek nor Roman, the clothing was of Iranic derivation (trousers, shoes), and the massive jewellery worn by the female figures is strongly reminiscent of Persian goldsmithery. The city's focal point was the caravan route that crossed the oasis: for about a kilometre of its path through the city it was lined by columns (the so-called Great Colonnade), opened by a great arch, and lined by shops. From east to west it linked the two oldest settlements, the areas of the Temple of Bêl and Diocletian's Camp, where there is an immense tomb that mirrors the form of a temple. The Corinthian columns, which stand more than 9 metres (30 feet) tall,

have a bracket halfway up their height, meant to hold statues of civic dignitaries. The road is not perspectival in its progress: since the two zones are not on a line with each other, it takes a sharp turn and then straightens out at the three-aperture Triumphal Arch dating from the Severan Period (late second and early third centuries A.D.), undergoing a further adjustment on a line with the so-called Tetrapile, two pairs of floral columns symmetrically arranged on tall monumental bases. The complex dedicated to the cult of Bêl was built between the first and second centuries A.D. in an area that in Hellenistic times featured a sanctuary dedicated to all the gods honoured in the oasis: the temple proper, built in A.D. 32, stood at the centre of a sacred precinct that was later bounded (late first and early second centuries A.D.) by a broad porticoed *peribolos* with a double order of

1. Temple of Bêl
2. Museum
3. Valley of the tombs
4. Theatre
5. Monumental Nymphaeum
6. Via Sacra
7. Great Colonnade
8. Tetrapile

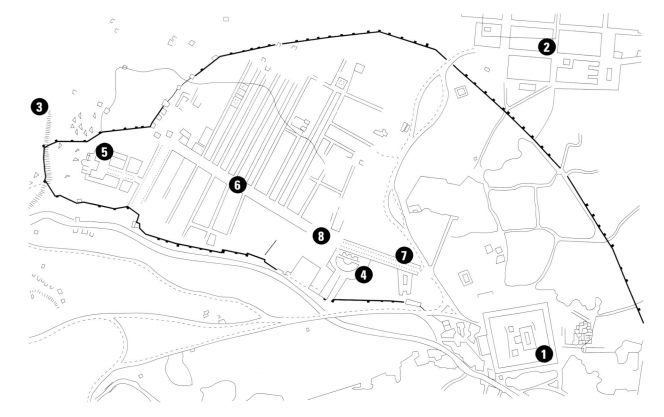

ZENOBIA, QUEEN OF THE EAST

About her the Emperor Aurelian, who defeated her, wrote: 'I am accused of failing to act as a man in triumphing over Zenobia. But the same ones who disapprove of me would not be able to find words sufficient to sing my praises if they knew what a woman she is, if they knew the wisdom of her decisions, her firmness in carrying them out, her severity towards her soldiers, if they knew how she can be generous and cruel, as necessity calls'. In fact, because of Zenobia's extraordinary nature, she captured the imagination of her contemporaries, who portrayed her with fanciful features not very different from those depicted in such famous figures as Semiramis and Cleopatra. She was an intelligent woman, who knew several languages and who wrote a compendium of Eastern history, and was extraordinarily beautiful: 'She had a dark face, with a brownish complexion, dark and lively eyes, the bearing of a goddess, and extraordinary beauty. Her teeth were so glittering white that many thought they were pearls' — that is how she is described in the *Lives of the Thirty Tyrants* that forms part of the *Historia Augusta* (Chapter 30). She was however also a warrior queen who caused Rome to tremble: she would address her soldiers dressed like a Roman emperor, with a helmet on her head and a purple cape, she knew how to alternate clemency and severity, and she withstood hardships more and better than any man, to the point that she loved to ride horseback and sometimes marched on foot alongside her soldiers. The myth of Zenobia, constructed from the account of the *Historia Augusta* which described the queen as the incarnation of the finest male and female virtues, would outlive the collapse of the ancient world: we find her again in Petrarch's *Triumph of Fame*, in the *Illustrious Women* by Boccaccio, in the painting by Giambattista Tiepolo, *Queen Zenobia Addressing Her Soldiers* (1730), in Rossini's opera, *Aurelian in Palmyra* (1813), and finally even in the movies: in 1959 the film *Nel Segno di Roma* was released, with the contribution of Michelangelo Antonioni, in which Zenobia was played by Anita Ekberg, and Aurelian by Gino Cervi.

Portrait of Zenobia, Queen of Palmyra.

Marble bas-relief with Bêl, the sun god, and probably Baalshamîn.

Funerary portrait of a young man, now in the National Museum of Damascus.

Detail of a sarcophagus.

columns on the interior, punctuated on the exterior by elegant Corinthian pilaster strips. One enters the temple via a staircase; the temple still has its cella intact, along with much of the peristyle. On either side of the entry door there are still many fragments of the frieze, carved on both sides with ritual scenes. A partly similar structure can be found in the Temple of Nabu dating from the first century A.D., set on the southern side of the Great Colonnade, which offers an interesting example of a mixture of elements of Greek and Eastern tradition, with the use of a peristyle alongside the courtyard: it is in fact constituted by a high podium with a Corinthian *peristasis* and a porticoed courtyard. Also on the southern side of the road was the theatre, its *scaena*, now reduced to a single storey, featuring a distinctive circular exedra in the middle, similar to those in the theatres of Sabratha and Leptis Magna, and the *agora*, enclosed by porticoed walls, which is reached by doors, like a basilica. Outside of the inhabited town, along the four main access roads to the city, stood four other necropolises, which feature three types of tombs. The oldest (first to second centuries A.D.) and most distinctive variety is represented by the funerary towers, tall multi-storey sandstone buildings belonging to the richest family groups. On the front of those that survive, foremost among them the Tower of Elahbel (A.D. 103), halfway up there is an arch with a sarcophagus, which in ancient times supported a reclining statue. The families who could not afford to build their own mausoleum instead purchased batches of loculi in very deep underground tombs (first to third centuries A.D.), which could contain numerous funereal niches. Corridors and rooms were subdivided by vertical bays of loculi, closed, as was the case in the funereal towers as well, by slabs of stone carved with the image of the deceased and painted in lively colours. Beginning in the middle of the second century, it became common instead among the wealthier families to make use of temple-tombs. These tombs provide us, thanks to the many funerary reliefs unearthed and now conserved in part at the Archaeological Museum of Palmyra, a formidable and fascinating figurative patrimony, a crowd of faces, men and women with remote gazes, described by an art characterized by a frontal view and a profusion of minor details.

Great Colonnade on the
caravan road.

View of the esastyle front
of a temple at Palmyra.

Kandy

The name Kandy derives from an Anglicized version of *Kanda Uda Fata,* which in the Sinhalese language means 'the land of mountains'. But when the city was founded, between 1357 and 1374, under King Wickramabahu III, it was called Senkadagalapura. We are uncertain about the origin of this name; Senkadagala was a colourful stone found in this place; Senkanda was the name of a Brahmin who lived in a nearby cave, and more especially, it was the name of the king's wife, the queen.

It was only during the reign of Senasammata Wickremabahu (1473-1511) that the city became the capital of the Kingdom of Kandy. So it remained with his successor, Jayaweera Astan, until 1551, when the new King Karalliyadde Bandara preferred to make Sitawaka his capital. The true period of the city's flourishing, however, corresponded with the reign of Konappu Bandara, better known by the name of Wimaladharmasuriya I. In order to consolidate his power, this king embraced Buddhism, a religion that had been brought to Sri Lanka by Mahinda, the son of the Indian Emperor Ashoka, as early as the third century B.C., and by this point was deeply rooted in the Sinhalese population, which in fact was never absorbed into the more dominant Indian civilization. Wimaladharmasuriya I brought the relic of the tooth of the Gautama Buddha from a place called Delgamuwa, and ordered the construction of an enormous temple to house it, the Dalada Maligawa. Today this *stupa*, the characteristic Buddhist building in which relics are preserved, stands on a granite base along the artificial lake built, between 1803 and 1807, at the orders of the last king, Sri Wickrema Rajasinghe, who was exiled to southern India by the English in 1815.

The relic is displayed only on special occasions: one of the most important ones is certainly the ceremony of *Esala Perahera* in which processions of hundreds of richly decorated elephants escort the case in which the tooth is housed around the city. The relic is housed within a system of Chinese boxes: no fewer than seven containers made of the purest gold and decorated with pearls, rubies, emeralds, and diamonds.

The holy status of Kandy is documented by its buildings. Indeed, not only is it the most important city to Sinhalese Buddhism, but its history in close contact with invading peoples, both conquerors and colonizers, ranging from the Muslims and the Portuguese to the Dutch and the English, as well as the tolerance of its sovereigns, always ready to welcome persecuted refugees of any religion, made its territory a Muslim religious centre with the Mosque of Meeramakkam and the Christian Cathedral of Saint Paul. Even the Temple of Dalada Maligawa is surrounded by the four *Mahas*, Natha, Pattini, Katharagama, and Vishnu, deities of the Hindu religion.

UNESCO declared Kandy a World Heritage Site in 1988.

General view of the Dalada Maligawa, seventeenth-eighteenth centuries.

Detail of a stupa, *a characteristic reliquary construction.*

Opposite page
Colossal statue of the Buddha in meditation in the Vihara *(Temple) of Kandy.*

THE BUDDHA'S TOOTH

The earliest Buddhist tradition seems to make no mention of the relic of the tooth. The *Digha Nikaya*, one of the most important texts in the Buddhist religion, features the description of the cremation of the Buddha and mentions the eight recipients into which the Brahmin Drona shared out the remains of the pyre, distributing them afterwards to eight different followers. All the same the tooth is not mentioned and the King of Kalinga, its first owner, does not appear as one of the eight guardians of the relics. The kingdom of Kalinga, in the state of Orissa in India, is mentioned subsequently in connection with a tooth preserved in that site and which formed part of the ten — no longer eight — canopic jars. In the thirteenth century this probable interpolation of the text made it possible to claim that one of the cremators removed the left tooth directly from the pyre prior to the division of the remains, and then took it to Dantapura, appropriately enough, 'the city of the tooth', in the kingdom of Kalinga. The relic seems to have been taken to the island of Sri Lanka in the fourth century B.C. by a female Brahmin. Legend has it that it was Ranmali, daughter of the King of Kalinga Guhasiva, who, in order to obey her father's will, escaped from his kingdom disguised as an ascetic, carrying with her the display case containing the tooth following her father's defeat in battle. Both the princess and the relic were protected by King Kittisirimeghavanna. Subsequent events took the relic back and forth between an Indian kingdom and the island of Sri Lanka several times, often without the precious container. It even fell into the hands of the Portuguese in 1560, who burned it instead of trading it for the large sum of money made available by the sovereign of Kandy as promised. The Sinhalese in any case denied that the true tooth had been plundered and burned, and in 1566 they exhibited for adoration by the faithful what they claimed was the true tooth of the Buddha.

Elephant decorated for the ceremony of Esala Perahera during which the relic of the tooth of the Buddha is displayed.

BUDDHISM

The Buddhist religion, originally from India, from the territories neighbouring Nepal and Audh, was founded by the Sakyamuni Buddha, whose existence is historically accepted. The doctrine that he preached spread in the second half of the sixth century B.C. throughout eastern India, even though nothing was put in written form during the Buddha's lifetime. After the Buddha's attainment of enlightenment (about 480 B.C.) it was generally thought necessary to gather and unify the elements of his doctrines concerning discipline, *vinaya*, dogma and law, *dharma*, and metaphysics, *abhidharma*. With this purpose in mind, the councils of Rajagriha (about 477 B.C.), Vaiala (377 or 367 B.C.), and Pataliputra (249 or 242 B.C.) were held. The conversion of the Emperor Ashoka (about 250-249 B.C.) gave new energy to Buddhism, which was declared a state religion and encouraged by the missions that spread it inside and outside of the empire. Political events and, in particular, the establishment of the Kushana Empire to the north, facilitated its expansion in China. Its greatest expansion was attained under the Gupta dynasty (fourth-sixth centuries A.D.), only to decline gradually as a result of the persecutions and invasions of the Huns. The decline of Buddhism was hastened by the growing popularity of Tantrism, Brahmanism, and especially Islam, which spread into India following the Muslim invasions at the end of the twelfth and the beginning of the thirteenth centuries. It is still one of the three most important religions in the world, with over 300 million adherents. Its doctrine preaches the perpetuity and indestructibility of elementary matter. Worlds live through *kalpa*, that is, cycles, of formation, development, decadence, and death, only to be rebuilt once again. Similar laws regulate the mortal soul of living beings. Only when a being is able to release its hold entirely on vices and, in a higher sense, even on virtues, will that being attain the state of *nirvana*. Hence the dogma of the 'Four Sacred Truths' (*Arya-Satyani*): the existence of sorrow, the cause of sorrow, the suppression of sorrow, and the path to follow in order to suppress it.

Interior of the Hall of Gold of the Buddhist Monastery.

Detail of the Dalada Maliwaga (Temple of the Tooth), seventeenth-eighteenth centuries, during the festivities of Esala Perahera.

Hierapolis

Turning one's gaze along the plain of Cürüksu one sees a white spot at the foot of the Cökelez Mountains. This is a plateau created by the calcareous water of limestone springs that, gushing down from above, leave behind them a coating of white sediments with refined shapes and a series of small pools. 'Castle of cotton', Pamukkele, was the name given it by the Turks when they conquered Anatolia in the eleventh century. But already in the second century B.C., the 'sacred city', or Hierapolis, was being built here. Founded by Eumenes II, King of Pergamum (197-159 B.C.), as a military colony sometime after 190 B.C., the year of the battle of Magnesia and of the expansion of the kingdom of Pergamum to the Taurus Mountains, it was consecrated to the cult of Phrygian Cybele, the Great Mother, personification of the Earth and linked to rituals of the death and rebirth of plants.

The excavations of the Italian archaeological mission, begun in 1957, and the protection of UNESCO since 1988, have made it possible to unearth the entire urbanistic layout, characterized by a rigorous grid of orthogonal streets. The main artery is constituted by the north-south road that opens with a monumental gate of honour with three apertures, flanked by two circular towers. According to the marble inscription in Greek and Latin set on the façade, bearing a dedication to the Roman Emperor Domitian, referring to his twelfth year as consul, it is possible to date the structure to around A.D. 86. It was therefore built during the great reconstruction project undertaken by the Roman emperor following the disastrous earthquake of A.D. 60, also mentioned by ancient sources. Immediately thereafter the two-aisle portico of the *agora* was built. The square in which the city's economic life took place occupies an enormous area extending 170 by 280 metres (about 560 by 920 feet). The side that extends towards the slope of the hill is occupied by a two-storey stoa/basilica. The façade of this building, which had the functions of a present-day tribunal, is punctuated by arches made of local marble, supported by semi-columns whose Ionic capitals are decorated with masks and vegetal festoons. If one follows the road back, one reaches the centre of the city, constituted by the baths and the Temple of Apollo. The baths were laid out with three main rooms, the *calidarium* and the *tepidarium*, covered by barrel vaults, the open area of the gymnasium linked to the cold pools, or *frigidarium*, and was part of the larger project of reconstruction of the city. The temple of the greatest deity of the imperial period, in-

Aerial view of the urban layout.

Detail of the capital with a lion biting a bull, in the propylaeum of the eastern stoa, second century B.C.

Opposite page
Initial stretch of the Via Frontinus with the honorary gate.

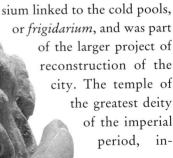

Central peristyle with the impluvium of the so-called House of the Ionic Capitals.

Ruins of the Martyrion of Saint Philip, the Apostle buried in Hierapolis.

Opposite page
Detail of the city baths with the niche of the caldarium which still bears traces of the pictorial decoration.

stead, overlapped the sacred area that was dedicated to the *Plutonion* prior to Hellenistic times: this was a natural cavern surrounded by a square enclosure in which purification rites were performed. Known from sources, it was considered one of the entrances to the Underworld because of the fumes and poisonous vapours of carbonic acid that still issue from it. The temple building, of which most of the ruins still exist, dates back to the third century A.D., while the construction on two terraces linked by a marble staircase leads us to think that other religious buildings, possibly earlier ones, may have existed, much like the Ionic portico whose orientation links it to the great main road. The dedication can be deduced from two small stelae made of marble that feature the double-headed axe and the appellation *Kareios*, which can be connected to the chthonic and oracular character of Apollo. To the east, the theatre was reconstructed, using the hill for its *cavea*. In the substructures that supported the external seat-steps there are access galleries for the public and rooms with flying vaults that lead to the *diazoma*, or passageway. A new arrangement of the *scaena* and a structural consolidation were undertaken during the reign of Septimius Severus. A new earthquake in the middle of the fourth century A.D. reduced the size of the city, along with the recently built enclosure walls. Dating from this period is the construction on the summit of a hill to the east of the city of a central-plan building based around an octagonal hall identified as the Martyrion of Saint Philip, the Apostle of Jesus Christ who is in fact buried in Hierapolis.

View of the limestone pools.

1. Martyrion of Saint Philip
2. Necropolis
3. Agora
4. Monumental baths
5. Honorary gate north
6. Byzantine gate
7. City baths
8. Temple of Apollo
9. Nymphaeum
10. House of the Ionic Capitals
11. Theatre

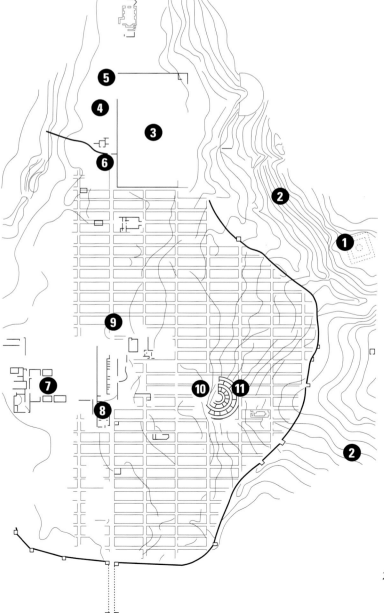

MIRACULOUS WATERS

With an average temperature of 35 °C (about 90 °F) and an average flow of some 40 cubic metres (about 52 cubic yards) per second, the curative waters of Hierapolis Pamukkale have been considered invaluable since ancient times. The architect Vitruvius and the geographer Strabo (first century B.C. - first century A.D.), while they were studying the rate at which the deposit left by the flowing water solidified, describe a landscape that is much different to that of the present day. The hot-spring oasis was criss-crossed by irrigation canals, which regulated the flow of the water in such a way that agriculture and industry could make the best possible use of its properties. From the existence of coins minted with an image of Dionysus, it has been deduced that the local production must have been well marketed. The gardens must have been numerous, to the point of justifying the existence of a guild of *kepourgòi*, or gardeners, mentioned in an inscription. The greatest use made of those non-potable waters involved their capacity to fix dyes on wool. Wool workers, dyers, and weavers were all organized into powerful guilds. The *porphyrabàphoi* acquired a dominant position because they had discovered that by using a plant native to this area, which scholars have identified as *Rhus cotinus* of the Coggygria family, they could dye fabrics purple without having to purchase the expensive *murex*. Even the characteristics of the famous local marble, a raw material for the funerary sarcophagi of the leading members of the local aristocracy, at first Greek and later Roman, were derived, according to Philostratus (first half of the third century A.D.), from the flow of hot water. When the waters pooled, they supposedly created a yellowish variety, while the clearer flowing water created a stone as clear as crystal, and the variegated qualities developed out of different conditions of sedimentation. Unfortunately the surviving sources are limited to the decorations and architectural elements of the buildings of the city; all the same, research has made it possible to narrow down the identification of the 'Hierapolis stone' to a variably transparent onyx or alabaster, but not colourful.

Opposite page
Panoramic view of the theatre with important ruins of the fixed scaena *and sculptural decorations.*

Marble slab with a scene of the Death of Adonis, *detail of the podium of the* scaena.

THE FRIEZE OF THE THEATRE

The extraordinary state of preservation of the frieze, which adorned the base of the colonnade that ran along the *frontis scaena* of the theatre, places this work among the most important complexes of theatrical decoration currently known in Asia Minor. In these buildings there is a prevalence of decorations with generic erotic figures and of the entourage of Dionysus, the deity of disguises and masquerades, and therefore the inspiration of acting and performance. The theatre of Hierapolis, although it still preserves its Dionysian frieze, also presents in the most important point in the structure, that is, along the platforms where the actors acted, a frieze consisting of forty-nine panels depicting the myths of Artemis and Apollo. The originality of the figurative themes does not draw on the usual motifs of the repertory, but rather appears to be linked to the cultural realities and the conditions in the city, the milieu of Asia Minor in which the mythological cycle concerning the two twins born of the goddess Latona is so often set, herself a deity originally from Asia Minor; the twins were venerated in the largest sanctuaries of Asia Minor, Artemis at Ephesus, Apollo in the oracular temples of Didyme and Clarus, as well as at Hierapolis. Through an organic iconographic programme, we pass from the glory of the city that flourished in the Hellenistic period to the grandeur of the current period, due to the Emperor Septimius Severus. The fulcrum of the entire narrative, in fact, is the high relief fastened to the architrave on a line with the main door: it depicts the apotheosis of the Emperor Septimius Severus in the garb of Zeus, crowned by Victory, surrounded by his wife, Julia Domna, and his sons, Caracalla and Geta, and by a series of personifications, courage, justice, fortune, under whose good auspices the theatrical competitions were held. The subtle correspondence between the iconography and the descriptions of the myths in the literary texts made it possible to hypothesize that the author may well have been Antipater, a Sophist philosopher.

Bukhara,
the Historic Centre

The Islamic city of Bukhara is located in the former Soviet Republic of Uzbekistan, in a broad oasis watered by the River Zeravsan. Its chief historic importance was that for centuries it had been a fundamental stopping point along the caravan routes, heavily travelled commercial routes that linked the most important centres of the Asian continent. The city was the capital of various major principalities, and was a lively artistic and cultural centre: its name is linked, among other things, with a precious type of carpet and a renowned school of painting that flourished in the sixteenth century, and which left a body of miniatures still preserved in important manuscripts. The historic centre of Bukhara, with its splendid monuments dating back to various eras and ruling peoples, constitutes an array of remarkable artistic and environmental importance.

The prosperity of Bukhara dates back to A.D. 709 when, following a period of Turkic invasions, it was annexed to the Arabic caliphate of Baghdad: the Iranian cultural matrix was a fundamental component of its history until the ninth century, when the progressive decline of Persian central authority encouraged the emergence of important new local dynasties. The city then enjoyed one of its greatest moments of splendour when, in the tenth century, it became the capital of the Samanid Kingdom, replacing Samarkand. Later, following a succession of different dominations, Bukhara enjoyed a new period of prestigious economic and cultural development with the advent of the Shaybanid dynasty (1500-1598): in the sixteenth century the Uzbek Prince Mohamed Jnibek Khan, of distant Mongol descent, in fact occupied the city and made it the political capital of his realm. Most of the monuments that survive date from this period, and are in some way linked to the cultural role assigned to Bukhara, which had

become a lively centre of Sunni Muslim teaching: the city's numerous Koranic schools played an important role in the tradition of Muslim orthodoxy. After the fall of the Shaybanid Khanate, there was a long phase of political decline, during which various dynasties succeeded one another in the rule of the city, which in 1868 became a protectorate of the Russian Empire.

The monumental buildings that contributed to the renown of Bukhara therefore date, for the most part, from the sixteenth century, but they are set in a distinctive urban structure that was already well defined in Samanid times. In the tenth century the city was already developing into three separate parts: a raised citadel with the royal palace and a mosque, a collection of suburbs, and a centre known as the *sahrestan* (city of the nobles). This last-named zone, joined with the others by a single enclosure wall, presented a precise rectangular layout, which was in turn enclosed by a wall with bastions and seven gates. On its interior, the *sahrestan* was subdivided into regular blocks, defined by a grid of perpendicular streets, the five largest ones on the east-west axis, and the nine smaller ones on the north-south axis. This unusual layout with street intersections, probably of Indo-Iranic derivation, can still be partially detected in the present-day urban grid, whose distinctive configuration in any case was established by the sixteenth century. The axes that join the main gates of the city still intersect at a perpendicular angle: the larger axis links the largest religious buildings, while on the north-south artery where the most important commercial road extends is a sort of linear, covered grand bazaar.

There are two distinctive features to the urban grid of Bukhara: the first lies in the capillary presence of water, while the second can be identified in the complex monumental

View of the skyline of Bukhara.

Opposite page
Chor Minar (the four minarets), a madrasa *built in 1807 for the Turkmen merchant Khalif Niyaz-kul.*

structures that stand at the intersection of the largest roads. Here massive domes arch over vaulted spaces, opening on four sides with pointed-arch doorways: these heavily trafficked areas were particularly sought after by vendors of precious merchandise, who set up their shops there. The largest of these buildings — of which only three now stand, compared with the five that the city once boasted — is located at the intersection of the main roadways: it is called Toki Zargaron and features a square plan and complex articulation. The Toki Telpak Feruson, instead, is located in the southern area of the city and is round. Another distinctive space in Bukhara is certainly the Lyabi Haruz Square, overlooked by several monumental buildings: its surface is partly occupied by a large open-air basin, a sort of swimming pool with stepped banks, surrounded by trees. This popular meeting place is only one of the numerous artificial basins that dot the city, often linked to religious institutions: sometimes in the form of simple covered cisterns, they were fed by the network of canals that ran through all the inhabited or cultivated areas enclosed by the outermost defensive wall.

Only a very few relics survive from the Samanid era: even the defensive walls that enclosed the town have vanished, badly damaged in the sack and plunder by Genghis Khan in 1220. All the same, one remarkable building survives to document the splendour of the ancient capital: this is the mausoleum of Ismail, which dates back to the end of the tenth century. The monument consists of a massive cubic structure surmounted by a cupola and opened on four sides by complex portals. The distinctiveness of this plan, a possible relic of the temples of the Mazdean religion, is in keeping with the unusual treatment of the wall surface. The building, erected entirely with simple bricks, is characterized by the remarkable chromatic and decorative values of its

DECORATIONS IN BRICK

The principal construction material for a great portion of the Asian continent, brick played a notable part in the definition of traditional architectural forms: its weakness in terms of resistance to traction, in fact, caused the extensive use of arches in place of the trabeation and vault and dome structures for roofing. The aesthetic implications of the use of this material, all the same, found a further ramification in this area, constituted by the development of a remarkable decorative technique. The oldest ornamental solutions (eighth century) consisted of simple raised ribbings, niches, and blind arches obtained simply by specially arranging bricks in the wall surface. In the Transoxiana region this technique was further perfected, leading to extraordinary results. In the buildings of Bukhara, the walls are entirely covered with ornamental motifs obtained by the placement of the little rectangles, arranged in an infinite array of combinations: here the contrast between bricks that jut out and bricks that are recessed creates remarkable effects of light and shadow. From the regions of Central Asia the so-called 'brick style' spread into Pakistan and Iran as well (eleventh-twelfth centuries).

Opposite page
Tomb of Ismail dating back to the end of the tenth century.

Detail of polychrome frieze that characterizes the façades of the most important buildings in the city.

Detail of the minaret of the Mosque of Kalyān, built in 1127 by the Qarāhānid Arslān Šah.

Façade of the Shir Dar madrasa, 1619-1636, Samarkhand.

Panoramic view of the Mosque of Kalyān with the shaft of the minaret in the foreground.

Opposite page
Porticoed courtyard of the Mosque of Kalyān.

surfaces, which are reminiscent in their plastic articulation of the interweaving of wicker or fabrics. This refined ornamentation is obtained exclusively with the bricks, arranged in various manners: in the pointed-arch portals the painstaking decoration is enriched with panels of carved terracotta and a rectangular frieze adorned with a sequence of circles.

Among the oldest buildings we should also mention the Kalyan Mosque, whose splendid minaret was rebuilt in 1127: here the brickwork decoration, arranged in horizontal strips, attains extraordinary levels of virtuosity, evident especially in the jutting of the balcony from which the *muezzin* calls the faithful to prayer. The sole touch of colour consists in the insert of an enamelled dark blue strip, set beneath the lower cornice.

The best-known monument from the Shaybanid period is certainly the imposing Mir Arab *madrasa*, a Muslim school of juridical and religious scholarship, where the pupils lived in the school. The plan of the building is classic for this type of structure: the rooms are arranged around a central courtyard, with the façade articulated in a double order of pointed arches stacked to form a loggia. The

central portal, of monumental size, is in the typical shape of the *iwan*: a high vault, entirely open on one side with a pointed arch, frames two smaller orders. There remain on the walls of the *madrasa* significant patches of the original polychromatic decoration, which has its focal point in the remarkable turquoise domes. Of great allure is also the façade of the *madrasa* of Nadin Diwanbegi, in which the central portal is decorated with predominantly dark-blue polychrome enamels: in the large upper panel stand out two exceedingly elegant figures of symmetrical facing peacocks.

Similarly, countless buildings of remarkable beauty are distributed throughout the urban fabric of Bukhara, which boasts, alongside the mosques and *madrasas* also a number of important secular buildings, including baths and caravanserais. The latter were special structures linked to the development of the great caravan routes, and they offered hospitality and shelter to people, animals, and goods. They therefore contained rooms for travellers, stables, and warehouses: these rooms overlooked porticoed courtyards and were often distributed over plans of astonishing complexity.

San'a

The capital of Yemen, San'a, stands at the centre of the country on a plateau 2,350 metres (7,710 feet) above sea-level and surrounded by mountains.

The pearl of Arabia Felix, the city traces its legendary origins back to Shem, the first-born son of Noah and the father of the Semitic race, who supposedly, arriving from northern Yemen, selected the setting for the original site through the indications of a bird (a small Jewish neighbourhood still survives in the capital). Legend also has it that at the beginning of the Christian era, during the reigns of Saba (Sheba) and Himyar, San'a housed the Ghumdan, a marvellous building twenty storeys tall, with a dome of translucent alabaster and bronze lions guarding every corner; at the end of the second century A.D., the King of Saba, Sha'r Awtar, supposedly built around the Palace of Ghumdan a wall, the original version of the city's enclosure wall of which only the gate, known as the Bab al-Yemen, now survives, and from this originated both the city and its name, which literally means, 'fortified city'. Following Saba and Himyar, and the conquest of the territory by the Ethiopian Aksumite (A.D. 525), there followed a brief phase of Christianization of the country; the construction of the Qualis, an imposing cathedral made of teak with silver and gold spires, dates back to this period; no trace of it remains today.

Fifty years later, a Persian army occupied the territory and expelled the Ethiopians; in A.D. 628 the satrap of San'a embraced Islam, ordered the destruction of the buildings of all non-Muslims, and made use of the ruins to build the city's Great Mosque.

The new religion spread rapidly and the history of the country almost constantly mirrored that of the various Muslim powers of the East. The ancient realm fell under the control of the Omayyads, then under the Abbasid Caliphs of Baghdad; it was during the war that Yemen waged to free itself from their domination that, in A.D. 803, San'a was destroyed. The Abbasids were succeeded by the Zaydi *imams*, the Fatimids of Egypt, and the Ayyubids of Saladin. At the start of the sixteenth century it was the turn of the Mamelukes, followed in 1548 by the long rule of the Ottoman Empire, which only ended in 1636.

More than 200 years later, in 1872, the Turks reconquered the Yemeni highlands, only to withdraw again in 1912. Just six years later, San'a became the capital of the Independent Islamic Kingdom of Yemen, ruled by an *imam*. In 1962 the *imam* was overthrown and the proclamation of the Republic was followed by a civil war that lasted almost ten years. In 1990 North and South Yemen were reunited and San'a became the capital of the New Republic of Yemen.

In the 1960s, the modernization of the country led to the exponential growth of the city, which witnessed the creation of new residential neighbourhoods and areas meant to house the centres of power; the expansion entailed the demolition of long stretches of the city walls and the absorption of adjoining villages and fields. The Old City, practically abandoned, was thus able, for the most part, to preserve its ancient structures.

What makes San'a extraordinary is its historic centre, characterized by an architecture that is at once mimetic and exceedingly lively, considerably different to that of any other Arab country or any country on earth; even the modern buildings that have been built there followed the 1,000-year-old model of the legendary Palace of Ghumdan, sometimes configuring themselves as miniature replicas. The houses of San'a stand six or seven storeys high and generally combine a lower section in basalt (usually a dark grey, less frequently a dark reddish colour) with a section

Detail of the Wadi Dhahr, the so-called Palace on the Rock.

Opposite page
Aerial view of the Old City of San'a.

One of the monumental gates to the city, a favourite site for the market.

Dome and minaret of Al-Jami' al-Kabir (the Great Mosque), built at the westernmost end of the Suq al-Milh in A.D. 630 and restored in the twelfth century.

of the upper storeys in exposed brick or covered with mud plaster; the external walls, on the characteristic background of bricks and earth, present a white chalk plaster that includes arabesques and filigrees of various sizes and styles.

Alabaster is also used there, a material employed in the Palace of Ghumdan, and progressively replaced in modern buildings by coloured glass. The distinctive windows, made up of polychrome panels, are crucial to the fascinating appearance of the city within the enclosure walls or along the internal lanes, usually made of dirt, and used equally by cars, goats, and pedestrians.

From the Great Mosque, which dates back to A.D. 630, and from the *funduq* (small inns) it is possible to make one's way into the colourful spice market, until you reach Bab al-Yemen. In the inexhaustible variety of its elements, which belonged to various eras and dominations, blending with the unique local idiosyncrasies, the city continues to amaze: from the *hammam*, public baths that largely date from the Turkish era, to the gardens within the houses, for the most part closed to tourists; and from the *madaris* (Islamic theological schools) on the high floors of the buildings to the *mafraj*, where guests assemble to smoke and chew *qat*, a widely used invigorating plant.

It was the Italian director Pier Paolo Pasolini, who was in Yemen in 1971 to shoot his film *Fiore delle Mille e una notte* (Flower of the Thousand and One Nights), who launched an appeal to UNESCO on behalf of the city through his documentary film *Le mura di Sana'a* (The Walls of San'a). His appeal found a response in the international campaign to safeguard the Old City, undertaken in 1984.

THE LEGENDARY REALM OF THE QUEEN OF SHEBA

Yemen is the land of the fabulous Kingdom of Saba, or Sheba, whose existence is documented as far back as the eighth century B.C. It was a prosperous state that extended from southern Arabia to the coasts of Abyssinia, and famed for its legendary queen, celebrated in Hebrew, Greek, Abyssinian, and Islamic sources. Memorable was her encounter with King Solomon, to whom she posed subtle riddles and to whom she brought 120 pounds of gold, spices, precious stones, and ivory. Christian culture was fascinated by this Eastern queen and her splendid realm, and interpreted her as a prefiguring of the Church. Artists and clients wanted to depict her on the portals of Romanesque cathedrals and in cycles of Renaissance frescoes.

Interior of a noble house with the niche that indicates the direction of Mecca.

Front view of the 'Palace on the Rock' (Wadi Dhahr) featuring white plaster decoration that contrasts with the baked-brick wall.

Significant examples of façades of buildings making up the structure of the Old City, characterized by a sharp contrast between the *construction material and the whitewash that covers the decorative details.*

Opposite page
A road of the city.

245

Algiers

Marrakesh

Leptis Magna

MOROCCO

TUNISIA

Cairo

WESTERN
SAHARA

ALGERIA

LIBYA

EGYPT

Thebes

MAURITANIA

CAPE
VERDE

MALI

NIGER

CHAD

ERITREA

GAMBIA

SENEGAL

DJIBUTI

GUINEA
BISSAU

BURKINA
FASO

NIGERIA

SUDAN

GUINEA

SIERRA LEONE

IVORY
COAST

GHANA

TOGO

BENIN

CENTRAL
AFRICA
REP.

ETHIOPIA

SOMALIA

LIBERIA

CAMEROON

EQUATORIAL
GUINEA

SÃO TOME
AND
PRINCIPE

GABON

CONGO

ZAIRE

UGANDA

KENYA

RWANDA

BURUNDI

TANZANIA

SEYCHELLES

ANGOLA

COMOROS

MALAWI

MOZAMBIQUE

MAURITIUS

ZAMBIA

NAMIBIA

ZIMBABWE

MADAGASCAR

BOTSWANA

SWAZILAND

LESOTHO

SOUTH AFRICA

AFRICA Africa

Algiers, the Casbah

The first and the literal meaning of *casbah* has to do with the fortified enclosure walls of a city, a citadel. As time passed, the term grew to include an entire quarter, typical of the Arab cities of northern Africa, generally set high atop a hill, characterized by narrow twisting lanes and labyrinths of steep and winding staircases. What these quarters usually had in common, making them in a certain sense homogeneous, was their irregular plan, without any particular focal points, and their architecture. The casbah of Algiers extended along the bay which the city overlooked, around the ancient castle of the *Bey*. Its configuration, which alternated military architecture with stretches of popular and residential architecture, is a priceless example of Arab and Turkish urbanistic organization and its overall development during the sixteenth and seventeenth centuries in a Mediterranean city. According to legend, the city of Algiers was founded by twenty comrades of the Greek hero Hercules who were separated from him during a voyage across the Mediterranean. It has been historically determined that in the sixth century B.C. it was a Punic trading emporium called *Ikosim*, a Phoenician word that offers three different possible interpretations: island of thorns, island of owls, or island of seabirds. The corresponding Greek term is *eikosis,* which means 'twenty', thus linking back to the legend of Hercules's comrades. In the last third of the first century B.C., the city was conquered from the Carthaginians by the Romans who renamed it Icosium. Under Vespasian, it became a fully fledged Latin colony. After a period of Byzantine rule, the city fell subject to continual occupations by various Berber peoples, such as the Almoravids, the Almohads, and Merinids, and others still. In the seventh century it was conquered by the Arabs and renamed Marana, but the city continued to hold an entirely marginal role in the flourishing commercial traffic that was criss-crossing the Mediterranean Sea. No ancient ruins or other trace from this period is visible in the modern city. During the summary excavations undertaken in the nineteenth century, only a few ruins and other fragments were uncovered and are now in the Stéphan Gsell Museum. The modern city was founded in the tenth century by the Berbers, and until the sixteenth century it was ruled by Arab dynasties, with the exception of a few brief intervals of independence. The great fortune of Algiers, and the interest that it has always exerted, depends primarily on its strategic geographic position. Besides being protected towards the interior by the hill of Bouzaréa, it also enjoyed an excellent system of natural defences towards the sea. In fact, a series of rocky islands lies in front of the bay, later connected to the mainland, which served as a protective screen; these islands, in Arabic *al-Jazair*, gave the city its name. Throughout the Berber domination, Algiers enjoyed a rich and flourishing period, but the apex of its splendour, as well as its period of greatest power, came about 1516 when the pirates Aruj and Khayr ad-Din (or Barbarossa) liberated the city from the Spanish. In that period, Algiers, under Turkish dominion, constituted a serious threat to the rest of the Mediterranean. Clustered on the steep slopes of the hill was the casbah, the sixteenth-century fortress that long symbolized the city's invulnerability. Algiers has withstood repeated bombardments from the sea (in 1541 by the fleet of Charles V, by the English fleet in 1662, by the French fleet in 1682 and 1683, and by the Spanish fleet in 1775) until 1830, when it finally surrendered to the French. From that point on, the city began to change its appearance. The French settlement in the Turkish city led to numerous changes in terms of urbanistic and architec-

View of the casbah of Algiers.

Opposite page
Stairway among the alleys of the casbah, with the distinctive jutting rooms of the houses.

tural structure: old buildings were knocked down, especially in the lower section of the city, and were gradually replaced by more modern structures; broad streets and squares were built, along with a system of staircases on the ancient Turkish walls. Protected in a certain sense, the higher section of the casbah avoided much of the destruction, though it too bore the inexorable marks of French domination. The old neighbourhood of the casbah, originally constituted by the citadel alone, within which stood the palace of the *Bey*, the highest authority who ruled the city in the Turkish period, developed as a pulsating labyrinth of intense and frenetic commercial trade. In Islamic cities the quarter was known as the *medina*, which meant the stretch of city linked to the bazaar and the mosque, where personal relations were densest and most intricate. The houses, built in the Arab-Mediterranean style, known as *ed-dar*, stood immediately next to one another, cheek-by-jowl as it were, and recalled in their joint structure some huge and fully fledged palace. They developed around a central courtyard, often embellished and enriched with majolica of various colours, with a well and a cistern, and they feature a distinctive roof terrace. At times they are flanked by other small constructions called *dwera*. There are never windows on the façade overlooking the street, so that the family life of the Muslims could be carried on privately inside the home. Just as the internal courtyard represented the core of the Moorish palace, so the casbah, with its maze of lanes and narrow alleys, staircases and unexpected views, constituted the ancient heart of the city of Algiers.

Detail of the modern minaret of the casbah, visible from every point in the Old City.

Aerial view of the casbah
with the port of Algiers
in the background.

MIGUEL DE CERVANTES: ILLUSTRIOUS PRISONER OF THE CASBAH OF ALGIERS

As early as 1568 Cervantes (born Alcali de Henares 1547 – died Madrid 1616), a personal and sharp-eyed interpreter of the problems of humanity at the point of transition from the Renaissance to the Baroque and author of the renowned novel, *The Adventures of the Ingenious Gentleman Don Quixote de la Mancha (El Ingenioso Hidalgo Don Quijote de La Mancha)*, was in Italy. Here he set out on the soldier's career that led him to take part in numerous expeditions. In 1575, in order to travel to Spain, he took passage in Naples aboard the galley 'Sol'. Near the delta of the River Rhône, the ship was attacked by three vessels packed with Turkish corsairs, and Cervantes was taken prisoner and transported to Algiers. Sold into slavery, he remained a prisoner in the fortress of the city for five years, attempting to escape more than once, but in vain. It was during this long enforced stay in the casbah of Algiers, before taking ship once again for Spain in October of 1580, that Miguel de Cervantes composed two plays, *El trato de Árgel* and *Los baños de Árgel*.

Detail of a projecting
room in a dar (*typical
house of the casbah*).

The casbah of Algiers,
seen from the sea in an
eighteenth-century print.

Detail of the loggia of an interior courtyard of a dar, overlooked by all of the upper rooms in the house.

Detail of a typical roof terrace of an Algerian dar.

Portal of a dar.

View along a stairway that runs over the hill of the casbah.

Detail of the portal of a dar *with a sculpted rosette decoration.*

Muslim Cairo

The capital of a country with thousands of years of history, Cairo preserves vestiges of the Egypt of the Pharaohs only on its outskirts, where the ancient Heliopolis once stood, while the heart of the city is entirely Islamic in its history. Here, mosques, minarets, palaces, and even the multicoloured shops of the twisting lanes all testify to the glory of the legendary Fatimid and Mameluke sultans who ruled there.

The oldest urban structure stood on the right bank of the Nile, near the island of ar-Roda, built by the Romans, who called the city Babylon 'on the river': it included a fort, fragments of which have survived. In early Christian times, the Coptic community took up residence there, and built the Churches of Saint Barbara and Saint Michael, as well as the Church of Saint Sergius (*Abu Sergha*) which, according to tradition, stood on the site where the Holy Family found shelter during the flight into Egypt.

In the seventh century, following the death of Mohammed, the founder of Islam, Arab armies marched with great speed to conquer neighbouring lands. In A.D. 640, the army of the Caliph Omar, commanded by Amr Ibn al-As, reached the Nile and, by bringing to Egypt the Arab religion, language, and culture, changed the course of history. Amr occupied Babylon and founded across from it his own capital, al-Fustat (from the Arabic word for 'tent', or, according to others, from the Latin 'fossatum', meaning 'moat' or 'ditch'), surrounded by an enclosure wall. There he built the Mosque of Amr Ibn al-As, the oldest mosque in Egypt, which was built on the model of the Mosque of the Prophet in Medina: enclosing a simple courtyard surrounded by brick walls, it perfectly embodies early Islam, severe and almost military in character.

During the domination of the Abbasids, al-Fustat gradually declined in importance and was replaced by the northern suburb of al-Askar ('the Army'), the military camp that gradually gathered more and more buildings: the palace of the governor, houses, shops, and a mosque. In A.D. 870, the new Governor Ahmed Ibn-Tulun made Egypt independent of the Abbasid Caliphate and founded in the north-eastern area a splendid new capital, al-Qatai ('the fief'). The city was destroyed at the beginning of the tenth century, when the Abbasids regained control of the country; they spared the Great Mosque of Ibn-Tulun which still today, with its large courtyard (*sahn*) surrounded by the porticoes intended for teaching (*riwaq*), punctuated by elegantly decorated round arches, probably the work of Iraqi artists, represents one of the most admirable monuments in Cairo.

The great period of the city's splendour began at the end of the tenth century, when Egypt was conquered by the powerful Shi'ite Muslim dynasty of the Fatimids, who decided to build a new capital capable of rivalling even the illustrious Baghdad. And so it was that, in A.D. 969, to the north of al-Qatai, the city of al-Qahira was founded (Arabic name meaning 'the victorious', the name from which the English name 'Cairo' derives). In the heart of the new capital, which summoned talented artists from all over the Muslim world, stood the residence of the *imam*, the administrative buildings, and most important, the two great Fatimid Palaces, with 4,000 rooms, splendid gardens, fountains and the cloisters lined with mosaics, of which nothing, sadly, survives today; what does survive, however, from this golden age of Islamic art, are the Mosque and the University of al-Azhar, still an imposing Islamic cultural centre that has converted to Sunni orthodoxy. The present-day quarter of al-Azhar preserves other monuments from the Fatimid era, such as the three large gates (Bab Zuwayla, Bab al-Futuh, and Bab an-Nasr) and

Aerial view of the Muslim city.

Opposite page
Detail of the domes of the Mosque of al-Ahzar, 970-972.

the huge square towers of the city's enclosure walls, and, especially, five mosques. Of these, the Mosque of al-Hakim, should be mentioned, the last example of a 'military' mosque, a symbol of an expanding and self-confident Islam, built at the behest of the cruel and extravagant caliph after whom it is named. It is a compact and severe building, with a broad open courtyard that, with the adjacent walls, makes up a medieval architectural compound of remarkable power. The Mosque of al-Azhar, 'the most resplendent mosque', was also built by the Fatimids, though it gathers around its central core buildings from different eras that extend over a very large surface area (five minarets, six gates, and 300 marble columns): it was built between 970 and 972, under the Caliph Muizz, to serve as a sanctuary, but also as a meeting place for the citizenry. Beginning in 988, at the behest of the Caliph al-Aziz, it also housed a university that, initially meant for the propagation of the Shi'ite cult, was soon opened to the teaching of philosophy, chemistry, and astronomy, becoming an important centre for Islamic studies, active to the present day. The exceedingly refined present-day appearance of the complex, with its Persian-arch porticoes, its decorated gates, the immense prayer hall (*iwan*) punctuated by nine aisles of columns, the principal *mihrab* (the niche inside the mosque that indicates the direction of Mecca, in order to help orient the faithful) richly decorated with mosaics, the variously shaped minarets, adorned with lacy carved stone, is the product of a series of embellishment projects.

After the brief and bloody incursions of the Seljuk Turks, and the even bloodier attacks of the Crusaders, who burned al-Fustat, in 1172 Egypt fell into the hands of the celebrated Saladin, founder of the Ayyubid dynasty.

But the period of Cairo's greatest splen-

Aerial view of the Mosque of General Ahmed ibn-Tulun, built to the west of the Old City in the Fustat zone, in the second half of the ninth century.

Mosque of Muhammad Alì, built to plans by the Greek architect Jusnf Bushnaq, in the first half of the nineteenth century.

Opposite page
Courtyard of the Mosque of Ibn-Tulun: dome of a fountain built at the end of the thirteenth century.

257

Detail of the fountain set at the centre of the courtyard of the al-Gawhara Palace.

Interior of the madrasa *Al Iwan with the vaulted hall opening out on to a courtyard.*

Square towers of the Bab el-Nasr Gate, incorporated into the city walls at the end of the eleventh century.

dour coincided with the advent of the dynasty of the Mamelukes, the feudal functionaries, probably of Turkish origin, who replaced the Ayyubids in 1257 and remained in power until 1517. The new sultans, definitively expelling the Crusaders from the East and thrusting the Mongol invaders back within the boundaries of Persia, encouraged the economic prosperity of their country, whose capital was enriched with great architectural creations, such as aqueducts, hospitals, mosques, *madrasa* (schools of doctrine), and splendid mausoleums. The first Mameluke mosque was built in 1266 by the Sultan Baibars, crowned by an immense dome that represented the tangible sign of the power of the ruling dynasty. In 1340, the Emir al-Mardani ordered the construction of the mosque that bears his name, with columns of every shape and size, taken from Pharaonic, Graeco-Roman, and Coptic temples; particularly exquisite is the rare pierced-wood screen that separates its eastern *riwaq* from the courtyard, the window grills made of enamelled ceramic, and the magnificent star-spangled *mihrab* with mother-of-pearl, red stone, and dark-blue enamel. Dating from the decades that followed (1356-63) was the *madrasa*-mosque that the Sultan Hasan

SALADIN

The heart of the city of Cairo still preserves monuments from the rule of the legendary soldier and Sultan Saladin (Salah al-Din, 1138-93), celebrated and commemorated over the centuries, both in East and West, as a champion of the Islamic faith and defender of the chivalric ideal. The future conqueror of Jerusalem, who defeated both the Fatimids and the Crusaders, restored Egypt to the Turkish sultans of Syria and changed the appearance of Cairo, joining the ancient quarter of al-Fustat with the Fatimid quarter of al-Qahira. Saladin, in order to protect the new urban complex from invasions and heresies (such as the Shi'ite heresy that took hold during the Fatimid era) built a stone enclosure wall, which he was unable to complete because of his departure for the war against the Crusaders. This was crowned by the Citadel, built in 1179 on a spur of the Muqattam, the powerful fortress rising above the residential area, which until the nineteenth century was to be the residence of all the governors of Egypt, from the Mameluke sultans to the Ottoman pashas. The Citadel contained the Mosque of Mohammed Alì, also known as the 'Alabaster Mosque' for the abundance of this material in its decoration, and the al-Gawhara Palace.

View of the courtyard of the Mosque of Al-Azhar, 970-972.

THE MAUSOLEUM OF QAITBEY

In the site that accommodated, from 1382, the 'Tombs of the Caliphs', that is, of the Circassians, the last dynasty of the Mamelukes, stands the mausoleum of Qaitbey, one of the most significant works of Arabic art of the fifteenth century. Adorned on the exterior with decorations with delicate chiaroscuro effects, it contains a mosque with a cross-shaped plan and also contains a *minbar* (the elevated pulpit which, in mosques, is reserved for the *imam* to deliver the Friday prayer) decorated with precious encrustations, as well as the tombs of the sultan and his sister, surmounted respectively by a dome and a baldachin. The stained-glass windows, high in the walls, suffuse the light that enhances the elaborate arabesques, the marble mosaics, and the stucco decorations.

VII ordered built, requisitioning the possessions of the victims of an outbreak of the plague that had decimated the population of Cairo. The impressive building, whose cross-shaped plan develops around a central courtyard, with the elegant pavilion of the fountain for ritual ablutions, was built with the use of material taken largely from the pyramids. The stern and massive appearance of the construction is balanced by the thrusting vertical power of the dome that arches over the sultan's tomb, and the sole minaret of the original four to have survived, which stands 90 metres high, the tallest in Cairo. According to legend, when this mosque, considered one of the greatest masterpieces of Arab architecture, was finished, the Sultan Hasan ordered that the hands of the architect who had designed it be cut off, so that he could never build anything to rival it. Also dating from the Mameluke era is the Mosque of Aq-Sunqur, built in 1348, but especially famous for the interior decoration with white and light-blue decorated ceramics that gave it the name of the 'Blue Mosque', which was executed during its reconstruction in 1652 under Ottoman domination.

Aside from religious structures, the sultans and the nobles of the golden age of Cairo built splendid mausoleums, concentrated in the 'City of the Dead', the huge necropolis to the east of the city proper. In the sumptuous buildings that were erected there, proper residences for deceased sultans, *imams*, and princesses, one can see the cultural imprint of the Egypt of the Pharaohs.

Opposite page
Domed tomb of the Sultan Qaitbal, 1472-1474.

Detail of the minarets in el-Rafai Mosque.

View through Bab el-Zueilah Gate, which dates back to the end of the eleventh century, later surmounted by minarets at the beginning of the fifteenth century at the behest of the Mameluke Al-Muayyad.

Thebes and the Royal Tombs

Thebes contains the finest relics of the history, art, and religion of ancient Egypt, of which it was the capital in its period of greatest splendour. Hundreds of sovereigns, from pharaohs to Roman emperors, glorified the city with architecture, obelisks, and sculpture. According to Homer, 'Thebes of the Hundred Gates' possessed such wealth that it could only be exceeded by the number of grains of sand. The exaltation of life found expression in the 'Thebes of the Living', identifiable in the fabulous sites of Luxor and Karnak, on the right bank of the Nile, site of the temples dedicated to the divine triad of Montu, Amon, and Mut, while the celebration of death took shape in the 'Thebes of the Dead', i.e. in the magnificent necropolises along the left bank of the great river.

From the Middle Kingdom to the end of the ancient era, the city was sacred to the ancient god Amon, supreme sun god: to him were dedicated temples of incomparable splendour and size. Among the ceremonies that were performed there, the most magnificent was the one that was performed on the occasion of the new year, during which the gilded vessels of the gods would set out from the sanctuaries of Karnak and sail across the Nile to the forest of columns in the Temple of Luxor. Here would take place the rite that legitimized the power of the pharaoh, that is to say, his conjunction with the 'ka', the supernatural essence of the gods. The Temple of Luxor, built by Amenophis III and Ramesses II, was connected to the great sanctuary of Karnak by a long triumphal boulevard lined by sphinxes that led to the entrance, preceded by a pair of obelisks made of pink granite. Upon the obelisk that has remained in place are engraved vertical bands of hieroglyphics painted red and a small scene in which Ramesses II adores Amon; the other obelisk, donated in 1831 to Louis Philippe, now stands in the Place de la Concorde in Paris. The entrance to the temple, lined by the colossal seated figures of Ramesses II, Queen Nefertari, and their daughter Meritamon, is adorned with scenes from the Syrian and Hittite military campaign and leads to the great courtyard of Ramesses II and to the chapel that served as a storehouse for the boats, dedicated to the triad of Amon, the father, Mut, the mother, represented in the form of a vulture or a lion, and Khonsu, the lunar son of the couple. The second complex, with a magnificent and immense entrance and colonnade, a porticoed courtyard, and a hall crowded with tall columns, was built at the command of Amenophis III, the protagonist of the decorations of the 'chamber of birth', in which his divine origin is illustrated, right from conception.

About three kilometres (two miles) from Luxor is the monumental complex of Karnak, composed of three temples, one of which is consecrated to Mut, one to the warrior god Montu, and one to Amon. The building dedicated to the father of the gods, girded by massive walls in which there are eight stone gates, is the product of a series of ingenious projects of expansion and renovation ordered by pharaohs eager to leave behind marvellous testimonials to their reigns: the immense courtyard at the centre of which stands the enormous aedicule of Taharqa, stopping place for the vessel of Amon; the portico of Bubastis, flanked by two rows of sphinxes; the Temple of Sethi II, where the boats of the Theban triad would stop; the colossi of the Pharaohs Thutmosis III and Ramesses I and II; the great hypostyle hall with its astounding forests of 134 colossal columns; the six monumental entrances that follow one after the other; the granite pillars and obelisks; the rooms decorated with religious and military scenes and the hall of the 'botanical garden' which featured the exotic plants so loved by

Aerial view of the site of ancient Thebes.

Opposite page
Monumental entrance to the hypostyle hall of the Ramesseum, funerary Temple of Ramesses II, depicted in the four large statues on the front, XIX dynasty, c. 1235 B.C.

THE COLOSSI OF MEMNON: THE STONES THAT SING

In 27 B.C. an earthquake opened a long fissure in the northern colossus that ran down to its waist. This triggered a famous physical phenomenon whereby the statue, at dawn, emitted a sound similar to the vibration of a guitar string as it began to lose its nocturnal moisture. For that reason the Greeks thought that the colossus could be identified as the god Memnon, who came back to life each day at the warm caress of the rays of sunlight of his mother Aurora (and so the name, strictly speaking, should be applied only to the north colossus). As is documented by the numerous writings that discuss this statue, the oldest of which dates back to the year A.D. 120, the myth attracted a great number of Greek and Roman visitors. On the legs of the colossus you can also read four epigrams, left here by the court poetess Julia Balbilla, who accompanied the Emperor Hadrian on his visit to Egypt in 130. Septimius Severus, at the beginning of the third century, ordered the restoration of the monument, which from that point forward lost its voice.

Opposite page
Colonnaded courtyard built at the behest of Amenophis III (1413-1377 B.C.) at Luxor.

Papyriform colonnade of the temple dedicated to Amon, Mut, and Khonsu at Luxor.

Detail of the statue of Amenophis III placed in the courtyard of the Temple of Luxor.

Funerary Temple of Queen Hatshepsut (1501-1480) at Deir el-Bahari.

Temple of the god Serapis at Luxor, from the Hellenistic era.

Aerial view of the sacred zone with the temples of Luxor overlooking the Nile.

the pharaohs; the sacred lake flanked by store-houses for offerings and a cage for acquatic birds; other buildings for the boats to stop, with engraved and carved decorations, set on terraces that could be reached by ramps; the temple dedicated to the hippopotamus-goddess Opet, placed on the site in which she is said to have given birth to Osiris; and, finally, the Southern Propylaea, four portals adorned with bas-reliefs, columns, obelisks, and colossi, which adorned the sacred way that led to the Temple of Mut.

On the opposite bank of the river there grew up over the centuries the 'Thebes of the Dead'. For almost fifteen centuries, great funerary temples were built at the foot of the hills so that they would be accessible to the visits and homages of worshippers. They were entirely separate from their corresponding tombs, which instead were dug out of the mountains, safe from violation and tomb-robbers. To the north were built the Temple of Qurna al-Gedida, dedicated to Amon-Re, and the temple consecrated to Hathor, the goddess of sweetness and joy who was venerated in the form of a cow. It was commissioned by Queen Hatshepsut for herself and for her father Thutmosis I. This masterpiece of Egyptian architecture, built in the natural terrace of Deir al-Bahri, was accessible via an uphill road lined with sphinxes and a series of terraces cut into the mountain, connected by ramps supported by porticoed walls. Even better known is the magnificent funerary Temple of Ramesses II (*Ramesseum*), a building situated at the edge of the cultivated fields which, because of its courtyards, *sacraria* filled with statues, decorations and colossi, was admired by many ancient writers. All that remains from the Temple of Amenophis III are the colossi of Memnon, two impressive quartz monoliths that depict the pharaoh sitting on his throne, accompanied by the figures of his mother and his wife.

The tombs of the pharaohs, of their dignitaries, priests, and princesses are instead hidden in the bowels of the mountains and form the great necropolises of al-Asasif, al-Khokha, Qurnet Mura, Deir al-Medina, and the Valley of the Kings and Valley of the Queens.

Among the underground tombs of the Valley of the Kings, the British explorers Lord Carnarvon and Howard Carter found in 1922 a small tomb that soon became the most renowned in Egypt, the tomb of the young pharaoh Tutankhamen, whose spectacular tomb furnishings included a group of objects that today constitutes one of the most precious treasures of the Cairo Museum.

Tomb of Queen Tiyi, bride of Amenophis III; details of the pictorial decoration in the chamber of the sarcophagus.

Tomb of Thutmosis IV; detail of the frieze depicting the rite of the Opening of the Mouth, in the presence of Isis, Osiris, and Anubis.

THE TOMB OF REKHMIRE

In the necropolis of Sheikh Abd al-Qurna, which contains tombs of high officials of Thebes from the XVIII dynasty, is the tomb of Rekhmire, 'Governor of the city and vizier' during the reigns of Thutmosis III and Amenophis II, one of the best preserved of the great civil tombs of the period. In the vestibule are depicted, aside from agricultural scenes, ceremonies of the presentation of tribute on the part of foreign peoples. This vividly realistic depiction is of great historic and artistic interest, with the five groups of men well characterized by their facial features and the gifts that they bear: Somalians, with short clothing, offer ebony, ivory, ostrich plumes, leopards, and chimpanzees; Cretans, with elaborate hairstyles, bring goblets, vases, and objects of goldsmithery; and black Africans, their flanks girded with panther skins, proffer ebony, ivory, animal pelts, ostrich eggs, feathers, precious minerals, gold rings, and animals, such as a jaguar, chimpanzees, and a giraffe.
The paintings in the royal tombs are of major importance due to their depiction of rituals of resurrection, scenes of royal life and images of the gods. Some of the best-preserved cycles are those in the tomb of Queen Nefertari, who was the wife of Ramesses II, the decoration in the tomb of Queen Tiyi, in which the royal falcon spreads his wings to protect the sarcophagus, and in the tomb of Thutmosis IV, in which individual gods open the pharaoh's mouth so that his soul can embrace eternal life. The iconography and types of scenes depicted remained unaltered over time — due to their intrinsic sacredness — with the exception of the 'realism' seen, uniquely, during the reign of Amenhotep IV.

Leptis Magna

In the fifteenth century Arab travellers in their notes described Leptis Magna as a ghost city preserved carefully by the desert. In 1921, Italian archaeologists were the first to excavate the entire city, fully three kilometres (two miles) in length. Now there is only desert here, but in antiquity this was a very favourable location in which to found a city: close by a natural harbour and in the centre of a zone made particularly fertile by the many mountain streams that poured down to the sea (among them, the Wadi Lebdah, from which the name Leptis derived). All around there extended a veritable sea of olive trees that in imperial Roman times made Leptis Magna the leading supplier of oil to the Eternal City. Founded by the Phoenicians between the tenth and the eighth centuries B.C., the city owed its importance to its port, one of the few natural harbours along the extensive coasts of Libya, which in turn channelled the trade of the peoples of the hinterlands in the interior. Originally a tributary of Carthage, at the beginning of the second century B.C. it was incorporated into the Berber Kingdom of Numidia: during the Jugurthine War which, between 112 and 105 B.C., saw bloody combat between the Roman army and the army of the Numidians, Leptis allied itself with the Romans, becoming a Roman *socia et amica*; around the middle of the first century A.D. the town was made a Roman *municipium*, and in A.D. 110 Trajan conferred upon it the status of *colonia*. But its period of greatest splendour coincided with the rule of the Severi, who were originally from Leptis: in A.D. 193 Septimius Severus awarded it *ius italicum*. Later, like in the rest of the empire, there was a process of decadence that was exacerbated by the destruction wrought in A.D. 455 by Vandals and Berbers; in the sixth century A.D. there was a brief moment of recovery with the Byzantines, only to be definitively abandoned two centuries later, as a result of the Arab invasions.

The first emperor to come from a province outside of Europe was Septimius Severus, born in Leptis Magna in A.D. 146 to a family that was not particularly illustrious. He began his career as a senator, which allowed him to occupy important military posts under the last of the Antonines; in the disorders that followed the murder of Commodus (December 192) he became emperor by defeating the other pretenders to the purple at the command of his legions. His government was based on the power of the army and was constantly at war, in Asia Minor and in Britain, where he died. His *Autobiography* has been lost, and all that remains of him are accounts of a man with frizzy hair, who never lost his strong Punic accent and who had few or no ties to the Roman Senate and the Italic tradition; he came from a distant, outlying province, and he married a learned Eastern woman profoundly rooted in Syrian cultural and religious traditions, Julia Domna (A.D. 158-217) who gathered around her a circle of scholars that included the wise men Philostratus and Aelian, the physician Galen, and the philosopher Diogenes Laertius. Septimius died in A.D. 211; the ensuing history of the family is punctuated by acts of violence. Only a year later his son Caracalla, in order to gain power, killed his younger brother Geta, possibly in the presence of his mother, even

Detail of one of the large statues set on either side of the cavea *of the theatre.*

Statue depicting Aesculapius, the Roman god of medicine.

Opposite page
Detail of the cavea *and the* scaena *of the theatre built during the reign of Emperor Augustus, first century A.D.*

though his father had planned for them to rule jointly. Caracalla, famous for his edict of A.D. 212 which awarded Roman citizenship to all the free inhabitants of the empire, died in 217, murdered in his turn by his Praetorian prefect Macrinus, who replaced him as emperor. From this point on, the female members of the family played a decisive role in the events of the Severian dynasty. Julia Maesa, the sister of Julia Domna, together with her daughters Julia Soaemias and Julia Mamaea, succeeded in reconquering power by having her eldest grandson Elagabalus proclaimed emperor (A.D. 218) at the age of fourteen, but he proved to be a poor choice, since the Praetorian Guard was hostile to the excesses and extravagance of the new dynasty, whose sole interest was to introduce in Rome the worship of the god Baal, of whom he was a priest and from whom he took his name. Julia Maesa then forced Elagabalus to adopt his cousin Alexander Severus (A.D. 221), which triggered more family conflict: the Praetorian Guard murdered Elagabalus and his mother Julia Soaemias and placed his cousin, still a minor, on the throne, with his grandmother, Julia Maesa, and his mother, Julia Mamaea, as regents. During the rule of Alexander Severus 'classical' jurisprudence enjoyed its highest development through the work of jurists such as Ulpianus and Julius Paulus.

When Leptis Magna first re-emerged from the desert, in the seventeenth century, the French consul Lemaire probably could not believe his eyes: he packed up a good number of columns, which are still in the Parisian Church of Saint-Germain-des-Prés, just as the English took some to embellish Windsor Castle. All the same, plundered though it was, Leptis Magna remained a veritable forest of columns. It is possible to distinguish two phases in the urbanistic development of the city: in a first phase, coinciding with the reign

THE ARCH OF SEPTIMIUS SEVERUS AND THE CRISIS OF CLASSICAL NATURALISM

The most famous monument in Leptis Magna is the great four-fronted arch built in A.D. 203 on the orders of Septimius Severus, in his own honour: the man who had come from that poverty-stricken, sun-baked area, one of the least valued corners of the entire Roman Empire, had risen to the dizzying height of the imperial throne, and upon his apotheosis he was determined to celebrate himself and his native city with a monument analogous to the one that he had ordered built in the same period in Rome on the occasion of the tenth anniversary of his rise to power. Set at the intersection of the *cardo maximus* and the *decumanus maximus*, the arch, consisting of four piers supporting a cap dome, did not present a structure that was innovative or particularly daring, and the same can be said of the Corinthian columns, the plinths, and the trabeation: the only exception are the half pediments at the top, which confer an anti-classical unfinished look to the structure as a whole. It presented a rich vegetal-motif decoration. On the interior of the piers and on the attic, instead, were placed large-scale reliefs depicting scenes of triumph and sacrifice: in particular, one façade was dedicated to the advent of Severus, one was dedicated to the sacrifice in honour of Julia Domna, one was dedicated to the investiture of Geta, and one was dedicated to the triumph of Caracalla. These ornamental high reliefs, now in the Museum of the Castle of Tripoli, provide the earliest documentation of new artistic principles which, by venturing away from the technique of detached relief and from the rational perspective typical of the classical visual language, marked the beginning of the vision of late antiquity. Indeed, the marble was worked with a drill, which, through its distinctive effect of chiaroscuro (light-shadow), conferred upon the composition an effect that was more colouristic than plastic. Most important, in the depiction of the triumphal scenes, it is frontality that dominates. One eloquent example is offered by the panel that describes the triumph of Caracalla, where, after the two rows of knights shown in profile, the imperial chariot is presented, with a forced perspective, 'frontal', so that the figures of the Severi appear in their full majesty.

Opposite page
Portrait of Julia Domna, wife of the Emperor Septimius Severus and the mother of Caracalla.

Detail of the Basilica of Septimius Severus with the columns of pink granite from Aswan and the Corinthian capitals.

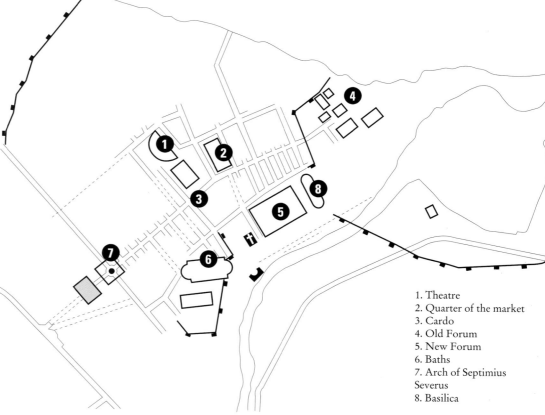

1. Theatre
2. Quarter of the market
3. Cardo
4. Old Forum
5. New Forum
6. Baths
7. Arch of Septimius Severus
8. Basilica

of Octavian Augustus, the preponderant merchant class did the most to rebuild in travertine on the Roman model the old unbaked-earth buildings of the Carthaginians. They also built the Old Forum, the heart of the city set close to the sea, the quarter of the market and the theatre. The theatre was one of the earliest in the Roman world, second only to Pompey's theatre in Rome, and it preserves intact its *cavea*, the *scaena* bristling with columns and decorated with elegant statues, as well as the natural backdrop of a glittering bright blue sea. Dating from the age of Hadrian were the baths (A.D. 126-127), not monumental but all the more significant in that they preserve intact the allure and vividness of another time. Septimius Severus also lavished special efforts in making his native city monumental, endowing it with grand and imposing buildings, which required the use of a vast quantity of Greek marble, since the area had absolutely none: one crucial element of the 'Severian addition' is the colonnaded triumphal way that runs from the sea, where

the monumental basin of the nymphaeum stands, and runs all the way to the new urban centrepiece, the Severian Forum. Built on the model of Trajan's Forum in Rome, it was surrounded on the three interior sides by a portico whose columns featured bases and capitals with the names of the Greek stonecutters engraved in them; set upon them were arches adorned with tondoes depicting heads of Medusa or Scylla. An analysis of these protomas, which in some cases show a clear adherence to the Graeco-Hellenistic tradition, in other cases more expressive references, and in yet other cases a hasty and slapdash execution, allows us to suppose the existence of a model imported from another centre and copied, in some cases with considerable variations, by local sculptors. On a short side of the forum stands the basilica, nearly 100 metres of columns made of red granite and white marble, closed on the sides by two apses upon which stood pillars richly decorated with acanthus leaves and grape vines, framing protomas, animals, and mythological scenes.

Detail of the cavea *and the second storey of the* scaena *of the theatre.*

Marrakesh

View of the Old City with the structure of the mosque.

Opposite page
Aerial view of the historic centre of Marrakesh.

The first dynasty to rule over Morocco was that of the Almoravids, nomadic Berbers from the Sahara, who founded an empire that extended at its high point from the Sahara to the River Ebro and from the Atlantic Ocean to Algeria. Around the year 1000, from an encampment on the northern slope of the nascent empire, the city of Marrakesh grew and developed, the splendid capital of the realm of Yusuf Ibn Tachfin. At the foot of the Atlas mountain range, surrounded by an immense palm grove, girded by massive walls, Marrakesh justifies its inclusion (1985) as a World Heritage Site because of its role in documenting the art and history of a complex and refined Middle Eastern culture, in which the Berber element was enriched by the influences of Black Africa, constituting a civilization that became a literary commonplace, a place that in turn was a symbol of the Middle East that had stimulated the Western imagination since ancient times. It was an allure built on buildings such as the ruins of the casbah of Abu Bakr, of the Mosque of Ibn Tachfin, and the Palace of Ali Ibn Yusuf, the last remaining traces of the Almoravid dynasty which capitulated in 1147 in the face of a new and intransigent religious movement, that of the Almohads. Under this new dynasty, relations became closer with southern Spain, and the fruit of this acculturation was the Mosque of Koutoubia (or Qutubiyya), with its minaret, identical and coeval with the Giralda of Seville, becoming the symbol of the capital and one of the first creations of an artistic dialogue that was almost never interrupted. Under the rule of this dynasty, moreover, the walls were enlarged and a vast new fortified casbah was built, which included all the structures that were typical of an independent city. In 1269 the capital was moved to Fez by the new ruling dynasty, the Marinids, or Banu Marin. Yet this period of decline allowed the construction of such important buildings as the *madrasa* of Ibn Yusuf.

A new period of flourishing art was encouraged by the advent of the Sa'adi princes who in 1510 rebuilt Marrakesh as the capital of a newly unified realm. In this period, an architecture developed that would found certain aesthetic paradigms of Islamic art, taking form in buildings such as the Sa'adi Tombs and the el-Badi Palace, or again in the reconstruction of the Mosque and *madrasa* of Ibn Yusuf, or the Mosque and *madrasa* of Sidi bel Abbes es Sebti, buildings that are exceptional examples of a golden period in the history of the capital, which lasted until 1659. The dynasty that still rules in Morocco is that of the Alawids, who moved the capital to Meknès. But Marrakesh continued to be a privileged spot, favoured by the benevolence of the kings, enriched with palaces and private residences of important personages of the court, and the Palace of Bahia is one of the finest examples. Gardens like the Aguedal and parks like the Mènara offer sites of ascetic contemplation; they are the result of parameters of construction that obey ancient canons, calling for porticoes, cloisters, and artificial lakes loaded with symbolic significance to the Garden of Delights where Mohammed was taken by the Archangel Gabriel.

Marrakesh also represents one of the places in which Islamic art most powerfully characterized its direction. For Islam the city is the fundamental location of the structures of power, and the architectural structures that it adopts are limited in number and extremely functional. The first in absolute terms is the mosque, and Marrakesh offers some splendid examples in the various solutions adopted by the ruling dynasties. The mosque in its numerous typologies is characterized as an enclosure with a portico on three sides; the

Geometric decoration on the tiles in an interior.

Detail of a bab *(gate) of the city. Their characteristic structure had square towers set on either side of the entry portal.*

side that points towards Mecca is generally deeper. The hall destined for prayer tends to be wider than it is long, in order to allow the greatest possible number of worshippers to pray towards the wall that faces Mecca. Another constituent element is the minaret, a structure that can be compared to the Christian campanile or bell tower, serving a similar function, with the *muezzin* who calls the faithful to prayer. An element that is often present is the *hammam* (bath), necessary for the ritual of purification. Typical is the *madrasa* (school), an institution in which the basics of the Koran are taught in the education of the learned in theological and juridical questions. The non-religious architecture includes the *suq* and the *bazaar*: markets have played a fundamental role in the *medina*, the historical centre of the city. As for the forms

of an essentially decorative art, the principal iconography of Islam is Arabic writing. From the Muslim iconoclasty which condemns idols and their worship, divine art has found its own form of expression in the invention of a script endowed with its own aesthetic value, obtained through an elaboration of the forms that is the product of a rigorous study of geometric ratios. A fundamental role is destined to the geometric decoration that is based on a repertory involving flat figures and their integration into lines of harmony; a harmony that is incorporated, with an almost vegetal repertory of styles, by the arabesque, which is technically characterized as an abstract floral motif.

Detail of the decoration of the courtyard of a madrasa *(Islamic theological school), fourteenth century.*

THE MOSQUE OF KOUTOUBIA

The Koutoubia is one of the largest mosques in the Muslim west. It is characterized by an Hispanic-Moorish style, and beneath an apparent simplicity it conceals a luxury of form and colour. It has a square tower made of pink sandstone, adorned with a delicate sculptural decoration. The minaret terminates in a lantern which is also square and decorated, topped by a ribbed dome. A first mosque, built after 1147, was later destroyed because its orientation towards Mecca was incorrect. The foundations of the first mosque are still visible today. The construction of the present-day mosque, built in accordance with the directives of Abd el-Moumen, was completed in 1158, at the behest of Yacoub el-Mansour. This splendid piece of Muslim architecture is subdivided into sixteen aisles and a larger central nave. The luxurious Almoravid ornamentation and the decoration of Andalusian inspiration, whose influence would affect much of the architectural work of Marrakesh, exalt sobriety and purity of line in a creation of exceptional artistic value.

Detail of the rich polychrome decoration for the main façade of a madrasa.

View of the loggia in the courtyard of a mosque; at the centre is a fountain.

USA

C A N A D A

UNITED STATES

MEXICO

Chichén Itzá

Teotihuacan

Havana BAHAMAS

CUBA

DOMINICAN REP.

JAMAICA

GUATEMALA BELIZE

HAITI

Copán HONDURAS

EL SALVADOR NICARAGUA

COSTA RICA

PANAMA

VENEZUELA GUYANA

SURINAME

COLOMBIA FRENCH GUYANA

ECUADOR

PERU

B R A Z I L

Machu-Picchu

Nazca *Cuzco* *Brasilia*

BOLIVIA

PARAGUAY

CHILE

ARGENTINA

URUGUAY

AMERICA America

Brasilia

This modern Brazilian capital was built at the prompting of President Juselino Kubitschek; it was begun in September of 1956 and completed in the very early 1960s. Since 1987 it has been considered a World Heritage Site by UNESCO, because it is one of the greatest examples and most organic expressions of the modern architectural movement of the twentieth century.

Brasilia stands on a plateau at an elevation of about 1,0000 metres, in the interior of the eleventh State of the Federation, created specially to house the capital. It lies about 1,000 kilometres from Rio de Janeiro and from the Atlantic coast in general. This considerable degree of isolation explains the city's still scanty population, even though its urban layout was conceived to accommodate about 800,000 persons.

The project of transferring the capital to the interior in place of the outlying city of Rio de Janeiro was initiated in 1956, and with that piece of legislation the plan was to encourage the population and economic development of the western regions, till then sparsely populated because of the concentration of almost all the population in the Atlantic coastal regions, and especially in the cities of Rio and Saõ Paulo.

Brasilia, designed and built by Lucio Costa and Oscar Neimeyer in the middle of the 1950s, caused a crisis in the progressive development of Brazilian architecture, a crisis destined to provoke a worldwide reaction against the precepts of the Modern Movement which permeated the entire project, not merely at the level of individual buildings, but also and especially on the scale of the entire overall project.

As with Le Corbusier at Chandigarh (1951), the conceptual dichotomy between the monumental isolation of the government centre and the rest of the city was to surface in Brasilia as well.

While Chandigarh paid apparent homage to the logic consecrated over time, i.e. the colonial chequer-board, or grid, Brasilia, despite its regular structure of *supercuadras*, was fundamentally based upon a cross-shaped plan.

The plan resulted in the development of two separate cities: the monumental governmental and business city, and the city of slums, or *favelas*.

The layout, based on an intentionally simple and elementary image, is formed by two intersecting axes.

The north-south axis is conceived as a modern highway, and it conveys traffic through the heart of the city. Along this axis are arranged all the residential areas, while at the intersection of the axis with the penetrating cross streets, specially equipped with multi-level platforms, are arranged recreational centres.

The east-west axis links the various executive and office districts and forms the monumental artery of the new political centre; the most important buildings (the executive office building, the Supreme Court building, and the Congress) are arranged around a triangular square, the Praça dos Três Poderes, while the cathedral is located in a separate isolated area, in or-

Detail of the bronze group of the Os Guerreiros (The Warriors) by Bruno Giorni that stands in front of the Palácio do Planalto.

The monumental granite Statue of Justice adorns the façade of the Ministry of Justice.

OSCAR NIEMEYER

Oscar Niemeyer was born on 5 December 1907 in Rio de Janeiro. In 1929 he enrolled in the National Academy of Fine Arts in Rio, where he studied architecture, with Alfonso Reidy, Helio Uchoa, Fernando Brito, and Milton Roberto.

He worked at Lucio Costa's studio in the Avenida Rio Branco.

From his meeting with Le Corbusier, which took place when the European architect travelled to Brazil for the modification of the overall urban regulatory plan of Rio in 1929, Niemeyer gathered the entire array of Le Corbuser's motifs (heavy reinforced concrete pillars plan, roof-gardens, free façades, window strips). Believing strongly in the potential offered by engineering technology and the expressive manipulation of reinforced concrete, Niemeyer reconciled the freedom of visual arts with building technology.

The first specific design collaboration involved the Brazilian master working interactively with Le Corbusier for the design of a new building for the Ministry of Education and Health in Rio, in which he polemically declared a radical rejection of the traditional construction techniques, touting the role of reinforced concrete as a material capable of triggering 'a true architectural revolution', because of the ease with which its shape could be manipulated.

In 1956, at the request of the Brazilian President Kubitschek and on the basis of the overall urban plan conceived by Lucio Costa, Niemeyer began to design the main buildings of Brasilia, inaugurating a construction yard that was to remain in operation until 1986. Among his creations was the Brazilian Pavilion at the New York World's Fair (1939), a manifesto of the modernist renewal of Brazilian architecture, and the residential complex of Pampulha near Belo Horizonte (1940). Forced, because of his Communist beliefs, to leave Brazil when the military took over in 1965, he left his imprint in France, Algeria, the Middle East, and Italy.

The twin towers of the Congress building overlook the man-made Lake Paranoa.

Overall view of the cathedral with its large, reinforced concrete ribs that support the frame of the construction and separate the polychrome windows.

Previous page
The dome of the Cathedral of Nossa Senhora Aparecida, designed by Oscar Niemeyer, with windows by Marianne Peretti and angels by the sculptor, Ceschiatti.

der to accentuate its monumental value.

The residential zones are arranged in very large super-blocks, designed as single units.

The absence of spatial restrictions made it possible to design a genuine ideal city. This was the masterpiece of Niemeyer, who has been nicknamed the poet of cement for the harmonious way in which he joined planes and lines together into a composition that made the most of the material used, in a repertoire of symbols that are found scattered through the city, for instance, the sword hilt in front of the Ministry of Defense.

Spread along the shores of Lake Paranoa, the plan of Brasilia was designed in the shape of an aeroplane, with the residential neighbourhoods on the wings and the ministries and embassies in the body of the imaginary aircraft.

It is a city with chiefly political and administrative functions; trade and industry have failed to develop there due to the lack of adequate infrastructure that isolates the city from the outside world.

Deserving special attention are: the national theatre, shaped like an Aztec pyramid; the television broadcast tower, 218 metres tall, with a viewing area at an altitude of 75 metres; the cathedral, considered one of the loveliest churches of the twentieth century; and the Praça dos Três Poderes (or Square of the Three Powers, in reference to the three branches of government), the centrepiece of the architectural creation assembled by the two architects.

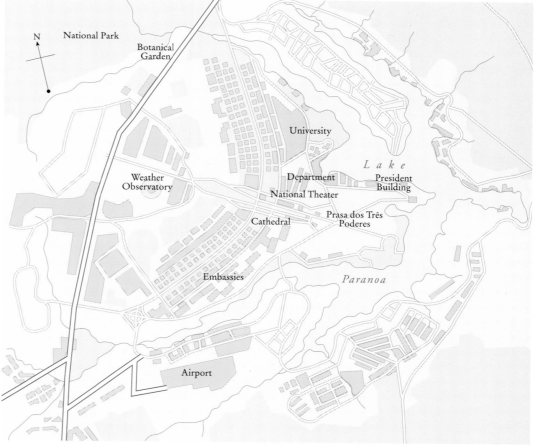

Aerial view of the city centre seen from the weather observatory. The Congress building can be seen on the far side of Lake Paranoa.

Plan of Brasilia in the form of an aeroplane.

Havana, the Old City

Detail of the façade of the cathedral, 1777.

Opposite page
One of the peculiar things about the Old City of Havana is the free-form association of typological models of all sorts, from the Arab horseshoe arch to Indian columns, while the array of colours selected for the plasters follows the whims of the population.

Havana has long been a popular destination for famous travellers, who sometimes reached the city in flight from a Mother Europe that had been all too stingy towards their yearnings for justice and liberty, for example, Giuseppe Garibaldi, and sometimes in search of a place offering a new outlet for their creative imaginations, as was the case with Federico Garcia Lorca and Ernest Hemingway. Situated on the Atlantic coast in a well-sheltered bay, the city was founded in 1515 by Diego Velasquez de Cuellar, who was also its first governor, with the name of San Cristòbal de la Habana, as a tribute to Christopher Columbus, who discovered the island, and to Habaquanax, an indigenous tribal chief: in 1607 it replaced Santiago de Cuba as the seat of the Spanish Governor and capital of the island with the simple name of La Habana. If on the one hand the history of the island has been determined over the centuries by its status as a Spanish colony, on the other, the intervention of the English-speaking peoples was a decisive factor not once, but twice, in imposing a new direction on Cuban affairs. A first great change took place in 1762 when English troops under Admiral Sir George Pocock, after a siege lasting forty-four days, took the city by attacking it from behind by land; they held the city for ten months, allowing the landholders, the merchants, and the shipowners to trade with the rest of the world. In fact, upon their return, the Spaniards found themselves obliged to modify their colonial policies and in part at least give up the monopolistic regime that they had imposed upon their colonial possession. Impatience with Spanish domination and the slave-based economy that prevailed in the plantations of the island grew throughout the nineteenth century, and finally exploded in the second half of the century in various independence movements, one of whose protago-

nists was the poet José Martì, who died before seeing a free Cuba, but who is still considered by the Cubans the father of their independence. In 1898 the explosion of the American battleship *Maine* in Havana harbour, the site of violent anti-Spanish demonstrations, gave an excuse to the United States to re-initiate hostilities against Spain and to occupy the island, which after four years of administration by the United States was to win its independence in 1902. Over the course of the first half of the twentieth century, Cuba found itself tied increasingly closely to the United States, which intervened repeatedly in its internal affairs, supporting now this and now that president or imposing various dictators. The Americans exerted great influence in economic terms and in terms of lifestyle: in Havana, great hotels and office blocks were built along the broad French-style boulevards built in the nineteenth century around the historic centre, while elegant new neighbourhoods were developed along the sea, crowded with luxurious villas and gardens. During the 1950s, under the dictatorship of Fulgencio Batista, while corruption ran rampant at every level, the city, which appeared to the *gringos* as an Eldorado where every sort of adventure was possible, teemed with businessmen in search of easy pickings, tourists in quest of legal gambling and promiscuous sex, adventurers and spies. All of this came to an end in a traumatic manner with the revolution of the *barbudos*, who, commanded by Fidel Castro, took power on 1 January 1959.

Habana vieja

Havana 'is the yellow of Cadiz, in a slightly darker hue, the pink of Seville, verging on carmine, and the green of Granada, but slightly phosphorescent like the scales of a fish': that is how Garcia Lorca resolved into pure terms of colour the powerful impression that

The Cathedral of Havana dominates the Old City with an architecture that was still influenced by the dictates of late European Baroque; it was completed in 1777 by Pedro Medina.

Details of the Castillo della Real Forza, rebuilt and consolidated between 1558 and 1577 because of the attack of the pirate Jacques de Sores.

TREASURES AND PIRATES

There were two underlying factors in the great wealth of the island of Cuba, first colonized in 1511. First of all, the island's fertility, because of which it was cultivated extensively with coffee, sugar, and tobacco plantations. The second factor involved its position: it lay athwart the routes of the galleons that transported precious cargoes from Central America to Spain, and this made its capital, Havana, an indispensable stop-over for technical and logistical requirements prior to setting off on the long and dangerous Atlantic crossing. Naturally, the steady flow of such immense wealth attracted pirates and corsairs: French, English, and Dutch buccaneers and filibusters, led by chiefs who were often shrouded in an aura of legend, such as Henry Morgan, all worked to sack and plunder Spanish ships and possessions. Havana did not escape their attentions: among the many who preyed on the city, let us mention the Frenchman Jacques de Sores, who took the city's garrison in 1554 and demanded a ransom of 30,000 pesos before he would leave, and the Englishmen John Hawkins and Francis Drake. Documentation of this violent and adventuresome history of attacks and plunder is offered by the city's impressive system of fortification, which over the course of two centuries took on a square configuration and basically made Havan invulnerable. The sole original fortress of the city, the Castillo della Real Forza, reconstructed and consolidated between 1558 and 1577 after the city's sacking by Jacques de Sores, was reinforced at the end of the sixteenth century by the addition of two other fortifications: the decision was made, in fact, to take advantage of the bay's bottle-neck shape to raise two strongholds on either side, the Castillo de los Tres Reyes del Morro and the Castillo di San Salvador de la Punta, both designed by the Italian military architect Battista Antonelli and completed in 1610. The two forts allowed a crossfire to be concentrated on the entrance to the bay, and also allowed a chain to be drawn across the narrows to close the entrance to the bay. In 1774, after the expulsion of the English, another fortress was built, the most powerful, the Fortaleza de San Carlos de la Cabana, meant to defend the city even from possible attacks from inland.

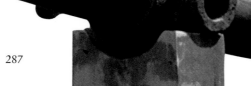

A square in the Old City gives the best view of the stronghold known as The Castle.

Aerial view of the city centre, with the dome of the Congress building and the Garcia Lorca Theatre.

this city — so distant and yet so evocative of the atmosphere of his own Andalusia — made upon him. The historic centre of the capital, the largest colonial nucleus of Latin America that has survived to the present day, developed along the bay and preserved its original regular grid of narrow lanes. If the Church of San Francisco (1719-38) is the most emblematic relic of the earliest Spanish period, the one just prior to the brief interval of English domination in 1762, in the last decades of the eighteenth century colonial Baroque also became common in Cuba. The architectural fervour here was not caused by the intervention of wealthy mine-owners, nor by the massive religious orders, as was the case in Mexico and in Peru; rather it was promoted primarily by the Spanish Crown, which ordered the construction of many brand new public buildings. The result was a monumental style enriched by indigenous characteristics, marked by lively but severe lines. The inexpensive materials used, a porous local stone that was poorly suited to carving and wood, was made up for by the

skilful use made of the architectural elements to confer movement to the façades and the taste for bright and lively colours. The architects Pedro de Medina, a Spaniard, and Antonio Fernandez de Trevejos y Zaldivar, a Cuban, were the chief masterminds of this renovation which focused primarily on two points in the city: the Plaza de Armas and the Plaza of the Cathedral. The Plaza de Armas was the centre of civil and secular power: on its western side stood the Palacio de los Capitanes Generales (1776-91), now transformed into the Museo de la Ciudad, a sumptuous residence arranged around a patio, enclosed by two orders of imposing stone arcades. This building, originally the seat of the island's governors, and then of the first presidents after the proclamation of the republic, and finally the city hall until 1958, served as the model in the nineteenth century for numerous other buildings in the city and on the island. During the restoration that was carried out on the building, the original wooden flooring was restored in the part of the square before it, intended to muffle the noise of

The façade of the Garcia Lorca Theatre, built in the second half of the nineteenth century, borrowing typologies from Parisian architecture of the period.

Detail of the equestrian monument to Antonio Maceo, overlooking the ocean.

Sign of the legendary bar, the Floridita, frequented by Ernest Hemingway, where the daiquiri was invented.

*View of a house in the
Old City of Havana in
which the modernist style
of the late nineteenth
century was varied in a
floral motif.*

*Opposite page
The historic centre of the
Cuban capital,
miraculously preserved,
shows the interesting
continuity of colonial
architecture and local*

*versions of international
modernism and Art
Deco.*

the carriage wheels and horseshoes. On the
northern side of the Plaza de Armas is another
noteworthy example of the local Baroque, the
Palacio del Segundo Cabo (1772-1776) or, as it
was originally called, the Casa de Correos: it
had been built as the headquarters of the Royal Post, and in republican times it was first the
seat of the senate and later of the supreme
court. It now houses various public offices.
Completing this plaza, alongside the nineteenth-century Palace of the Count of San-
tovenia, is El Templete, a small building erected in Neo-classical style in 1828 in order to
commemorate the mass that was said here on
16 November 1519 on the occasion of the first
settlement of San Cristobal de la Habana. The
Plaza de la Catedral, a marshy area throughout
the entire seventeenth century (it was in fact
called the 'Plaza de Ciénaga', or marsh), is
dominated by the façade of the cathedral: completed in 1777 by Pedro Medina on the site of
the previous Church of the Company of Jesus
(Jesuits), it represents the riches and most interesting example of Baroque religious architecture on the island. On the other three sides
of the square are elegant porticoed palaces,
private residences of the local nobility, built
in rivalry to the spectacular elegance of the
public buildings: these are the homes of the
Counts de Arcos (1741), Count Lombillo
(mid-eighteenth century), the older Palace of
the Counts de casa Bayona (1720), which still
preserves its eighteenth-century façade and,
lastly, the Palace of the Marquesses de Aguas
Claras. In these buildings we find exquisite
wrought-iron balustrades, instead of the wood-
en balconies painted a light blue so typical of
eighteenth-century Cuba, though they are also
present along the internal staircases; wood
painted light blue also covers the ceilings of
many of the rooms. UNESCO, in 1982, listed
the historic centre of the city as a World Heritage Site.

Copán

John Lloyd Stephens and Frederick Catherwood were the first outsiders to visit Copán in 1839. The enthusiasm and intelligence of John Lloyd Stephens, together with the talent as an illustrator of Frederick Catherwood, ensured the fame of the ruins and soon drew the attention of scholars. With the expedition of the Peabody Museum of Harvard, which began its work in 1891, Copán was the first Maya site subjected to scientific research. Today it is protected by the archaeological park of Paseo Quetzal, and in 1980 UNESCO added it to the World Heritage List.

This city stood in a small valley covering 24 square kilometres (about 9 square miles), surrounded by low mountains which presented tall column-like formations of volcanic tufa stone. Even though the earliest buildings in the Mayan metropolitan area date back to roughly two centuries earlier, the true urban development of the town of Copán took place between A.D. 400 and A.D. 900, the so-called Classic Period, thanks to the settlement of a Mayan dynastic institutional power that introduced hieroglyphic writing and new aesthetic standards. Rigid systems of hierarchical structure of social classes and centralization of political, economic, and religious life were introduced. The army became a system parallel to the oligarchic power, expressing legalized force, while the ruling dynasty became the element upon which the supremacy of the state was based, expressed in strategic alliances, dominations, and wars waged to conquer small towns and centres, some quite distant, in order to exact tribute.

The city extended its residential quarters around a central zone known as the Principal Group. This district was configured as a complex of structures that presented, to the north, a vast low expanse of public squares and, to the south, an artificially raised acropolis. The Great Square to the north contained a series of stelae all dedicated by the thirteenth sover-

eign, Waxaklalun ubah K'awil, on the occasion of great ceremonies that he organized in order to keep his realm in harmony with the powerful forces of the cosmos. The steps that surround it could accommodate 3,000 people, without counting the space available in the square itself, probably occupied by the part of the populace that was taking part directly in the ceremonies. After the death of this king, which took place during the course of a battle against his former vassal of the site of Quiriguá, the Great Square remained unmodified by his successors; his martyrdom so shocked the royal dynasty that his strongholds were considered a sacred heritage upon which later kings could no longer build.

The square, further south, was enclosed by the Ball Court, the Staircase of the Hieroglyphics with its temple, and by Temple 11. Information derived from the glyphs and from the excavation of the structures indicate that the Ball Court was built in its final version by the thirteenth sovereign. The platform upon which the field is set is divided into two parts: the area towards the north is fairly broad, while the other part was narrowed by the construction of two side scarps. The Staircase of the Hieroglyphics which rises up the pyramid of Temple 26 was built by the fifteenth sovereign, 'Sea shell Smoke' in honour of the last six sovereigns who had preceded him. Five of them, presented as great warriors and sacrificers, are depicted seated in the central axis of the staircase. In the high section of the pyramid, the sixth king, standing, is placed against the platform that held up the temple, since destroyed. On the risers of the steps we find a long text that recounts two centuries of dynastic history. As a whole, the building represents the cosmos: the underworld was depicted, at the foot of the stairs, by an altar in the form of a skull inhabited by snakes; the temple, decorated with parrots, symbols of

Aerial view of the archaeological site of Copán.

Opposite page
Carved head of a deity, a significant example of Mayan art.

Two views of the archaeological ruins of the 'City of Stone' of Copán.

the sun, represented the sky; the staircase is a serpent with its head facing downward that joins the upper and lower worlds, and supports on his back, between heaven and earth, the great ancestors. Temple 11 taken as a whole is a transposition of the universe, in which the upper level represents heaven or the sky, and the lower level, the earth and the underworld. The plan of the ground level is a cross oriented towards the cardinal points of the compass, as indicated by the four entrance doors, and the central hall was enclosed by glyphic panels depicting the skeletal maws of serpents, animals that symbolize the earth. It is surprising to find the same form in the cosmographic depiction featured in the *Tzolkin* of the Codex of Madrid. Since the lower space was better suited to circulation than to occupation, we may suppose that it was used for ritual processions, which certainly took into account the four directions indicated by the arms of the cross, reproducing the course of time.

The summit of the acropolis was crowned by Temple 16, which thus occupied the geographic centre of the complex and which extended out over the eastern and western courtyards. This monument was erected by Yax Pasah, 'Rising Sun', the last King of Copán, who died in A.D. 830, in memory of K'inich Yax K'uk Mo', the founder of the dynasty. A T-shaped block, at the top of the first flight of the staircase that runs up the pyramid, was decorated with rows of skulls accompanied by *kan* crosses, a symbol that signifies 'yellow' or 'precious'. At the far end of the western hall of the temple, a niche in the shape of a snake's jaw contained the statue of a king, his legs hidden by bird legs, bearing a severed head in one hand. This personage seems to be the same as the founder of the dynasty, who appears on Altar Q, at the foot of the pyramid. Here he presents the royal sceptre to Rising Sun on the day of his accession to the throne, surrounded by the preceding fourteen sovereigns. To all

THE MAYA CIVILIZATION

The Mayan Empire extended across south-eastern regions of Mexico, Belize, northern and central Guatemala, and north-western Honduras and El Salvador. Over the course of time that includes the Ancient Preclassical Period (2500-850 B.C.) the cultural elements that characterized the Maya people were defined. They developed their own urbanistic models with settlements in large villages constituted by houses built with perishable materials on platforms designed to insulate the houses from the moisture of the ground. In the Middle and Late Preclassical Period (850 B.C.-A.D. 200) there was a considerable increase in the number of settlements followed by a far-reaching transformation, both in social and cultural terms. The decoration of artefacts included complex symbolic content that emphasized the political and social changes ensuing from the evident triumph of an élite class in close conjunction with religious power. In the field of architecture, techniques were perfected. A further change was produced by the maturing urbanistic model represented by the presence of a ceremonial nucleus in the interior of the city, sharply differentiated from the ring-like bands of residences that ran around that nucleus. This period also witnessed the first use of a system of writing. During the Classic Period (A.D.-200-900) in the area of the central and southern plains, a social and political model was established on the foundation of the activities of a majority of city states, linked but basically independent. This phase of Mayan civilization can be considered as the period in which the phenomenon of expression in the various technological and artistic fields shows a clear degree of consolidated maturity. This period corresponds to the construction of the major monumental centres. The balance between the powers of the city state was not always constant and could be one of the causes for the decline of the most important centres at the end of the Classic Period and throughout the Postclassic Period (A.D. 900-1546). Other causes might be linked to catastrophic environmental events (floods or droughts) or excessive population growth.

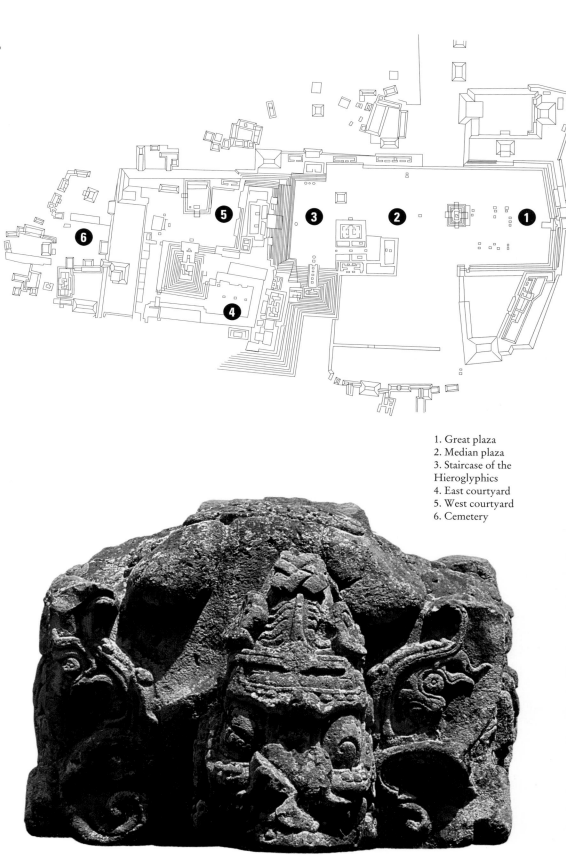

1. Great plaza
2. Median plaza
3. Staircase of the Hieroglyphics
4. East courtyard
5. West courtyard
6. Cemetery

View of the altar of a stele with its multiple carved faces.

of them were offered as a sacrifice the fifteen jaguars found in a stone cist, or tomb, carved into the ground right behind the altar.

Temple 18 is located in the south-eastern corner of the acropolis. A hieroglyphic text on the western wall of the inner chamber bears a date that corresponds to the year A.D. 800. A staircase that extends the full length of the temple provides access to the first room that opens towards the north. Beneath the bottom room there is a vaulted tomb, consisting of an antechamber in which a crypt has been dug. Originally, one could reach the tomb from Temple 18 via an interior staircase. The façade included four niches surrounded by feather decorations and separated by white lily flowers, featuring statues with masks of terrestrial monsters. The upper part of the walls was adorned with serpents with the same flowers in their maws. Anthropomorphic medallions set against a background of pearls, monsters, and serpents' heads with white wa-terlilies decorated the ceiling. Far from evok-ing death, this iconography focused on rebirth and fertility. The posts of the two doors bear carved portraits of 'Rising Sun' standing upon a mask of a terrestrial monster or an emblem of the earth. The sovereign is depicted as a victorious warrior armed with a spear and shield or else in the act of brandishing a scep-tre adorned with a roaring jaguar head, weighed down with trophy heads and ropes intended for use in binding his prisoners. The funerary monument of the king is a carved stele that was originally placed at the far end of the temple: the king is depicted dead and with his body sunk halfway into the underworld, represented by sea shells and bones.

Opposite page
View of several of the numerous carved stelae on the Great Plaza of Copán.

Detail of a carved deity, a significant epression of the Mayan civilization.

Detail of a sculpture depicting a seated man on the steps of Temple 12.

CALENDAR AND WRITING

The Maya had two ways of counting time. The Ritual Calendar, called the *Tzolkin*, was formed by the combination of the names of 20 days with the numbers from 1 to 13 and was linked to divinatory ritual. The first day of the cycle was '*1 Imix*', and before this particular combination could occur again, 260 days would have to pass. The Civil Calendar, instead, corresponded to the solar years, and was composed of 360 days, divided into 18 parts, similar to our months, each with 20 days. At the end of each year, in order to complete the cycle of the sun, a period of 5 days — considered unlucky — was added. According to the second type of calendar the agricultural cycles and numerous festivities were established. The combination of the two cycles took place once every 52 years, originating what was known as the Calendrical Wheel. The subdivision of time allowed this people to adopt another system to record the important dates of their history: it has been called variously the Initial Series or the Long Count, since it contained 20 years of 360 days, the *katun*. Thanks to the use of the Zero sign, considered an element of completion, this calendar covered a period of 5,125 years, whose 'year zero' was calculated to be 13 August of 3114 B.C. Numbers and dates were expressed through a 'glyphic' writing system. Each symbol engraved in stone or painted on strips of paper or parchment could have an ideographic value, expressing a complete concept, or else a phonetic value, so that a series of glyphs in succession could equal a word. Mayan writing was deciphered only recently, after lengthy study of the materials unearthed in excavations, such as stelae, and four codices that survived the Conquista: the Dresden Codex, the Madrid Codex, the Paris Codex, and the Grolier Codex.

Broad view of a number of archaeological ruins of the 'City of Stone'.

One of the numerous altars of the stelae, an exquisite example of the mastery of the Maya sculptors.

Opposite page
View of the archaeological ruins of Copán, one of the most important research centres for scholars of the Mayan civilization.

Chichén Itzá

Located on a limestone plateau extending over 300 hectares (about 750 acres) to the north-east of the Yucatàn peninsula, overlooking the Gulf of Mexico, stands Chichén Itzá. At the turn of the tenth century in the central area of the Mayan Empire, the cultural activities that had characterized the Classic Period (third to tenth centuries A.D.) came to a halt. Mayan sources, such as the *Chilam Balam*, tell of the arrival in the lowlands of groups of outsiders, headed by Kulkulcán, an historic personage whose name was translated by the Maya as Quetzalcoatl. One of these groups was the Maya-Toltec people of the Itzá. The social and political picture changed with the ensuing supremacy of military hierarchies over the authority of the priestly groups.

The date of foundation of Chichén Itzá is placed at A.D. 987. The name means 'Well Head of the Itzá', and refers to the distinctive feature of this territory, characterized by vast reserves of water, *cenotes*, circular in shape, produced by the collapse of the vaults of caverns where water runs, filtering through the porous surface stone.

The city developed around a main square upon which the monumental sacred edifices were built. The architecture of the Itzá, in contrast with the typical Mayan architecture, calls for the creation of very spacious interiors, while the effect of vertical reach had no functional purpose, but was strictly aesthetic in character, intended to arouse amazement in those who attended ceremonies and functions, especially crowds of soldiers who needed large spaces to assemble. The fusion of Mayan culture with Toltec culture is evident in the simultaneous use of richly decorated columns and flat roofs supported by beams. Toltec iconography dominates the architectural decoration of the buildings and exemplifies the reinforcement of

military power and the warrior spirit that pervaded the new vision of the cosmos: the Tzompantlis is a platform whose base is decorated with a sequence of human skulls, from which it takes its name, where perhaps prisoners of war were sacrificed. Just a bit to the south stands the Temple of the Jaguars, named for the procession of big cats carved into the architrave: inside were numerous rooms decorated with exceedingly colourful wall paintings with military scenes, while the columns of the various entrances present the king enthroned or military chiefs in war garb, carrying tribute offerings. Jaguars also appear in the so-called Platform of the Eagles and Jaguars, represented in the frieze of the lower dado as they devour human hearts. Probably this structure was used for the ceremonies preceding a battle, officiated by the priests in order to ensure the favour of the gods. The same type of decoration with an infinite series of warriors, from which it takes its name, is found also in the Temple of the Warriors. The jaguar appears as a sculptural depiction of the god Chac, a deity associated with rain and water, a fundamental element for human life, to whom precious gifts were offered and, less frequently than people seem to think, human sacrifices, as is shown by the materials uncovered in the Cenote Sagrado.

At the centre of the great plain stands the Pyramid of Kulkulkán, or the Castillo, which is astronomically oriented and marks the rise of the sun on the summer solstice and the setting of the sun on the

Aerial view of the site.

Detail of the figure of the god Chac-Mool: an altar upon which the sacrificial victims were lain.

Opposite page
Detail of the top of the sacred staircase of the Temple of the Warriors with a praying figure on the head of the feathered serpent Quetzacoatl.

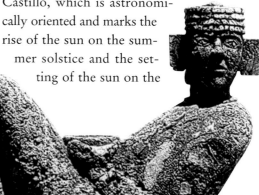

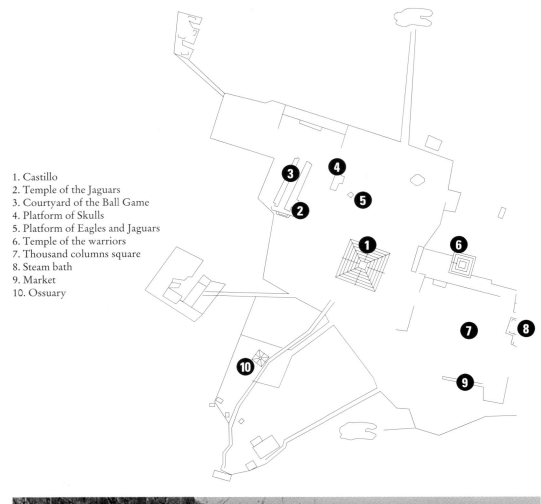

1. Castillo
2. Temple of the Jaguars
3. Courtyard of the Ball Game
4. Platform of Skulls
5. Platform of Eagles and Jaguars
6. Temple of the warriors
7. Thousand columns square
8. Steam bath
9. Market
10. Ossuary

THE BALL GAME

The presence of a playing field on the Olmec site of La Venta documents the antiquity of this custom. The Spanish Conquistadores forbade this practice, not only for religious reasons, but also because the Aztecs had a habit of betting heavily on the outcome, risking their lands, their property, even their own personal liberty. Before the Conquista, sometimes matches were held to resolve controversies over land or even politics. The Ball Game, in reality, was a true sacred ritual honouring the gods. Two teams of players were required to hurl a heavy rubber ball into the opposing territory, often with the aim of sending it through a stone ring set on the side walls bounding the field, quite high off the ground. To judge from the depictions of the players, engraved in stone or in the form of clay statues, we know that the players were covered with protective leather at the knees, the chest, and the head. It is thought that this game was played in order to assure the continuity and regularity of astronomic, meteorological, and agricultural cycles. It seems to have been meant to represent, in fact, the movement of the celestial bodies, with the ball playing the role of the sun. The sacred nature of this rite seems to have reserved participation to males only, and from the élite classes. Almost certainly the game culminated in a human sacrifice, but, according to the various theories of the scholars, it was thought that the victim was either the captain of the winning team, whose power and courage honoured the gods, or else the players of the losing team, who had failed to keep the ball — and therefore the sun — high.

Detail of the stone ring fastened on to the walls of the Courtyard of the Ball Game, through which the players tried to hurl a rubber ball.

Opposite page
View of the pyramid El Castillo that overlooks the great central esplanade of Chichén Itzá.

Panoramic view of the Temple of the Warriors, built in the thirteenth century, with distinct elements of the architecture and sculpture of the Toltecs.

View of the Temple of the Warriors, with the pillars decorated at their base with the head of the feathered serpent and the altar-statue of Chac-Mool.

Opposite page
Detail of a bas-relief with a ritual scene in the wall of the Courtyard of the Ball Game.

Detail of the frieze of skulls on the platform called the Tzompantli upon which, according to tradition, the heads of the human sacrificial

victims were hoisted on to pikes.

THE MAYA RELIGION

The literary sources drawn up by the Conquistadores and the first men of letters who came into contact with the Meso-American civilizations note that, according to the Mayan culture, the universe was created by the action of divine energies in order to perpetuate their own existence through a being different from all the others because of its self-awareness, man, who would therefore become the fulcrum of the world. The Mayan gods were invisible forces that could manifest themselves through natural phenomena or by assuming the semblances of animals or humans, and could materialize into the simulacra created by mere humans. Since the cosmos was in constant movement and change, even the gods could transform themselves, and above all they lived and died. They could be four in number, like the directions of the cosmos, thirteen, like the deities of the heavens, or nine, like the deities of the subterranean world.

The deciphering of the Mayan writing has allowed us to learn the creation myths of humans that were common in the Classic Period (A.D. 200-900). According to this cosmogony, sculpted on to the temples of the city Palenque, the First Father was born in 3114 B.C. He performed prodigious deeds and conquered death by reviving. The resurrection from the World Below transformed him into a young woman of extraordinary beauty who brought to earth the precious corn seeds. Corn appears as well in the myth handed down in the *Popol Vuh*, a text written in the *quiche* language. According to this version the primordial divine couple put an end to the chaos of the universe and organized the world by creating a pair of Divine Twins. They extracted from the mountains substances for nourishment, white and yellow corn: they ground it up nine times and with the precious flour they shaped the bodies of the first humans.

winter solstice, with an effect of light and shadow that is projected on to the head of the serpent with its undulating body stretching out along the parapet of the main staircase. Rising 55 metres high, the structure consists of nine stacked platforms, the last of them enclosed in a hall decorated with images of the god Chac. The access staircases each have 365 steps, the number of the days of the year. According to popular imagination, this pyramid represents the mountain where the First Mother shaped with a corn paste the first humans. Surely tied to astronomical activity is the round building rising from two rectangular platforms of the *Caracol*, literally 'snail', for the spiralling shape of its roof; this is a true work of architectural and scientific mastery. It is circular in shape and has numerous windows opening out from the spiral tower that make it possible to observe the movement of the stars, following their path created by the rotation of the earth.

The monumental complex possesses the largest ball court in Meso-America. This is an exceedingly long plaza, bounded on its long sides by two high walls, upon which were located the bastions and temples in which the inaugural rites were performed for the game, and upon which were placed two stone rings on each side, used in the Ball Game, or *Juego de la Pelota*.

The three principal cities of the Itzá people, Chichén Itzá, Uxmal, and Mayapán, joined together in an alliance known as the League of Mayapán, which lasted two centuries during which Toltec influence spread through the territory of Yucatán, with the resulting formation of a network of trade roads, which had been intensifying as far back as the Classic Period. But in 1194 war broke out and Mayapán conquered Chichén Itzá, which was destroyed. In 1441 the organization of a general revolt by the subject peoples caused the centralized system of the peninsula to collapse, establishing a series of local lordships too weak to keep from falling to Spanish power in 1531. The monumental ruins of the city were declared a World Heritage Site by UNESCO in 1988.

Teotihuacán

Although it was one of the greatest cities of ancient Mexico and, today, one of the largest archaeological sites on the American continent, it has no name. A UNESCO World Heritage Site since 1987, Teotihuacán was the name given it by the Aztecs when they occupied it towards the end of the first millennium of the Christian era, and because of its size they called it, in their language, *nahuatl*, 'birthplace of the gods'.

The systematic archaeological research begun in 1962 under the supervision of the National Institute of Anthropology and History of Mexico focuses on the typological analysis of the ceramics and on stratigraphic data correlated with carbon-14 dating; it has made it possible to break down the span of occupation of the city into six phases, beginning in the first century A.D. and culminating in the seventh century. In the first phase, Patlachique, the first settlement was built, but it was in the two successive centuries, between A.D. 100 and 200, the Tzacualli and Miccaotli phases, that the first monuments were built. The development of the city seems to have taken place due to the migration of peoples in search of natural resources for subsistence, land to farm and convenient sources of water. Later, the increase of agricultural production and the introduction of technological inventions that led to the formation of a system of long-range trade imposed the need for a complex and articulated political and social organization in the form of a theocratic state run by a priestly class. For four centuries, the Tlamimilolpa and Xolalpan phases, Teotihuacán spread its influence over the surrounding territory, attaining an expansion over 20 square kilometres (about 8 square miles), still evident today thanks to the ruins of the foundations of the buildings, and a population of 125,000 inhabitants. The collapse of the system of government and the invasion by warrior peoples from the north, such as the Toltecs and then Aztecs, led to the abandonment of the settlement around A.D. 600-650 (Metepec phase).

The city lies 48 kilometres (thirty miles) to the north of Mexico City in a fertile valley watered by two rivers, the Rio San Juan and the Rio San Lorenzo. The main thoroughfare along which the numerous sacred and residential buildings were developed was the Boulevard of the Dead (Avenida de los Muertos). Some two and one-half kilometres (one and one-half miles) in length, it was probably designed at the moment of the foundation of the urban centre, since along its entire length, from north-east to south-west, it is lined with sacred buildings. To the south it intersects perpendicularly with the canal that was excavated to regulate the flow of the Rio San Juan and into which the water drains from beneath the road paving. The artery's width ranges from 40 to 95 metres (130 to 310 feet) and it appears that it runs to the mountains which rise to the south of the city. The northern part of the road opens into a plaza that lies in front of the Pyramid of the Moon, which is oriented southward and comprises five staggered platforms. If you position yourself at a certain distance from it while remaining on the main road, you can align the height of the pyramid exactly with that of the mountain behind, the Cerro Gordo. The plaza is surrounded by fifteen other pyramid structures, including the Palace of Qutzalpapalotl. On the eastern side of the road, midway along its length and square in the centre of the urban complex, oriented in accordance with the trajectory of the sun, stands the Pyramid of the Sun. The original building measured 215 metres (705 feet) on each side and 63 metres (207 feet) tall, but over the course of time it was renovated twice so that it is now 225 metres (738 feet) long on each side. In contrast with

View of the Pyramid of the Moon.

Opposite page
Detail of a frieze.

Detail of the massive flight of steps in the Pyramid of Tlàloc-Quetzalcoatl.

The frieze from the Pyramid of Tlàloc-Quetzalcoatl allegorically represents the alternation between the god of rain and the supreme deity of the Aztec pantheon as a symbol of the equilibrium of the universe.

MEXICAN CIVILIZATIONS

The earliest civilization, known only through archaeological finds, was that of the Olmecs. It was Bernardino de Sahagún in the first half of the sixteenth century who gave this name to the natives who lived in the coastal jungle on the Gulf of Mexico; it means 'peoples of caoutchouc'. They settled in the present-day territories of the Mexican states of Veracruz and Tabasco around 1800 B.C. Worshippers of the jaguar god, they spread throughout central and southern Mexico only to disappear mysteriously around 300 B.C. Their monumental art, which includes the well-known Olmec basalt heads and countless stelae are their most important relics. Later, around 200 B.C., the Zapotecs and Mixtecs took power; their superior culture can be recognized in the astronomical notions according to which the sacred buildings of the city of Monte Albán were erected.

From the end of the eighth century A.D., Mexico was invaded by the Toltecs, a population from the north. Organized in military clans, they overlapped with other tribes of *nahua* descent and assimilated their culture. The distinctive features of their civilization are large constructions, such as pyramidal temples, playing fields, and their remarkable statuary, prevalently zoomorphic, depicting their pantheon of deities in the form of jaguars and feathered serpents. The last pre-Conquest civilization, and the best known thanks to their contacts with the Spanish who conquered their territory, was the Aztecs. According to Mexican tradition, the migration of the Aztecs

began around 1160, from the northern regions of
Mexico. At the end of the twelfth century the cultural
unity that had developed in Teotihuacán around the
Toltecs broke down in the wake of the struggles
between tribes and the invasions of the Chichimecs,
who came from the north. The Aztecs settled in the
north-western regions of Mexico in the fourteenth
century. They were governed by Colhuacan, and then
by Atzcapotzalco. Later they took refuge on the
islands of Lake Texcoco where they founded a
kingdom whose capital was Tenochtitlán and whose
ruling dynasty was begun by Acamapichtli in 1375.
Under Montezuma I (1440-69) the war extended
southward; his son, Axayacatl (1469-81), advanced
victoriously as far as Oaxaca. After Axayacatl and
Tizoc (1481-86) Ahuitzotl took the throne in 1486 and
extended his dominions as far as Guatemala. His
successor Montezuma II, or Motecuhzoma (1503-
20), the son of Axayacatl, was faced with the
Spanish invasion. The Spanish led by Cortes, after
various episodes, took control of Tenochtitlán and
captured Montezuma II, who died in prison, while his
brother and his nephew, Cuitlahuac and
Cuauhtemoc, tried in vain to organize a last-ditch
resistance and were hanged in 1525. The countless
Aztec deities represented the various forces of
nature. A place of honour belonged to Huitzilopochtli,
god of war, manifestation of the sun, and lord of the
world: he placated hunger and thirst with the flesh
and blood of his enemies, and therefore numerous
victims were regularly sacrificed from among the
prisoners of war.

*Detail of bas-relief with
the figure of an eagle in
one of the pillars in the
central courtyard of the
Palace of Quetzalpapatl.*

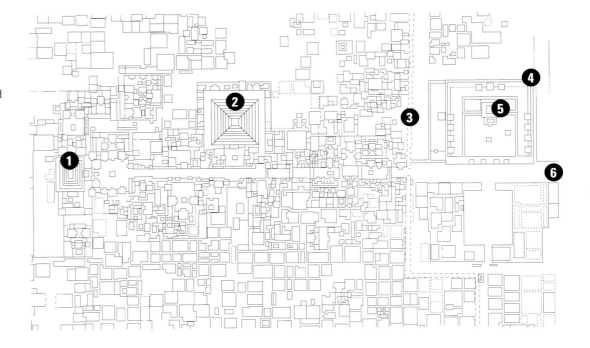

View from the Pyramid of the Sun of one of the smaller temple structures of the city.

1. Pyramid of the Moon
2. Pyramid of the Sun
3. Rio San Juan
4. Ciudadela
5. Pyramid of the Feathered Serpent
6. Boulevard of the Dead

the Pyramid of the Moon, it had four platforms; the fifth platform that we see today was reconstructed by mistake by the first scholar of the site, Leopoldo Batres, at the beginning of the twentieth century.

The city is divided into two sections by the canal of the Rio San Juan to the south of which lies the sacred complex called the Ciudadela. This presents itself as a broad plaza 400 metres (about 1,300 feet) on each side to the east of the Avenida de los Muertos, surrounded by four platforms topped by pyramids in the north, west, and south sectors. The eastern side is occupied by three other pyramids along the edge of the plaza, and by another enormous structure shifted towards the centre. Called the Pyramid of the Feathered Serpent, it is the most important monument in the city. It was built around A.D. 200 atop an existing building, of which a few traces of flooring and walls remain in the underlying sectors. It is 65 metres (213 feet) long on each side, and it is now only 19.4 metres (about 64 feet) tall. It is rather difficult to say

exactly how many platforms it comprised, though the most recent research suggests six or seven. All four sides of the temple structure are covered by blocks of worked stone and are decorated with elaborate sculptures. Today only the main façade remains almost perfectly preserved; it was covered by another structure built later, around the fourth century, known as the Adosada platform. The excavation of this building unearthed architectural fragments in an iconographic style similar to that of the sculptures of the Temple of the Pyramid of the Feathered Serpent. Other materials uncovered in the same context bear traces of an exposure to high temperatures, leading us to suppose that the sacred complex had been burned. The ruins of the structure, inasmuch as they were sacred, were not destroyed but instead buried with the construction of the Adosada. The iconographic motifs, carved on the interior of the rectangular cornices on the walls that constitute the platforms, mostly depict serpents whose feathered bodies slither across the stone background. The head with its gaping jaw is carved in full-relief on both the walls and on the parapets of the staircases. The bodies of the different serpents are divided by images depicting the heads of zoomorphic creatures. Their identification with the iconography of the gods is still quite difficult to decipher: it is possible to recognize Tlaloc, the god of storms; Youalcoatl, in the shape of a feathered serpent with different and specific characteristics compared to the supreme god; Itzpapalotl, in the shape of a butterfly; Cipactli, the crocodile also depicted in Aztec codices, and Xiuhcoatl, the Serpent of Fire.

The excavations around and inside the platform, begun in 1917 by Ignacio Marquina and still under way, are conducted by the Mexican Institute in collaboration with the Department of Anthropology of the University of Arizona. So far they have uncovered some two hundred burial sites. Of particular importance seem to be a number of tombs in specific locations in the interior of the temple structure. The stratigraphy of the inhumations shows that the burials were done in conjunction with the construction of the building. Despite the lack of definite proof from studies of the bones concerning the cause of death, many of the individuals were found with their wrists tied behind their backs. This allows us to guess that these were victims of human sacrifice.

View of the Pyramid of the Sun from the plaza of the Pyramid of the Moon on the thoroughfare of the Boulevard of the Dead, or Miccaotli.

Detail of the mighty staircase of the Pyramid of Tlàloc-Quétzacoatl.

Cuzco

Cuzco, or *Qosqo* in the ancient language of the Quechua, is located in the depression of the valley of the Rio Huatanay at about 3,360 metres (about 11,000 feet) above sea-level. On three sides, the mountains rise up sheer, while on the south-east side the valley opens out, extending for miles between two walls of mountains, a succession of fertile plains and marshy expanses.

Archaeological research has made it possible to date to around 1000 B.C. the earliest human presence in the valley, documented by finds of ceramic artefacts. Subsequently, the territory formed part of the Chanapata culture, which takes its name from a suburb of Cuzco where fragments of ceramics, bone tools, weapons, and clay figurines indicate the presence of a long-ago settlement. It was not until A.D. 750 that solid structures began to be built under the reign of the Wari. It has now been shown that the Inca civilization began to evolve around the year 1200, in agreement with mythical tradition. The moment of maximum expansion of the Inca Empire dates back to 1400 and it would appear that Cuzco was rebuilt in accordance with a good regulatory plan in exactly this period under the ninth Inca, Pachacuti Yupanqui, in 1438.

Starting from the central square, called Huaycapata, and following the regular grid of the streets, extended the twelve circumscriptions of the city, divided into roughly four sections, which represented the four principal orientations or cantons of the world that gave the empire its name: *Tahuantisuyo*. Around it stood the monumental residences of the Incas and the Palace of the Chosen Virgins, Acclahuasi, which, along with the houses of the nobles, structures that rose as high as three storeys, formed Lower Cuzco, *Hurin*. These buildings, even today, surprise us for the skill of the workers in laying huge stones one atop the other without the help of modern machinery. The most widely accepted thesis holds that the hewn stones were pushed on wooden rollers with the help of pounded earth ramps, and then hoisted using as handles rock protuberances that had been specially left in place. It was only in a second phase that the walls were carefully cut and smoothed. The external parts of the buildings were left undecorated, but the most important buildings were covered with sheet gold; most of the gold plunder that came from Cuzco, which was meant to pay the ransom of the Inca Atahuallpa, consisted of sheet gold that had evidently been taken from the external walls. The more modest neighbourhoods in Upper Cuzco, *Hanan*, had low houses made of sun-baked mud, painted red or yellow, and covered with a thick layer of straw.

In that period the two rivers that flowed in from the north were channelled between banks of worked stone. To the south the towering Temple of the Sun occupied the highest eminence. This complex structure consisted of six principal buildings: the sanctuaries of the Sun, Moon, Stars, Lightning, and Rainbow, as well as a sort of refectory for the priests of the Sun; all of these buildings surrounded the *Inti Pama*, the Field of the Sun. In its vast central section, there was a gold-plated fountain upon which was engraved an image of the sun. The exterior of the building was sheathed in sheet-gold that was so massive that each panel weighed between 4 and 10 pounds. The roof was covered with thick layers of plant matter, but it is generally agreed that amongst that material there were also gold threads that each day reflected the rays of the sun at sunset; the Field of the Sun itself was a reproduction of a garden with leaves of grass, corn cobs, flowers, and animals, all in cast and wrought gold. Adjoining the temple was the other most important building of Cuzco: the Coricancha, on the site where legend recount-

View of Inca constructions in the area of Cuzco.

Opposite page
View of one of the colonial quarters of the city.

ed that the first building had been erected by the first Inca. Here the priests, the Virgins of the Sun, and the Inca performed rites in honour of the Father God Inti. Nearly every month (the Incas had a twelve-month calendar), feasts of purification of the earth and its rebirth in the springtime were celebrated. The most important feast was *Inti Raimi,* in June, dedicated to the sun.

To the north of the city stands Sacsahuamán, an enormous fortress, the *pucara* of Cuzco. It was begun by Pachacuti, 'He Who Causes the Earth to Tremble', after 1438. The most important fortifications look northward; on this side there is an uninterrupted wall almost 400 metres (about 400 yards) in length. This Cyclopean wall is formed by three orders of stone, with forty-six terraces inserted in as many points; the three parapets that rise to a total height of some 20 metres (about 60 feet) are built with salients, recessed angles, and buttresses. There were only three gates. At the two extremities of the subterranean passages there were two square military towers (*mayumarcas*), an enormous water cistern with stone-lined aqueducts, in which the water ran from one place to another, a palace for the Inca of extremely refined construction, storehouses for provisions and weapons, lodgings for soldiers and for the persons in charge of defence and regular maintenance.

With Francisco Pizarro's entry into Cuzco in 1533 the city was transformed into what it is today. The Church of Santo Domingo was built on the structure of the Corichanca while the Palace of the Virgins became the Convent of Santa Catalina. One of the Inca palaces overlooking the Huaycapata, transformed into the Plaza de Armas, houses the Baroque Church of the Compañía.

We offer translations of a number of passages taken from reports written by the Con-

THE INCA EMPIRE

The origin of the Incas and the foundation of the city of Cuzco are linked to the same myth. Legend has it that the god Inti, which in the spoken language of the Andean people, the Quechua, means 'sun', forefather of the human race, sent two of his sons to gather the natives into a community and to teach them the arts of civilized life. Manco Capac and Mama Oello Huaco, brother and sister, husband and wife, set out therefore from Lake Titicaca in search of a place to found the new civilization. According to the instructions of their father the god, they were to reach a plain in which the golden staff that they had been given would sink completely into the earth, disappearing forever. The prophecy came true in the valley where Cuzco now stands, a name that in the language of the Incas is said to mean 'navel'.

The archaeological documentation and the reports left by the Spaniards make it possible to reconstruct a more plausible scenario whereby the inhabitants of the valley of Cuzco, because of the constant conflicts with neighbouring peoples for possession of the fertile valley, adopted a policy of constant aggression that led them to build a vast empire: *Tahuantisuyu*. The realm was divided into four regions, or *suyu*: starting from the centre, that is, from Cuzco, it extended eastward into the territories covered by Amazonian forest, the *Antisuyu*; to the south-west, from Lima to Chile, was the *Cuntisuyu*; to the south-east, Lake Titicaca, Bolivia, and mountainous bulwarks of Argentina formed the *Collasuyu*; the entire territory to the north of Cuzco, part of Peru and all of Ecuador with the city of Quito, formed part of the *Chinchasuyu*. The administration of the empire was based on the planning of production through the division of labour. The population was subdivided into *ayllus*, communities that devoted themselves to certain forms of work in order to pay the sovereign a *mita*. This was a tax that took the form of work or service, which might be agricultural in nature, such as raising corn or llamas, or else artisanal, such as the production of fabrics, or service-related; for instance, the village of Curahuasi had the obligation to keep the rope bridge over the Apurimac Gorge in perfect operating condition. This organization kept the entire population safe and well fed, since the Inca himself, in collaboration with his officials, divided up among one and all his *puric*, or subjects, the revenue and yield of production.

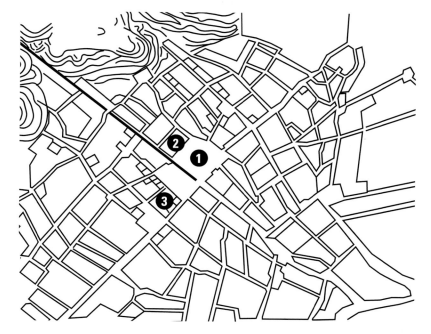

1. Plaza de Armas
2. Church of the Compañía
3. Cathedral

Ruins of the giant megalithic walls of the capital of the Inca Empire.

Opposite page
Masonry from Inca settlements in the area of Cuzco.

INCA LITERATURE

Pedro Sarmiento de Gamboa was commissioned by the Viceroy of Peru to write an official history of the Inca, intended as a justification of the Spanish Conquista. He began work in 1569, gathering all the tribal chiefs who knew the past history of the Inca. Since there was no system of writing, the accounts of the various Indios were based on oral tradition, which each father handed down to each son, insisting on repetition and relying on the mnemonic assistance of the *quipo*. The *quipo*, in Quechua, means simply 'knot', and is an instrument formed by a main cord to which smaller cords of various colours are attached, featuring knots at regular distances. The knots were meant to represent numbers, while the little cords represented a certain object. The *quipos* found in the tombs today are silent, because no one has yet succeeded in attributing to each length of twine or elaborate knot its real significance. Among the information that has come down to us from the Spaniards who heard the translations of the *quipo*, we still preserve a legend that was apparently performed as a drama, with songs and dances, during festivities. It is known as the *Drama of Ollantay*. This Ollantay, who gave his name to his native village, Ollantaytambo, which still exists, was a feudal noble who asked for the hand in marriage of an Inca princess. The sovereign grew enraged at this presumptuous act, since marriages took place only within specific classes, and he sent his daughter to the *Acclahausi*, the residence of the Virgins of the Sun, with the assigned task of tending to rites honouring the father god. Ollantay violated the boundaries of the sacred precinct to visit her and was captured. He managed to flee, however, and instigated a revolt against the Inca. When a frontal attack failed, the Inca's fortress was taken by treachery. In 1780, this account was transformed into a full-fledged theatrical opera by Antonio Valdez of Tinta in Peru.

One characteristic of Inca architecture is the masonry assembly of dry-walled polygonal stones in which the apertures are generally trapezoidal in shape.

Fortified façade of the Jesuit church, built on the ruins of the royal Inca palace.

The complex structure of the vaults of the cathedral cover the ruins of one of the Inca royal palaces of Cuzco.

quistadores after they reached Cuzco, to document the astonishment that this city, the creation of a supposedly primitive people, created in them: 'This city was very great and rich in enormous buildings and was divided up into quarters; when the Spaniards entered it for the first time there was a great many people, a populace of over forty thousand families in the city itself and two hundred thousand in the quarters surrounding the city for a distance of at least twelve leagues; it was the most populous city of the entire kingdom. This city is the finest and the largest that has ever existed on earth, especially in India, and I say to Your Majesty that it was so fine and rich in magnif-

icent buildings that it is truly something to see. It has streets paved for many leagues. The square itself is made of many small stones, all of the houses of the nobles are made of carved and hewn stone. On the slope of a mountain that looms over the city is a fortress made with such fine stonework that the Spaniards, who have travelled widely through strange lands, say that they have never seen anything of the sort. Through the city and out into the plains for at least twenty leagues there flows a river within a paved canal, something that has never been seen or heard of'.

In 1983 UNESCO declared Cuzco a World Heritage Site.

The emphatic style of colonial architecture, with the ample use of decorative elements borrowed from Spanish culture, can be found in the magnificent wooden choir of the cathedral.

View of the Plaza de Armas with the Cathedral and the Jesuit Church.

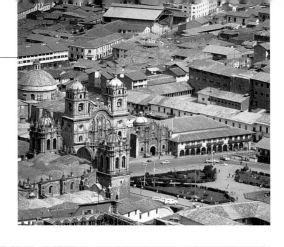

320

View, from the roof of the Jesuit Church, of the façade of the cathedral and the valley of Cuzco.

The monumental Baroque façade of the cathedral, overlooking the Plaza de Armas, displays a typology inherited from European Baroque culture, with the double bell tower.

Machu Picchu

Following the route of the *Capac Nan*, the Royal Road, setting out from Cuzco and heading north into the canyon created by the waters of the Rio Urubamba, at an elevation of about 3,000 metres (9,850 feet), one reaches the city of mystery *par excellence*. Perfectly set in the saddle between two peaks, no one knows its actual name; everyone knows it as Machu Picchu, or Old Mountain, which refers to the highest peak, while further north stands the Huayna Picchu, or Young Mountain.

The elevation, the blanket of clouds, the forest, and the architecture that is perfectly integrated with the surrounding landscape, all conspired to keep it concealed from the world until 1911, when it was discovered by Hiram Bingham, an archaeologist from Yale University.

The Cyclopean walls that protect it also served the function of retaining the distinctive terraces, or *andenes,* seen throughout the Andean Cordillera, carved into the rock and created in order to increase the amount of living and farming space; a daunting task because the earth was brought up, carried on human shoulders, in baskets, all the way from the valley below. The city, as is always the case in Inca urbanistics, is subdivided into quarters: in the upper part stood the royal residences and the sacred areas; down below stood the houses of the populace, divided by a large public square, Intipampa, and by the House of the Virgins of the Sun, Acclahuasi. The buildings are all made with perfectly cut blocks of stone, joined together without mortar or any type of adhesive.

The entrance has the appearance of a great square tower with five doors opening in it and decorated by nine trapezoidal niches. The road, now wedged between building and often made up of staircases, leads to the Torreon del Sol, whose worked blocks, following the slightest irregularity of the rocky spur on which it

stands, protect the underground cavern, the site of a tomb. The three trapezoidal windows offer a view that includes the whole city towards the rising sun. On the same terrace stand the royal apartments and, to the north, the Inticancha, the Sacred Square, facing the main temple: two walls run from the base wall, adorned with niches at their top, while the altar stands in the middle, a rectangular megalith more than 4 metres (12 feet) long. Immediately adjacent is the Temple of the Three Windows, consisting of a long hall, opening out in three windows, as the name suggests, which are as always trapezoidal. Much higher up, on the steep upper plane, the Intihuatana dominates the city. The 'Place to Bind the Sun', as its name signified, stands at the top of a long staircase. On the upper terrace, small halls and chapels adorned by the characteristic horizontal windows probably served as service areas for the personnel performing the ceremonies. The chief structure consists of a large boulder carved to form a horizontal plane upon which a vertical column stands, creating a meridian, a sundial. The shadows cast by the column indicated the month and the season, according to which the Indios conducted their lives. The sun, symbolically linked to the stone, was celebrated at the winter solstice, on the darkest day, to beg it not to abandon its children.

The city's discoverer believed that he had found Vilcabamba, the city to which the last Inca fled with his entourage to escape the Spaniards, who in fact never caught him. This belief was bolstered by the fact that many of the mummies found in the mountain necropolises were women, and therefore possibly Virgins of the Sun who had accompanied the Inca in his flight.

Certainly, the city had never been seen by the Spaniards, as it is not mentioned in any of the accounts of the Conquistadores and, most important, it shows no trace of the destruction that

View of the archaeological site.

Opposite page
The settlement of Machu Picchu was built in the cordillera of Vilcabamba along the course of the River Urubamba and divided into quarters with the royal residences and the sacred areas in the upper section. In the distance is the summit of Huayna Picchu.

Detail of the royal quarter and the sacred area of the city, built between 1460 and 1470 by the Inca Pachacuti Yupanqui.

Detail of the terracing, with dry-wall retaining walls running along the slope.

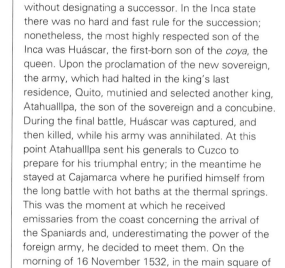

1. Sacred rock
2. Central plaza
3. Temple of the Three Windows
4. House of the Great Priest
5. Ceremonial baths
6. Monumental entrance
7. Residential quarter
8. Funerary rock

THE END OF THE INCA EMPIRE

When Pizarro sailed along the Peruvian coast for the first time, the Inca Empire was going through a period of crisis. The last king, Huayna Capac, had died without designating a successor. In the Inca state there was no hard and fast rule for the succession; nonetheless, the most highly respected son of the Inca was Huáscar, the first-born son of the *coya*, the queen. Upon the proclamation of the new sovereign, the army, which had halted in the king's last residence, Quito, mutinied and selected another king, Atahualllpa, the son of the sovereign and a concubine. During the final battle, Huáscar was captured, and then killed, while his army was annihilated. At this point Atahualllpa sent his generals to Cuzco to prepare for his triumphal entry; in the meantime he stayed at Cajamarca where he purified himself from the long battle with hot baths at the thermal springs. This was the moment at which he received emissaries from the coast concerning the arrival of the Spaniards and, underestimating the power of the foreign army, he decided to meet them. On the morning of 16 November 1532, in the main square of Cajamarca, Atahualllpa was captured by treachery after witnessing the slaughter of his entire army which had come unarmed in honour of the visitors. During his imprisonment he became acquainted with his enemy and understood that they had been lured to his lands by a thirst for gold. And so he struck a deal with Pizarro to free him after the delivery of a lavish ransom. All of the subjects of the realm were summoned to deliver as much gold as they could: the gold coverings of the buildings were disassembled, all of the recipients of the royal household were gathered together, statues of the gods were confiscated. After splitting up all the plunder, the Spaniards decided that it would not be safe to release the Inca, because he could gather a number of armies to fight them. On 29 August 1533, following a false trial, Atahualllpa was sentenced to death.

The funerary fort with, in the foreground, the building known as the House of the Guardian of the Tombs.

Details of the construction methods of the Inca civilization that used roughly hewn boulders; they also made walls incorporating large rocks hewn to exceedingly precise geometric shapes.

Opposite page
One of the terraces built to defend the city on the slopes of the mountain.

they had visited on all Inca religious buildings.

Some scholars believe that it was built about 100 years before Pizarro's conquest of Peru; others believe that it is much older. The type of architecture (listed as the last style by scholars, polygonal and monumental, characterized by the custom of building walls at a slight incline, so that the base was wider and therefore better suited to support the weight of the stones above) suggests that it was built during the reign of the Pachacuti Inca Yupanqui, the great rebuilder of the empire.

The ease with which it could be defended, so high on the mountain slopes was it perched, and the protection provided by two enclosure walls, an interior wall and an exterior wall, suggests that from the beginning this was a military fortress or a very important bulwark in the empire, one that would be staunchly defended: a sanctuary dedicated to the cult of the ancestors and the sun god.

It is also possible, however, that Machu Picchu was an imperial *llacta*. The *llactas* offer the best evidence of the imperial spirit of the Inca and their urge to dominate permanently the peoples that they had conquered. These were settlements built along the Royal Road, intended to control and administer the economy of the various regions conquered; these were bureaucratic cities, in which the administrators and officials of the Inca court resided, and inasmuch as they were self-sufficient cities, they had their own servants, craftsmen, warriors, and Virgins of the Sun.

Nazca

One of the largest figures traced in the rocky desert of Nazca is the geoglyph of the so-called chimpanzee.

Opposite page
One of the great trapezoidal spaces that are considered ceremonial plazas dedicated to the seasonal rites of the Nazca culture.

In 1994 UNESCO added the Lines and Geoglyphs of Nazca and Pampas de Jumana to the list of World Heritage Sites. This cultural expression of the pre-Inca civilization known as the Nazca civilization extends over some 450 square kilometres (about 175 square miles) in the coastal desert of southern Peru, between the present-day city of Nazca and Palpa, in the alluvial plain of Pampa de Nazca between the Rio Ingenio and the Rio Grande. This zone is characterized by a sandy soil covered by a layer of alluvial detrital material, an ideal situation in which to 'cut into the earth', as the term geoglyph indicates. The geoglyphs are, in fact, made by simply removing the stones and leaving the lighter clayey soil, beneath, uncovered. The technique of execution includes two variants: in the first, probably the older, the fine rubble was moved towards the interior of the figure that was to be 'drawn', leaving a sort of negative of the geoglyph on the ground; in the second case, which is more frequent, the stones were used to create the outline itself, in some cases formed little walls of 20 centimetres (about 8 inches) or even one metre (about one yard). What is most surprising today, to the point that some have attributed these creations to extraterrestrials, is the size: they range from 30 to 300 metres (about 90 to 900 feet). In 1977 Josué Lancho proved empirically that a dozen people using only wooden poles and ropes and relying on the general system of the pantograph, could draw a line of 180 metres (about 60 feet) in less than half an hour.

There is in fact very little chronological information. The carbon-14 dating done on a number of organic items found near the lines points to a span of time ranging from 200 B.C. to A.D. 1430. In 1959 Julio C. Tello, an eminent Peruvian archaeologist, found a ceramic vase from the Paracas Caverns phase, prior to the Nazca phase, associated with a glyph. All the same research on the ceramic materials linked to the geoglyphs, gathered during the survey done by the Smithsonian Institution of Cambridge in 1969, attributed most of the 'engravings' to the Nazca cultural phase. Nowadays we prefer to use a relative dating system that is based on the stratification and overlapping of the designs, whereby for instance it is clear that the circular spiral motif, but also the square of meandering spirals, are the oldest, and that newer glyphs have been laid over them or, in the most recent phases, new designs have even been integrated with them. This type of study is supported by the iconographic analysis of the finds of cultural material. In the desert Pampas, the same anthropomorphic and zoomorphic motifs that are present are utilized to decorate ceramics and fabrics: we find the motif of the killer whale, the shark, and the spider all emblems linked to the water cult and the fertility cult, already present in the earlier cultures of Paracas that originated on the coast of the Pacific Ocean. Subsequently, the influences of Andean culture, which was to manifest itself in the Huari culture and, later, the Tihuanaco culture, introduced the ornithomorphs, such as the condor, the hummingbird, the heron, all representations of the rain-bearing bird which brings water, and hence, life. The final, and therefore the most recent, overlappings are those of the great geometric motifs of the lines, rectangles, triangles, trapezoids, and the huge squares, *los campos barridos*, that cover the entire plain.

It was these latest creations that were the first to be studied. In 1927 Toribio Mejia Xesspe wrote that the system of geoglyphs was a set of sacred spaces, where the ancient natives gathered to celebrate their religious ceremonies in honour of gods and ancestors, linked by ritual paths. While the local population identified them as the *caminos incaicos,* or roads of the Inca, Paul Kosok, an American

Detail of the geoglyph of
the so-called whale.

Carved in the sand on
the Pacific coast, it is
possible to make out the
form refered to as a
'candelabrum' when seen
from a great distance.

professor from the University of Long Island, thought that they were a calendar. On the afternoon of 21 June 1941, the day of the winter solstice in the southern hemisphere, Kosok noted that the sun set directly atop a line, which had therefore been drawn in order to indicate this important date for the agricultural calendar of the ancient population. The most important supporter of the theory of the Astronomical Calendar was the scholar of physics and mathematics, Maria Reiche, who spent her entire life on research into and conservation of the lines. Even now, certain points are called 'astronomical observatories' precisely because, located as they are in agricultural areas and raised above the level of the plain, they make it possible to observe the sky. All the same, the astrophysicist Gerald Hawkins, at the request of the National Geographic Society, proved in 1967 that most of the lines had no connection with any particu-

lar astronomical event that occurred from 5000 B.C. to the present day.

The most widely supported theory links the geoglyphs and the lines to the cults of water and fertility both in terms of iconography and structure. It has been noted that many of the lines actually connect with surrounding mountains, rich in water, such as the Illa Kata and the Tunga, while others mark underground channels where water runs from the Cordillera and which, because of a particular geological configuration of the soil, sand overlaid upon a base of impermeable clay, can only rise to the surface in the most low-lying areas. An Aymara legend says that the god of water, setting out from the top of the Andes, reached the coast by flying, bringing with him this precious gift, giving life to the plains. And so, to propitiate the god, the population designed huge figures on the ground as a sign of offering, and so the god could see them from above.

Geoglyph depicting the so-called killer whale, or orca.

NAZCA CULTURE

The pre-Inca culture of Nazca takes its name from the Peruvian city near which three necropolises were unearthed which conserved materials that were different from those that had been studied until then by archaeologists who were working on pre-Columbian civilizations in 1905. Over the course of the years that followed, further investigation led to a subdivision of the ceramic materials into no fewer than ten phases, which covered a span of time from 500 B.C. to A.D. 700. Today, the best-known feature of this culture is the gigantic glyphs traced in the desert. And yet the population that settled in the coastal desert of southern Peru developed a full-fledged state-run system. Architectural documentation consists of ruins of homes linked to storehouses for the preservation of foodstuffs (Tambo Viejo), and ceremonial centres with adjoining zones for the production of ceramics and fabrics (Cahuachi), as well as irrigation canals (*puquio*), which exploited underground water tables or mountain torrents to make much of the desert territory arable. Most of the material culture comes from tombs: ceramic vases, fabrics, ornamental objects. The outstanding characteristics of Nazca ceramics are unquestionably their colour and iconography, clearly linked to a mythical and ceremonial milieu: relatively stylized depictions of the jaguar, the killer whale, serpents, and the water-bearing bird, in the form of the condor, heron, and hummingbird, make it possible to reconstruct the Nazca pantheon. Research seems to show that the society had developed a theocratic state in which every member of the community would have a productive role, whether as fewners or craftsmen, even though it is not possible to establish a division into classes, with economic differentiations. Because there seems to have been no money in the Nazca culture, the government was probably controlled by the hieratic class, and not directed towards the accumulation of wealth; because they were in regular contact with the gods, they were considered to be the best suited people to organize the state system, allowing the greatest proportion of the population to survive.

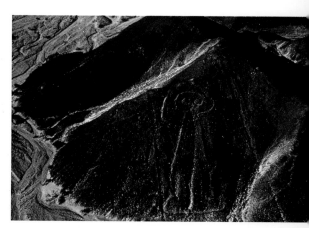

Small polychrome ceramic carafe belonging to the Nazca culture, on which is painted an image that refers to the geoglyph of the killer whale.

On the side of the mountain is depicted an image of an anthropomorphic deity with the head of an owl.

The most renowned geoglyph from the Nazca desert is the hummingbird: a figure linked to the cults of water and fertility.

Opposite page
A figure with two large paws, perhaps a representation of a frog or toad in the grasslands of Ingenio.

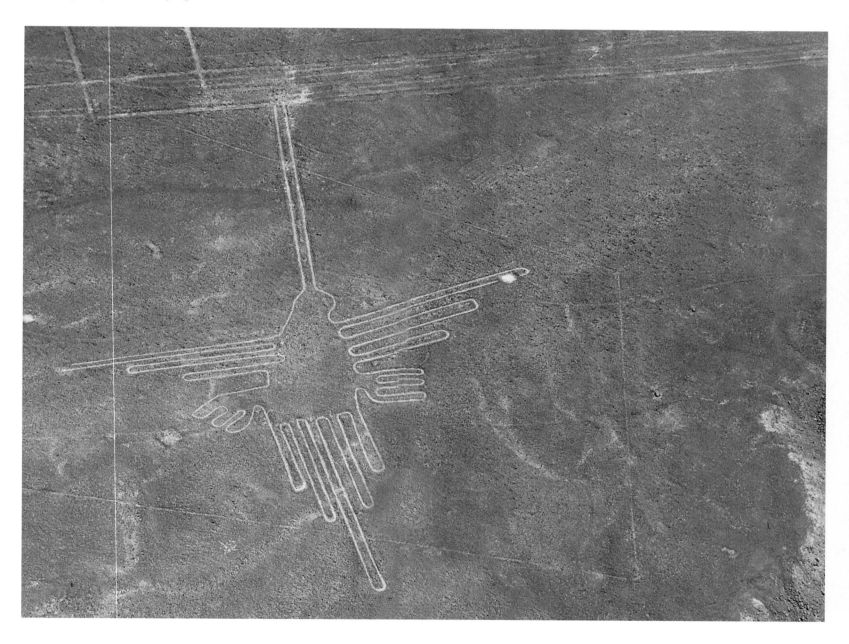

UNESCO Unesco

Unesco

World Heritage Sites   *The Convention*

Aerial view of Muslim Cairo.

Africa

ALGERIA

Al Qal'a of Beni Hammad

In a mountainous site of extraordinary beauty, the ruins of the first capital of the Hammadid Emirs, founded in 1007 and demolished in 1152, provide an authentic picture of a fortified Muslim city. The mosque, whose prayer room has thirteen aisles with eight bays, is one of the largest in Algeria.

Djémila

Situated 900 metres (2,925 feet) above sea-level, Djémila, or Cuicul, with its forum, temples, basilicas, triumphal arches and houses, is an interesting example of Roman town planning adapted to a mountain location.

M'Zab Valley

A traditional human habitat, created in the tenth century by the Ibadites around their five *ksour* (fortified cities), has been preserved intact in the M'Zab valley. Simple, functional and perfectly adapted to the environment, the architecture of M'Zab was designed for community living, while respecting the structure of the family. It is a source of inspiration for today's urban planners.

Timgad

Timgad lies on the northern slopes of the Aurès mountains and was created *ex nihilo* as a military colony by the Emperor Trajan in A.D. 100. With its square enclosure and orthogonal design based on the *cardo* and *decumanus*, the two perpendicular routes running through the city, it is an excellent example of Roman town planning.

Tipasa

On the shores of the Mediterranean, Tipasa was an ancient Punic trading post conquered by Rome and turned into a strategic base for the conquest of the kingdoms of Mauritania. It comprises a unique group of Phoenician, Roman, Palaeochristian and Byzantine ruins alongside indigenous monuments such as the Kbor er Roumia, the great royal mausoleum of Mauritania.

BOTSWANA

Tsodilo

With one of the highest concentrations of rock art in the world, Tsodilo has been called the 'Louvre of the Desert'. Over 4,500 paintings are preserved in an area of only 10 square kilometres (4 square miles) of the Kalahari Desert. The archaeological record of the area gives a chronological account of human activities and environmental changes over at least 100,000 years. Local communities in this hostile environment respect Tsodilo as a place of worship frequented by ancestral spirits.

EGYPT

Abu Mena

The church, baptistry, basilicas, public buildings, streets, monasteries, houses and workshops in this early Christian holy city were built over the tomb of the martyr Menas of Alexandria, who died in A.D. 296.

ETHIOPIA

Aksum

The ruins of the ancient city of Aksum are found close to Ethiopia's northern border. They mark the location of the heart of ancient Ethiopia, when the Kingdom of Aksum was the most powerful state between the Eastern Roman Empire and Persia. The massive ruins, dating from between the first and the thirteenth century A.D., include monolithic obelisks, giant stelae, royal tombs and the ruins of ancient castles. Long after its political decline in the tenth century, Ethiopian emperors continued to be crowned in Aksum.

Fasil Ghebbi, Gondar Region

In the sixteenth and seventeenth centuries, the fortress-city of Fasil Ghebbi was the residence of the Ethiopian Emperor Fasilides and his successors. Surrounded by a 900-metres (975-yards) wall, the city contains palaces, churches, monasteries and unique public and private buildings marked by Hindu and Arab influences, subsequently transformed by the Baroque style brought to Gondar by the Jesuit missionaries.

Lower Valley of the Awash

This area, in the centre of Ethiopia, is one of the most important fossil beds in Africa. Many remains of hominids, indispensable for furthering studies of *Australopithecus* and *Homo sapiens*, and various animal species have been found there.

Lower Valley of the Omo

A prehistoric site near Lake Turkana, the lower valley of the Omo is renowned the world over. The discovery of many fossils there, especially *Homo gracilis*, has been of fundamental importance in the study of human evolution.

Rock-hewn Churches, Lalibela

The eleven medieval monolithic cave churches of this thirteenth-century 'New Jerusalem' are situated in a mountainous region in the heart of Ethiopia near a traditional village with circular-shaped dwellings. Lalibela is a high place of Ethiopian Christianity, still today a place of pilgrimage and devotion.

Tiya

Tiya is among the most important of the roughly 160 archaeological sites discovered so far in the Soddo region, south of Addis Ababa. The site contains thirty-six monuments, including thirty-two carved stelae covered with symbols, most of which are difficult to decipher. They are the remains of an ancient Ethiopian culture whose age has not yet been precisely determined.

GHANA

Asante Traditional Buildings

To the north-east of Kumasi, these are the last material remains of the great Asante civilization, which reached its peak in the eighteenth century. The dwellings, made of earth, wood and straw, are gradually being destroyed by the effects of time and weather.

Forts and Castles, Volta Greater Accra, Central and Western Regions

The remains of fortified trading posts, erected between 1482 and 1786, can still be seen along the coast of Ghana between Keta and Beyin. They were links in the trade routes established by the Portuguese in many areas of the world during their era of great maritime exploration.

KENYA

Lamu Old Town

Lamu Old Town is the oldest and best-preserved Swahili settlement in East Africa, retaining its traditional functions. Built in coral stone and mangrove timber, the town is characterized by the simplicity of structural forms enriched by such features as inner courtyards, verandas, and elaborately carved wooden doors. Lamu has hosted major Muslim religious festivals since the nineteenth century, and has become a significant centre for the study of Islamic and Swahili cultures.

LIBYA

Archaeological Site of Cyrene

A colony of the Greeks of Thera, Cyrene was one of the principal cities in the Hellenic world. It was Romanized, and remained a great capital until the earthquake of 365. One thousand years of history is written in its ruins, famous since the eighteenth century.

Archaeological Site of Sabratha

A Phoenician trading post that served as an outlet for the products of the African hinterland, Sabratha was part of the short-lived Numidian Kingdom of Massinissa before being Romanized and rebuilt in the second and third centuries A.D.

Old Town of Ghadamès

Built in an oasis, Ghadamès, 'the pearl of the desert', is one of the oldest pre-Saharan cities and an outstanding example of a traditional settlement. Its architecture is characterized by the different functions assigned to each storey — the ground floor used to store supplies, another floor extending over dark enclosed passages forming a system of passageways, and the open-air terraces reserved for women.

Rock-Art Sites of Tadrart Acacus

On the border of Tassili N'Ajjer in Algeria, also a World Heritage Site, this rocky massif contains thousands of cave paintings in very different styles, dating from 12,000 B.C. to A.D. 100. They bear witness to marked changes in the fauna and flora and to the different ways of life of the populations that succeeded one another in this Saharan region.

MALI

Cliffs of Bandiagara (Land of the Dogons)

These cliffs protect architectural structures of great beauty (houses, granaries, altars, sanctuaries and *toguna* — meeting places), which have been for centuries the soul of traditional, secular Dogon culture. The Bandiagara plateau is one of the most impressive geological and landscape features in West Africa.

Old Towns of Djenné

Inhabited since 250 B.C., Djenné developed into a market centre and a link in the trans-Saharan gold trade. In the fifteenth and sixteenth centuries, it became one of the spiritual centres for the dissemination of Islam. Its traditional houses, of which close to 2,000 have survived, are built on hillocks (*toguere*) and adapted to the environment of seasonal floods.

Timbuktu

Home of the prestigious Koranic Sankore University and other *medersas*, Timbuktu was in the fifteenth and sixteenth centuries an intellectual and spiritual capital and a centre for the expansion of Islam throughout Africa. Its three great mosques, the Djingareyber, Sankore and Sidi Yahia, speak of Timbuktu's Golden Age. Although restored in the sixteenth century, these monuments are today threatened by the encroachment of sand.

MAURITANIA

The Ancient *Ksour* of Ouadane, Chinguetti, Tichitt and Oualata

These towns were founded in the eleventh and twelfth centuries as trading and religious centres serving the caravans crossing the Sahara, and became focal points of Islamic culture. They have ably preserved an urban fabric built up between the twelfth and sixteenth centuries. Houses with patios crowd narrow streets around a mosque with a square minaret. They illustrate a traditional way of life centred on the nomadic culture of the people of the Western Sahara.

MOROCCO

Archaeological Site of Volubilis

The Mauritanian capital, founded in the third century B.C., became an important outpost of the Roman Empire and was graced with many fine buildings. Substantial remains of these survive in the archaeological site, located in a fertile agricultural area. It was later to become briefly the capital of Idris I, founder of the Idrissid dynasty, who is buried at nearby Moulay Idriss.

Historic City of Meknes

Founded in the eleventh century by Almoravid rulers as a military town, Meknes became a capital under Sultan Moulay Ismaïl (1672-1727), the founder of the Alaouite dynasty. The sultan turned it into an impressive city in Spanish-Moorish style surrounded by high walls with great doors which show today the harmonious blending of Islamic and European styles of the seventeenth-century Maghreb.

Ksar of Aït-Ben-Haddou

The Ksar, a group of earthen buildings surrounded by high walls, is a traditional pre-Saharan habitat. Aït-Ben-Haddou is a striking example of the architecture of southern Morocco.

Medina of Fez

Founded in the ninth century, Fez reached its height first in the fourteenth century under the Marinids and again in the seventeenth century. In 1912, when France established Rabat as the new capital, its political importance declined, but its religious and cultural role continues today, centred as it is around the two famous Mosques of Al-Qarawiyin and Al-Andalus in the heart of the medina.

Medina of Tétouan (Titawin)

Fringing the Atlantic coast, the park is made up of sand dunes, coastal swamps, small islands and shallow coastal waters. The austerity of the desert and the biodiversity of the marine zone result in a land and seascape of exceptional contrasting natural value. A wide variety of migrating birds spend the winter there. Several species of sea turtle and dolphin, which fishermen use to attract shoals of fish, can also be found.

NIGERIA

Sukur Cultural Landscape

The cultural landscape of Sukur, with the Palace of the Hidi (Chief) on a hill dominating the villages below, its terraced fields and their sacred symbols, and the extensive remains of a former flourishing iron industry, is a remarkably intact physical expression of a society and its spiritual and material culture.

SENEGAL

Island of Gorée

Off the coast of Senegal, facing Dakar, Gorée was, from the fifteenth to the nineteenth century, the largest slave trading centre on the African coast. Ruled, in succession, by Portuguese, Dutch, English and French powers, its architecture is characterized by the contrast between the dark slave-quarters and the elegant houses of the slave traders. Today it continues to serve as a reminder of human exploitation and as a sanctuary for reconciliation.

Island of Saint-Louis

Founded as a French colonial settlement in the seventeenth century, the Island of Saint-Louis was urbanized in the mid-nineteenth century. It was the capital of Senegal from 1872 to 1957 and played an important cultural and economic role in the whole of West Africa. The location of the town on an island at the mouth of the Senegal River, its regular town plan, the system of quays, and the characteristic colonial architecture give Saint-Louis its particular quality and identity.

SOUTH AFRICA

The Fossil Hominid Sites of Sterkfontein, Swartkrans, Kromdraai, and Environs

The many caves in the Sterkfontein Valley have produced abundant scientific information on the evolution of modern man over the past 3.5 million years, on his way of life, and on the animals with which he lived and on which he fed. The landscape also preserves many features of that of prehistoric man.

TANZANIA

Ruins of Kilwa Kisiwani and Ruins of Songo Mnara

On two small islands near the coast, the remains of two great East African ports admired by early European explorers can be found. From the thirteenth to the sixteenth centuries, the merchants of Kilwa traded gold, silver, pearls, perfumes, Arabian crockery, Persian earthenware and Chinese porcelain, much of the trade in the Indian Ocean thus passing through their hands.

Stone Town of Zanzibar

The Stone Town of Zanzibar is a fine example of the Swahili coastal trading towns of East Africa. It retains its urban fabric and townscape virtually intact and contains many fine buildings that reflect its particular culture, which has brought together and homogenized disparate elements of the cultures of Africa, the Arab region, India, and Europe over more than a millennium.

TUNISIA

Carthage

Founded in the ninth century B.C. on the Gulf of Tunis, Carthage developed, from the sixth century, into a great trading empire covering much of the Mediterranean and was home to a brilliant civiliza-tion. In the course of long Punic wars, Carthage occupied territories belonging to Rome, which finally destroyed its rival in 146 B.C. A Roman-Carthage was then established on the ruins of the first.

Dougga/Thugga

Before the Roman annexation of Numidia, the town of Thugga, built on an elevated site overlooking a fertile plain, was the capital of an important Libyan-Punic state. It flourished under Roman and Byzantine rule, but declined in the Islamic period. The ruins visible today bear impressive witness to the resources of a small Roman town on the edges of the empire.

Kairouan

Founded in 670, Kairouan flourished under the Aghlabid dynasty in the ninth century. Despite the transfer of the political capital to Tunis in the twelfth century, Kairouan remained the first holy city of the Maghreb. Its rich architectural heritage includes the Great Mosque with its columns in marble and porphyry and the ninth-century Mosque of the Three Gates.

Medina of Sousse

Sousse, an important commercial and military port in the times of the Aghlabites (800-909), is a typical example of a town dating from the first centuries of Islam. With its casbah, its ramparts, its medina (with the Great Mosque), the Bu Ftata Mosque and its typical ribat, at the same time a fort and religious building, Sousse formed part of a coastal defence system.

Medina of Tunis

Under the reign of the Almohave and the Hafsid dynasties, from the twelfth to the sixteenth centuries, Tunis was considered one of the greatest and wealthiest cities of the Islamic world. Some 700 monuments, including palaces, mosques, mausoleums, *medersas* and fountains, speak of this remarkable past.

Punic Town of Kerkuane and its Necropolis

This Phoenician city, probably abandoned during the First Punic War (around 250 B.C.), and as a result not rebuilt by the Romans, constitutes the only remains of a Phoenician-Punic city, which has survived. Its houses were built to a standard plan in accordance with a very developed form of town planning.

UGANDA

Tombs of Buganda Kings at Kasubi
The Tombs of Buganda Kings at Kasubi constitute a site embracing almost 30 hectares of hillside within Kampala district.

Most of the site is agricultural, farmed by traditional methods. At its core on the hilltop is the former Palace of the Kabakas of Buganda, built in 1882 and converted into the royal burial ground in 1884.

Four royal tombs now lie within the Muzibu Aza-ala Mpanga, the main building which is circular and surmounted by a dome. It is a major example of an architectural achievement in organic materials, principally wood, thatch, reed, wattle and daub. The site's main significance lies, however, in its intangible values of belief, spirituality, continuity and identity.

ZIMBABWE

Khami Ruins National Monument
Khami, developed after the capital of Great Zimbabwe had been abandoned in the mid-sixteenth century, is of great archaeological interest. The discovery of objects from Europe and China reveals that Khami had long been a centre of trade.

*Nasca, Peru: image
of a deity with the head
of an owl.*

America

ARGENTINA

Cueva de las Manos, Río Pinturas

The Cueva de las Manos, Río Pinturas, contains an exceptional assemblage of cave art, executed between 13,000 and 9,500 years ago. It takes its name (Cave of the Hands) from the stencilled outlines of human hands in the cave, but there are also many depictions of animals, such as guanacos (*Lama guanicoe*), which are still common in the region, as well as hunting scenes. The people who were responsible for the paintings may have been the ancestors of the historic hunter-gatherer communities of Patagonia found by European settlers in the nineteenth century.

ARGENTINA/BRAZIL

Jesuit Missions of the Guaranis

The ruins of São Miguel das Missões in Brazil, and those of San Ignacio Miní, Santa Ana, Nuestra Señora de Loreto and Santa María la Mayor in Argentina, lie at the heart of a tropical forest. They are the impressive remains of five Jesuit missions, built in the land of the Guaranis during the seventeenth and eighteenth centuries. Each is characterized by a specific layout and a different state of conservation.

BOLIVIA

City of Potosí

City of Potosí in the sixteenth century, this area was regarded as the world's largest industrial complex. The extraction of silver ore relied on a series of hydraulic mills. The site consists of the industrial monuments of the Cerro Rico, where water is provided by an intricate system of aqueducts and artificial lakes; the colonial town with the Casa de la Moneda; the Church of San Lorenzo; several patrician houses; and the *barrios mitayos*, the areas where the workers lived.

Fuerte de Samaipata

The archaeological site of Samaipata consists of two parts: the hill with its many carvings, believed to have been the ceremonial centre of the old town (fourteenth-sixteenth centuries), and the area to the south of the hill, which formed the administrative and residential district. The huge sculptured rock, dominating the town below, is a unique testimony to pre-Hispanic traditions and beliefs, and has no parallel anywhere in the Americas.

Historic City of Sucre

Sucre, the first capital of Bolivia, was founded by the Spanish in the first half of the sixteenth century. Its many well-preserved sixteenth-century religious buildings, such as San Lázaro, San Francisco and Santo Domingo, illustrate the blending of local architectural traditions with styles imported from Europe.

Jesuit Missions of the Chiquitos

Between 1696 and 1760, six ensembles of *reducciones* (settlements of Christianized Indians) inspired by the 'ideal cities' of the sixteenth-century philosophers were founded by the Jesuits in a style that married Catholic architecture with local traditions. The six that remain — San Francisco Javier, Concepción, Santa Ana, San Miguel, San Rafael and San José — make up a living heritage on the former territory of the Chiquitos.

Tiwanaku: Spiritual and Political Centre of the Tiwanaku Culture

The city of Tiwanaku, capital of a powerful pre-Hispanic empire that dominated a large area of the southern Andes and beyond, reached its apogee between 500 and 900 A.D. Its monumental remains testify to the cultural and political significance of this civilization, which is distinct from any of the other pre-Hispanic empires of the Americas.

BRAZIL

Historic Centre of Salvador de Bahia

As the first capital of Brazil, from 1549 to 1763,

Salvador de Bahia witnessed the blending of European, African and Amerindian cultures. It was also, from 1558, the first slave market in the New World, with slaves arriving to work on the sugar plantations. The city has managed to preserve many outstanding Renaissance buildings. A special feature of the old town is the brightly coloured houses, often decorated with fine stucco-work.

Historic Centre of São Luis

The late seventeenth-century core of this historic town, founded by the French and occupied by the Dutch before coming under Portuguese rule, has preserved the original rectangular street plan in its entirety. Thanks to a period of economic stagnation in the early twentieth century, an exceptional number of fine historic buildings have survived, making this an outstanding example of an Iberian colonial town.

Historic Centre of the Town of Diamantina

Diamantina, a colonial village set like a jewel in a necklace of inhospitable rocky mountains, recalls the exploits of diamond prospectors in the eighteenth century and testifies to the triumph of human cultural and artistic endeavour over the environment.

Historic Centre of the Town of Goiás

Goiás testifies to the occupation and colonization of the lands of central Brazil in the eighteenth and nineteenth centuries. The urban layout is an example of the organic development of a mining town, adapted to the conditions of the site. Although modest, both public and private architecture form a harmonious whole, thanks to the coherent use of local materials and vernacular techniques.

Historic Centre of the Town of Olinda

Founded in the sixteenth century by the Portuguese, the town's history is linked to the sugar-cane industry. Rebuilt after being looted by the Dutch, its basic urban fabric dates from the eighteenth century.

The harmonious balance between the buildings, gardens, twenty Baroque churches, convents and numerous small *passos* (chapels) all contribute to Olinda's particular charm.

Historic Town of Ouro Preto

Founded at the end of the seventeenth century, Ouro Preto (Black Gold) was the focal point of the gold rush and Brazil's golden age in the eighteenth century. With the exhaustion of the gold mines in the nineteenth century, the city's influence declined but many churches, bridges and fountains remain as a testimony to its past prosperity and the exceptional talent of the Baroque sculptor Aleijadinho.

CANADA

Historic District of Québec

Québec was founded by the French explorer Champlain in the early seventeenth century. It is the only North American city to have preserved its ramparts, together with the numerous bastions, gates and defensive works which still surround Old Québec. The Upper Town, built on the cliff, has remained the religious and administrative centre, with its churches, convents and other monuments like the Dauphine Redoubt, the Citadel and Château Frontenac. Together with the Lower Town and its medieval districts, it forms an urban ensemble which is one of the best examples of a fortified colonial city.

L'Anse aux Meadows National Historic Site

At the tip of the Great Northern Peninsula of the island of Newfoundland, the remains of an eleventh-century Viking settlement are evidence of the first European presence in North America. The excavated remains of wood-framed peat-turf buildings are similar to those found in Norse Greenland and Iceland.

Old Town, Lunenburg

Lunenburg is the best surviving example of a planned British colonial settlement in North America. Established in 1753, it has retained its original layout and overall appearance, based on a rectangular grid pattern drawn up in the home country. The inhabitants have managed to safeguard the city's identity throughout the centuries by preserving the wooden architecture of the houses, some of which date from the eighteenth century.

Sgaang Gwaii (Anthony Island)

The village of Ninstints (Nans Dins) is located on a small island off the west coast of the Queen Charlotte Islands (Haida Gwaii). Remains of houses, together with carved mortuary and memorial poles, illustrate the Haida people's art and way of life. The site commemorates the living culture of the Haida people and their relationship to the land and sea, and offers a visual key to their oral traditions.

CHILE

Churches of Chiloé

The churches of Chiloé represent a unique example in Latin America of an outstanding form of ecclesiastical wooden architecture. They represent a tradition initiated by the Jesuit Peripatetic Mission in the seventeenth and eighteenth centuries, continued and enriched by the Franciscans during the nineteenth century and still prevailing today. These churches embody the intangible richness of the Chiloé Archipelago, and bear witness to a successful fusion of indigenous and European culture, the full integration of its architecture in the landscape and environment, as well as to the spiritual values of the communities.

COLOMBIA

Historic Centre of Santa Cruz de Mompox

Founded in 1540 on the banks of the River Magdalena, Mompox played a key role in the Spanish colonization of northern South America. From the sixteenth to the nineteenth century the city developed parallel to the river, with the main street acting as a dyke. The historic centre has preserved the harmony and unity of the urban landscape. Most of the buildings are still used for their original purposes, providing an exceptional picture of what a Spanish colonial city was like.

National Archaeological Park of Tierradentro

Several monumental statues of human figures can be seen in the park, which also contains many hypogea dating from the sixth to the tenth centuries. These huge underground tombs, with some burial chambers up to 12 metres (39 feet) wide, are decorated with motifs that reproduce the internal decor of homes of the period. They reveal the social complexity and cultural wealth of a pre-Hispanic society in the northern Andes.

Port, Fortresses and Group of Monuments, Cartagena

Situated in a bay in the Caribbean Sea, Cartagena has the most extensive fortifications in South America. A system of zones divides the city into three neighbourhoods: San Pedro, with the cathedral and many Andalusian-style palaces; San Diego, where merchants and the middle class lived; and Gethsemani, the 'popular quarter'.

San Agustin Archaeological Park

The largest group of religious monuments and megalithic sculptures in South America stands in a wild, spectacular landscape. Gods and mythical animals are skilfully represented in styles ranging from abstract to realist. These works of art display the creativity and imagination of a northern Andean culture that flourished from the first to the eighth centuries.

CUBA

Archaeological Landscape of the First Coffee Plantations in South-East Cuba

The remains of the nineteenth-century coffee plantations in the foothills of the Sierra Maestra are unique evidence of a pioneering form of agriculture in a difficult terrain. They throw considerable light on the economic, social, and technological history of the Caribbean and Latin American region.

Trinidad and the Valley de los Ingenios

Founded in the early sixteenth century in honour of the Holy Trinity, the city was a bridgehead for the conquest of the American continent. Its eighteenth- and nineteenth-century buildings, such as the Palacio Brunet and the Palacio Cantero were built in its days of prosperity from the sugar trade.

DOMINICAN REPUBLIC

Colonial City of Santo Domingo

After Christopher Columbus's arrival on the island in 1492, Santo Domingo became the site of the first cathedral, hospital, customs house and university in the Americas. This colonial town, founded in 1498, was laid out on a grid pattern that became the model for almost all town planners in the New World.

ECUADOR

City of Quito

Quito, the capital of Ecuador, was founded in the sixteenth century on the ruins of an Inca city and stands at an altitude of 2,850 metres (9,262 feet). Despite the 1917 earthquake, the city has the best-preserved, least altered historic centre in Latin America. The Monasteries of San Francisco and Santo Domingo, and the Church and Jesuit College of La Compañía, with their rich interiors, are pure examples of the 'Baroque school of Quito', which is a fusion of Spanish, Italian, Moorish, Flemish and indigenous art.

Historic Centre of Santa Ana de los Ríos de Cuenca

Santa Ana de los Ríos de Cuenca is set in a valley surrounded by the Andean mountains in the south of Ecuador. This inland colonial town (*entroterra*), now the country's third city, was founded in 1557 on the rigorous planning guidelines issued thirty years earlier by the Spanish King Charles V. Cuenca still observes the formal orthogonal town plan that it has respected for 400 years. One of the region's agricultural and administrative centres, it has been a melting pot for local and immigrant populations. Cuenca's architecture, much of which dates from the eighteenth century, was 'modernized' in the economic prosperity of the nineteenth century as the city became a major exporter of quinine, straw hats and other products.

EL SALVADOR

Joya de Ceren Archaeological Site

Joya de Ceren was a pre-Hispanic farming community that, like Pompeii and Herculaneum in Italy, was buried under a volcanic eruption around A.D. 600. Because of the exceptional condition of the remains, the site provides a view of the daily lives of the Central American populations who worked the land at that time.

GUATEMALA

Antigua

Antigua, the capital of the Captaincy-General of Guatemala, was founded in the early sixteenth century. Built 1,500 metres (4,875 feet) above sea-level in an earthquake-prone region, it was largely destroyed by an earthquake in 1773 but its principal monuments are still preserved as ruins. In the space of under three centuries the city, which was built on a grid pattern inspired by the Italian Renaissance, acquired a number of superb monuments.

Archaeological Park and Ruins of Quirigua

Inhabited since the second century A.D., Quirigua had become during the reign of Cauac Sky (723-84) the capital of an autonomous and prosperous state. The ruins of Quirigua contain some outstanding eighth-century monuments and an impressive series of carved stelae and sculpted calendars that constitute an essential source for the study of Mayan civilization.

Tikal National Park

In the heart of the jungle, surrounded by lush vegetation, lies one of the major sites of Mayan civilization, inhabited from the sixth century B.C. to the tenth century A.D. Its ceremonial centre contains superb temples and palaces, and ramps leading to public squares. Remains of dwellings are scattered throughout the surrounding countryside.

HAITI

National History Park — Citadel, Sans-Souci, Ramiers

These monuments of Haiti dating from the beginning of the nineteenth century when Haiti proclaimed its independence — the Palace of Sans Souci, the buildings at Ramiers and, especially, the Citadel — serve as a universal symbol of liberty, as they were the first to be built by black slaves who had gained their freedom.

MEXICO

Archaeological Monuments Zone of Xochicalco

Xochicalco is an exceptionally well-preserved example of a fortified political, religious, and commercial centre from the troubled period of A.D. 650-900 that followed the breakdown of the great Meso-American states such as Teotihuacán, Monte Alban, Palenque, and Tikal.

Archaeological Zone of Paquimé, Casas Grandes

Paquimé Casas Grandes, which reached its apogee in the fourteenth and fifteenth centuries, played a key role in trade and cultural contacts between the Pueblo culture of the south-western United States of America and northern Mexico and the more advanced civilizations of Meso-America. Its extensive remains, only part of which have been excavated, bear eloquent testimony to the vitality of this culture, well adapted to its physical and economic environment, which would disappear abruptly at the time of the Spanish Conquest.

El Tajin, Pre-Hispanic City

Located in the state of Veracruz, the pre-Hispanic site of El Tajin was inhabited from the early ninth to the early thirteenth centuries and so dates from between the great empires of Teotihuácan and Mexico-Tenochtitlán. It is composed of a series of richly decorated public squares and pyramids, the best known of which is the so-called 'Pyramid of the Niches'. The well-preserved site, by virtue of its artistic and architectural importance, attests to the grandeur of the pre-Columbian cultures of Mexico.

Historic Centre of Mexico City and Xochimilco

Built in the sixteenth century by the Spanish upon the ruins of Tenochtitlan, the old Aztec capital, the city is today one of the largest and most densely populated cities in the world. Besides the five Aztec temples, there is also the cathedral, and nineteenth- and twentieth-century public edifices such as the Palacio de las Bellas Artes. Xochimilco, 28 kilometres (17 miles) south of the city, with its network of canals and artificial islands, is an exceptional testimony of the efforts of the Aztec people to build a habitat amid an unfavourable environment.

Historic Centre of Morelia

Constructed in the sixteenth century around a Franciscan monastery, Morelia's 249 historic monuments are built mostly in warm pink stone following a strict chess-board design. All have retained their structure and show the vital cultural and economic life that flourished in the city in the seventeenth century.

Historic Centre of Oaxaca and Archaeological Site of Monte Alban

Inhabited over a period of 1500 years by a succession of peoples — Olmecs, Zapotecs and Mixtecs — the terraces, dams, canals, pyramids and artificial mounds of Monte Alban were literally carved out of the mountain and are the symbols of a sacred topography. Nearby, the chess-board design of Oaxaca is a good example of Spanish colonial architecture.

Historic Centre of Puebla

About 100 kilometres (62 miles) east of Mexico City, at the foot of Popocatépetl volcano, Puebla was founded *ex nihilo* in 1531. The great religious buildings of Puebla, such as the cathedral (sixteenth and seventeenth centuries), superb palaces like the old Archbishop's Palace, as well as a host of houses whose walls are covered in tiles (*azulejos*), have been preserved.

Historic Centre of Zacatecas

Founded in 1546 after the discovery of a very rich silver lode, Zacatecas' prosperity reached its height in the sixteenth and seventeenth centuries. Built on the steep slopes of a narrow valley, the town offers a breathtaking panorama. Many old buildings, both religious and civil, remain. The cathedral, built between 1730 and 1760, dominates the centre of the town. It is outstanding in its design and in its façades, which are decorated in both European and indigenous styles.

Historic Fortified Town of Campeche

The historic centre of Campeche is a harbour town typical of the Spanish colonial period in the New World. It has kept its outer walls and system of fortifications, constructed to defend this Caribbean port against attacks from the sea.

Historic Monuments Zone of Querétaro

The old colonial town of Querétaro is unusual in retaining side by side the original street patterns of both the native Indian inhabitants and the Spanish conquerors. The twisting streets of the Indian quarters contrast with the geometrically laid out section of the Spanish. The Otomi, the Tarasco, the Chichimeca and the Spanish lived peacefully together in the town, notable for its many extravagantly adorned civil and religious Baroque monuments from its golden age in the seventeenth and eighteenth centuries.

Historic Monuments Zone of Tlacotalpan
Tlacotalpan, a Spanish colonial river port on the Gulf Coast of Mexico, founded in the mid-sixteenth century, has preserved its original urban fabric to an exceptional degree. Its qualities are to be found in its outstanding townscape of wide streets, colonnaded houses built in an exuberant variety of styles and colours, and many mature trees in the public open spaces and private gardens.

Historic Town of Guanajuato and Adjacent Mines
Founded by the Spaniards in the early sixteenth century, it became the world's leading silver extraction centre in the eighteenth century. This past can be seen in its 'subterranean streets' and the 'Boca del Infierno', a mineshaft that plunges a breathtaking 600 metres (1,950 feet). Its churches, La Compañía and La Valenciana, are considered to be among the most beautiful examples of Baroque architecture in Central and South America.

Pre-Hispanic City and National Park of Palenque
A prime example of a Mayan sanctuary of the Classical Period, Palenque was at its height between A.D. 500 and 700 and had a great influence on the entire basin of the Usumacinta River. The elegance and craftsmanship of the construction, as well as the lightness of the sculpted reliefs illustrating Mayan mythology, attest to the creative genius of this civilization.

Pre-Hispanic Town of Uxmal
The Mayan town of Uxmal, in the Yucatàn, was founded in about 700 and had about 25,000 inhabitants. Its buildings, which date from between 700 and 1000, are arranged according to astronomical knowledge of the period. The Pyramid of the Soothsayer, as the Spanish called it, dominates the ceremonial centre which comprises carefully designed buildings richly decorated with symbols and with sculptures depicting Chac, the rain god. The ceremonial sites of Uxmal, Kabáh, Labná and Sayil together represent the pinnacle of Mayan art and architecture.

Rock Paintings of the Sierra de San Francisco
In the reserve of El Vizcaino, in Baja, California, the Sierra de San Francisco, from about 100 B.C. to A.D. 1300, was home to a population now disappeared, which left one of the most outstanding collections of rock paintings in the world. Remarkably well preserved because of the dry climate and the inaccessibility of the site, the paintings illustrate people and many animal species (mammals, fish, reptiles and birds), using extremely varied colours and techniques.

NICARAGUA

Ruins of León Viejo
León Viejo is one of the oldest Spanish colonial settlements in the Americas. It did not develop and so its ruins are outstanding testimony to the social and economic structures of the Spanish Empire in the sixteenth century. The site has immense archaeological potential.

PANAMA

Fortifications on the Caribbean Side of Panama: Portobelo-San Lorenzo
Magnificent examples of seventeenth- and eighteenth-century military architecture, these Panamanian forts on the Caribbean coast form part of the defence system built by the Spanish Crown to protect transatlantic trade.

Historic District of Panamá, with the Salón Bolivar
Panamá was the first European settlement on the Pacific coast of the Americas, founded in 1519 by the *conquistador* Pedrarias Dávila. The Historic District, which developed after 1671, preserves in its street pattern the early layout; the architecture is an unusual mixture of Spanish, French, and Early American styles. The Salón Bolivar was the venue for the unsuccessful effort made by *El Libertador* in 1826 to establish a multinational continental congress.

PARAGUAY

Jesuit Missions of La Santisima Trinidad de Parana and Jesus de Tavarangue
In addition to their artistic interest, these missions represent the social and economic initiatives that accompanied the Christianization of the Río de la Plata Basin by the Society of Jesus in the seventeenth and eighteenth centuries.

PERU

Chavin (Archaeological site)
This archaeological site gave its name to the culture that developed in this high valley of the Peruvian Andes between 1500 and 300 B.C. The architecture of this complex of terraces and squares, surrounded by structures of dressed stone, and its largely zoomorphic ornamental structure, give a striking appearance to this former place of worship, one of the earliest and best-known pre-Columbian sites.

Chan Chan Archaeological Zone
The Chimu Kingdom, of which Chan Chan was the capital, reached its peak in the fifteenth cen-

tury, not long before falling under the Incas. The planning of this huge city, the biggest in pre-Columbian America, reflects a strict political and social strategy, marked by its division into nine 'citadels' or 'palaces' forming independent units.

Historic Centre of Arequipa

The Historic Centre of Arequipa, built in volcanic sillar rock, represents an integration of European and native building techniques and characteristics, expressed in the admirable work of colonial masters and criollo and Indian masons. It is illustrated by its robust walls, archways and vaults, courtyards and open spaces, and the intricate Baroque decoration of its façades.

Historic Centre of Lima

Although severely damaged by earthquakes (in 1940, 1966, 1970 and 1974), this 'City of Kings' was, until the middle of the eighteenth century, the capital and most important city of the Spanish do-minions in South America. Many of its buildings, such as the San Francisco Convent (the biggest in this part of the world) are the result of joint cre-ations between local craftsmen and masters from the Old Continent.

UNITED STATES OF AMERICA

Cahokia Mounds State Historic Site

About 15 kilometres (9 miles) north of Saint-Louis (Missouri), Cahokia provides the most complete source of information on pre-Columbian civilizations in the regions of the Mississippi. It is a striking example of a pre-ur-ban sedentary structure that allows for the study of a kind of social organization about which no written traces exist.

Chaco Culture National Historical Park

This national park, in north-west New Mexico, con-tains the most important remains of the Chaco cul-ture, which was at its height between about 1020 and 1110. It was characterized by a very elaborate sys-tem of urban dwellings surrounded by villages and linked by a network of roads

La Fortaleza and San Juan Historic Site in Puerto Rico

The defensive structures built over four centuries (fifteenth to nineteenth) to protect the city and the Bay of San Juan, a vital strategic point in the Caribbean Sea, have left a rich display of European military architecture adapted to the harbours of the American continent.

Monticello and the University of Virginia in Charlottesville

Excellent examples of Neo-classicism, seen in the re-lationship of the buildings with nature and the blending of functionalism and symbolism, the Man-sion of Monticello and the University of Virginia re-flect the design of their architect, Thomas Jefferson (1743-1826), who was strongly influenced by the Enlightenment.

URUGUAY

Historic Quarter of the City of Colonia del Sacramento

Founded by the Portuguese in 1680 on the Rio de la Plata, the city fulfilled a strategic function against the Spanish Empire. Disputed for a century, it was finally lost by its founders. Its preserved urban landscape, a mixture of solemnity and intimacy, is an example of the successful fusion of the Portuguese, Spanish and post-colonial styles.

VENEZUELA

Ciudad Universitaria de Caracas

The Ciudad Universitaria de Caracas, built to the design of the architect Carlos Raúl Villanueva from the 1940s to the 1960s, is an outstanding example of the Modern Movement in architecture. The university campus integrates the large number of buildings and functions into a clearly articulated ensemble, including masterpieces of modern architecture and visual arts, such as the Aula Magna with the *Clouds* of Alexander Calder, the Olympic Stadium, and the Covered Plaza.

Coro and its Port

Built in an earthen style unique to the Caribbean, the city is the only surviving example of a rich fusion of local traditions, Spanish *mudejar* and Dutch architectural techniques. One of the first colonial towns, it was founded in 1527 and contains some 602 historic buildings.

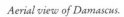

Aerial view of Damascus.

Asia

Cathedral and Churches of Echmiatsin and the Archaeological Site of Zvartnots

The Cathedral and churches of Echmiatsin and the archaeological remains at Zvartnots graphically illustrate the evolution and development of the Armenian central-domed cross-hall type of church, which exerted a profound influence on architectural and artistic development in the region.

AZERBAIJAN

Walled City of Baku with the Shirvanshah's Palace and Maiden Tower

Built on a site inhabited since the Paleolithic period, the Walled City of Baku reveals evidence of Zoroastrian, Sassanian, Arabic, Persian, Shirvani, Ottoman, and Russian presence in cultural continuity. The Inner City (Icheri Sheher) has preserved much of its twelfth-century defensive walls. The twelfth-century Maiden Tower (Giz Galasy) is built over earlier structures dating from the seventh and sixth centuries B.C., and the fifteenth-century Shirvanshah's Palace is one of the pearls of Azerbaijan's architecture.

BANGLADESH

Historic Mosque City of Bagerhat

Situated in the suburbs of Bagerhat, at the meeting point of the Ganges and Brahmaputra Rivers, this ancient city, formerly known as Khalifatabad, was founded by the Turkish General Ulugh Khan Jahan in the fifteenth century. The city's infrastructure reveals considerable technical skill, and an exceptional number of mosques and early Islamic monuments, many built of brick, can be seen there.

CHINA

Ancient City of Ping Yao

Ping Yao is an exceptionally well-preserved example of a traditional Han Chinese city, founded in the fourteenth century. Its urban fabric shows the evolution of architectural styles and town planning in Imperial China over five centuries. Of special interest are the imposing buildings associated with banking, for which Ping Yao was the major centre for the whole of China in the nineteenth and early twentieth centuries.

Ancient Villages in Southern Anhui — Xidi and Hongcun

The two traditional villages of Xidi and Hongcun preserve to a remarkable extent the appearance of non-urban settlements of a type that largely disappeared or was transformed during the last century. Their street plans, their architecture and decoration, and the integration of houses with comprehensive water systems are unique surviving examples.

Classical Gardens of Suzhou

Classical Chinese garden design, which seeks to recreate natural landscapes in miniature, is nowhere better illustrated than in the nine gardens in the historic city of Suzhou. They are universally acknowledged to be masterpieces of the genre. Dating from the sixteenth to eighteenth centuries, the gardens reflect the profound metaphysical importance of natural beauty in Chinese culture in their meticulous design.

Dazu Rock Carvings

The steep hillsides of the Dazu area contain an exceptional series of rock carvings dating from the ninth to the thirteenth centuries. They are remarkable for their aesthetic quality, their rich diversity of subject matter, both secular and religious, and the light that they shed on everyday life in China during this period. They provide outstanding evidence of the harmonious synthesis of Buddhism, Taoism and Confucianism.

Imperial Tombs of the Ming and Qing Dynasties

The Ming and Qing Imperial Tombs are natural

sites modified by human influence, carefully chosen in accordance with the principles of geomancy (*Fengshui*) to house numerous buildings of traditional architectural design and decoration. They illustrate the continuity over five centuries of a world view and concept of power specific to feudal China.

Longmen Grottoes

The grottoes and niches of Longmen contain the largest and most impressive collection of Chinese art of the late Northern Wei and Tang dynasties (316-907). These works, entirely devoted to the Buddhist religion, represent the high point of Chinese stone carving.

Lushan National Park

Mount Lushan, in Jiangxi, is one of the spiritual centres of Chinese civilization. Buddhist and Taoist temples, along with landmarks of Confucianism, where the most eminent masters taught, blend effortlessly into a strikingly beautiful landscape which has inspired countless artists who developed the aesthetic approach to nature found in Chinese culture.

Mogao Caves

Situated at a strategic point along the Silk Route, at the crossroads of trade as well as religious, cultural and intellectual influences, the 492 cells and cave sanctuaries in Mogao are famous for their statues and wall paintings, spanning 1,000 years of Buddhist art.

Mountain Resort and its Outlying Temples, Chengde

The Mountain Resort (the Qing dynasty's summer palace), in Hebei Province, was built between 1703 and 1792. It is a vast complex of palaces and administrative and ceremonial buildings. Temples of various architectural styles and imperial gardens blend harmoniously into a landscape of lakes, pastureland and forests. In addition to its aesthetic interest, the Mountain Resort is a rare historic vestige of the final development of feudal society in China.

Mount Emei Scenic Area, including Leshan Giant Buddha Scenic Area

The first Buddhist temple in China was built here in Sichuan Province in the first century A.D. in very beautiful surroundings atop Mount Emei. The addition of other temples turned the site into one of Buddhism's principal holy places. Over the centuries, the cultural treasures grew in number. The most remarkable was the Giant Buddha of Leshan, carved out of a hillside in the eighth century and looking down on the confluence of three rivers. At 71 metres (231 feet) high, it is the largest Buddha in the world. Mount Emei is also notable for its very diverse vegetation, ranging from subtropical to subalpine pine forests. Some of the trees are more than 1,000 years old.

Mount Qincheng and the Dujiangyan Irrigation System

Construction of the Dujiangyan irrigation system began in the third century B.C. This system still controls the waters of the Minjiang River and distributes it to the fertile farmland of the Chengdu plains. Mount Qingcheng was the birthplace of Taoism, which is celebrated in a series of ancient temples.

Mount Taishan

In *c.* 220 B.C., under Qin Shi Huang, sections of earlier fortifications were joined together to form a united defensive system against invasions from the north. Construction continued up to the Ming dynasty (1368-1644), when the Great Wall became the world's largest military structure. Its historic and strategic importance is matched only by its architectural significance.

Mount Wuyi

Mount Wuyi is the most outstanding area for biodiversity conservation in south-east China and a refuge for a large number of ancient, relict species, many of them endemic to China. The serene beauty of the dramatic gorges of the Nine Bend River, with

its numerous temples and monasteries, many now in ruins, provided the setting for the development and spread of Neo-Confucianism, which has been influential in the cultures of East Asia since the eleventh century. In the first century B.C. a large administrative capital was built at nearby Chengcun by the Han dynasty rulers. Its massive walls enclose an archaeological site of great significance.

Old Town of Lijiang

The Old Town of Lijiang, which is perfectly adapted to the uneven topography of this key commercial and strategic site, has retained a historic townscape of high quality and authenticity. Its architecture is noteworthy for the blending of elements from several cultures that have come together over many centuries. Lijiang also possesses an ancient water-supply system of great complexity and ingenuity that still functions effectively today.

Peking Man Site at Zhoukoudian

Scientific work at the site, which lies 42 kilometres (26 miles) south-west of Beijing, is still under way. So far, it has led to the discovery of the remains of *Sinanthropus pekinensis*, who lived in the Middle Pleistocene, along with various objects, and remains of *Homo sapiens sapiens* dating as far back as 18,000-11,000 B.C. The site is not only an exceptional reminder of the prehistoric human societies of the Asian continent, but also illustrates the process of evolution.

Temple of Confucius, Cemetery of Confucius, and Kong Family Mansion in Qufu

The temple, cemetery and family mansion of Confucius, the great philosopher, politician and educator of the sixth to fifth centuries B.C., are located at Qufu, in Shandong Province. Built to commemorate him in 478 B.C., the temple has been destroyed and reconstructed over the centuries; today it comprises more than 100 buildings. The cemetery contains Confucius's tomb and the remains of more than 100,000 of his descendants. The small house of the

Kong family developed into a gigantic aristocratic residence, of which 152 buildings remain. The Qu-fu complex of monuments has retained its outstanding artistic and historic character due to the devotion of successive Chinese emperors over more than 2,000 years.

Yungang Grottoes

The Yungang Grottoes, in Datong city, Shanxi Province, with their 252 caves and 51,000 statues, represent the outstanding achievement of Buddhist cave art in China in the fifth and sixth centuries. The Five Caves created by Tan Yao, with their strict unity of layout and design, constitute a classical masterpiece of the first peak of Chinese Buddhist art.

GEORGIA

City-Museum Reserve of Mtskheta

The historic churches of Mtskheta, former capital of Georgia, are outstanding examples of medieval religious architecture in the Caucasus. They show the high artistic and cultural level attained by this ancient kingdom.

Upper Svaneti

Preserved by its long isolation, the Upper Svaneti region of the Caucasus is an exceptional example of mountain scenery with medieval-type villages and tower-houses. The village of Chazhashi still has more than 200 of these very unusual houses, which were used both as dwellings and as defence posts against the invaders who plagued the region.

INDIA

Agra Fort

Near the gardens of the Taj Mahal stands the important sixteenth-century Mughal monument known as the Red Fort of Agra. This powerful fortress of red sandstone encompasses, within its enclosure walls, the imperial city of the Mughal rulers. It comprises many fairy-tale palaces, such as

the Jahangir Palace and the Khas Mahal, built by Shah Jahan; audience halls, such as the Diwan-i-Khas; and two very beautiful mosques.

Buddhist Monastery at Sanchi

On a hill overlooking the plain, about 40 kilometres (25 miles) from Bhopal, the site of Sanchi comprises a group of Buddhist monuments (monolithic pillars, palaces, temples and monasteries), all in different states of conservation and mainly dating back to the second and first centuries B.C. It is the oldest Buddhist sanctuary in existence and was a major centre of Buddhism in India until the twelfth century A.D.

Churches and Convents of Goa

The churches and convents of Goa, the former capital of the Portuguese Indies — particularly the Church of Bom Jesus, which contains the tomb of St Francis-Xavier — illustrate the Evangelization of Asia. These monuments were influential in spreading forms of Manueline, Mannerist and Baroque art in all the countries of Asia where missions were established.

Elephanta Caves

The 'City of Caves', on an island in the Sea of Oman close to Bombay, contains a collection of rock art linked to the cult of Shiva. Here, Indian art has found one of its most perfect expressions, particularly the huge high reliefs in the main cave.

Ellora Caves

These thirty-four monasteries and temples, extending over more than 2 kilometres (1.5 miles), were dug side by side in the wall of a high basalt cliff, not far from Aurangabad, in Maharashtra. Ellora, with its uninterrupted sequence of monuments dating from A.D. 600 to 1000, brings the civilization of ancient India to life. Not only is the Ellora complex a unique artistic creation and a technological exploit but, with its sanctuaries devoted to Buddhism, Hinduism and Jainism, it illustrates the spirit of tolerance that was characteristic of ancient India.

Fatehpur Sikri

Built during the second half of the sixteenth century by the Emperor Akbar, Fatehpur Sikri (the City of Victory) was the capital of the Mughal Empire for only some ten years. The complex of monuments and temples, all in a uniform architectural style, includes one of the largest mosques in India, the Jama Masjid.

Group of Monuments at Hampi

The austere, grandiose site of Hampi was the last capital of the last great Hindu Kingdom of Vijayanagar. Its fabulously rich princes built Dravidian temples and palaces which won the admiration of travellers between the fourteenth and sixteenth centuries. Conquered by the Deccan Muslim Confederacy in 1565, the city was pillaged over a period of six months before being abandoned.

Group of Monuments at Khajuraho

The temples at Khajuraho were built during the Chandella dynasty, which reached its apogee between 950 and 1050. Only about twenty temples remain; they fall into three distinct groups and belong to two different religions — Hinduism and Jainism. They strike a perfect balance between architecture and sculpture. The Temple of Kandariya is decorated with a profusion of sculptures that are among the greatest masterpieces of Indian art.

Group of Monuments at Mahabalipuram

This group of sanctuaries, founded by the Pallava kings, was carved out of rock along the Coromandel coast in the seventh and eighth centuries. It is known especially for its *rathas* (temples in the form of chariots), *mandapas* (cave sanctuaries), giant open-air reliefs such as the famous 'Descent of the Ganges', and the Temple of Rivage, with thousands of sculptures to the glory of Shiva.

Group of Monuments at Pattadakal

Pattadakal, in Karnatâka, illustrates the apogee of an eclectic art which, in the seventh and eighth centuries A.D., under the Châlukya dynasty, achieved a harmonious blend of architectural forms from the north and south of India. An impressive series of nine Hindu temples, as well as a Jain sanctuary can be seen there. In this group, one masterpiece stands out — the Temple of Virûpâksha, built around 740 by Queen Lokamahadevi to commemorate her husband's victory over the kings from the south.

Qutb Minar and its Monuments, Delhi

Built in the early thirteenth century a few miles south of Delhi, the red sandstone tower of Qutb Minar is 72.5 metres (236 feet) high, tapering from 2.75 metres (8 feet) in diameter at its peak to 14.32 metres (46 feet) at its base, and alternating angular and rounded flutings. The surrounding archaeological area contains funerary buildings, notably the magnificent Alai-Darwaza Gate, the masterpiece of Indo-Muslim art (built in 1311), and two mosques, including the Quwwatu'l-Islam, the oldest in northern India, built of materials reused from some twenty Brahmin temples.

INDONESIA

Sangiran Early Man Site

Excavations here from 1936 to 1941 led to the discovery of the first hominid fossil at this site. Later, fifty fossils of *Meganthropus palaeo* and *Pithecanthropus erectus/Homo erectus* were found — half of all the world's known hominid fossils. Inhabited for the past one and a half million years, Sangiran is one of the key sites for the understanding of human evolution.

IRAN

Tchoga Zanbil

The ruins of the holy city of the Kingdom of Elam, surrounded by three huge concentric walls, are found at Tchogha Zanbil. Founded *c.* 1250 B.C., the city remained unfinished after it was invaded by Ashurbanipal, as shown by the thousands of unused bricks left at the site.

IRAQ

Hatra

A large fortified city under the influence of the Parthian Empire and capital of the first Arab Kingdom, Hatra withstood invasions by the Romans in A.D. 116 and 198 thanks to its high, thick walls reinforced by towers. The remains of the city, especially the temples where Hellenistic and Roman architecture blend with Eastern decorative features, attest to the greatness of its civilization.

ISRAEL

Masada

The site of the self-immolation of approximately 1,000 Jewish patriots in the face of a large Roman army, Masada is a symbol of the ancient Kingdom of Israel. Built as a palace complex and place of refuge by Herod the Great, King of Judaea (reigned 37-4 B.C.), Masada's extensive remains survive on the summit of this seemingly impregnable fortress, set in a rugged natural landscape of great beauty. The siege works of the Roman army and other related sites lie unexcavated at the base of the rock.

Old City of Acre

The historic townscape of the walled port city of Acre is characteristic of Islamic town planning, with narrow winding streets and fine public buildings and houses. Beneath the eighteenth- and nineteenth-century Ottoman Acre, lie almost intact the remains of its predecessor, the Crusader city, dating from 1104 to 1291. Crusader Acre is today mostly subterranean and has only recently begun to be revealed.

Old City of Jerusalem and its Walls

As the holy city for Judaism, Christianity and Islam, Jerusalem has always had a high symbolic value. Among the 220 historic monuments is the stunning Dome of the Rock, built in the seventh century and decorated with beautiful geometric and floral motifs. It is recognized by all three religions as the site of

Abraham's sacrifice. The Wailing Wall delimits the quarters of the different religious communities whilst the Resurrection Rotonda protects Christ's tomb.

JAPAN

Buddhist Monuments in the Horyuji Area

There are some forty-eight Buddhist monuments in the Horyu-ji area, in the Nara Prefecture. Masterpieces of wooden architecture, they are the oldest of their type in Japan. Eleven of them were constructed before or during the eighth century, and marked an important date in the history of art — illustrating the adaptation of Chinese Buddhist architecture and layouts to Japanese culture, as well as in the history of religion — since their construction coincides with the introduction of Buddhism to Japan.

Gusuku Sites and Related Properties of the Kingdom of Ryukyu

Five hundred years of Ryukyuan history (twelfth to seventeenth century) are represented by this group of sites and monuments. The ruins of the castles, on imposing elevated sites, are evidence of the social structure over much of that period, whilst the sacred sites provide mute testimony to the rare survival of an ancient form of religion into the modern age. The wide economic (and hence cultural) contacts of the Ryukyu islands over that period are illustrated by the unique culture that emerged.

Historic Villages of Shirakawa-go and Gokayama

Located in a mountainous region that was cut off from the rest of the world for a long time, the gassho-style villages survived from growing mulberry trees and rearing silkworms. Their large houses with double, steeply pitched, thatched roofs are unique in Japan. Despite economic upheavals, the villages of Ogimachi, Ainokura and Suganuma are still exceptional examples of how the traditional way of life was perfectly suited to their environment and social function.

Historic Monuments of Ancient Nara

The historic monuments of Nara — temples, shrines, the excavated remains of the great imperial palace — provide a vivid picture of the capital of Japan in the eighth century A.D., a period of profound political and cultural change.

Shrines and Temples of Nikko

The Nikko shrines and temples, together with their natural surroundings, have for centuries formed a sacred site known for its architectural and decorative masterpieces. They are closely associated with the history of the Tokugawa Shoguns.

JORDAN

Quseir Amra

Built in the early eighth century, this desert castle, which is exceptionally well-preserved, was a fortress that from time to time was used both as a garrison and a residence for the Omayyad caliphs. The most outstanding features of this small pleasure palace are the reception halls and the baths, all richly decorated with figurative murals that reflect the secular art of the time.

KOREA

Changdeokgung Palace Complex

In the early years of the fifteenth century, the Emperor T'aejong ordered the construction of a new palace at an auspicious site. A Bureau of Palace Construction was set up to create the ensemble, which consists of a number of official and residential buildings set in a garden that closely conforms with the uneven topography of the 58 hectares site. The result is an exceptional example of Far Eastern palace architecture and design, harmoniously integrated with its surrounding natural landscape.

Gochang, Hwasun, and Ganghwa Dolmen Sites

The prehistoric cemeteries at Gochang, Hwasun, and Gangwha contain many hundreds of examples of dolmens, tombs from the first millennium B.C. constructed of large stone slabs. They form part of the Megalithic culture, to be found in many parts of the world, but nowhere in such a concentrated form.

Gyeongju Historic Areas

The Gyeongju Historic Areas contain a remarkable concentration of outstanding examples of Korean Buddhist art, in the form of sculptures, reliefs, pagodas, and the remains of temples and palaces from the flowering, between the seventh and the tenth centuries, of this form of unique artistic expression.

Haeinsa Temple Janggyeong Panjeon, the Depositories for the Tripitaka Koreana Woodblocks

The Temple of Haeinsa, on Mount Kaya, is home to the Tripitaka Koreana, the most complete collection of Buddhist texts, engraved on 80,000 woodblocks between 1237 and 1249. The buildings of Janggyeong Panjeon, which date from the fifteenth century, were constructed to house the woodblocks, which are also revered as an exceptional work of art. As the oldest repository of the Tripitaka, they reveal an astonishing mastery of the devising and implementation of conservation techniques.

Seokguram Grotto and Bulguksa Temple

Established on the slopes of Mount T'oham in the eighth century, the Seokguram cave contains a monumental statue of Buddha looking at the sea in the *bhumisparsha mudra* position. With the surrounding portrayals of gods, *Bodhisattvas* and disciples, realistically and delicately sculpted in high relief and low relief, it makes up a masterpiece of Buddhist art in the Far East. The Temple of Bulguksa, built in 752, and the cave form a body of religious architecture of exceptional significance.

LAOS

Town of Luang Prabang

This town reflects the exceptional fusion of traditional architecture and urban structures built by nineteenth — and twentieth — century European colonial rulers. Its unique township is remarkably well preserved, illustrating a key stage in the blending of these two distinct cultural traditions.

Vat Phou and Associated Ancient Settlements within the Champasak Cultural Landscape

The Champasak cultural landscape, including the Vat Phou Temple complex, is a remarkably well-preserved planned landscape more than 1,000 years old. It was shaped to express the Hindu vision of the relationship between nature and humanity, using an axis from mountain top to river bank to lay out a geometric pattern of temples, shrines and waterworks extending over some 10 kilometres (6 miles). Two planned cities on the banks of the Mekong River are also part of the site, as well as Phou Kao mountain. The whole represents a development ranging from the fifth to fifteenth centuries, mainly associated with the Khmer Empire.

LEBANON

Anjar

The ruins of Anjar, a city founded by Caliph Walid I at the beginning of the eighth century, has a very methodical layout, reminiscent of the palace-cities of ancient times. It is a unique testimony to Omayyad city planning.

Byblos

Byblos is the site of the multi-layered ruins of one of the most ancient cities in Lebanon, inhabited since Neolithic times and closely tied to the legends and history of the Mediterranean region for many thousands of years. Byblos is directly associated with the history of the diffusion of the Phoenician alphabet.

Tyre

Tyre, where, according to legend, purple dye was invented, was the great Phoenician city that ruled the seas and founded prosperous colonies such as Cadiz and Carthage. Its historical role declined at the end of the Crusades. It conserves important archaeological remains, mainly from Roman times.

NEPAL

Kathmandu Valley
At the crossroads of the great civilizations of Asia, seven groups of Hindu and Buddhist monuments, as well as the three residential and palace areas of the royal cities of Kathmandu, Patan and Bhadgaon, illustrate Nepalese art at its height. Among the 130 monuments are pilgrimage centres, temples, shrines, bathing sites and gardens — all sites of veneration by both religious groups.

Lumbini, the Birthplace of the Lord Buddha
Siddharta Gautama, the Lord Buddha, was born in 623 B.C. at the famous gardens of Lumbini, which soon became a place of pilgrimage. Among the pilgrims was the Indian Emperor Ashoka, who erected one of his commemorative pillars there. The site is now being developed as a Buddhist pilgrimage centre, where the archaeological remains associated with the birth of the Lord Buddha form a central feature.

OMAN

Archaeological Sites of Bat, Al-Khutm and Al-Ayn
The protohistoric site of Bat, near a palm grove within the Sultanate of Oman, constitutes, along with the neighbouring sites, the most complete collection of settlements and necropolises of the third millennium B.C.

The Frankincense Trail
The frankincense trees of Wadi Dawkah and the remains of the caravan oasis of Shisr, and the ports of Khor Rori and al-Balid vividly illustrate the trade in frankincense that flourished in this region for many centuries, as one of the most important trading activities of the ancient and medieval world.

PAKISTAN

Archaeological Ruins at Moenjodaro
The ruins of an immense city in the valley of the Indus, Moenjodaro was built entirely of unbaked brick in the third millennium B.C. The site contains an acropolis, built on large embankments, ramparts, and a lower town laid out according to strict rules, evidence of an early system of town planning.

Buddhist Ruins at Takht-i-Bahi and Neighbouring City Remains at Sahr-i-Bahlol
The 'throne of origins', a beautifully preserved first-century Buddhist monastery, can be seen on the top of a high hill, close to the ruins of Sahr-i-Bahlol, a small fortified city, dating from the same period.

Historic Monuments of Thatta
The capital of three successive dynasties and later ruled by the Mogul emperors of Delhi, Thatta was constantly embellished from the fourteenth to the eighteenth centuries. The remains of the city and its necropolis provide a unique view of the Sind civilization.

Taxila
From the ancient neolithic tumulus of Saraikala to the ramparts of Sirkap (200 B.C.), to the city of Sirsukh dating from the first century A.D., Taxila illustrates the different stages in the development of a city on the Indus, alternately influenced by Persia, Greece and Central Asia and which, from the fifth century B.C. to the second century A.D., was an important Buddhist centre of learning.

PHILIPPINES

Baroque Churches of the Philippines
These churches, located in Manila, Santa Maria, Paoay and Miag-ao, the first of which was built in the late sixteenth century by Spain, are unique. They represent the fusion of European Baroque as reinterpreted by Chinese and Philippine craftsmen.

Historic Town of Vigan
Vigan, established in the sixteenth century, is the best-preserved example of a planned Spanish colonial town in Asia. Its architecture reflects the coming together of cultural elements from elsewhere in the Philippines and from China with those of Europe to create a unique culture and townscape without parallel anywhere in East and South-East Asia.

SRI LANKA

Ancient City of Polonnaruwa
The second capital of Sri Lanka after the destruction of Anuradhapura in 993, Polonnaruwa comprises, besides the Brahmanic monuments built by the Cholas, the monumental ruins of the fabulous garden-city created by Parakramabahu I in the twelfth century.

Ancient City of Sigiriya
On the steep slopes and the summit of a granitic peak some 370 metres (1200 feet) high — the 'Lion's Rock', which dominates the jungle on all sides - lie the ruins of the capital built by the parricidal King Kassapa I (477-95). A series of galleries and staircases which emerge from the mouth of a gigantic lion constructed of bricks and plaster provide access to the site.

Old Town of Galle and its Fortifications
Founded in the sixteenth century by the Portuguese, Galle reached the height of its development in the eighteenth century, before the arrival of the British. It is the best example of a fortified city built by Europeans in South and South-East Asia, illustrating the interaction of European architecture and South Asian traditions.

Sacred City of Anuradhapura
This sacred city was established around a cutting from the 'tree of enlightenment', Buddha's fig tree, brought there in the third century B.C. by Sanghamitta, the founder of an order of Buddhist nuns.

Anuradhapura, a Ceylonese political and religious capital that flourished for 1,300 years, was abandoned after an invasion in 993.

SYRIA

Ancient City of Aleppo

Located at the crossroads of various trade routes since the second millenium B.C., Aleppo was ruled successively by the Hittites, Assyrians, Arabs, Mongols, Mamelukes and Ottomans. Its thirteenth-century citadel, its twelfth-century Great Mosque and various seventeenth-century *medersas*, palaces, caravanserais and hammams give it a cohesive and unique urban fabric, now threatened by overpopulation.

Ancient City of Bosra

Once the capital of the Roman province of Arabia, an important stopover on the ancient caravan route to Mecca, Bosra has conserved within its thick walls a magnificent Roman theatre from the second century, early Christian ruins and several mosques.

Ancient City of Damascus

Founded in the third millenium B.C., it is one of the oldest cities in the Middle East. In the Middle Ages Damascus was the centre of a flourishing artisan industry (swords and laces). Amongst the 125 monuments from the different periods of its history, the eighth-century Great Mosque of the Umajjads is one of the most spectacular, built on the site of an Assyrian sanctuary.

THAILAND

Ayutthaya and Associated Historic Towns

Founded in about 1350, Ayutthaya became the second Siamese capital after Sukhotai. It was destroyed by the Burmese in the eighteenth century. Its remains, characterized by its *prang* or reliquary towers and gigantic monasteries, give an idea of its past splendour.

Ban Chiang Archaeological Site

Considered the most important prehistoric settlement so far discovered in South-East Asia, Ban Chiang was the centre of a remarkable phenomenon of human cultural, social and technological evolution. The site presents the earliest evidence of farming in the region and of the manufacture and use of metals.

Sukhothai and Associated Historic Towns

Capital of the first Kingdom of Siam in the thirteenth and fourteenth centuries, a number of notable monuments, which illustrate the beginnings of Thai architecture, can be seen in Sukhotai.

TURKMENISTAN

Historical and Cultural Park 'Ancient Merv'

Merv is the oldest and most completely preserved of the oasis cities along the Silk Route in Central Asia. The remains in this wide oasis span 4,000 years of human history and a number of monuments are visible, particularly from the last two millennia.

UZBEKISTAN

Historic Centre of Bukhara

Situated on The Silk Road, Bukhara is more than 2,000 years old. It is the most complete example of a medieval city in Central Asia, with an urban fabric that has remained largely intact. The monuments of interest include Ismail Samani's famous tomb, a masterpiece of tenth-century Muslim architecture, and a number of seventeenth-century *medersas*.

Historic Centre of Shakhrisyabz

The historic centre of Shakhrisyabz contains a collection of exceptional monuments and ancient quarters which bear witness to the centuries of its history, and particularly to the period of its apogee, under the Empire of Timur, in the fifteenth century.

Itchan Kala

Itchan Kala is the inner town, protected by brick walls about 10 metres (33 feet) high, of the old Khiva oasis, which was the last resting place of caravaneers before crossing the desert to Iran. Although few very old monuments still remain there, it is a coherent and well-preserved example of Muslim architecture of Central Asia.

VIETNAM

Complex of Hué Monuments

Established as the capital of unified Vietnam in 1802, Hué was not only the political but also the cultural and religious centre under the Nguyen dynasty until 1945.

Hoi An Ancient Town

Hoi An constitutes an exceptionally well-preserved example of a South-East Asian trading port from the period of the fifteenth to nineteenth centuries. Its buildings and its street pattern reflect the influences, both indigenous and foreign.

My Son Sanctuary

Between the fourth and the thirteenth centuries a unique culture developed on the coast of contemporary Vietnam which owed its spiritual origins to the Hinduism of India. This is illustrated by the remains of a series of impressive tower temples.

YEMEN

Historic Town of Zabid

The domestic and military architecture of this city and its urban plan make it a site of outstanding archaeological and historical value. Zabid was the capital of Yemen from the thirteenth to the fifteenth centuries.

Old Walled City of Shibam

Surrounded by a fortified wall, the sixteenth-century city of Shibam is one of the oldest and best examples of urban planning based on the principle of vertical construction.

Aerial view of Paestum.

Europe

ALBANIA

Butrint

Butrint occupies a small peninsula between the Straits of Corfu and Lake Butrint. Inhabited since prehistoric times, Butrint has been the site of a Greek colony, a Roman city, and a bishopric. Following a period of prosperity under Byzantine administration, then a brief occupation by the Venetians, the city was abandoned in the late Middle Ages after marshes formed in the area. The present archaeological site is a repository of the ruins representing each period in the city's development. The limits of the World Heritage Site were extended in 1999 to include not only the walled city from the Greek and Roman period (approximately 16 hectares), but an additional 184 hectares to better protect the site.

AUSTRIA

Historic Centre of Graz

Graz is a particularly fine example of the living heritage of a Central European urban complex that was under Habsburg rule for many centuries. The old city is a harmonious blend of the architectural styles and artistic movements that have succeeded one other since the Middle Ages, together with cultural influences from neighbouring regions.

Historic Centre of the City of Salzburg

Salzburg has managed to preserve an extraordinarily rich urban fabric, developed over the period from the Middle Ages to the nineteenth century when it was a city-state ruled by a prince-archbishop. Its Flamboyant Gothic art attracted many craftsmen and artists before the city became even better known through the work of the Italian architects Vincenzo Scamozzi and Santini Solari, to whom the centre of Salzburg owes much of its Baroque appearance. This meeting point of northern and southern Europe perhaps sparked the genius of Salzburg's most famous son, Wolfgang Amadeus Mozart, whose name has been associated with the city ever since.

Historic Centre of Vienna

Vienna developed from early Celtic and Roman settlements into a medieval and Baroque city, the capital of the Austro-Hungarian Empire. It played an essential role as a leading European centre of music, from the great age of Viennese Classicism through until the early part of the twentieth century. The historic centre of Vienna is rich in architectural ensembles, including Baroque castles and gardens, as well as the late-nineteenth-century Ringstrasse lined with grand buildings, monuments and parks.

BELGIUM

Belfries of Flanders and Wallonia

The thirty belfries in Flanders and Wallonia, invariably found in an urban setting, are imposing belltowers of medieval origin, generally attached to the town hall and occasionally to a church. In addition to their outstanding artistic value, the belfries are potent symbols of the transition from feudalism to the mercantile urban society that played a vital role in the development of late medieval Europe.

Flemish Béguinages

The *Béguines* were women who dedicated their lives to God without retiring from the world. In the thirteenth century they founded the *béguinages*, enclosed communities designed to meet their spiritual and material needs. The Flemish *béguinages* are architectural ensembles composed of houses, churches, ancillary buildings and green spaces, with a layout of either urban or rural origin and built in styles specific to the Flemish cultural region. They are a fascinating reminder of the tradition of the *Béguines* that developed in north-western Europe in the Middle Ages.

Historic Centre of Brugge

Brugge is an outstanding example of a medieval historic settlement, which has maintained its historic fabric as it evolved over the centuries, and where original Gothic constructions form part of the town's identity. As one of the commercial and cultural capitals of Europe, Brugge developed cultural links to different parts of the world. It is closely associated with the school of Flemish Primitive painting.

BULGARIA

Ancient City of Nessebar

Situated on a rocky peninsula on the Black Sea, the more than 3,000-year-old site of Nessebar was originally a Thracian settlement (Menebria). At the beginning of the sixth century B.C., the city became a Greek colony. The city's remains, which date mostly from the Hellenistic period, include the acropolis, a temple of Apollo, an agora and a wall from the Thracian fortifications. Among other monuments, the Stara Mitropolia Basilica and the fortress date from the Middle Ages, when this was one of the most important Byzantine towns on the west coast of the Black Sea. Wooden houses built in the nineteenth century are typical of the Black Sea architecture of the period.

CROATIA

Historic City of Trogir

Trogir is a remarkable example of urban continuity. The orthogonal street plan of this island settlement dates back to the Hellenistic period and it was embellished by successive rulers with many fine public and domestic buildings and fortifications. Its beautiful Romanesque churches are complemented by the outstanding Renaissance and Baroque buildings from the Venetian period.

Historic Complex of Split with the Palace of Diocletian

The ruins of Diocletian's Palace, built during the late third and early fourth centuries A.D., can be found throughout the city. The cathedral was built in the Middle Ages, reusing materials from the ancient mausoleum. Twelfth- and thirteenth-century

Romanesque churches, medieval fortifications, fifteenth-century Gothic palaces and other palaces in Renaissance and Baroque style make up the rest of the protected area.

CYPRUS

Choirokoitia

The Neolithic settlement of Choirokoitia, occupied from the seventh to the fourth millennium B.C., is one of the most important prehistoric sites in the eastern Mediterranean. Its remains and the finds from the excavations there have thrown much light on the evolution of human society in this key region. Since only part of the site has been excavated, it forms an exceptional archaeological reserve for future study.

Paphos

Paphos has been inhabited since the Neolithic period. It was a centre of the cult of Aphrodite and of pre-Hellenic fertility deities. Aphrodite's legendary birthplace was on this island, where her temple was erected by the Myceneans in the twelfth century B.C. The remains of villas, palaces, theatres, fortresses and tombs mean that the site is of exceptional architectural and historic value. The mosaics of Nea Paphos are among the most beautiful in the world.

CZECH REPUBLIC

Historic Centre of Cesky Krumlov

Situated on the banks of the Vltava River, the town was built around a thirteenth-century castle with Gothic, Renaissance and Baroque elements. It is an outstanding example of a small Central European medieval town whose architectural heritage has remained intact thanks to its peaceful evolution over more than five centuries.

Historic Centre of Telc

The houses in Telc, which stands on a hilltop, were originally built of wood. After a fire in the late

fourth century, the town was rebuilt in stone, surrounded by walls and further strengthened by a network of artificial ponds. The town's Gothic castle was reconstructed in High Gothic style in the late fifteenth century.

Holasovice Historical Village Reservation

Holasovice is an exceptionally complete and well-preserved example of a traditional Central European village. It has a large number of outstanding eighteenth- and nineteenth-century vernacular buildings in a style known as 'South Bohemian folk Baroque', and preserves a ground plan dating to the Middle Ages.

Kutná Hora: Historical Town Centre with the Church of Saint Barbara and the Cathedral of Our Lady at Sedlec

Kutná Hora developed as a result of the exploitation of the silver mines. In the fourteenth century it became a royal city endowed with monuments that symbolized its prosperity. The Church of Saint Barbara, a jewel of the late Gothic period, and the Cathedral of Our Lady at Sedlec, which was restored in line with the Baroque taste of the early eighteenth century, were to influence the architecture of Central Europe. These masterpieces today form part of a well-preserved medieval urban fabric with some particularly fine private dwellings.

DENMARK

Jelling Mounds, Runic Stones and Church

The Jelling burial mounds and one of the runic stones are striking examples of pagan Nordic culture, while the other runic stone and the church illustrate the Christianization of the Danish people towards the middle of the tenth century.

ESTONIA

Historic Centre (Old Town) of Tallinn

The origins of Tallinn date back to the thirteenth

century, when a castle was built there by the crusading knights of the Teutonic Order. It developed as a major centre of the Hanseatic League, and its wealth is demonstrated by the opulence of the public buildings (the churches in particular) and the domestic architecture of the merchants' houses, which have survived to a remarkable degree despite the ravages of fire and war in the intervening centuries.

FINLAND

Bronze Age Burial Site of Sammallahdenmäki

This Bronze Age burial site features more than thirty granite burial cairns, providing a unique insight into the funerary practices and social and religious structures of northern Europe more than three millennia ago.

Old Rauma

Situated on the Gulf of Botnia, Rauma is one of the oldest harbours in Finland. Built around a Franciscan monastery, where the mid-fifteenth-century Holy Cross Church still stands, it is an outstanding example of an old Nordic city constructed in wood. Although ravaged by fire in the late seventeenth century, it has preserved its ancient vernacular architectural heritage.

FRANCE

Cathedral of Notre-Dame, Former Abbey of Saint-Rémi and Palace of Tau, Reims

The outstanding handling of new architectural techniques in the thirteenth century, and the harmonious marriage of sculptural decoration with architecture, have made Notre-Dame in Reims one of the masterpieces of Gothic art. The former abbey still has its beautiful ninth-century nave, in which lie the remains of Archbishop St Rémi (440-533), who instituted the Holy Anointing of the kings of France. The former archiepiscopal palace known as the Tau Palace, which played an important role in

religious ceremonies, was almost entirely rebuilt in the seventeenth century.

Decorated Grottoes of the Vézère Valley

The Vézère valley contains 147 prehistoric sites dating from the Palaeolithic and twenty-five decorated caves. It is particularly interesting ethnologically and anthropologically as well as aesthetically because of its cave paintings, especially those of the Lascaux Cave, whose discovery in 1940 was of great importance to the history of prehistoric art. The hunting scenes show some 100 animal figures, which are remarkable for their detail, rich colours and lifelike quality.

Historic Centre of Avignon

In the fourteenth century, this city in the South of France was the seat of the papacy. The Palais des Papes, an austere-looking fortress lavishly decorated by Simone Martini and Matteo Giovanetti, dominates the city, the surrounding ramparts and the remains of a twelfth-century bridge over the Rhône. Beneath this outstanding example of Gothic architecture, the Petit Palais and the Romanesque Cathedral of Notre-Dame-des-Doms complete an exceptional group of monuments that testify to the leading role played by Avignon in fourteenth-century Christian Europe.

Historic Fortified City of Carcassonne

Since the pre-Roman period, a fortified settlement has existed on the hill where Carcassonne now stands. In its present form it is an outstanding example of a medieval fortified town, with its massive defences encircling the castle and the surrounding buildings, its streets and its fine Gothic cathedral. Carcassonne is also of exceptional importance because of the lengthy restoration campaign undertaken by Viollet-le-Duc, one of the founders of the modern science of conservation.

Historic Site of Lyons

The long history of Lyons, which was founded by

the Romans in the first century B.C. as the capital of the Three Gauls and has continued to play a major role in Europe's political, cultural and economic development ever since, is vividly illustrated by its urban fabric and the many fine historic buildings from all periods.

Paris, Banks of the Seine

From the Louvre to the Eiffel Tower or the Place de la Concorde to the Grand and Petit Palais, the evolution of Paris and its history can be seen from the river. The Cathedral of Notre-Dame and the Sainte-Chapelle are architectural masterpieces while Haussmann's wide squares and avenues influenced late nineteenth-and twentieth-century urbanism the world over.

Place Stanislas, Place de la Carrière, and Place d'Alliance in Nancy

Nancy, the temporary residence of a king without a kingdom — Stanislas Leszczynski, later to become Duke of Lorraine — is paradoxically the oldest and most typical example of a modern capital where an enlightened monarch proved to be sensitive to the needs of the public. Built between 1752 and 1756 by a brilliant team led by the architect Héré, this was a carefully conceived project that succeeded in creating a capital that not only enhanced the sovereign's prestige but was also functional.

Provins, Town of Medieval Fairs

The fortified medieval town of Provins is situated in the former territory of the powerful Counts of Champagne. It bears witness to early developments in the organization of international trading fairs and the wool industry. The urban structure of Provins, which was built specifically to host the fairs and related activities, has been well preserved.

Roman and Romanesque Monuments of Arles

Arles is a good example of the adaptation of an ancient city to medieval European civilization. It has some impressive Roman monuments, of which the earliest — the arena, the Roman theatre and the *cryptoporticus* (subterranean galleries) — date back to the first century B.C. During the fourth century Arles experienced a second golden age, as attested by the baths of Constantine and the necropolis of Alyscamps. In the eleventh and twelfth centuries, Arles once again became one of the most attractive cities in the Mediterranean. Within the city walls, Saint-Trophime, with its cloister, is one of Provence's major Romanesque monuments.

Roman Theatre and its Surroundings and the 'Triumphal Arch' of Orange
Situated in the Rhône valley, the ancient theatre of Orange, with its 103 metre (335 feet) façade, is one of the best preserved of all the great Roman theatres. Built between A.D. 10 and 25, the Roman arch is one of the most beautiful and interesting surviving examples of a provincial triumphal arch from the reign of Augustus. It is decorated with low reliefs commemorating the establishment of the Pax Romana.

Routes of Santiago de Compostela in France
Santiago de Compostela was the supreme goal for countless thousands of pious pilgrims who converged there from all over Europe throughout the Middle Ages. To reach Spain pilgrims had to pass through France, and the group of important historical monuments included in this inscription marks out the four routes by which they did so.

Royal Saltworks of Arc-et-Senans
The Royal Saltworks of Arc-et-Senans, near Besançon, was built by Claude-Nicolas Ledoux. Its construction, begun in 1775 during the reign of Louis XVI, was the first major achievement of industrial architecture, reflecting the ideal of progress of the Enlightenment. This vast, semi-circular complex was designed to permit a rational and hierarchical organization of work and was to have been

followed by the building of an ideal city, a project that was never realized.

Strasbourg, Grande Ile
Surrounded by two arms of the River Ill, the Grande Ile (Big Island) is the historic centre of the Alsatian capital. It has an outstanding complex of monuments within a fairly small area. The cathedral, the four ancient churches and the Palais Rohan — former residence of the prince-bishops — far from appearing as isolated monuments, form a district that is characteristic of a medieval town and illustrates Strasbourg's evolution from the fifteenth to the eighteenth centuries.

The Loire Valley between Sully-sur-Loire and Chalonnes
The Loire Valley is an outstanding cultural landscape of great beauty, containing historic towns and villages, great architectural monuments (the châteaux), and cultivated lands formed by many centuries of interaction between their population and the physical environment, primarily the River Loire itself. The site includes the Château and Estate of Chambord, which was inscribed on the World Heritage List in 1981.

GERMANY

Bauhaus and its sites in Weimar and Dessau
Between 1919 and 1933, the Bauhaus School, based first in Weimar and then in Dessau, revolutionized architectural and aesthetic concepts and practices. The buildings designed and decorated by the school's professors (Walter Gropius, Hannes Meyer, Laszlo Moholy-Nagy and Wassily Kandinsky) launched the Modern Movement, which shaped much of the architecture of the twentieth century.

Classical Weimar
In the late eighteenth and early nineteenth centuries the small Thuringian town of Weimar witnessed a

remarkable cultural flowering, attracting many writers and scholars, notably Goethe and Schiller. This development is reflected in the high quality of many of the buildings and of the parks in the surrounding area.

Collegiate Church, Castle, and Old Town of Quedlinburg
Quedlinburg, in the *Land* of Sachsen-Anhalt, was a capital of the East Franconian German Empire at the time of the Saxonian-Ottonian ruling dynasty. It has been a prosperous trading town since the Middle Ages. The number and high quality of the timber-framed buildings make Quedlinburg an exceptional example of a medieval European town. The Collegiate Church of Saint Servatius is one of the masterpieces of Romanesque architecture.

Hanseatic City of Lübeck
Lübeck — the former capital and Queen City of the Hanseatic League — was founded in the twelfth century and prospered until the sixteenth century as the major trading centre for northern Europe. It has remained a centre for maritime commerce to this day, particularly with the Nordic countries. Despite the damage it suffered during the Second World War, the basic structure of the old city, consisting mainly of fifteenth- and sixteenth-century patrician residences, public monuments (the famous Holstentor brick gate), churches and salt storehouses, remains unaltered.

Mines of Rammelsberg and Historic Town of Goslar
Situated near the Rammelsberg Mines, Goslar held an important place in the Hanseatic League because of the rich Rammelsberg metallic ore deposits. From the tenth to the twelfth centuries it was the seat of the Holy Roman Empire of the German Nation. Its historic centre, dating from the Middle Ages, is perfectly preserved with some 1,500 semi-timbered houses built between the fifteenth and nineteenth centuries.

Palaces and Parks of Potsdam and Berlin

With 500 hectares of parks and 150 buildings constructed between 1730 and 1916, the complex of palaces and parks of Potsdam form an artistic whole, whose eclectic nature reinforces its sense of uniqueness. It extends into the district of Berlin-Zehlendorf, with the palaces and parks which line the banks of the Havel and the Glienicke Lakes. Voltaire stayed in the Sans-Souci Palace, built under Frederick II, between 1745 and 1757.

Roman Monuments, Cathedral of Saint Peter and Church of Our Lady in Trier

Trier, which stands on the Moselle River, was a Roman colony from the first century A.D. and then a great trading centre beginning in the next century. It became one of the capitals of the Tetrarchy at the end of the third century, when it was known as the 'Second Rome'. The number and quality of the surviving monuments are an outstanding testimony to Roman civilization.

The Luther Memorials in Eisleben and Wittenberg

These places in Saxony-Anhalt are all associated with the lives of Martin Luther and his fellow reformer Melanchthon. They include Melanchthon's house in Wittenberg, the houses in Eisleben where Luther was born in 1483 and died in 1546, his room in Wittenberg, the local church and the castle church where, on 31 October 1517, Luther posted his famous '95 Theses', which launched the Reformation and a new era in the religious and political history of the Western world.

The Zollverein Coal Mine Industrial Complex in Essen

The Zollverein industrial landscape in *Land* Nordrhein-Westfalen consists of the complete infrastructure of a historical coal-mining site, with some twentieth-century buildings of outstanding architectural merit. It constitutes remarkable material evidence of the evolution and decline of an essential industry over the past 150 years.

Völklingen Ironworks

The ironworks, which cover some 6 hectares, dominate the city of Völklingen. Although they have recently gone out of production, they are the only intact example, in the whole of Western Europe and North America, of an integrated ironworks that was built and equipped in the nineteenth and twentieth centuries and remained intact.

GREAT BRITAIN

Blaenavon Industrial Landscape

The area around Blaenavon bears eloquent and exceptional testimony to the pre-eminence of South Wales as the world's major producer of iron and coal in the nineteenth century. All the necessary elements can be seen *in situ*: coal and ore mines, quarries, a primitive railway system, furnaces, the homes of the workers, and the social infrastructure of their community.

Canterbury Cathedral, Saint Augustine's Abbey, and Saint Martin's Church

For 300 years the seat of the spiritual leader of the Church of England, Canterbury, in Kent, houses the modest Church of Saint Martin, the oldest in England, the ruins of the Abbey of Saint Augustine, a reminder of the evangelizing role of the saint in the Heptarchy from 597, and the superb Christ Church Cathedral, a breathtaking mixture of Romanesque and Gothic perpendicular styles, where Archbishop Thomas Becket was assassinated in 1170.

Castles and Town Walls of King Edward in Gwynedd

In the former principality of Gwynedd, in northern Wales, the castles of Beaumaris and Harlech, thanks largely to the greatest military engineer of the time, James of Saint George, and the fortified complexes of Caernarfon and Conwy, all extremely well-preserved, bear witness to the works of colonization and defence carried out throughout the reign of Edward I, King of England (1272-1307), and to the military architecture of the time.

City of Bath

Founded by the Romans as a thermal spa, Bath became an important centre of the wool industry in the Middle Ages. In the eighteenth century, under George III, it developed into an elegant town with Neo-classical buildings inspired by Palladio, which blended harmoniously with the Roman thermal complex.

Durham Castle and Cathedral

Built in the late eleventh and early twelfth centuries to house the relics of Saint Cuthbert, the evangelist of Northumbria, and the Venerable Bede, the cathedral attests to the importance of the early Benedictine monastic community and is the largest and best example of Norman-style architecture in England. The innovative audacity of its vaulting foreshadowed Gothic architecture. Behind the cathedral is the castle, an ancient Norman fortress which was the residence of the prince-bishops of Durham.

Hadrian's Wall

Built on the orders of Emperor Hadrian in about A.D. 122 on the border between England and Scotland, the 118 kilometres (74 miles) long wall is a striking example of the organization of a military zone, which illustrates the techniques and strategic and geopolitical views of the Romans.

Heart of Neolithic Orkney

The group of Neolithic monuments on Orkney consist of a large chambered tomb (Maes Howe), two ceremonial stone circles (the Stones of Stenness and the Ring of Brodgar), and a settlement (Skara Brae), together with a number of unexcavated burial, ceremonial, and living sites. The group constitutes a major relict of a cultural landscape that graphically depicts life in this remote archipelago north of the coast of Scotland 5,000 years ago.

Historic Town of Saint George and Related Fortifications, Bermuda

The town of Saint George is an outstanding example of the earliest English urban settlement in the New World. Its associated fortifications graphically illustrate the development of English military engineering from the seventeenth to the twentieth centuries, being adapted to take account of the development of artillery over this period.

Ironbridge Gorge

In Ironbridge, known worldwide as the symbol of the Industrial Revolution, all the elements of progress developed in an eighteenth-century industrial region can be found, from the mines themselves to the railway lines. Nearby, the blast furnace of Coalbrookdale, built in 1708, is a reminder of the discovery of coke, which, together with the bridge at Ironbridge, the first metallic bridge in the world, had considerable influence on the evolution of technology and architecture.

Maritime Greenwich

The ensemble of buildings at Greenwich, near London, and the park in which they are set, are distinguished symbols of English artistic and scientific endeavour in the seventeenth and eighteenth centuries. The Queen's House by Inigo Jones was the first Palladian building in the British Isles, whilst the complex that was until recently the Royal Naval College was designed by Christopher Wren. The park, laid out on the basis of an original design by André Le Nôtre, contains the original Royal Observatory, the work of Wren and the scientist Robert Hooke.

Old and New Towns of Edinburgh

Edinburgh, capital of Scotland since the fifteenth century, presents the dual face of an old city dominated by a medieval fortress and a new Neo-classical city whose development from the eighteenth century onwards exerted a far-reaching influence on European urban planning. The harmonious juxtaposition of these two highly contrasting historic areas, each containing many buildings of great significance, is what gives the city its unique character.

Saltaire

Saltaire, West Yorkshire, is a complete and well-preserved industrial village from the second half of the nineteenth century. Its textile mills, public buildings and workers' housing are built in a harmonious style of high architectural standards and the urban plan survives intact, giving a vivid impression of Victorian philanthropic paternalism.

GREECE

Archaeological Site of Delphi

The pan-Hellenic sanctuary of Delphi, where the oracle of Apollo spoke, was the site of the *omphalos*, the 'navel of the world'. Blending harmoniously with the superb landscape and charged with sacred meaning, Delphi in the sixth century B.C. was indeed the religious centre and symbol of unity of the ancient Greek world.

Archaeological Site of Epidaurus

In a small valley in the Peloponnesus, the site of Epidaurus sprawls out over several levels. The cult of Asclepius first began there in the sixth century B.C., but the principal monuments, particularly the theatre — considered one of the purest masterpieces of Greek architecture — date from the fourth century. The vast site is a tribute to the healing cults of Greek and Roman times, with temples and hospital buildings devoted to its gods.

Archaeological Sites of Mycenae and Tiryns

The archaeological sites of Mycenae and Tiryns are the imposing ruins of the two greatest cities of the Mycenaean civilization, which dominated the eastern Mediterranean world from the fifteenth to the twelfth centuries B.C. and played a vital role in the development of classical Greek culture. These two cities are indissolubly linked to the Homeric epics, the *Iliad* and the *Odyssey*, which have influenced European art and literature for more than three millennia.

Archaeological Site of Olympia

The site of Olympia, in a valley in the Peloponnesus, has been inhabited since prehistoric times. In the tenth century B.C., Olympia became a centre for the worship of Zeus. The Altis — the sanctuary to the gods — has one of the highest concentrations of masterpieces from the ancient Greek world. In addition to temples, there are the remains of all the sports structures erected for the Olympic Games, which were held in Olympia every four years beginning in 776 B.C.

Archaeological Site of Vergina

The city of Aigai, the ancient first capital of the Kingdom of Macedonia, was discovered in the nineteenth century near Vergina, in northern Greece. The most important remains are the monumental palace, lavishly decorated with mosaics and painted stuccoes, and the burial ground with more than 300 tumuli, some of which date from the eleventh century B.C. One of the royal tombs in the Great Tumulus is identified as that of Philip II, who conquered all the Greek cities, paving the way for his son Alexander and the expansion of the Hellenistic world.

Delos

According to Greek mythology, Apollo was born on this tiny island in the Cyclades archipelago. Apollo's sanctuary attracted pilgrims from all over Greece, and Delos became a prosperous trading port. The island bears traces of the succeeding civilizations in the Aegean world, from the third millennium B.C. to the Palaeochristian era. The archaeological site is exceptionally extensive and rich and conveys the image of a great cosmopolitan Mediterranean port.

Historic Centre (Chorá) with the Monastery of Saint John 'the Theologian' and the Cave of the Apocalypse on the Island of Pátmos

The small island of Pátmos in the Dodecanese is reputed to be where Saint John the Theologian wrote both his *Gospel* and the *Apocalypse*. A monastery dedicated to the 'Beloved Disciple' was founded there in the late tenth century and it has been a place of pilgrimage and of Greek Orthodox learning continuously since that time. The fine monastic complex dominates the island, and the old settlement of Chorá associated with it, which contains many religious and secular buildings.

Medieval City of Rhodes

The Order of Saint John of Jerusalem occupied Rhodes from 1309 to 1523 and set about transforming the city into a stronghold. It subsequently came under Turkish and Italian rule. With the Palace of the Grand Masters, the Great Hospital and the Street of the Knights, the Upper Town is one of the most beautiful urban ensembles of the Gothic period. In the Lower Town, Gothic architecture coexists with mosques, public baths and other buildings dating from the Ottoman period.

Meteora

In a region of almost inaccessible sandstone peaks, monks settled on these 'columns of the sky' from the eleventh century onwards. Twenty-four of these monasteries were built, despite incredible difficulties, at the time of the great revival of the eremetic ideal in the fifteenth century. Their sixteenth-century frescoes mark a key stage in the development of post-Byzantine painting.

Monasteries of Daphni, Hossios Luckas and Nea Moni of Chios

Although geographically distant from each other, these three monasteries (the first is in Attica, near Athens, the second in Phocida near Delphi, and the third on an island in the Aegean Sea, near Asia Minor) belong to the same typological series and share the same aesthetic characteristics. The churches are built on a cross-in-square plan with a large dome supported by squinches defining an octagonal space. In the eleventh and twelfth centuries they were decorated with superb marble works as well as mosaics on a gold background, all characteristic of the 'second golden age of Byzantine art'.

Mystras

Mystras, the 'wonder of the Morea', was built as an amphitheatre around the fortress erected in 1249 by the Prince of Achaia, William of Villehardouin. Reconquered by the Byzantines, then occupied by the Turks and the Venetians, the city was abandoned in 1832, leaving only the breathtaking medieval ruins, standing in a beautiful landscape.

Palaeochristian and Byzantine Monuments of Thessalonika

Founded in 315 B.C., the provincial capital and sea port of Thessalonika was one of the first bases for the spread of Christianity. Among its Christian monuments are fine churches, some built on the Greek cross plan and others on the three-aisle basilica plan. Constructed over a long period, from the fourth to the fifteenth centuries, they constitute a diachronic typological series, which had considerable influence in the Byzantine world. The mosaics of the rotunda, Saint Demetrius and Saint David are among the great masterpieces of early Christian art.

Pythagoreion and Heraion of Samos

Many civilizations have inhabited this small Aegean island, near Asia Minor, since the third millennium B.C. The remains of Pythagoreion, an ancient fortified port with Greek and Roman monuments and a spectacular tunnel-aqueduct, as well as the Heraion, temple of the Samian Hera, can still be seen.

HUNGARY

Budapest, the Banks of the Danube and the Buda Castle Quarter

This site has the remains of monuments such as the Roman city of Aquincum and the Gothic Castle of Buda, which have had a considerable influence on the architecture of various periods. It is one of the world's outstanding urban landscapes and illustrates the great periods in the history of the Hungarian capital.

Hollokö

An outstanding example of a deliberately preserved traditional settlement, this village, which was developed mainly during the seventeenth and eighteenth centuries, is a living example of rural life before the agricultural revolution of the twentieth century.

The Pécs (Sopianae) Early Christian Cemetery

In the fourth century, a remarkable series of decorated tombs were constructed in the cemetery of the Roman provincial town of Sopianae (modern Pécs). These are important both structurally and architecturally, since they were built as underground burial chambers with memorial chapels above the ground. The tombs are important also in artistic terms, since they are richly decorated with murals of outstanding quality depicting Christian themes.

IRELAND

Archaeological Ensemble of the Bend of the Boyne

The three main prehistoric sites of the Brúna Bóinne Complex, Newgrange, Knowth and Dowth, are situated on the north bank of the River Boyne, 50 kilometres (32 miles) north of Dublin. This is Europe's largest and most important concentration of prehistoric megalithic art. The monuments there had social, economic, religious and funerary functions.

ITALY

Archaeological Area and the Patriarchal Basilica of Aquileia

Aquileia, one of the largest and wealthiest cities of the Early Roman Empire, was destroyed by Attila in the mid-fifth century. Most of it still remains unexcavated beneath fields, and as such it constitutes the greatest archaeological reserve of its kind. Its Patriarchal Basilica, an outstanding building with an exceptional mosaic pavement, also played a key role in the Evangelization of a large region of Central Europe.

Archaeological Area of Agrigento

Founded as a Greek colony in the sixth century B.C., Agrigento became one of the leading cities of the Mediterranean world. Its supremacy and pride are demonstrated by the remains of the magnificent Doric temples that dominate the ancient town, much of which remains intact under latter-day fields and orchards. Selected excavated areas throw light on the later Hellenic and Roman town and on the burial practices of its Palaeochristian inhabitants.

Assisi, the Basilica of San Francesco and Other Franciscan Sites

Assisi, an ancient sanctuary and a medieval hill town, is the birthplace of Saint Francis and fundamentally associated with the work of the Franciscan Order. The masterpieces of medieval art, such as the Basilica of San Francesco and the paintings by Cimabue, Simone Martini, Pietro Lorenzetti, and Giotto, have made Assisi a fundamental reference point for the development of Italian and European art and architecture.

Cathedral, Torre Civica and Piazza Grande, Modena

The magnificent twelfth-century Cathedral of Modena is a supreme example of Romanesque art, the work of two great artists (Lanfranco and Wiligelmo). With its associated piazza and the soaring tower, it testifies to the strength of the faith of its builders and the power of the Canossa dynasty who commissioned it.

Cilento and Vallo di Diano National Park with the Archaeological Sites of Paestum and Velia, and the Certosa di Padula

The Cilento area is a cultural landscape of exceptional quality. Dramatic chains of sanctuaries and settlements along its three east-west mountain ridges vividly portray the historical evolution of the area as a major route for trade and for cultural and political interaction during the prehistoric and medieval periods. It was also the boundary between the Greek colonies of Magna Grecia and the indigenous Etruscan and Lucanian peoples, and so preserves the remains of two very important classical cities, Paestum and Velia.

City of Verona

The historic city of Verona was founded in the first century A.D. It flourished particularly under the rule of the Scaliger family in the thirteenth and fourteenth centuries and as part of the Republic of Venice from the fifteenth to eighteenth centuries. Verona, a city of culture and art, has preserved a remarkable number of monuments from antiquity and the medieval and Renaissance periods, and represents an outstanding example of a military stronghold.

Historic Centre of Florence

Built on the site of an Etruscan settlement, Florence, the symbol of the Renaissance, rose to economic and cultural pre-eminence under the Medici in the fifteenth and sixteenth centuries. Its 600 years of extraordinary artistic activity can be seen above all in the thirteenth-century cathedral (Santa Maria del Fiore), the Church of Santa Croce, the Uffizi and the Pitti Palaces, and the work of great masters such as Giotto, Brunelleschi, Botticelli and Michelangelo.

Historic Centre of Naples

From the Neapolis founded by Greek settlers in 470 B.C. to the city of today, Naples has retained the imprint of the successive cultures that emerged in Europe and the Mediterranean Basin. This makes it a unique site, with a wealth of outstanding monuments such as the Church of Santa Chiara and the Castel Nuovo.

Historic Centre of San Gimignano

'San Gimignano delle belle Torri' is situated in Tuscany, 56 kilometres (35 miles) south of Florence. It served as an important relay point for pilgrims on the Via Francigena to and from Rome. The patrician families, who controlled the city, built some seventy-two tower-houses (up to 50 metres high) as symbols of their wealth and power. Only fourteen have survived but San Gimignano has retained its feudal atmosphere and appearance. The city also contains masterpieces of fourteenth-and fifteenth-century Italian art.

Historic Centre of Siena

Siena is the embodiment of a medieval city. Its inhabitants pursued their rivalry with Florence right into the area of urban planning. Throughout the centuries, they preserved their city's Gothic appearance, acquired between the twelfth and fifteenth centuries. During this period the work of Duccio, the Lorenzetti brothers and Simone Martini was to influence the course of Italian and, more broadly, European art. The whole city of Siena, built around the Piazza del Campo, was devised as a work of art that blends into the surrounding landscape.

Historic Centre of Urbino

Urbino is a small hill town that experienced an astonishing cultural flowering in the fifteenth century, attracting artists and scholars from all over Italy and beyond, and influencing cultural developments elsewhere in Europe. Owing to its economic and cultural stagnation from the sixteenth century onwards, its Renaissance appearance has been remarkably well preserved.

Rock Carvings in Valcamonica

Valcamonica, in the foothills of the Lombardy Alps, has one of the greatest collection of prehistoric petroglyphs to be found — more than 140,000 signs and figures carved in rock over a period of 8,000 years, depicting themes of agriculture, navigation, war and magic.

Su Nuraxi at Barumini

During the late second millennium B.C., in the Bronze Age, a special type of defensive structure, known as *nuraghi*, for which no parallel exists anywhere else, was developed on the island of Sardinia. The complex consists of circular defensive towers in the form of truncated cones built of dressed stone, with corbel-vaulted internal chambers. The complex at Barumini, which was extended and strengthened in the first half of the first millennium under Carthaginian pressure, is the finest and most complete example of this remarkable form of prehistoric architecture.

The Sassi of Matera

This is the most outstanding, intact example of a troglodyte settlement in the Mediterranean region, perfectly adapted to its terrain and ecosystem. The first inhabited zone dates from the Palaeolithic, while later settlements illustrate a number of significant stages in human history. Matera is in the southern region of Basilicata.

The Trulli of Alberobello

The *trulli*, limestone dwellings found in the southern region of Puglia, are remarkable examples of dry-wall (mortarless) construction, a prehistoric building technique still in use in this region. The *trulli* are made of roughly worked limestone boulders collected from neighbouring fields. Characteristically, they feature pyramidal, domed or conical roofs built up of corbelled limestone slabs.

Venice and its Lagoon

Founded in the fifth century and spread over 118 small islands, Venice became a major maritime power in the tenth century. The whole city is an extraordinary architectural masterpiece in which even the smallest building contains works by some of the world's greatest artists such as Giorgione, Titian, Tintoretto, Veronese and others.

LATVIA

Historic Centre of Riga

Riga was a major centre of the Hanseatic League and prospered from its trade with central and eastern Europe in the thirteenth to fifteenth centuries. The urban fabric of its medieval centre reflects this prosperity, although most of its earlier buildings have been destroyed by fire and war. In the nineteenth century it became a very important economic centre, and the suburbs of the medieval town were built, first in imposing wooden buildings in classical style and then in *Jugendstil*. It is generally recognized that Riga contains the finest concentration of Art Nouveau buildings in Europe.

LITHUANIA

Vilnius Historic Centre

Political centre of the Grand Duchy of Lithuania from the thirteenth to the end of the eighteenth centuries, Vilnius has had a profound influence on the cultural and architectural development of much of Eastern Europe. Despite invasions and partial destruction, it has preserved an impressive complex of historic buildings.

LUXEMBOURG

City of Luxembourg: its Old Quarters and Fortifications

Because of its strategic position, Luxembourg was one of Europe's greatest fortresses from the sixteenth century until 1867, when it became neutral.

Repeatedly fortified as it passed from one great European power to another (the House of Burgundy, the Habsburgs, the French and Spanish kings, and the Holy Roman emperors), its fortifications were, until their partial dismantlement, an epitome of military architecture spanning several centuries.

MACEDONIA

Ohrid Region with its Cultural and Historical Aspect and its Natural Environment

Located on the shores of Lake Ohrid (inscribed as a natural World Heritage Site since 1979), the town of Ohrid is one of the oldest human settlements in Europe. Built mostly between the seventh and the nineteenth centuries, it has the most ancient Slav monastery (Saint Pantelejmon) and more than 800 icons of Byzantine style, painted between the eleventh and the end of the fourteenth centuries, which are considered to be, after those of the Tretiakov Gallery in Moscow, the most important collection in the world.

MALTA

City of Valetta

The capital of the Republic of Malta is irrevocably linked to the history of the military and charitable order of Saint John of Jerusalem. Ruled successively by the Phoenicians, Greeks, Carthaginians, Romans, Byzantines, Arabs and the Order of the Knights of Saint John, its 320 monuments, confined within an area of 55 hectares, make it one of the most concentrated historic areas in the world.

Megalithic Temples of Malta

Seven megalithic temples stand on the islands of Malta and Gozo, each a result of individual development. The Ggantija complex on the island of Gozo is remarkable for its superhuman achievements dating from the Bronze Age. On the island of Malta, the Temples of Hagar Qin, Mnajdra and Tarxien are unique architectural masterpieces, given the very limited resources of their builders. The Ta'Hagrat and Skorba complexes bear witness to the development of the temple tradition in Malta.

THE NETHERLANDS

Defence Line of Amsterdam
Extending 135 kilometres (84 miles) around the city of Amsterdam, this defence line, built between 1883 and 1920, is the only example of a fortification based on the control of water. Since the sixteenth century, the people of the Netherlands have used their special knowledge of hydraulic engineering for defence purposes. The protection of the centre of the country was ensured by a network of forty-five forts and their artillery acting in concert with temporary flooding from polders and an intricate system of canals and locks.

Historic Area of Willemstad, Inner City, and Harbour, Netherlands Antilles
The Dutch established a trading settlement at a fine natural harbour on the Caribbean island of Curaçao in 1634. The town developed continuously over the succeeding centuries. The modern town consists of several distinct historic districts whose architecture reflects both the European planning and styles of the Netherlands, and the Spanish and Portuguese colonial towns with which Willemstad engaged in trade.

Mill Network at Kinderdijk-Elshout
The contribution made by the people of 'the low countries' to the technology of handling water is enormous, and this is admirably demonstrated by the installations in the Kinderdijk-Elshout area. Hydraulic works to drain the land for agriculture and settlement began in the Middle Ages and have continued uninterruptedly to the present day. The site contains all the relevant elements of this technology — dikes, reservoirs, pumping stations, administrative buildings, and a series of impeccably preserved windmills.

NORWAY

Bryggen
Bryggen, the old wharf of Bergen, is a reminder of the town's importance as part of the Hanseatic League's trading empire from the fourteenth to the mid-sixteenth centuries. Many fires, the last in 1955, have ravaged the beautiful wooden houses of Bryggen but its main structure has been preserved. Many of the remaining fifty-eight buildings are now used as artists' studios.

Rock Carvings of Alta
This group of petroglyphs in the Alta Fiord, near the Arctic Circle, bears the traces of a settlement dating from 4200 to 500 B.C. The thousands of paintings and engravings add to our understanding of the environment and human activities at the boundaries of the Far North in prehistoric times.

Røros
Located on a mountainous site, its history is linked to the exploitation of copper mines, discovered in the seventeenth century and used for 333 years until 1977. Completely rebuilt after its destruction by Swedish troops in 1679, the city includes some eighty wooden houses, most of which are grouped around courtyards. Many of them still retain their dark-pitch log façades which give the town a medieval aspect.

POLAND

Historic Centre of Warsaw
In August 1944, during the Second World War, more than 85 per cent of Warsaw's eighteenth-century historic centre was destroyed by Nazi occupation troops. After the war, a five-year reconstruction campaign by its citizens resulted in today's meticulous reproduction of the churches, palaces and the market-place. It is an exceptional example of a total reconstruction of a span of history from the thirteenth to the twentieth centuries.

Medieval Town of Torun
Torun owes its origins to the Teutonic Order, which built a castle there in the mid-thirteenth century as a base for the conquest and Evangelization of Prussia. It quickly developed a commercial role as part of the Hanseatic League, and many of the imposing public and private buildings from the fourteenth and fifteenth centuries that survive in its Old and New Towns are striking testimony to its importance.

Old City of Zamosc
Zamosc was founded in the sixteenth century by the hetman (head of the army) Jan Zamoysky on the trade route linking western and northern Europe with the Black Sea. Modelled on the Italian trading cities and built during the Baroque period by the architect Bernando Morando, a native of Padua, Zamosc remains a perfect example of a Renaissance town of the late sixteenth century which retains its original layout and fortifications and a large number of buildings blending Italian and Central European architectural traditions.

Wieliczka Salt Mines
Mined since the thirteenth century, this deposit of rock salt in Wielicz-Bochniz is still actively worked. With over nine levels and 300 kilometres (190 miles) of galleries with famous works of art, altars, and statues sculpted in salt, it constitutes a fascinating pilgrimage into the past of a major industrial undertaking.

PORTUGAL

Central Zone of the Town of Angra do Heroismo in the Azores
Situated on one of the islands of the Azores archipelago, this was an obligatory port of call from the fifteenth century until the advent of the steamship, in the nineteenth century. Its 400-year-old San Sebastian and San Juan Baptista fortifications are a

unique example of military architecture. Damaged by an earthquake in 1980, Angra is being restored.

Cultural Landscape of Sintra

In the nineteenth century Sintra became the first centre of European Romantic architecture. Ferdinand II turned a ruined monastery into a castle where this new sensitivity was displayed in the use of Gothic, Egyptian, Moorish and Renaissance elements and in the creation of a park blending local and exotic species of trees. Other prestigious homes built along the same lines in the surrounding Serra created a unique combination of parks and gardens which influenced the development of landscapes in Europe.

Historic Centre of Evora

This museum-city, whose roots go back to Roman times, reached its golden age in the fifteenth century, when it became the residence of the Portuguese kings. Its unique quality stems from its sixteenth-to eighteenth-century whitewashed houses decorated with *azulejos* and wrought-iron balconies. Its monuments decisively influenced Portuguese architecture in Brazil.

Historic Centre of Guimarães

The historic town of Guimarães is associated with the emergence of the Portuguese national identity in the twelfth century. An exceptionally well-preserved and authentic example of the evolution of a medieval settlement into a modern town, its rich building typology exemplifies the specific development of Portuguese architecture from the fifteenth to nineteenth centuries through the consistent use of traditional building materials and techniques.

Historic Centre of Oporto

The city of Oporto, built along the hillsides that overlook the mouth of the Douro River, forms an exceptional urban landscape with a thousand-year history. Its continuous growth, linked to the sea (the Romans gave it the name Portus, or port), can

be seen in its many and varied monuments — from the cathedral with its Roman choir, via the Neo-classical Stock Exchange to the typically Portuguese Manueline Church of Santa Clara.

Prehistoric Rock-Art Sites in the Côa Valley

The exceptional concentration of rock engravings from the Upper Palaeolithic period, from 22,000 to 10,000 B.C., is the most outstanding example of the early manifestation of human artistic creation in this form anywhere in the world.

ROMANIA

Churches of Moldavia

With their painted exterior walls, decorated with fifteenth-and sixteenth-century frescoes, masterpieces of Byzantine art, these seven churches are unique in Europe.

Dacian Fortresses of the Orastie Mountains

The Dacian fortresses, six Late Iron-Age defensive works, were created in the first centuries B.C. and A.D. as protection against Roman conquest. Their extensive and well-preserved remains are located on a spectacular natural site and present a dramatic picture of a vigorous and innovative Iron Age civilization.

Historic Centre of Sighisoara

Founded by German craftsmen and merchants, known as the Saxons of Transylvania, the historic centre of Sighisoara has preserved in an exemplary way the features of a small, fortified, medieval town, which played an important strategic and commercial role at the edges of Central Europe for several centuries.

Villages with Fortified Churches in Transylvania

The Transylvanian villages with fortified churches provide a vivid picture of the cultural landscape of southern Transylvania. The seven villages inscribed

are characterized by the specific land-use system, settlement pattern, and organization of the family farmstead units preserved since the late Middle Ages, and dominated by their fortified churches, which illustrate building periods from the thirteenth to sixteenth centuries.

Wooden Churches of Maramures

The Maramures wooden churches represent a selection of eight outstanding examples of different architectural solutions from different periods and areas. They provide a vivid picture of the variety of design and craftsmanship expressed by narrow but high timber constructions with their characteristic tall, slim clock towers at the western end of the building, single-or double-roofed and covered by shingles. As such, they are a particular vernacular expression of the cultural landscape of that mountainous area of northern Romania.

RUSSIAN FEDERATION

Cultural and Historic Ensemble of the Solovetsky Islands

The Solovetsky archipelago is composed of six islands in the western part of the White Sea, covering 300 square kilometres (186 square miles). Inhabited since the fifth century B.C., important traces of human life from as far back as the third millennium B.C. can be found there. Since the fifteenth century, the archipelago has been the site of fervent monastic activity, and several churches, constructed between the sixteenth and nineteenth centuries, still remain.

SLOVAKIA

Banska Stiavnica

Over the centuries the town was visited by many outstanding engineers and scientists who contributed to its fame. The old medieval mining centre grew into a town with Renaissance palaces, sixteenth-century churches, elegant squares and castles.

The urban centre blends into the surrounding landscape which contains vital relics of the mining and metallurgical activities of the past.

Bardejov Town Conservation Reserve

Bardejov is a small but exceptionally complete and well preserved example of a fortified medieval town, which typifies the urbanization of this region. Among other remarkable features, it also contains a small Jewish quarter around a fine eighteenth-century synagogue.

Spissky Hrad and its Associated Cultural Monuments

One of the largest ensembles of thirteenth- and fourteenth-century military, political and religious buildings in eastern Europe, its Romanesque and Gothic architecture has remained remarkably intact.

Vlkolínec

In the centre of Slovakia, Vlkolínec is a remarkably intact settlement of forty-five buildings with the traditional features of a Central European village. It is the most complete grouping of its kind in the region, with traditional log houses, often found in mountainous areas.

SPAIN

Archaeological Ensemble of Mérida

The colony of Augusta Emerita, which became present-day Mérida in the Estremadura, was founded in 25 B.C. at the end of the Spanish Campaign, and was the capital of Lusitania. The remains of the old city, complete and well-preserved, include, in particular, a large bridge over the Guadiana, an amphitheatre, a theatre, a vast circus and an exceptional water supply system. It is an excellent example of a provincial Roman capital during the empire and in the years following.

Archaeological Ensemble of Tárraco

Tárraco (modern Tarragona) was a major adminis-trative and mercantile city in Roman Spain and the centre of the Imperial cult for all the Iberian provinces. It was endowed with many fine buildings, and parts of these have been revealed in a series of exceptional excavations. Although most of the remains are fragmentary, many preserved beneath more recent buildings, they present a vivid picture of the grandeur of this Roman provincial city.

Archaeological Site of Atapuerca

The caves of the Sierra de Atapuerca contain a rich fossil record of the earliest human beings in Europe, from nearly one million years ago and extending into the Christian Era. They represent an exceptional reserve of data, the scientific study of which provides priceless information about the appearance and the way of life of these remote human ancestors.

Catalan Romanesque Churches of the Vall de Boí

The steep-sided, narrow Vall de Boí, is situated in the high Pyrenees, in the Alta Ribagorça region. Each of the villages in the valley contains a Romanesque church, and is surrounded by a pattern of enclosed fields. There are extensive seasonal grazing lands on the higher slopes.

Historic City of Toledo

Successively a Roman *municipium*, the capital of the Visigothic Kingdom, a fortress of the Emirate of Cordoba, an outpost of the Christian kingdoms fighting the Moors and, in the sixteenth century, the temporary seat of the supreme power under Charles V, Toledo is the keeper of more than two millenia of history. Its masterpieces are the product of heterogeneous civilizations in an environment where the existence of three major religions — Judaism, Christianity and Islam — was a major factor.

Historic Walled Town of Cuenca

Built by the Moors on a defensive position in the heart of the Caliphate of Cordoba, Cuenca is a very well-preserved fortified medieval city. Conquered by the Castilians in the twelfth century, it became a royal town and bishopric rich with major buildings, such as Spain's first Gothic cathedral, and the famous *casas colgadas* (hanging houses), suspended from sheer cliffs overlooking the Huécar River. Admirably making the most of its location, the city crowns the magnificent countryside surrounding it.

Ibiza, Biodiversity and Culture

Ibiza, Biodiversity and Culture gives an excellent example of the interaction between the marine and coastal ecosystems. The dense prairies of oceanic *Posidonia* (seagrass), an important endemic species found only in the Mediterranean basin, contain and support a diversity of marine life. Ibiza preserves considerable evidence of its long history. The archaeological sites at Sa Caleta (settlement) and Puig des Molins (cemetery) testify to the important role played by the island in the Mediterranean economy in protohistory, particularly during the Phoenician-Carthaginian period. The fortified Upper Town (Alta Vila) is an outstanding example of Renaissance military architecture, which had a profound influence on the development of fortifications in the Spanish settlements of the New World.

La Lonja de la Seda of Valencia

Built between 1482 and 1533, this group of buildings, originally used for trading in silk (hence its name, The Silk Exchange), has always been a place of commerce especially in its strikingly grandiose Sala de Contratación (Contract or Trading Hall). A masterpiece of Late Gothic, it illustrates the power and wealth of a major Mediterranean mercantile city of the fifteenth and sixteenth centuries.

Monuments of Oviedo and the Kingdom of the Asturias

In the ninth century the flame of Christianity

was kept alive in the Iberian peninsula in the tiny Kingdom of the Asturias, where an innovative form of pre-Romanesque architecture was created that was to play a significant role in the development of the religious architecture of the peninsula. Its highest achievements can be seen in the Churches of Santa Maria del Naranco, San Miguel de Lillo, Santa Cristina de Lena, the Cámara Santa, and San Julián de los Prados, in and around the ancient capital city of Oviedo. Associated with them is the remarkable contemporary hydraulic engineering structure known as La Foncalada.

Mudejar Architecture of Aragon

The development in the twelfth century of Mudejar art in Aragon resulted from the particular political, social and cultural conditions that prevailed in Spain after the Reconquista. This art, influenced by Islamic tradition, also reflects various contemporary European styles, particularly the Gothic. Present until the early seventeenth century, it is characterized by an extremely refined and inventive use of brick and glazed tiles in architecture, especially in the belfries.

Old Town of Avila, including its Extra Muros Churches

Founded in the eleventh century to protect the Spanish territories from the Moors, this 'City of Saints and Stones', the birthplace of Saint Theresa and the burial ground of the Great Inquisitor Torquemada, has kept its medieval austerity. This purity of form can still be seen in its Gothic cathedral and its fortifications which, with eighty-two semi-circular towers and nine gates, are the most complete in Spain.

Old Town of Caceres

The city's history of battles between Moors and Christians is reflected in its architecture which is a blend of Roman, Islamic, Northern Gothic, and Italian Renaissance styles. From the Muslim period remain about thirty towers, of which the Torre del Bujaco is the most famous.

Old Town of Segovia and its Aqueduct

The Roman aqueduct of Segovia, probably built around A.D. 50, is remarkably well preserved. This impressive construction, with its two tiers of arches, forms part of the setting of the magnificent historic city of Segovia, where one can also visit the Alcazar, begun around the eleventh century, and the sixteenth-century Gothic cathedral.

Parque Güell, Palacio Güell and Casa Mila in Barcelona

Truly universal works in view of the diverse cultural sources from which they are inspired, the creations of Antonio Gaudí (1852-1926) in Barcelona represent an eclectic as well as a very personal architectural style which led to new styles, not only architecturally but also for gardens, sculpture and all forms of decorative art.

Rock-Art of the Mediterranean Basin on the Iberian Peninsula

The late prehistoric rock-art sites of the Mediterranean seaboard of the Iberian peninsula form an exceptionally large group in which the way of life in a critical phase of human development is vividly and graphically depicted in paintings that are unique in style and subject matter.

Route of Santiago de Compostela

Proclaimed the first European Cultural Capital by the Council of Europe, this is the route, from the French-Spanish border, which was — and still is — taken by pilgrims to Santiago de Compostela. Some 1800 buildings along the route, both religious and secular, are of great historic interest. The route played a fundamental role in facilitating cultural exchanges between the Iberian peninsula and the rest of Europe during the Middle Ages. It remains a testimony to the power of Christian faith in people of all social classes and all over Europe.

San Cristóbal de La Laguna

San Cristóbal de la Laguna has two nuclei, the original unplanned Upper Town, and the Lower Town, the first ideal 'city-territory' laid out according to philosophical principles. Its wide streets and open spaces contain a number of fine churches and public and private buildings from the sixteenth to eighteenth centuries.

Santiago de Compostela (Old Town)

This famous pilgrimage site in the north-west of Spain became a symbol in the Spanish Christians' struggle against Islam. Destroyed by the Muslims at the end of the tenth century, it was completely rebuilt in the following century. The Old Town of Santiago forms one of the world's most beautiful urban areas with Romanesque, Gothic and Baroque buildings. The oldest monuments are grouped around Saint James's tomb and the cathedral which contains the remarkable Pórtico de la Gloria.

SWEDEN

Birka and Hovgården

The Birka archaeological site, located on Björkö Island in Lake Mälar and occupied in the ninth and tenth centuries, and Hovgården, on the neighbouring island of Adelsö, make up an archaeological complex that illustrates the elaborate trading networks of Viking-Age Europe and their influence on the subsequent history of Scandinavia. Birka was also important as the site of the first Christian congregation in Sweden, founded in 831 by Saint Ansgar.

Church Village of Gammelstad, Luleå

Gammelstad, at the head of the Gulf of Bothnia, is the best-preserved example of a unique kind of town found in northern Scandinavia — the church town. Its 424 wooden houses crowded around the early fifteenth-century stone church were used only on Sundays and religious festivals to lodge worshippers who came in from the surrounding countryside and who could not return home in a single day because of the distance and difficult travelling conditions.

Engelsberg Ironworks

This site is the best preserved and most complete example of a Swedish ironworks, which produced the superior grades of iron that made Sweden a leader in this field in the seventeenth and eighteenth centuries.

Hanseatic Town of Visby

A former Viking site on the island of Gotland, Visby was the main centre of the Hanseatic League of the Baltic from the twelfth to the fourteenth centuries. Its thirteenth-century ramparts and more than 200 warehouses and trading establishments from the same period make it the best-preserved fortified commercial city in northern Europe.

Mining Area of the Great Copper Mountain in Falun

The enormous mining excavation known as the Great Pit at Falun is the most striking feature of a landscape that illustrates the survival of copper production in this region since at least the thirteenth century. The seventeenth-century planned town of Falun with its many fine historic buildings, together with the industrial and domestic remains of a number of settlements spread over a wide area of the Dalarna region, provide a vivid picture of what was for centuries one of the world's most important mining areas.

Rock Carvings in Tanum

The rock carvings in Tanum, in the north of Bohuslän, represent a unique artistic achievement due to their rich and varied motifs (depictions of humans and animals, weapons, boats and other objects) as well as their cultural and chronological unity. Their abundance and outstanding quality illustrate the life and beliefs of the people in the Bronze Age in Europe.

SWITZERLAND

Old City of Berne

Founded in the twelfth century on a hill site surrounded by the Aar River, Berne became the Swiss capital in 1848. The buildings in the Old City, from a variety of periods, include sixteenth-century arcades and fountains. The major part of the medieval town was renovated in the eighteenth century but its original character was preserved.

Three Castles, Defensive Wall and Ramparts of the Market-town of Bellinzona

The Bellinzona site consists of a group of fortifications centring on the castle of Castelgrande, which stands on the rocky peak looking out over the entire Ticino valley. Running from the castle, a series of fortified walls protect the ancient town and block the passage through the valley. A second castle forms an integral part of the fortifications; a third but separate castle (Sasso Corbaro) was built on an isolated rocky promontory south-east of the other fortifications.

TURKEY

Archaeological Site of Troy

Troy, with its 4,000 years of history, is one of the most famous archaeological sites in the world. The first excavations at the site were started in 1871 by the famous archaeologist Heinrich Schliemann. In scientific terms, its extensive remains are the most significant and substantial demonstration of the first contact between the civilizations of Anatolia and the Mediterranean world. Moreover, the siege of Troy by Spartan and Achaean warriors from Greece in the thirteenth or twelfth century B.C., immortalized by Homer in the *Iliad*, has inspired great creative artists throughout the world since that time.

City of Safranbolu

From the thirteenth century to the advent of the railway in the early twentieth century, Safranbolu was an important caravan station on the main east-west trade route. Its Old Mosque, Old Bath and Suleyman Pasha *medersa* were built in 1322. During its apogee in the seventeenth century, its architecture influenced urban development in a large part of the Ottoman Empire.

Hattusha

The former capital of the Hittite Empire, Hattusha is a remarkable archaeological site for its urban organization, the types of construction that have been preserved (temples, royal residences, fortifications), the rich ornamentation of the Lions' Gate and the Royal Gate, and the ensemble of rock art of Yazilikaya. The city exercised a considerable influence in Anatolia and northern Syria in the second millenium B.C.

Historic Areas of Istanbul

Strategically located on the Bosphorus peninsula between the Balkans and Anatolia, the Black Sea and the Mediterranean, Istanbul has been associated with major political, religious and artistic events for more than 2,000 years. Its masterpieces include the ancient Hippodrome of Constantine, the sixth-century Hagia Sophia and the sixteenth-century Suleymaniye Mosque, which are now jeopardized by overpopulation, industrial pollution and uncontrolled urbanization.

Nemrut Dag

The mausoleum of Antiochus I (69-34 B.C.) who reigned over Commagene, a kingdom founded north of Syria and the Euphrates after the breakup of Alexander's Empire, is one of the most ambitious constructions of Hellenic times. The syncretism of its pantheon, and the lineage of its kings, which can be traced back through two sets of legends, Greek and Persian, is evidence of the dual origin of this kingdom's culture.

Xanthos-Letoon

The capital of Lycia, this site illustrates the mixture

of Lycian traditions and Hellenic influence, especially through its funeral art. The epigraphic inscriptions are crucial for understanding the Indo-European language and the history of the Lycian people.

UKRAINE

L'viv — the Ensemble of the Historic Centre

The city of L'viv, founded in the later Middle Ages, flourished as an administrative, religious, and commercial centre for several centuries. It has preserved virtually intact its medieval urban topography, and, in particular, evidence of the separate ethnic communities who lived there, along with many fine Baroque and later buildings.

YUGOSLAVIA

Natural and Cultural-Historical Region of Kotor

This natural harbour on the Adriatic coast in Montenegro was an important artistic and commercial centre with famous masonry and iconography schools in the Middle Ages. A large number of its monuments, including four Romanesque churches and the town walls, were heavily damaged by an earthquake in 1979 but the town has been restored, mostly with UNESCO's help.

Stari Ras and Sopocani

On the outskirts of Stari Ras, the first capital of Serbia, there is an impressive group of medieval monuments, fortresses, churches and monasteries. The monastery at Sopocani is a reminder of the contacts made between Western civilizations and the Byzantine world.

Convention Concerning the Protection of the World Cultural and Natural Heritage

The General Conference of the United Nations Educational, Scientific and Cultural Organization meeting in Paris from 17 October to 21 November 1972, at its seventeenth session,

Noting that the cultural heritage and the natural heritage are increasingly threatened with destruction not only by the traditional causes of decay, but also by changing social and economic conditions which aggravate the situation with even more formidable phenomena of damage or destruction,

Considering that deterioration or disappearance of any item of the cultural or natural heritage constitutes a harmful impoverishment of the heritage of all the nations of the world,

Considering that protection of this heritage at the national level often remains incomplete because of the scale of the resources which it requires and of the insufficient economic, scientific, and technological resources of the country where the property to be protected is situated,

Recalling that the Constitution of the Organization provides that it will maintain, increase, and diffuse knowledge, by assuring the conservation and protection of the world's heritage, and recommending to the nations concerned the necessary international conventions,

Considering that the existing international conventions, recommendations and resolutions concerning cultural and natural property demonstrate the importance, for all the peoples of the world, of safeguarding this unique and irreplaceable property, to whatever people it may belong,

Considering that parts of the cultural or natural heritage are of outstanding interest and therefore need to be preserved as part of the world heritage of mankind as a whole,

Considering that, in view of the magnitude and gravity of the new dangers threatening them, it is incumbent on the international community as a whole to participate in the protection of the cultural and natural heritage of outstanding universal value, by the granting of collective assistance which, although not taking the place of action by the State concerned, will serve as an efficient complement thereto,

Considering that it is essential for this purpose to adopt new provisions in the form of a convention establishing an effective system of collective protection of the cultural and natural heritage of outstanding universal value, organized on a permanent basis and in accordance with modern scientific methods,

Having decided, at its sixteenth session, that this question should be made the subject of an international convention,

Adopts this sixteenth day of November 1972 this Convention.

I

Definition of the cultural and natural heritage

Article 1

For the purposes of this Convention, the following shall be considered as 'cultural heritage':
– monuments: architectural works, works of monumental sculpture and painting, elements or structures of an archaeological nature, inscriptions, cave dwellings and combinations of features, which are of outstanding universal value from the point of view of history, art or science;
– groups of buildings: groups of separate or connected buildings which, because of their architecture, their homogeneity or their place in the landscape, are of outstanding universal value from the point of view of history, art or science;
– sites: works of man or the combined works of

nature and man, and areas including archaeological sites which are of outstanding universal value from the historical, aesthetic, ethnological or anthropological point of view.

Article 2

For the purposes of this Convention, the following shall be considered as 'natural heritage':
– natural features consisting of physical and biological formations or groups of such formations, which are of outstanding universal value from the aesthetic or scientific point of view;
– geological and physiographical formations and precisely delineated areas which constitute the habitat of threatened species of animals and plants of outstanding universal value from the point of view of science or conservation;
– natural sites or precisely delineated natural areas of outstanding universal value from the point of view of science, conservation or natural beauty.

Article 3

It is for each State Party to this Convention to identify and delineate the different properties situated on its territory mentioned in Articles 1 and 2 above.

II

National protection and international protection of the cultural and natural heritage

Article 4

Each State Party to this Convention recognizes that the duty of ensuring the identification, protection, conservation, presentation and transmission to future generations of the cultural and natural heritage referred to in Articles 1 and 2 and situated on its territory, belongs primarily to that State. It will do all it can to this end, to the utmost of its own resources and, where appropriate, with any international assistance and co-operation, in particular, financial, artistic, scientific and technical, which it may be able to obtain.

Article 5

To ensure that effective and active measures are taken for the protection, conservation and presentation of the cultural and natural heritage situated on its territory, each State Party to this Convention shall endeavor, in so far as possible, and as appropriate for each country:
a. to adopt a general policy which aims to give the cultural and natural heritage a function in the life of the community and to integrate the protection of that heritage into comprehensive planning programmes;
b. to set up within its territories, where such services do not exist, one or more services for the protection, conservation and presentation of the cultural and natural heritage with an appropriate staff and possessing the means to discharge their functions;
c. to develop scientific and technical studies and research and to work out such operating methods as will make the State capable of counteracting the dangers that threaten its cultural or natural heritage;
d. to take the appropriate legal, scientific, technical, administrative and financial measures necessary for the identification, protection, conservation, presentation and rehabilitation of this heritage; and
e. to foster the establishment or development of national or regional centres for training in the protection, conservation and presentation of the cultural and natural heritage and to encourage scientific research in this field.

Article 6

1. Whilst fully respecting the sovereignty of the States on whose territory the cultural and natural heritage mentioned in Articles 1 and 2 is situated, and without prejudice to property right provided by national legislation, the States Parties to this Convention recognize that such heritage constitutes a world heritage for whose protection it is the duty of the international community as a whole to co-operate.
2. The States Parties undertake, in accordance with

the provisions of this Convention, to give their help in the identification, protection, conservation and presentation of the cultural and natural heritage referred to in paragraphs 2 and 4 of Article 11 if the States on whose territory it is situated so request.
3. Each State Party to this Convention undertakes not to take any deliberate measures which might damage directly or indirectly the cultural and natural heritage referred to in Articles 1 and 2 situated on the territory of other States Parties to this Convention.

Article 7

For the purpose of this Convention, international protection of the world cultural and natural heritage shall be understood to mean the establishment of a system of international co-operation and assistance designed to support States Parties to the Convention in their efforts to conserve and identify that heritage.

III

Intergovernmental committee for the protection of the world cultural and natural heritage

Article 8

1. An Intergovernmental Committee for the Protection of the Cultural and Natural Heritage of Outstanding Universal Value, called 'the World Heritage Committee', is hereby established within the United Nations Educational, Scientific and Cultural Organization. It shall be composed of 15 States Parties to the Convention, elected by States Parties to the Convention meeting in general assembly during the ordinary session of the General Conference of the United Nations Educational, Scientific and Cultural Organization. The number of States members of the Committee shall be increased to 21 as from the date of the ordinary session of the General Conference following the entry into force of this Convention for at least 40 States.

2. Election of members of the Committee shall ensure an equitable representation of the different regions and cultures of the world.

3. A representative of the International Centre for the Study of the Preservation and Restoration of Cultural Property (Rome Centre), a representative of the International Council of Monuments and Sites (ICOMOS) and a representative of the International Union for Conservation of Nature and Natural Resources (IUCN), to whom may be added, at the request of States Parties to the Convention meeting in general assembly during the ordinary sessions of the General Conference of the United Nations Educational, Scientific and Cultural Organization, representatives of other intergovernmental or non-governmental organizations, with similar objectives, may attend the meetings of the Committee in an advisory capacity.

Article 9

1. The term of office of States members of the World Heritage Committee shall extend from the end of the ordinary session of the General Conference during which they are elected until the end of its third subsequent ordinary session.

2. The term of office of one-third of the members designated at the time of the first election shall, however, cease at the end of the first ordinary session of the General Conference following that at which they were elected; and the term of office of a further third of the members designated at the same time shall cease at the end of the second ordinary session of the General Conference following that at which they were elected. The names of these members shall be chosen by lot by the President of the General Conference of the United Nations Educational, Scientific and Cultural Organization after the first election.

3. States members of the Committee shall choose as their representatives persons qualified in the field of the cultural or natural heritage.

Article 10

1. The World Heritage Committee shall adopt its Rules of Procedure.

2. The Committee may at any time invite public or private organizations or individuals to participate in its meetings for consultation on particular problems.

3. The Committee may create such consultative bodies as it deems necessary for the performance of its functions.

Article 11

1. Every State Party to this Convention shall, in so far as possible, submit to the World Heritage Committee an inventory of property forming part of the cultural and natural heritage, situated in its territory and suitable for inclusion in the list provided for in paragraph 2 of this Article. This inventory, which shall not be considered exhaustive, shall include documentation about the location of the property in question and its significance.

2. On the basis of the inventories submitted by States in accordance with paragraph 1, the Committee shall establish, keep up to date and publish, under the title of 'World Heritage List', a list of properties forming part of the cultural heritage and natural heritage, as defined in Articles 1 and 2 of this Convention, which it considers as having outstanding universal value in terms of such criteria as it shall have established. An updated list shall be distributed at least every two years.

3. The inclusion of a property in the World Heritage List requires the consent of the State concerned. The inclusion of a property situated in a territory, sovereignty or jurisdiction over which is claimed by more than one State shall in no way prejudice the rights of the parties to the dispute.

4. The Committee shall establish, keep up to date and publish, whenever circumstances shall so require, under the title of 'List of World Heritage in Danger', a list of the property appearing in the World Heritage List for the conservation of which major operations are necessary and for which assistance has been requested under this Convention.

This list shall contain an estimate of the cost of such operations. The list may include only such property forming part of the cultural and natural heritage as is threatened by serious and specific dangers, such as the threat of disappearance caused by accelerated deterioration, large-scale public or private projects or rapid urban or tourist development projects; destruction caused by changes in the use or ownership of the land; major alterations due to unknown causes; abandonment for any reason whatsoever; the outbreak or the threat of an armed conflict; calamities and cataclysms; serious fires, earthquakes, landslides; volcanic eruptions; changes in water level, floods and tidal waves. The Committee may at any time, in case of urgent need, make a new entry in the List of World Heritage in Danger and publicize such entry immediately.

5. The Committee shall define the criteria on the basis of which a property belonging to the cultural or natural heritage may be included in either of the lists mentioned in paragraphs 2 and 4 of this article.

6. Before refusing a request for inclusion in one of the two lists mentioned in paragraphs 2 and 4 of this article, the Committee shall consult the State Party in whose territory the cultural or natural property in question is situated.

7. The Committee shall, with the agreement of the States concerned, co-ordinate and encourage the studies and research needed for the drawing up of the lists referred to in paragraphs 2 and 4 of this article.

Article 12

The fact that a property belonging to the cultural or natural heritage has not been included in either of the two lists mentioned in paragraphs 2 and 4 of Article 11 shall in no way be construed to mean that it does not have an outstanding universal value for purposes other than those resulting from inclusion in these lists.

Article 13

1. The World Heritage Committee shall receive and study requests for international assistance for-

mulated by States Parties to this Convention with respect to property forming part of the cultural or natural heritage, situated in their territories, and included or potentially suitable for inclusion in the lists mentioned referred to in paragraphs 2 and 4 of Article 11. The purpose of such requests may be to secure the protection, conservation, presentation or rehabilitation of such property.

2. Requests for international assistance under paragraph 1 of this article may also be concerned with identification of cultural or natural property defined in Articles 1 and 2, when preliminary investigations have shown that further inquiries would be justified.

3. The Committee shall decide on the action to be taken with regard to these requests, determine where appropriate, the nature and extent of its assistance, and authorize the conclusion, on its behalf, of the necessary arrangements with the government concerned.

4. The Committee shall determine an order of priorities for its operations. It shall in so doing bear in mind the respective importance for the world cultural and natural heritage of the property requiring protection, the need to give international assistance to the property most representative of a natural environment or of the genius and the history of the peoples of the world, the urgency of the work to be done, the resources available to the States on whose territory the threatened property is situated and in particular the extent to which they are able to safeguard such property by their own means.

5. The Committee shall draw up, keep up to date and publicize a list of property for which international assistance has been granted.

6. The Committee shall decide on the use of the resources of the Fund established under Article 15 of this Convention. It shall seek ways of increasing these resources and shall take all useful steps to this end.

7. The Committee shall co-operate with international and national governmental and non-governmental organizations having objectives similar to those of this Convention. For the implementation of its programmes and projects, the Committee may call on such organizations, particularly the International Centre for the Study of the Preservation and Restoration of Cultural Property (the Rome Centre), the International Council of Monuments and Sites (ICOMOS) and the International Union for Conservation of Nature and Natural Resources (IUCN), as well as on public and private bodies and individuals.

8. Decisions of the Committee shall be taken by a majority of two-thirds of its members present and voting. A majority of the members of the Committee shall constitute a quorum.

Article 14

1. The World Heritage Committee shall be assisted by a Secretariat appointed by the Director-General of the United Nations Educational, Scientific and Cultural Organization.

2. The Director-General of the United Nations Educational, Scientific and Cultural Organization, utilizing to the fullest extent possible the services of the International Centre for the Study of the Preservation and the Restoration of Cultural Property (the Rome Centre), the International Council of Monuments and Sites (ICOMOS) and the International Union for Conservation of Nature and Natural Resources (IUCN) in their respective areas of competence and capability, shall prepare the Committee's documentation and the agenda of its meetings and shall have the responsibility for the implementation of its decisions.

IV
Fund for the protection of the world cultural and natural heritage

Article 15

1. A Fund for the Protection of the World Cultural and Natural Heritage of Outstanding Universal Value, called 'the World Heritage Fund', is hereby established.

2. The Fund shall constitute a trust fund, in conformity with the provisions of the Financial Regulations of the United Nations Educational, Scientific and Cultural Organization.

3. The resources of the Fund shall consist of:

a. compulsory and voluntary contributions made by States Parties to this Convention,

b. Contributions, gifts or bequests which may be made by:

i. other States;

ii. the United Nations Educational, Scientific and Cultural Organization, other organizations of the United Nations system, particularly the United Nations Development Programme or other intergovernmental organizations;

iii. public or private bodies or individuals;

c. any interest due on the resources of the Fund;

d. funds raised by collections and receipts from events organized for the benefit of the fund; and

e. all other resources authorized by the Fund's regulations, as drawn up by the World Heritage Committee.

4. Contributions to the Fund and other forms of assistance made available to the Committee may be used only for such purposes as the Committee shall define. The Committee may accept contributions to be used only for a certain programme or project, provided that the Committee shall have decided on the implementation of such programme or project. No political conditions may be attached to contributions made to the Fund.

Article 16

1. Without prejudice to any supplementary voluntary contribution, the States Parties to this Convention undertake to pay regularly, every two years, to the World Heritage Fund, contributions, the amount of which, in the form of a uniform percentage applicable to all States, shall be determined by the General Assembly of States Parties to the Convention, meeting during the sessions of the General Conference of the United Nations Educational, Scientific and Cultural Or-

ganization. This decision of the General Assembly requires the majority of the States Parties present and voting, which have not made the declaration referred to in paragraph 2 of this Article. In no case shall the compulsory contribution of States Parties to the Convention exceed 1% of the contribution to the regular budget of the United Nations Educational, Scientific and Cultural Organization.

2. However, each State referred to in Article 31 or in Article 32 of this Convention may declare, at the time of the deposit of its instrument of ratification, acceptance or accession, that it shall not be bound by the provisions of paragraph 1 of this Article.

3. A State Party to the Convention which has made the declaration referred to in paragraph 2 of this Article may at any time withdraw the said declaration by notifying the Director-General of the United Nations Educational, Scientific and Cultural Organization. However, the withdrawal of the declaration shall not take effect in regard to the compulsory contribution due by the State until the date of the subsequent General Assembly of States parties to the Convention.

4. In order that the Committee may be able to plan its operations effectively, the contributions of States Parties to this Convention which have made the declaration referred to in paragraph 2 of this Article, shall be paid on a regular basis, at least every two years, and should not be less than the contributions which they should have paid if they had been bound by the provisions of paragraph 1 of this Article.

5. Any State Party to the Convention which is in arrears with the payment of its compulsory or voluntary contribution for the current year and the calendar year immediately preceding it shall not be eligible as a Member of the World Heritage Committee, although this provision shall not apply to the first election.

The terms of office of any such State which is already a member of the Committee shall terminate at the time of the elections provided for in Article 8, paragraph 1 of this Convention.

Article 17

The States Parties to this Convention shall consider or encourage the establishment of national public and private foundations or associations whose purpose is to invite donations for the protection of the cultural and natural heritage as defined in Articles 1 and 2 of this Convention.

Article 18

The States Parties to this Convention shall give their assistance to international fund-raising campaigns organized for the World Heritage Fund under the auspices of the United Nations Educational, Scientific and Cultural Organization. They shall facilitate collections made by the bodies mentioned in paragraph 3 of Article 15 for this purpose.

V

Conditions and arrangements for international assistance

Article 19

Any State Party to this Convention may request international assistance for property forming part of the cultural or natural heritage of outstanding universal value situated within its territory. It shall submit with its request such information and documentation provided for in Article 21 as it has in its possession and as will enable the Committee to come to a decision.

Article 20

Subject to the provisions of paragraph 2 of Article 13, sub-paragraph (c) of Article 22 and Article 23, international assistance provided for by this Convention may be granted only to property forming part of the cultural and natural heritage which the World Heritage Committee has decided, or may decide, to enter in one of the lists mentioned in paragraphs 2 and 4 of Article 11.

Article 21

1. The World Heritage Committee shall define the procedure by which requests to it for international assistance shall be considered and shall specify the content of the request, which should define the operation contemplated, the work that is necessary, the expected cost thereof, the degree of urgency and the reasons why the resources of the State requesting assistance do not allow it to meet all the expenses. Such requests must be supported by experts' reports whenever possible.

2. Requests based upon disasters or natural calamities should, by reasons of the urgent work which they may involve, be given immediate, priority consideration by the Committee, which should have a reserve fund at its disposal against such contingencies.

3. Before coming to a decision, the Committee shall carry out such studies and consultations as it deems necessary.

Article 22

Assistance granted by the World Heritage Committee may take the following forms:

a. studies concerning the artistic, scientific and technical problems raised by the protection, conservation, presentation and rehabilitation of the cultural and natural heritage, as defined in paragraphs 2 and 4 of Article 11 of this Convention;

b. provisions of experts, technicians and skilled labour to ensure that the approved work is correctly carried out;

c. training of staff and specialists at all levels in the field of identification, protection, conservation, presentation and rehabilitation of the cultural and natural heritage;

d. supply of equipment which the State concerned does not possess or is not in a position to acquire;

e. low-interest or interest-free loans which might be repayable on a long-term basis;

f. the granting, in exceptional cases and for special reasons, of non-repayable subsidies.

Article 23

The World Heritage Committee may also provide international assistance to national or regional centres for the training of staff and specialists at all levels in the field of identification, protection, conservation, presentation and rehabilitation of the cultural and natural heritage.

Article 24

International assistance on a large scale shall be preceded by detailed scientific, economic and technical studies. These studies shall draw upon the most advanced techniques for the protection, conservation, presentation and rehabilitation of the natural and cultural heritage and shall be consistent with the objectives of this Convention. The studies shall also seek means of making rational use of the resources available in the State concerned.

Article 25

As a general rule, only part of the cost of work necessary shall be borne by the international community. The contribution of the State benefiting from international assistance shall constitute a substantial share of the resources devoted to each programme or project, unless its resources do not permit this.

Article 26

The World Heritage Committee and the recipient State shall define in the agreement they conclude the conditions in which a programme or project for which international assistance under the terms of this Convention is provided, shall be carried out. It shall be the responsibility of the State receiving such international assistance to continue to protect, conserve and present the property so safeguarded, in observance of the conditions laid down by the agreement.

VI

Educational programmes

Article 27

1. The States Parties to this Convention shall endeavor by all appropriate means, and in particular by educational and information programmes, to strengthen appreciation and respect by their peoples of the cultural and natural heritage defined in Articles 1 and 2 of the Convention.

2. They shall undertake to keep the public broadly informed of the dangers threatening this heritage and of the activities carried on in pursuance of this Convention.

Article 28

States Parties to this Convention which receive international assistance under the Convention shall take appropriate measures to make known the importance of the property for which assistance has been received and the role played by such assistance.

VII

Report

Article 29

1. The States Parties to this Convention shall, in the reports which they submit to the General Conference of the United Nations Educational, Scientific and Cultural Organization on dates and in a manner to be determined by it, give information on the legislative and administrative provisions which they have adopted and other action which they have taken for the application of this Convention, together with details of the experience acquired in this field.

2. These reports shall be brought to the attention of the World Heritage Committee.

3. The Committee shall submit a report on its activities at each of the ordinary sessions of the General Conference of the United Nations Educational, Scientific and Cultural Organization.

VIII

Final clauses

Article 30

This Convention is drawn up in Arabic, English, French, Russian and Spanish, the five texts being equally authoritative.

Article 31

1. This Convention shall be subject to ratification or acceptance by States members of the United Nations Educational, Scientific and Cultural Organization in accordance with their respective constitutional procedures.

2. The instruments of ratification or acceptance shall be deposited with the Director-General of the United Nations Educational, Scientific and Cultural Organization.

Article 32

1. This Convention shall be open to accession by all States not members of the United Nations Educational, Scientific and Cultural Organization which are invited by the General Conference of the Organization to accede to it.

2. Accession shall be effected by the deposit of an instrument of accession with the Director-General of the United Nations Educational, Scientific and Cultural Organization.

Article 33

This Convention shall enter into force three months after the date of the deposit of the twentieth instrument of ratification, acceptance or accession, but only with respect to those States which have deposited their respective instruments of ratification, acceptance or accession on or before that date. It shall enter into force with respect to any other State three months after the deposit of its instrument of ratification, acceptance or accession.

Article 34

The following provisions shall apply to those States Parties to this Convention which have a federal or non-unitary constitutional system:

a. with regard to the provisions of this Convention, the implementation of which comes under the legal jurisdiction of the federal or central legislative power, the obligations of the federal or central government shall be the same as for those States parties which are not federal States;

b. with regard to the provisions of this Convention, the implementation of which comes under the legal jurisdiction of individual constituent States, countries, provinces or cantons that are not obliged by the constitutional system of the federation to take legislative measures, the federal government shall inform the competent authorities of such States, countries, provinces or cantons of the said provisions, with its recommendation for their adoption.

Article 35

1. Each State Party to this Convention may denounce the Convention.

2. The denunciation shall be notified by an instrument in writing, deposited with the Director-General of the United Nations Educational, Scientific and Cultural Organization.

3. The denunciation shall take effect twelve months after the receipt of the instrument of denunciation. It shall not affect the financial obligations of the denouncing State until the date on which the withdrawal takes effect.

Article 36

The Director-General of the United Nations Educational, Scientific and Cultural Organization shall inform the States members of the Organization, the States not members of the Organization which are referred to in Article 32, as well as the United Nations, of the deposit of all the instruments of ratification, acceptance, or accession provided for in Articles 31 and 32, and of the denunciations provided for in Article 35.

Article 37

1. This Convention may be revised by the General Conference of the United Nations Educational, Scientific and Cultural Organization. Any such revision shall, however, bind only the States which shall become Parties to the revising convention.

2. If the General Conference should adopt a new convention revising this Convention in whole or in part, then, unless the new convention otherwise provides, this Convention shall cease to be open to ratification, acceptance or accession, as from the date on which the new revising convention enters into force.

Article 38

In conformity with Article 102 of the Charter of the United Nations, this Convention shall be registered with the Secretariat of the United Nations at the request of the Director-General of the United Nations Educational, Scientific and Cultural Organization.

Done in Paris, this twenty-third day of November 1972, in two authentic copies bearing the signature of the President of the seventeenth session of the General Conference and of the Director-General of the United Nations Educational, Scientific and Cultural Organization, which shall be deposited in the archives of the United Nations Educational, Scientific and Cultural Organization, and certified true copies of which shall be delivered to all the States referred to in Articles 31 and 32 as well as to the United Nations.

Photo credits

Abbas/Magnum/Contrasto: p. 145

Agenzia Fotografica Luisa Ricciarini, Milan: pp. 195, 196 left/Max Mandel: pp. 194 left, 196 right, 197, 199, 201 right

Archivio Fotografico della Missione Archeologica Italiana di Hierapolis di Frigia (Politecnico di Torino): pp. 228, 230, 231, 232, 233

Archivio Eric Lessing/Contrasto: pp. 33, 84, 85, 89 bottom, 99, 103, 111, 229, 174, 175, 177, 269, 301, 302, 305 right, 306 left, 309

Archivio Scala, Florence: pp. 5, 6, 7, 8, 9, 10, 12, 13, 14, 15, 16, 17, 30, 31, 53, 54, 55, 56, 57, 58, 59, 61, 62, 63, 64, 65, 67, 68, 69 top, 71, 73, 74, 75, 76, 77, 78, 79, 80, 81, 86, 87, 88, 89 top, 91, 92, 93, 94, 95, 96, 97, 98, 100, 101, 103, 104, 105, 107, 108, 109, 110, 111, 112, 114 right, 117 top, 118 right, 131, 132, 133 bottom, 136 top, 140, 141, 152, 153, 154, 155 left, 157, 158 left, 159, 160 top, 161 right, 162, 163, 190, 191, 192, 193 left bottom and right, 215, 248, 251, 264, 265, 266, 267 right, 323, 324 right, 325, 326

The Image Bank: p. 239/Claudio Ansaloni: pp. 316, 319 top, 321 bottom/Yann Arthus-Bertrand: p. 40 top/Giuliano Bandieri: p. 285/Alan Becker: p.130/Carolyn Brown: p. 216/Angelo Cavalli: p. 288 bottom/Wendy Chan: pp. 123, 124 bottom/Giuliano Colliva: pp. 179, 182 top/Paolo Curto: p. 304 bottom/Patrick Eden: p. 40 bottom/F. Hidalgo: p. 320 bottom/Alberto Incrocci: p. 303/Ronald R. Johonson: p. 158 bottom/A. Lanzellotto: p. 241/Nino Mascardi: p. 156/Ger-

ard Mathieu: p. 126 bottom/Aris Mihich: p. 255/Kaz Mori: pp. 178 left, 182 left bottom/Nick Nicholson: p. 330 top/Alberto Novelli: p. 269/Tom Owen Edmunds: p. 250/Marcella Pedone: p. 28 right/Andrea Pistolesi: pp. 122, 124 left and top, 307/Donata Pizzi: pp. 218 top, 266/D. Redfearn: p. 39/Marc Romanelli: p. 315 bottom/Guido Alberto Rossi: pp. 4, 42, 60, 66, 72, 82, 83, 102, 113, 129, 150, 151, 155 right, 224, 225, 227 left, 249 top right, 253 left , 254, 257 top, 262, 275, 283, 288 top, 289, 291, 300 left/Gian Luigi Scarfiotti: p. 237 right/Isy Schwart: p. 281/Studio Balladore: p. 257 bottom/Simon Wilkinson: p. 41 bottom

Unesco-Photographic Archive: pp. 26, 69 bottom, 138, 139, 142, 143 top, 144, 145, 146, 147, 148, 149, 178 right, 322, 331 middle/Andre Abbe: p. 194 right/N. Abou Khalil: pp. 242 bottom, 243 right, 245 bottom left/Felipe Alcoceba: pp. 160 bottom, 161 left, 208, 210 top, 277/Edouard Bailby: p. 238 bottom/Eduardo Barios: p. 268 right/Emil Bauer: pp. 28 left, 29/Bernard Benoit-Zabbal: pp. 204, 205, 206 bottom right and left, 207/M. Bouchenaki: p. 202/H. Boyer: pp. 304 top, 306 top/J. F. Breton: p. 242 top/B. Brougier: p. 173 bottom/Bruno Carnez: pp. 18, 22/Fabian Charafi: pp. 274, 276 bottom/Michel Claude: pp. 268 left, 270, 271, 272, 273/Eric Condominas: p. 240/Cournot: pp. 169 bottom, 172 bottom/Gérard Degeorges: pp. 211 left, 213, 214, 223 top, 258, 259, 260, 261/Winnie Denker: pp. 209, 210 bottom, 211 right, 212, 217, 218 left, 220, 221, 222, 223 bottom/Maochamp Desbrosses: pp. 307 right, 308, 309, 310, 311, 313/Donoso: p. 173 top/Franck

Donovan: p. 38/A. Eaton: p. 193 top left/E. Eichenberger: p. 237 top/Kudo Fubomichi: pp. 282 bottom, 290, 305 left, 317/P. Gasparini: pp. 293, 295, 296, 298 bottom/Francisco Gattoni: p. 277/G. Hyvert: p. 25 bottom/Alberto Jonquìeres: pp. 319, 321 top/Anthony Lacoudre: p. 41 top/E. Laskowska: pp. 125, 129/Misato Le Mignon: pp. 181 top, 183 left/Sabine Le Nechet: pp. 21, 24/D. Lefèvre: p. 25 top/A. Lopez: p. 287/Georges Malempré: pp. 324 left, 327/Pascal Mareshaux: pp. 243 left, 244 top left, 245/T. Margozzes: p. 312/Alain McKenzie: pp. 180, 181 bottom, 183 right/C. Moutarde: pp. 166, 170, 172 top/Béatrice Petit: p. 256/Daniel Riffet: p. 180 bottom/Dominique Rogier: pp. 20, 23, 43, 44, 45, 46 bottom, 47, 48, 49 right, 50, 51, 206 top, 253, 252, 253 bottom right, 280, 282 top/Taw Sarrafon: p. 236/A. Sillette: p. 286 top/P. Solar: p. 135 top/Marianne Spier-Donati: pp. 168 top, 169 top/Jane Taylor: pp. 184, 186, 187, 189/Nathalie Tirot: p. 276 top left/Vautier-Decool: pp. 314, 318, 320 top/Alexis N. Vorontozoff: pp. 46 top, 143 bottom, 284, 286 bottom/S. Weiss: p. 27

Bruno Barbey/Magnum/Contrasto: pp. 226, 227 right, 235, 238 top

Stefano Baroni, Ferrara: pp. 52-54 top

Gianni Berengo Gardin/Contrasto: pp. 114, 117, 118 left, 121 top

Bildarchiv Preussicher Kulturbesitz, Berlin: pp. 32, 34, 35, 36, 37

Rene Burri/Magnum/Contrasto: p. 185
Gaetano Citeroni, Rome: pp. 198, 200, 201 top and left

Fototecnica, Vicenza: pp. 115, 116

Hiroji Kubota/Magnum/Contrasto: p. 176

Steve McCurry/Magnum/Contrasto: pp. 167, 168 middle, 169, 171

Gueorgui Pinkhassov/Magnum/Contrasto: pp. 203, 234, 239

Ferdinando Scianna/Magnum/Contrasto: pp. 243 right, 244

Dennis Stock/Magnum/Contrasto: pp. 19, 22 left

Massimo Zanella: pp. 133 top, 134, 137

Drawings are by Studio Margil